FAILURE DIAGNOSIS AND PERFORMANCE MONITORING

L.F. Pau

Ecole Nationale Supérieure
des Télécommunications (ENST)
Paris

MARCEL DEKKER, INC.   New York and Basel

Library of Congress Cataloging in Publication Data

Pau, L.-F. (Louis-Francois), [date]
   Failure diagnosis and performance monitoring.

   (Control and systems theory; v. 11)
   "Adapted, expanded, and translated from Diagnostic des
pannes dans les systèmes"--Verso t.p. Published:
Toulouse : Cepadues-éditions, 1975.
   Bibliography: p.
   Includes index.
   1. Reliability (Engineering)--Statistical methods.
2. Maintainability (Engineering)--Statistical methods.
3. Quality control--Statistical methods. 4. Automatic
checkout equipment. 5. Pattern recognition systems.
I. Title. II. Series.
TS173.P3813   620'.00452'0724   81-4533
ISBN 0-8247-1018-5   AACR2

MARCEL DEKKER, INC.
270 Madison Avenue, New York, New York 10016

Current printing (last digit):
10 9 8 7 6 5 4 3 2

PRINTED IN THE UNITED STATES OF AMERICA

The main theme of this text is the application of different methodologies to the surveillance of a nondigital system (or device) or
of a control system throughout its entire operating lifetime so as
to obtain a diagnosis of failures and deteriorations and increase
the operational availability. The term <u>surveillance</u> is meant to
include the processing of all data records (of whatever nature)
taken during the fabrication, testing, or maintenance of the equipment as well as data obtained from the monitoring of system parameters during its operation. It is important to stress here that the
methods described presuppose the exclusive utilization of nondestructive tests or sensors which do not affect the system's functioning.

A second theme of this book is the generalization of the concept of failures to include classes of degraded performance. Within
the framework of continuous equipment monitoring it is generally
insufficient to characterize a breakdown by an excessive value of
just a single functional or maintenance parameter. Physical failures or breakdowns may also result from the joint occurrence of
deviations of several such parameters, with all the parameters remaining within specified tolerance values. To the notion of automatic classification of these deviation vectors one can quite naturally relate concepts of equipment condition and classes of degraded
performance.

This enables us to envisage connecting the monitoring device
to a condition indicator which activates an alarm whenever the level

of degraded performance drops too far. The use of such indicators
complies with the requirements of on-line failure diagnosis and
leads to a notable increase in the safety and availability of the
equipment to which they are connected.

Another objective of this book is to provide tools whereby one
can systematize the process of improving the design and characteristics of a device on the basis of quantitative and qualitative information obtained during its operational life span. As a general
rule, the manufacturer does not know the true behavior of the equipment under operational conditions. Therefore this information cannot
be used for design or maintenance purposes. Reliability and maintenance data banks are one of the elements making up this feedback
loop. It is necessary to process their contents and to have a useful and easily addressable format. Certain methods described here
will address these concerns, and provide tools and solutions.

It is important to underscore the fact that the methods described here do not generally permit the immediate localization of
faulty components. Initially, it is usually possible only to identify or diagnose the failure or degradation modes (taking into account the operating conditions and the operational environment).
One can then usually proceed with failure localization once the
failure mode is known. The most convenient procedure for this involves going through a failure search tree, complying with procedures
contained in the maintenance instruction manual pertaining to the
failure mode determined from initial analysis. A study of such
search sequences, and of questionnaires, is contained in Chapters
4 and 5.

Rather than detailing the technology of the diagnosis or test
devices, we shall stress numerical methods and diagnostic system
architectures. Most of these are presented here for the first time.
They have wide applicability in special-purpose digital or hybrid
processors for the monitoring and diagnosis of lowered performance
levels of nondigital equipment or control systems and in the partial automation of testing and quality control. The experiments

and practical setups designed by the author have made possible, to
a large extent, the validation of the approaches we have mentioned.
The main applications would appear to be, on the one hand, within the
domain of equipment for which the operational availability factor is
primordial (i.e., aerospace systems, nuclear power station equipment,
rotating machinery) and, on the other hand, for devices used to ac-
celerate maintenance and repair (i.e., maintenance recorders, automatic test systems for mechanical or electromechanical equipment).
Prospects are also promising for partial automation of quality control and automated monitoring of industrial processes.

　　Close parallels between the approaches we have outlined and the
motivations behind the development of diagnostic aids and monitoring
systems in medicine have convinced us that our methods may also have
some utility in medical research.

　　This text incorporates practical considerations and also theoretical contributions from pattern recognition, reliability theory,
automatic control, and mathematical statistics. Numerous practical
and theoretical questions are discussed and should motivate further
research. This book has been designed so that the prerequisite
knowledge required includes only a general engineering background
and some notions of signal theory, probability, and automatic control. However, mathematical detail has not been spared in certain
parts of the text. Chapter 1 covers much of the more elaborate
background material required. In Chapter 2 we define the basic notions involved in failure or degradation analysis and in performance
monitoring and the constraints on the class of nondigital systems
for which the techniques to be described actually apply.

　　Before considering the analysis of degradation data for purposes
of failure detection or diagnosis, it seems logical to present models
for the physical and performance degradation in those classes of
nondigital equipment specified earlier. This is done in Chapter 3.

　　In Chapters 4 and 5 we deal with a comparison of tests from
the point of view of efficiency in failure localization and diagnostic performance. The latter issue is a very important one which
affects the benefits to be expected from an automated diagnosis

system. The methods presented can be used to evaluate the tests and signals proposed by the technicians who are most familiar with the equipment under study.

Contemporary concern with reducing overall maintenance costs has given rise to many attempts to implement systems that evaluate equipment behavior under operational conditions, either with simple maintenance reports or with more involved forms of computerized data (as described in Chapter 6). Note that even when the problems of data collection, file updating, and file management have been solved, it may still be impossible to use properly all the information available. Methods for data analysis and data display are given in Chapters 7 and 8. Applications discussed in Chapter 9 show that it is possible to obtain diagnostic information from these files which may be used to modify the equipment or the operational conditions. Another important area of application of these methods is the comparative study of different types of equipment in operation, including the case of prototype evaluation.

In Chapter 10, we consider the relationship between pattern recognition and the automation of failure or degradation diagnosis in the static case. The procedures presented have led to operational implementations. Attention is given mainly to the diagnosis of failures and to follow-up procedures in a production line as well as to the concept of quality control throughout the fabrication process.

In Chapters 11-15 we deal with performance monitoring and failure diagnosis when dynamic measurements on the system are available. After recounting the different methodologies of internal and external diagnosis, an effort is made to develop original methods which, when combined with classical techniques of signal processing and classification, enable implementation of automatic diagnosis in important classes of nondigital equipment and control systems, such as those discussed in Chapter 2. Chapter 13 is devoted to on-line acoustic and vibration monitoring.

If the diagnosis can be made in an adaptive manner on a continuous basis that allows compensation for natural wear and the like,

it is then possible to implement "on-condition" maintenance procedures or to modify equipment tasks so as to correspond with the actual condition of each system. This provides a notable improvement
with respect to the arbitrary approaches normally used in choosing
maintenance procedures such as periodical overhauls and random replacements. Using the example of aircraft engines, we establish
methods in Chapter 15 that are appropriate for adaptive diagnosis
and that can also serve as preventive alarms warning of the probable
occurrence of certain degradation modes considered to be unacceptable.

In Chapters 14 and 15 we also discuss design concepts for
fault-tolerant control systems and redundancy management based on
failure diagnosis. This includes the case of sensor reconfiguration and filtering-based fictive sensors, and failure localization
in the presence of feedback.

The author hereby acknowledges support from the Ministry of
Culture (France) in the preparation of this book and the assistance
of Dr. H. J. Chizeck, M.I.T., in editing the preliminary manuscript.
He is also grateful for the experience gained in teaching this material since 1972, and the encouragement of Ecole Nationale Supérieure
de l'Aéronautique et de l'Espace, Ecole Nationale Supérieure des
Techniques avancées, Ecole Nationale Supérieure des Télécommunications, Technical University of Denmark, and Massachusetts Institute
of Technology.

Ecole Nationale Supérieure   L. F. Pau
  des Télécommunications

$\triangleq$	definition equation
$\#$	little different from
$\blacksquare$	end of result or example
$\in$	belongs to
$\forall$	for all
$\cap$	set intersection
$\cup$	set union
Card($\cdot$)	cardinal, or number of elements of a set ($\cdot$)
dim($\cdot$)	dimension of a vector or of a matrix ($\cdot$)
det($\cdot$)	determinant value of a matrix ($\cdot$)
I	identity matrix
$\otimes$	tensor product (matrix) of two vectors
f $\circ$ g	operator, function, or matrix obtained by composing together the operators, functions, or matrices f, g
Pr	probability
$\hat{x}$	sample-based estimate of x
$\|\cdot\|$	Euclidean or otherwise specified norm
$\mathscr{I}(\cdot)$	integer part of ($\cdot$)
p = 2π jf	complex variable p in the Laplace transformation
A/B	conditional statement A if B
p.d.f.	probability density function
f^{-1}	inverse of operator f, or inverse table look-up
[a,b)	interval $a \leq x < b$

FAILURE DIAGNOSIS AND PERFORMANCE MONITORING

1. MATRIX ALGEBRA

Throughout this book, matrix notation will generally be assumed, thus requiring a proper definition of some notation.

1.1 Matrix

(a) A matrix $A = [a_{ij}: i = 1, \ldots, n; j = 1, \ldots, m]$ is a two-dimensional array of scalar elements a_{ij}, where i is the row index and j the column index.

(b) The matrix A has n rows and m columns; we use the following dimension notation to express this:

$$\dim(A) = \binom{n}{m} \qquad A = \begin{bmatrix} a_{11} & \cdots & a_{1m} \\ \vdots & & \vdots \\ a_{n1} & \cdots & a_{nm} \end{bmatrix}$$

1.2 Matrix product

Let A and B be two matrices of dimensions

$$\dim(A) = \binom{n}{p} \qquad \dim(B) = \binom{p}{m}$$

The matrix product $C \triangleq AB$ is a matrix defined as follows:

$$C = [c_{ij}] \qquad \dim(C) = \binom{n}{m} \qquad c_{ij} = \sum_{k=1}^{p} a_{ik}b_{kj}$$

$$i = 1, \ldots, n; j = 1, \ldots, m$$

1.3   Trace of a Square Matrix

The trace of the square matrix A is the scalar sum of all diagonal elements:

$$\text{Trace}(A) \stackrel{\Delta}{=} \sum_{i=1}^{n} a_{ii} \qquad \dim(A) = \binom{n}{n}$$

1.4   Transpose of a Square Matrix

The transpose ^{t}A of the square matrix A is another square matrix of the same dimensions obtained by exchanging the rows and columns in A:

$$\dim(A) = \dim(^{t}A) = \binom{n}{n} \qquad ^{t}A = [b_{ij}] \qquad b_{ij} \stackrel{\Delta}{=} a_{ji}$$

$$i = 1, \ldots, n; \; j = 1, \ldots, m$$

Note that the t sign is placed before the matrix which is transposed. If A is rectangular, ^{t}A is still defined by $b_{ij} \stackrel{\Delta}{=} a_{ji}$, $i = 1, \ldots, n$, $j = 1, \ldots, m$, although A and ^{t}A do not have the same dimensions.

1.5   Inverse of a Square Matrix
      Assumed Invertible

If the square matrix A has an inverse, it is denoted by A^{-1} and characterized by the property

$$AA^{-1} = I = [\delta_{ij}] \qquad \delta_{ij} = \begin{cases} 0 & i \neq j \\ 1 & i = j \end{cases}$$

1.6   Pseudo Inverse of a Matrix

If the rectangular matrix A has a right pseudo inverse $A^{\dagger}$, it is characterized by

$$\forall X,Y \quad Y = AX \iff X = (^{t}AA)^{-1} \, ^{t}AY = A^{\dagger}Y$$

2.   PROBABILITY THEORY

In this section, we shall give a number of definitions pertaining to an n-dimensional random vector $X = (X_i : \; i = 1, \ldots, n)$.

2.1 Distribution Function

The distribution function $F(x)$ of X is defined by

$$x \stackrel{\Delta}{=} (x_i : \; i = 1, \ldots, n)$$

$$F(x) = Pr(X_1 \leq x_1 \text{ and } X_2 \leq x_2 \text{ and } \cdots \text{ and } X_n \leq x_n)$$

where Pr denotes the probability of the subsequent joint event.

2.2 Density Function

If it exists, the probability density function $f(x)$ of X is defined by

$$f(x) \, dx_1 \, dx_2 \cdots dx_n = Pr[x_1 \leq X_1 \leq (x_1 + dx_1) \text{ and } \cdots \text{ and }$$
$$x_n \leq X_n \leq (x_n + dx_n)]$$

2.3 Marginal Probability Density Function

The marginal probability density function is obtained by fixing one component (i.e., x_1):

$$f_1(x_1) = \int_{-\infty}^{+\infty} \cdots \int_{-\infty}^{+\infty} f(x_1, x_2, \ldots, x_n) \, dx_2 \cdots dx_n$$

2.4 Independent Random Variables

The scalar random variables $X_1, \ldots, X_n$ are said to be independent iff

$$\forall x \quad f(x) = f(x_1, \ldots, x_n) = f_1(x_1)f_2(x_2) \cdots f_n(x_n)$$

which means that the joint density is equal to the product of all marginal densities.

2.5 Mean or Expected Value of X

The mean or expected value $\overline{X}$ of the random vector X is defined by

$$\overline{X} = E(X) \triangleq \int_{\mathbb{R}^n} xf(x) \, dx$$

2.6 Variance and Covariance

(a) The variance, $Var(X)$, of X is the matrix

$$Var(X) \triangleq E[(X - E(X))^t(X - E(X))] \qquad dim(Var(X)) = \binom{n}{n}$$

$$Var(X) = E(X^tX) - E(X)^tE(X)$$

(b) If X and Y are two random vectors of dimension n, then the
covariance, Cov(X,Y), of X and Y is the matrix

$$\text{Cov}(X,Y) \triangleq E[(X - E(X))^t(Y - E(Y))] \qquad \dim(\text{Cov}(X,Y)) = \binom{n}{n}$$

2.7 Uncorrelated Random Vectors

The random vectors X and Y of dimension n are said to be uncorrelated iff

$$\text{Cov}(X,Y) = [0]$$

2.8 Conditional Density Function

Conditional density function of the random vector Y for given
X is denoted by $f_Y(\cdot|x)$:

i. $f_Y(y|x) \, dy = \dfrac{f((x,y)) \, dx \, dy}{f_X(x) \, dx} =$

$$\dfrac{\Pr(x \le X \le (x + dx) \text{ and } y \le Y \le (y + dy))}{\Pr(x \le X \le (x + dx))}$$

ii. $f_Y(y|x) \ge 0 \qquad$ for all $y \in \mathbb{R}^n$

iii. $\displaystyle\int_{-\infty}^{+\infty} f_Y(y|x) \, dy = 1$

2.9 Conditional Mean

Conditional mean of the random vector Y for given x is defined
by

$$E_y(Y|x) = \int_{-\infty}^{+\infty} y f_Y(y|x) \, dy$$

Thus

$$E_x E_y(Y|x) = E(Y)$$

The function $x \to E_y(Y|x)$ is called the regression of Y vs. X.

2.10 Orthogonal Representation of a Probability Density
       Function

(a) Let f(x) be the probability density of the random vector X,
all moments of which are assumed bounded. Provided some regularity

conditions are satisfied, there exists a unique series $\{p_m\}$ of polynomials p_m determined by the conditions:

      i. $p_m(x)$ is of degree m, and the coefficients of homogeneous
expressions of degree m are nonnegative.

      ii. $\displaystyle\int_{-\infty}^{+\infty} p_\ell(x)p_k(x)f(x)\ dx = \delta_{\ell k} = \begin{cases} 0 & \ell \neq k \\ 1 & \ell = k \end{cases}$

$\{p_m\}$ is called the sequence of orthogonal polynomials associated
with $f(x)$.

    (b) <u>Example</u>: Hermite polynomials associated with the scalar
normal distribution: Let $f(x)$ be the standard scalar normal distribution,

$$f(x) = \frac{1}{\sqrt{2\pi}}\ e^{-x^2/2}$$

and define the Hermite polynomials $H_n(x)$ by the recursive relation:

$$\left(\frac{d}{dx}\right)^n e^{-x^2/2} = (-1)^n H_n(x) e^{-x^2/2}$$

$$H_0(x) = 1 \qquad H_1(x) = x \qquad H_2(x) = x^2 - 1$$

$$H_3(x) = x^3 - 3x \qquad H_4(x) = x^4 - 6x^2 + 3$$

$$H_5(x) = x^5 - 10x^3 + 15x \qquad H_6(x) = x^6 - 15x^4 + 45x^2 - 15$$

    Then it can be shown that $\{H_n/\sqrt{n!}\}$ is the unique sequence of
orthogonal polynomials associated with the standard normal density.
Thus one obtains the following series representation for $|t| < 1$
(see Charlier [A-29] and Cramer [A-28]:

$$\frac{1}{\sqrt{1-t^2}}\ \exp\left[-\frac{t^2x^2 + t^2y^2 - 2txy}{2(1-t^2)}\right] = \sum_{n=0}^{\infty} \frac{H_n(x)H_n(y)}{n!}\ t^n$$

$$\exp\left[-\left(\frac{t^2}{2} + tx\right)\right] = \sum_{n=0}^{\infty} \frac{H_n(x)}{n!}\ t^n \qquad \blacksquare$$

3. THE BAYES THEOREM

3.1 Discrete Case

    Let A and B be two events. The purpose of the Bayes theorem
is to relate the basic events A and B with the conditional events
"A if B is true" and "B if A is true."

$$Pr(A/B) = \frac{Pr(A) \cdot Pr(B/A)}{Pr(B)} \qquad Pr(B) \neq 0$$

where

$$Pr(A/B) = Pr(A \text{ given that } B \text{ is true})$$

$$Pr(B/A) = Pr(B \text{ given that } A \text{ is true})$$

Example 1: If B represents some condition on the measurements and
A the hypothesis "the machine is faulty," then the Bayes theorem
tells us how the truth of statement A is modified by the data. ■

Example 2: Failure detection with an imperfect failure detector:
Consider the events

F: Failure of the machine and corresponding a priori probabil-
    ity

$\overline{F}$: No failure of the machine and corresponding a priori prob-
    ability

D: The failure detector judges the machine to have a failure

$\overline{D}$: The failure detector does not judge the machine to have a
    failure

First, by application of the definition of conditional probabilities
we have

$$Pr(D) = Pr(F)\, Pr(D/F) + Pr(\overline{F})\, Pr(D/\overline{F})$$

Next, by application of the Bayes theorem we have:

    i. Probability of correct detection:

$$Pr(D/F) = \frac{Pr(D) \cdot Pr(F/D)}{Pr(F)}$$

    ii. Probability of false alarm:

$$Pr(D/\overline{F}) = \frac{Pr(D) \cdot [1 - Pr(F/D)]}{1 - Pr(F)}$$

    iii. Probability of rejection:

$$Pr(\overline{D}/F) = \frac{[1 - Pr(D)]\, Pr(F/\overline{D})}{Pr(F)}$$

■

3.2 Continuous Case

Let X and Y be two random vectors. Using the notation of Section 2.8 for conditional densities, we obtain

$$f_Y(y|x) = \frac{f_X(x|y)f_Y(y)}{\int_{-\infty}^{+\infty} f_X(x|y)f_Y(y)\ dy}$$

4.   STOCHASTIC PROCESSES AND TIME SERIES

In this section, we assume all processes to be time sampled.

4.1   Time Series and Stochastic Processes

(a)   Let $Z_1, \ldots, Z_n$ be n consecutive observations of a random measurement at times 1, ..., n; such a sequence of measurements is called a time series.

(b)   A time series is generated by a stochastic process $\{x_t\}$, which is defined here, for simplicity, as an indexed set of uncorrelated random variables x_t. Any such random variable x_t will affect all subsequent measurements x_τ, $\tau \geq t$.

4.2   Stationary Stochastic Process

The stochastic process $\{x_t\}$ is said to be (strongly) stationary iff the first two moments of x_t are invariant to a shift of the time axis:

$$\forall\tau\ \forall t\quad [E(x_{t+\tau}) = E(x_t)\qquad Var(x_{t+\tau}) = Var(x_t)]$$

(see Figure 1-1).

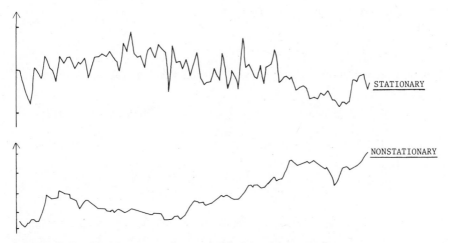

FIGURE 1-1   Stationary and nonstationary time series.

4.3 Autoregressive Moving Average (ARMA) Model

(a) Let $\{x_t\}$ be a stochastic process such that $E(x_t) = 0$, $\text{Var}(x_t) = R$, and $\text{Cov}(x_t, x_{t+\tau}) = 0$ for $\tau \neq 0$. The general ARMA model of order (p,q) is defined by

$$Z_t = a_1 Z_{t-1} + \cdots + a_p Z_{t-p} + x_t - b_1 x_{t-1} - \cdots - b_q x_{t-q} + b_0$$

where $a_1, \ldots, a_p, b_0, \ldots, b_q$ are coefficients to be estimated.

(b) ARMA models are generally estimated via recursive least-squares algorithms (see Box and Jenkins [A-22] and Graupe [A-6]). Grenander and Rosenblatt [A-27] give the asymptotic distribution of the coefficients of an autoregressive scheme.

Examples

i. ARMA $(1,0)$: $Z_t = a_1 Z_{t-1} + x_t$

(also called the autoregressive model of order 1)

ii. ARMA $(0,1)$: $Z_t = x_t - b_1 x_{t-1}$

(also called the moving average model of order 1)

4.4 Autoregressive Integrated Moving Average (ARIMA) Model

(a) If the process $\{x_t\}$ is nonstationary, and especially if there are periodic fluctuations or a trend in the measurements Z_t, ARMA models are inappropriate.

(b) The ARIMA technique consists in the study of difference measurements such as

$$W_{t,1} \triangleq Z_t - Z_{t-1}$$

whereby many nonstationary processes and time series can be studied again as ARMA models of $W_{t,1}$.

The ARIMA process of order (p,d,q) is such that the d-differences of Z_t obey an ARMA (p,q) process:

$$W_{t,d} = Z_t - Z_{t-d} = a_1 W_{t-1,d} + \cdots + a_p W_{t-p,d} + x_t - b_1 x_{t-1}$$
$$- \cdots - b_q x_{t-q} + b_0$$

The coefficient b_0 corresponds to a deterministic trend in the Z_t measurements.

For further details, see Box and Jenkins [A-22].

Example:

ARIMA $(0,1,1)$: $Z_t - Z_{t-1} = x_t - b_1 x_{t-1}$

4.5 Distributed Lag Model

A distributed lag model with input Z_t, output Y_t, geometric lags, and an uncorrelated residual is of the following form:

$$Y_t - \lambda Y_{t-1} = \alpha Z_t + \underbrace{x_t + \beta x_{t-1} + \gamma}_{\text{residual } n_t} = \alpha Z_t + n_t + \gamma$$

In such models, the residual n_t is an ARMA model; thus the residuals are autocorrelated. For further details, see Dhrymes [A-23].

4.6 Regression Model

(a) A regression model is a special distributed lag vector model in which Z_t includes all k exogenous variables at time t and α is a linear mapping represented by a matrix:

$$Y_t = \alpha Z_t + n_t = \sum_{i=1}^{k} \alpha_i Z_{ti} + n_t \qquad \dim(Y_t) = \binom{n}{1} \qquad \dim(\alpha) = \binom{n}{n}$$

$$n_t = a_1 n_{t-1} + \cdots + a_p n_{t-p} + x_t - b_1 x_{t-1} - \cdots - b_q x_{t-q}$$

Here n_t is an ARMA (p,q) model.

(b) If $n_t = x_t$ is a normal random vector of mean 0 and variance $\sigma^2 I$, then the maximum likelihood estimate of α is

$$\hat{\alpha} = Y_t {}^t Z_t (Z_t {}^t Z_t)^{-1} \qquad \dim(\hat{\alpha}) = \binom{n}{n}$$

and the approximate distribution of that estimate is

$$\hat{\alpha} \sim N(\alpha, \sigma^2 (Z_t {}^t Z_t)^{-1})$$

4.7 Orthogonal Representation of a Stochastic Process

The idea is to represent $\{x_t\}$ by a functional series representation of its probability density function $f(x_t)$ in a known orthogonal base $\{\varphi_i(t)\}$ (see Section 2.10):

$$f(x_t) = c_1 \varphi_1(t) + \cdots + c_n \varphi_n(t) + \cdots$$

$$\int_{-\infty}^{+\infty} {}^{t}\varphi_i(t)\varphi_j(t)u(t) \, dt = \delta_{ij} \qquad u: \quad \text{kernel function}$$

Thereby the process $\{x_t\}$ is characterized by the time-independent sequence of coefficients $\{c_i\}$. For further details, see, e.g., Grenander and Rosenblatt [A-27].

5. STATISTICAL FILTERING

5.1 Introduction

The basic objective of statistical filtering is to make the best possible use of a set of accessible noisy measurements $Z(t)$ in order to extract an estimate $\{\hat{x}(t)\}$ of the stochastic process $\{x(t)\}$ which has generated $Z(t)$. There is no access to $x(t)$ because of the sensor or measurement errors. Moreover, we want the filter to have the following properties:

    i. Unbiasedness: $E(\hat{x}(t)) = x(t)$

    ii. Minimum variance: $P(t) = \text{Var}(\hat{x}(t) - x(t))$ has a minimum trace.

All filtering procedures assume some model relating $x(t)$ to $Z(t)$ and noise. This measurement model is generally linear:

$Z(t) = H(t)x(t) + v(t)$

$\dim(x) = \begin{pmatrix} n \\ 1 \end{pmatrix} \qquad \dim(Z) = \begin{pmatrix} N \\ 1 \end{pmatrix} \qquad N > n \qquad \text{Rank}(H) = n$

x and y uncorrelated

$v:$ white Gaussian stationary noise: $E(v(t)) = 0$

$$E(v(t)^t v(t)) = R > 0$$

The $v(t)$ noise models the measurement errors in addition to actual noise.

5.2 Wiener Filter: Minimum Variance Estimate $\hat{x}(t)$

The Wiener filter is well adapted for analog implementations.

(a) The Wiener filter expresses the estimate $\hat{x}(t)$ as a linear time-invariant combination of all available measurements $Z(t)$:

$\hat{x}(t) = AZ(t)$

In other words, the Wiener filter synthesizes the transfer function of an optimal linear filter with $Z(t)$ as input and $\hat{x}(t)$ as output. This method is implementable in practice (analog filters) only if:

   i. $x(t)$ is stationary.

   ii. $H(t) \equiv H$.

   iii. The variance functions $C_{xx}(t)$, $C_{vv}(t)$ (see Section 2.6) have rational spectra and are given.

   (b) The minimum-variance Wiener filter is then

$$\hat{x}(t) = [(^{t}HR^{-1}H)^{-1}\ ^{t}HR^{-1}]Z(t) = AZ(t)$$

and the covariance matrix is

$$P = (^{t}HR^{-1}H)^{-1}$$

$$\hat{x}(t) = P^{t}HR^{-1}Z(t)$$

5.3   Wiener Filter: Maximum Likelihood Estimate $\hat{x}(t)$

   (a) The maximum-likelihood criterion consists of taking as an estimate $\hat{x}(t)$ the value of $x(t)$ which maximizes the probability density of the random variable $[Z(t) - Hx(t)]$ for given $Z(t)$.

   (b) It can be shown that the formulas for the maximum-likelihood Wiener filter are identical to those for the minimum-variance case.

5.4   Recursive Kalman-Bucy Filtering

   The recursive Kalman-Bucy technique is suitable for digital filtering only. However, it is able to process nonstationary processes $\{x(t)\}$. In the following, we assume the process and the measurements to be time sampled, thus the notation x_k and Z_k.

   (a) The Kalman filter expresses the estimate $\hat{x}_k$ as a linear combination of the measurements Z_k and of the predicted x_k value, denoted $\hat{x}'_k$, inferred from x_{k-1}, x_{k-2}, ... (see Figure 1-2):

$$\hat{x}_k = \hat{x}'_k + K_k(Z_k - H_k\hat{x}'_k)$$

   This requires a plant process model to be specified in addition to the measurement model.

   i.   Plant equation: $x_k = \varphi(k, k-1)x_{k-1} + w_{k-1}$ $k = 1, \ldots$

   ii. Measurement equation: $Z_k = H_k x_k + v_k$

   The additional assumptions are the following:

$$E(v) = E(w) = 0$$

$$Cov(w_k, w_j) = Q_k \delta_{kj}$$

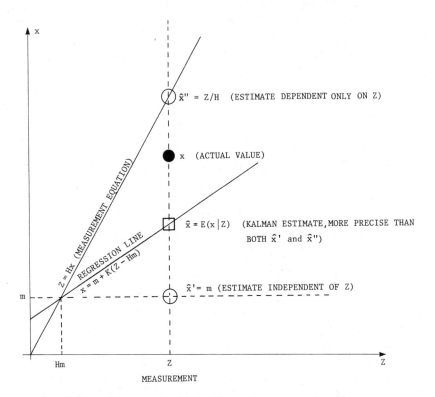

FIGURE 1-2   Kalman filtering: the various estimates.

$$\text{Cov}(v_k, v_j) = R_k \delta_{kj}$$

$$\text{Cov}(w_k, v_j) = C_k \delta_{kj}$$

Before any measurements are taken, the best estimates are given by

$$\hat{x}_0 = m \qquad \text{Var}(\hat{x}_0 - x_0) = P_0$$

(b) Filter equations in the case of correlated noises v, w (see Figure 1-3):

    i. Before observing Z_k, the best estimate is

$$\hat{x}'_k = \varphi(k, k-1)\hat{x}_{k-1} + A_{k-1}\left[Z_{k-1} - H_{k-1}\hat{x}'_{k-1} \right]$$

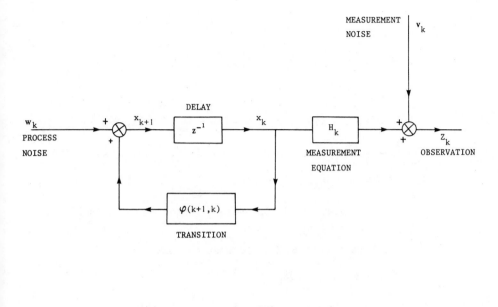

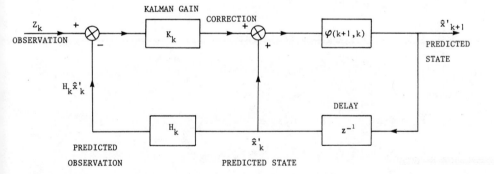

FIGURE 1-3 System implementation and flow graph of the discrete
Kalman filter; z is here the z transfer function variable.

ii.   Once Z_k has been observed, the best estimate is

$$\hat{x}''_k = H_k Z_k$$

iii. Kalman optimal estimate:

$$\hat{x}_k = \hat{x}'_k + K_k(Z_k - H_k \hat{x}'_k)$$

where

$$A_{k-1} = C_{k-1}[H_{k-1}\bar{P}_{k-1}{}^t H_{k-1} + R_{k-1}]^{-1}$$

$$K_k = \bar{P}_k{}^t H_k [H_k \bar{P}_k{}^t H_k + R_k]^{-1}$$

$$\bar{P}_k = \varphi(k,\ k-1)P_{k-1}{}^t\varphi(k,\ k-1) + Q_{k-1} - \varphi(k,\ k-1)K_{k-1}{}^t C_{k-1}$$

$$\qquad - C_{k-1}{}^t K_{k-1}{}^t \varphi(k,\ k-1) - A_{k-1}[H_{k-1}\bar{P}_{k-1}{}^t H_{k-1} + R_{k-1}]^{-1}{}^t A_{k-1}$$

$$P_k = \mathrm{Var}(x_k - \hat{x}_k) = \bar{P}_k - K_k H_k \bar{P}_k$$

(c) Filter equations in the case of uncorrelated noises v, w
(C_k = 0, and thus A_k = 0)

  i. Before observing Z_k, the best estimate is

$$\hat{x}'_k = \varphi(k,\ k-1)\hat{x}_{k-1}$$

  ii. Once Z_k has been observed, the best estimate is

$$\hat{x}''_k = H_k Z_k$$

  iii. Kalman optimal estimate:

$$\hat{x}_k = \hat{x}'_k + K_k(Z_k - H_k \hat{x}'_k)$$

where

$$\bar{P}_k = \varphi(k,\ k-1)P_{k-1}{}^t\varphi(k,\ k-1) + Q_{k-1}$$

$$K_k = \bar{P}_k{}^t H_k [H_k \bar{P}_k{}^t H_k + R_k]^{-1} = P_k{}^t H_k R_k^{-1}$$

$$P_k = \bar{P}_k - K_k H_k \bar{P}_k$$

$$P_k = (I - K_k H_k)\bar{P}_k{}^t(I - K_k H_k) + K_k R_k{}^t K_k$$

(d) Steady-state Kalman gain $K_{\infty,k}$: This constant gain matrix
is used whenever possible. It can be computed by setting
$\varphi(k,\ k-1)$ = I in the preceding system; thus $x_k = x_{k-1} + w_{k-1}$:

$$K_{\infty,k} = P_0{}^t H_k R_k^{-1}$$

6. SPECTRAL ANALYSIS

6.1 Prefiltering

(a) Spectral analysis can only be applied to stationary time series. It is therefore necessary to filter out any trend of the signal s(t) sampled at the period $\tau = 1$ (see, e.g., Jenkins and Watts [H-25]):

    i. First difference filter: $Y_1(t) = s(t) - s(t - 1)$

    ii. Trend correction for a known trend m(t): $Y_2(t) = s(t) - m(t)$

Example: Log-polynomial filter for which $\ln m(t) = a_0 + a_1 t + a_2 t^2$.

(b) Only trend-corrected signals (such as Y_1 or Y_2) will be considered in the remainder of this section.

(c) If s(t) is noisy, it should be passed through an analog or digital low-pass or band-pass filter. One such filter with cutoff frequency 1/T is the Hamming window, the impulse response f(t) and spectrum F(ω) of which are

$$f(t) = \begin{cases} 0.54 + 0.46 \cos\left(\dfrac{2\pi t}{T}\right) & -\dfrac{T}{2} \le t \le \dfrac{T}{2} \\ 0 & t > \dfrac{T}{2} \end{cases}$$

$$F(\omega) = T \frac{0.54(2\pi/T)^2 - 0.08\omega^2}{(2\pi/T)^2 - \omega^2} \frac{\sin(\omega T/2)}{\omega T/2}$$

Digital filtering is extensively discussed in Refs. A-8 and A-31.

6.2 Fourier Transform and Inverse Fourier Transform

(a) Fourier analysis is based on the Fourier transform pair of the stationary signal s(t):

$$S(\omega) = \frac{1}{2\pi} \int_{-\infty}^{+\infty} s(t) \exp(-j\omega t)\, dt \qquad \text{direct Fourier transform}$$

$$\text{(6.1)}$$

$$s(t) = \int_{-\infty}^{+\infty} S(\omega) \exp(j\omega t)\, d\omega \qquad \text{inverse Fourier transform}$$

where

$$S(\omega) \overset{\Delta}{=} \mathcal{F}(s(t)) \qquad s(t) \overset{\Delta}{=} \mathcal{F}^{-1}(S(\omega)) \qquad \omega = 2\pi f$$

This defines the (complex) frequency component $S(\omega)$ of $s(t)$ for each angular frequency ω (or frequency f). $S(\omega)$ is usually called the spectrum of $s(t)$.

(b) The discrete equivalents of (6.1) are the discrete Fourier transforms (DFTs) of the signal $s(t)$ sampled at the period $\tau = 1$:

$$S(k) = \frac{1}{N} \sum_{n=0}^{N-1} s(n) \exp\left(-\frac{2\pi jkn}{N}\right) \qquad \text{discrete Fourier transform} \tag{6.2}$$

$$s(k) = \sum_{n=0}^{N-1} S(k) \exp\left(\frac{2\pi jkn}{N}\right) \qquad \text{inverse discrete Fourier transform}$$

This transform pair has properties very similar to those of the continuous transform. However, it is periodic in both the time and frequency domains. Discrete Fourier transforms are obtainable using commercially available spectrum analyzers that implement the so-called fast Fourier transform (FFT). To calculate N values of $S(k)$ via the FFT requires about $N \log_2 N$ additions and as many multiplications [A-43].

(c) The distribution and confidence intervals for spectral estimates are discussed by Grenander and Rosenblatt [A-27].

6.3 Spectrum of a Periodic Signal with Amplitude Modulation
Define:

    i. A periodic signal of frequency f_1: $s_1(t) = a \sin 2\pi f_1 t$

    ii. A low-frequency signal $s_2(t)$ such that $|s_2(t)| \leq 1$, for example, $s_2(t) = \sin 2\pi f_2 t$, where $f_2 \ll f_1$

The signal $s(t)$ is obtained through amplitude modulation of s_1 by s_2 at the rate m:

$$s(t) = a[1 + ms_2(t)] \sin 2\pi f_1 t \qquad m \leq 1$$

Figure 1-4 represents the amplitude spectra of s_1 and the amplitude-modulated signal s. The spectral rays at frequencies $\pm f_1 \pm f_2$ are called lateral bands (or sidebands).

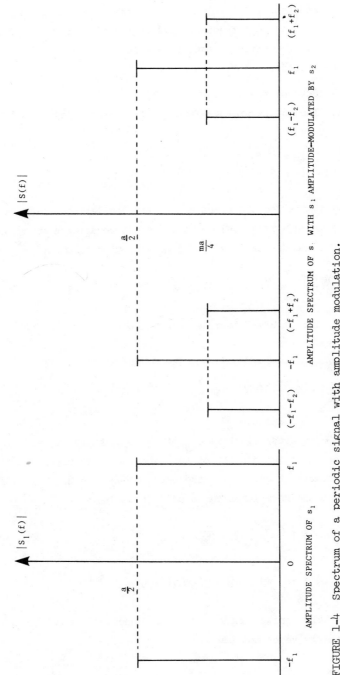

FIGURE 1-4 Spectrum of a periodic signal with amplitude modulation.

The important point to remember is that for a large number of periodic processes (of frequency f_1) degradations may be revealed by some kind of amplitude modulation which can then be best detected via lateral bands.

6.4 Autocovariance Function

(a) The autocovariance function of a stationary signal $s(t)$ is defined by

$$C(t) \triangleq \int_{-\infty}^{+\infty} s(u)\ s^*(u - t)\ du$$

where s^* stands for the transpose of the complex conjugate value.

(b) When s is a real scalar, the autocovariance function is related to the spectrum by the Wiener-Kynchine formula:

$$S(\omega) = \int_{-\infty}^{+\infty} C(t)\ \exp(-j\omega t)\ dt$$

(c) The Parseval formula then relates $s(t)$ to the total spectral energy:

$$\int_{-\infty}^{+\infty} s(t)\ s^*(t)\ dt = \frac{1}{2\pi} \int_{-\infty}^{+\infty} |S(\omega)|^2\ d\omega$$

6.5 Cross Spectra

(a) The cross spectrum S_{AB} of two stationary signals s_A and s_B indicates the power density at each angular frequency ω common to both signals. It also gives the phase between them. S_{AB} is computed from the covariance function C_{AB}:

$$C_{AB}(t) \triangleq \int_{-\infty}^{+\infty} s_A(u) s_B^*(u - t)\ dt$$

$$S_{AB}(\omega) \triangleq \int_{-\infty}^{+\infty} C_{AB}(t)\ \exp(-j\omega t)\ dt$$

(b) The finite sample covariance function estimation can be either recursive or nonrecursive:

$$\hat{C}_{AB}(k) = \frac{1}{N} \sum_{i=1}^{N-k} [s_A(k) - \overline{s_A}][s_B(i + k) - \overline{s_B}]^*$$

$$\hat{C}_{AB}^{(n+1)}(k) = \frac{1}{n + 1} \{n\hat{C}_{AB}^{(n)}(k) + [s_A(n + 1 - k) - \overline{s_A}][s_B(n + 1) - \overline{s_B}]^*\}$$

Nonlinear systems may be classified on the basis of a procedure (Chapter 10) applied to the $C_{AB}(\cdot)$ feature vector, where s_A is the input and s_B the output.

6.6 Cross-correlation Function
Between Two Stationary Signals s_A and s_B

$$R_{AB}(t) \triangleq \frac{C_{AB}(t)}{C_A(0)C_B(0)}$$

6.7 Coherence Function

Suppose that we sample a signal s_A at the input of a linear system and the signal s_B at the output. The frequency response function of the linear system is $H(\omega)$.

(a) The output s_B may contain system noise as well as components arising from the input s_A. The cross spectrum between s_A and s_B measures the common part:

$$H_1(\omega) \triangleq \frac{S_{AB}(\omega)}{S_A(\omega)}$$

(b) In the absence of noise, the rms response would be the square root of the ratio of the individual power spectra:

$$H_2(\omega) \triangleq \sqrt{\frac{S_B(\omega)}{S_A(\omega)}}$$

The ratio of the two frequency responses H_1 and H_2 is unity when there is no system noise. The square $[H_1(\omega)/H_2(\omega)]^2$ of this ratio is called the coherence function $\mathcal{C}_{AB}(\omega)$:

$$\mathcal{C}_{AB}(\omega) \triangleq \frac{S_{AB}^2(\omega)}{S_A(\omega)S_B(\omega)} \leq 1$$

It tends toward zero as more and more noise becomes included in s_B; hence s_B and s_A become independent.

7. RELIABILITY THEORY

In this short introduction to the field, we shall discuss the concept of failure rate and present a few typical failure distributions used as a priori models in the failure diagnosis and localization procedures of the following chapters.

7.1 Reliability at Time t of a Binary State Device

(a) A device is assumed to be in either of the following exclusive states:

E_0: operating E_1: failed

(b) The reliability $R(t)$ is the probability distribution of the instant τ at which the failure occurs (transition from E_0 to E_1), when the device is activated at $t = 0$:

$$R(t) \triangleq Pr(\tau > t)$$

7.2 Failure Rate at Time t

(a) The failure rate $Z(t)$ is the time-dependent function defined by

$$Z(t) \triangleq - \frac{dR(t)}{dt}$$

(b) If we consider a population $N(o)$ of initially identical devices and call $n(t)$ the number of failures taking place during the operating time interval $[t, t + \Delta t]$, then

$$Z(t) = \frac{1}{N(o)} \lim_{\Delta t \to 0} \frac{n(t)}{\Delta t}$$

7.3 Instantaneous Failure Rate at Time t
     (Also Called the Hazard Rate)

(a) The instantaneous failure rate $\lambda(t)$ is the time-dependent function defined by

$$\lambda(t) \triangleq - \frac{1}{R(t)} \frac{dR(t)}{dt}$$

(b) If we consider a population $N(o)$ of initially identical devices and call $N(t)$ the number of surviving devices after t operating hours, then

$$\lambda(t) = \frac{1}{N(t)} \lim_{\Delta t \to 0} \frac{n(t)}{\Delta t}$$

(c) The reliability $R(t)$ can be expressed in terms of the instantaneous failure rate $\lambda(t)$ (see Figure 1-5):

$$R(t) = \exp\left(-\int_0^t \lambda(u)\ du\right)$$

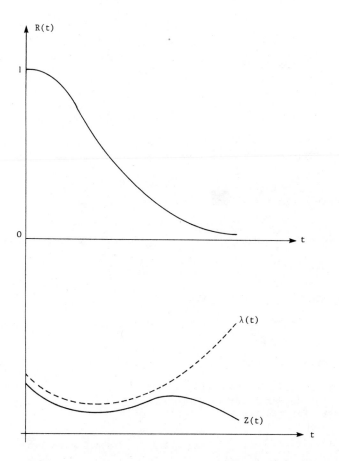

FIGURE 1-5 Evolution of the reliability $R(t)$, of the failure rate $Z(t)$, and of the instantaneous failure rate (hazard rate) $\lambda(t)$.

7.4   Mean Time Between Failures (MTBF)

The MTBF is the expected value of the time τ to failure:

$$\text{MTBF} \triangleq E(\tau) = \int_{0}^{+\infty} t \; dR(t)$$

7.5   Poisson Failure Distribution

The Poisson failure distribution is characterized by a constant hazard rate:

$$R(t) = e^{-\lambda t}$$
$$\lambda(t) = \lambda$$
$$\text{MTBF} = \frac{1}{\lambda}$$

7.6   Normal Failure Distribution
with Mean m and Standard Deviation σ

$$R(t) = \frac{1}{\sigma\sqrt{2\pi}} \int_{t}^{+\infty} \exp\left[-\frac{(t - m)^2}{2\sigma^2} \right] dt$$

$$Z(t) = \frac{1}{\sigma\sqrt{2\pi}} \exp\left[-\frac{(t - m)^2}{2\sigma^2} \right]$$

7.7   Gamma Failure Distribution
with Parameters $a > -1$ and $b > 0$

$$Z(t)_{\star} = \frac{1}{b\Gamma(a + 1)}\left(\frac{t}{b}\right)^{a} \exp\left(-\frac{t}{b}\right)$$

$$\text{MTBF} = b(a + 1)$$

The hazard rate is

$$\begin{cases} \text{Decreasing for } a < 0 \\ \text{Constant for } a = 0 \\ \text{Increasing for } a > 0 \text{ (bounded)} \end{cases}$$

7.8   Weibull Failure Distribution
with Location Parameter λ, Dispersion $\delta > 0$,
and Shape Parameter $a > 0$

$$R(t) = \begin{cases} \exp\left[-\left(\dfrac{t - \lambda}{\delta}\right)^{a} \right] & \text{for } t \geq \lambda \qquad \text{see Figure 1-6} \\ 0 & \text{for } t < \lambda \end{cases}$$

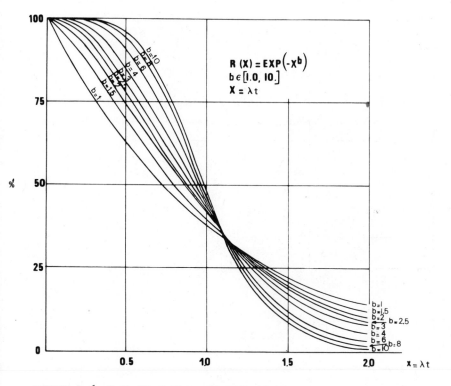

FIGURE 1-6 Weibull failure distribution.

$$\lambda(t) = \left(\frac{a}{\delta}\right)(t - \lambda)^{a-1} \qquad \text{for } t \geq \lambda$$

$$\text{MTBF} = \lambda + \delta^{1/a}\Gamma\left(1 + \frac{1}{a}\right)$$

The hazard rate is

$$\begin{cases} \text{Decreasing for } a < 1 \\ \text{Constant for } a = 1 \\ \text{Increasing for } a > 1 \text{ (unbounded)} \end{cases}$$

For further details about the Weibull law and the estimation of its parameters, see Mann et al. [C-3].

7.9 Experimental Instantaneous Failure Rates

It is essential to remember the following:

i. The instantaneous failure rates observed in practice are time dependent--hence the importance of such distributions as the Weibull and gamma distributions.

INSTANTANEOUS
  FAILURE
    RATE

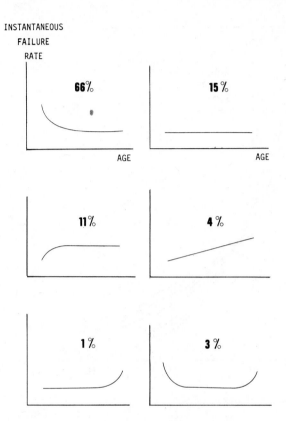

FIGURE 1-7   Main types of instantaneous failure rate evolutions and
frequencies of occurrence in aerospace components subject to maintenance.

     ii.   Those variations $\lambda(t)$ observed in practice are very often
monotonic and generally monotonically decreasing. Figure 1-7 gives
the distribution of the $\lambda(t)$ vs. shape for a large number of aerospace components. See also Broberg [E-22].

     iii. The instantaneous failure rates $\lambda(t)$ depend largely on
the environment. A model for this dependency is the following:

$$\lambda(t) = \lambda_{max}(t) \left[\frac{\lambda_{min}(t)}{\lambda_{max}(t)} \right]^{b} \qquad 0 \leq b \leq 1$$

where b is related to the operational environment and component
specifications, while λ_{min} and λ_{max} are lower and upper confidence
or experimental limits (i.e., RADC - TR - 67 - 108).

7.10 Bilateral Confidence Interval on the Estimate of an
      Exponential Instantaneous Failure Rate

Consider a lifetime estimation experiment where N identical
devices are tested for T cumulative hours with an observation of r
failures. A confidence interval $(\lambda_{min},\lambda_{max})$ for λ at the level
$(1 - \alpha)$ is given by (Gnedenko [C-30])

$$\lambda_{min} = \frac{\chi^2_{2r,\alpha/2}}{2NT} \qquad \lambda_{max} = \frac{\chi^2_{2(r + 1),(1 - \alpha/2)}}{2NT}$$

where $\chi^2_{m,\beta}$ is the β quantile of the chi-square distribution with m
degrees of freedom, and

$$Pr(\lambda_{min} \le \lambda \le \lambda_{max}) = 1 - \alpha$$

8. STATISTICAL TESTS

8.1 χ^2 (Chi-square) Test

(a) When dealing with the frequency of occurrence of events,
the properties of the χ^2 distribution are used to evaluate significance via the χ^2 or Pearson test.

(b) Define:

N = total number of occurrences observed

P_i = true probability of an event belonging to class i,
     i = 1, ..., k

n_i = number of occurrences observed in class i, i = 1, ..., k

and

$$\chi^2 \triangleq \sum_{i=1}^{k} \frac{(n_i - Np_i)^2}{Np_i}$$

If ℓ is the number of parameters to be tested for significance
at the level α, then χ^2 should be distributed as a $\chi^2_{k-\ell-1}$ distribution with $(k - \ell - 1)$ degrees of freedom. The test is:

ℓ significant parameters $\Leftrightarrow \chi^2 < \chi^2_{(k-\ell-1),\alpha}$

where $\chi^2_{m,\beta}$ is the β-quantile of the χ^2_m distribution.

Example 1: Test the significance of the ℓ estimated parameters of a failure distribution. The classes i, i = 1, ..., k, are then sub-intervals of $[0,\infty)$, and n_i is the number of failures observed in one such subinterval, while p_i is the distribution-based frequency of them.   ■

Example 2:

   (a) Assume that the number of bearing failures in an experi-mental apparatus over a period of 1 year are as follows:

Position on prototype	1	2	3	4	Total
Failures	55	24	52	49	180

The problem is as follows: is there something different about posi-tion 2 which results in relatively fewer failures? Or, equivalently, is there a significant difference between the results for the second and the other positions? The χ^2 test can be used to compare the ob-served frequencies with the values to be expected if there are no differences between bearing positions.

   (b) If there are no differences, then the expected failure frequency would be

$$p = \frac{180}{4} = 45 \text{ failures per position per year}$$

The differences between the observed and expected values are

Position	1	2	3	4	Total
Difference	10	(-21)	7	4	0

Thus

$$\chi^2 = \frac{10^2 + 21^2 + 7^2 + 4^2}{45} = 13.47$$

Since there are k = 4 positions and ℓ = 0 parameter, the number of

degrees of freedom is $k - \ell - 1 = 3$, and hence a χ^2 value of 13.47
is shown to be significant at the 0.5% level with 3 degrees of freedom. ■

8.2 Snedecor Test to Detect Systematic Failures of a Device with an Exponential Failure Distribution

(a) The Snedecor test is based on the fact that if a device
has an instantaneous failure rate λ and if r failures have been observed after T hours of testing, then $2\lambda T$ is distributed as χ^2_{2r}.

(b) We shall test the hypotheses

$$H_0: \quad \lambda_0 = \lambda_1 \qquad H_1: \quad \lambda_0 \neq \lambda_1$$

using the fact that the ratio of two independent χ^2 variables to
their respective degrees of freedom follows a Snedecor F distribution:

$$\frac{2\lambda_0 T_0 / 2r_0}{2\lambda_1 T_1 / 2r_1} = \frac{\lambda_0 T_0 r_1}{\lambda_1 T_1 r_0} = F(2r_0, 2r_1)$$

If $F_\alpha(2r_0, 2r_1)$ is the α-quantile, then the test outcome is

$$H_0: \quad \frac{T_0 r_1}{T_1 r_0} \leq F_\alpha(2r_0, 2r_1)$$

T_i = cumulated hours of testing of the population with failure rate λ_i

$$H_1: \quad \frac{T_0 r_1}{T_1 r_0} > F_\alpha(2r_0, 2r_1)$$

r_i = cumulated number of failures of this population

8.3 Wald's Sequential Probability Ratio Test (SPRT) and the Generalized Sequential Probability Ratio (GSPRT)

The SPRT and GSPRT are sequential hypothesis testing procedures
requiring only a small amount of computation and are well suited for
failure detection. They both use a likelihood ratio function.

Let X: $\{X_1, \ldots, X_k\}$ be a rolling and increasing sequence of k
independent consecutive identically distributed measurements for
which we assume a joint probability distribution $f(X_1, \ldots, X_k | H_i)$,
conditioned on the hypothesis H_i (e.g., operating vs. failed).

(a) <u>Two-hypothesis testing by SPRT</u>: We consider two hypotheses
H_0 and H_1 and define the likelihood ratio functions:

$$\lambda_k \triangleq \frac{f(X_1, \ldots, X_k | H_1)}{f(X_1, \ldots, X_k | H_0)} \qquad \Lambda_k \triangleq \ln\left[\frac{f(X | H_1)}{f(X | H_0)}\right]$$

together with two bounds on the classification errors:

$$\alpha = \Pr(H_1 / H_0) \qquad \beta = \Pr(H_0 / H_1)$$

Assuming f to be a normal distribution, the optimal sequential testing procedure is the following:

$$\begin{cases} \lambda_k > A: & H_1 \text{ true} \\ \lambda_k < B: & H_0 \text{ true} \\ B \le \lambda_k \le A: & \text{request an additional measurement, and set} \\ & \quad k = k + 1 \end{cases}$$

where A and B are stopping bounds given approximately by Wald and Wolfwitz [D-21]:

$$A = \frac{1 - \beta}{\alpha} \qquad B = \frac{\beta}{1 - \alpha} \qquad \alpha + \beta < 1 \tag{8.1}$$

The expected number of measurements N_i required to select the hypothesis H_i (i = 0, 1) is approximated by

$$N_0 = \frac{\beta \ln B + (1 - \beta) \ln A}{E(\Lambda)}$$

$$N_1 = \frac{(1 - \alpha) \ln B + \alpha \ln A}{E(\Lambda)}$$

(b) <u>m-Hypothesis testing by GSPRT</u>: For m classes (m ≥ 2) the generalized sequential likelihood function must be used:

$$u_{ik} \triangleq \frac{f(X_1, \ldots, X_k | H_i)}{\left[\displaystyle\prod_{j=1}^{m} f(X_1, \ldots, X_k | H_j)\right]^{1/m}} \qquad i = 1, \ldots, m$$

The testing procedure is then (see Reed [D-6]):

H_i true $\qquad \begin{cases} u_{ik} > A_i, & \text{and} \\ (\forall j = 1, \ldots, m) \ j \ne i \end{cases} \qquad\qquad u_{jk} \le A_j$

Request an additional
measurement and set k = k + 1 $\qquad (\forall j = 1, \ldots, m) \quad u_{jk} \le A_j$

(c) <u>Stopping bounds selection</u>: If only a finite number of
measurements N are available for hypothesis testing, the stopping
bounds should be made dependent on that number. If truncation occurs after more than twice the expected number of measurements N_i,
the effect of truncation is negligible. If not, $A(k)$ and $B(k)$ must
be monotonically nonincreasing and nondecreasing functions of k,
respectively. For example,

$$A(k) = A_0 \left(1 - \frac{k}{N} \right)^{r_1} \qquad B(k) = B_0 \left(1 - \frac{k}{N} \right)^{r_2} \qquad 0 \leq r_1, r_2 \leq 0$$

with A_0, B_0 given by (8.1).

(d) <u>Nonparametric SPRT</u>: In many cases, one of the major weak-
nesses of the SPRT and GSPRT as described is the requirement to know
a priori the conditional probability density functions of each of
the m classes. A nonparametric SPRT is described in Ref. A-45 in
which the statistic λ_k is replaced by a recursive statistic Z_k computed from the signed ranks $R(X_j)$ of the measurements X_j in the set
$\{X_1, \ldots, X_k\}$:

$$R(X_j) \triangleq \begin{cases} 1, \ldots, \ell, \ldots, k & \text{if } X_j > 0 \text{ is the } \ell\text{th} \\ & \quad \text{measurement} \\ -1, \ldots, -\ell, \ldots, -k & \text{if } X_j \leq 0 \text{ is the } \ell\text{th measure-} \\ & \quad \text{ment when ranked by} \\ & \quad \text{increasing values} \end{cases}$$

$$Z_k \triangleq \frac{R(X_1)}{1} + \frac{R(X_2)}{2} + \ldots + \frac{R(X_k)}{k}$$

(e) <u>Application</u>: Detection of a degradation in a dynamic
<u>system</u>: Consider a dynamic system modeled with additive noise.
Take X_i to be the estimated noise at time i, obtained by computing
the residual in the plant equation (see Section 5-4). Take for H_0
and H_1 the Gaussian and white noise distributions, respectively.
If the SPRT, operating on a sequence of noise estimates, indicates
a change of the distribution, this can be taken as evidence that a
degradation has occurred. The SPRT used in this way has been extensively applied to inertial measurement units [F-66].

9. DISTANCE MEASURES FOR CLASSIFICATION

Distance and similarity measures are quite essential at the classification stage of an automatic diagnostic system. We list here the
most important among them.

9.1 Distances Between Sets

Let $X = \{x\}$, $Y = \{y\}$ be two sets, and let $d(x,y)$ be a distance
measure between elements in the space. We then have the following
set distances:

1. Nearest neighbor metric:

$$D(X,Y) \triangleq \min_{x \in X, y \in Y} d(x,y)$$

2. Farthest neighbor metric:

$$D(X,Y) \triangleq \max_{x \in X, y \in Y} d(x,y)$$

3. Average metric:

$$D(X,Y) \triangleq \frac{\Sigma\, d(x,y)}{\text{Card}(X) \cdot \text{Card}(Y)}$$

4. Centroid metric:

$$D(X,Y) \triangleq d(\overline{x},\overline{y}) \qquad \overline{x} = E(x) \qquad \overline{y} = E(y)$$

5. Compactifying metric: $w(X)$ is the within-set sum of the
square distances:

$$D(X,Y) \triangleq w(X \cup Y) - w(X) - w(Y)$$

$$w(X) = 0.5 \left[\frac{\sum\limits_{\substack{x_1 \in X \\ x_2 \in X}} d^2(x_1,x_2)}{\text{Card}(X)} \right]$$

6. General distance:

$$D(X,Y) \triangleq \frac{|X \triangle Y|}{|X \cup Y|} \in [0,1]$$

where

$\triangle$:   symmetric difference operator

$|\cdot|$:   set measure

7. Hausdorff metric for topological vector spaces:

$$D(X,Y) \triangleq \inf\{c \in \mathbb{R} : X \subseteq (Y + cN) \text{ and } Y \subseteq (X + cN)\}$$

where N is a convex neighborhood in the vector space.

9.2 Geometric Distance Measures

Assuming X and Y to be subsets of $\mathbb{R}^n$, we denote by $x = (x_i)$ and $y = (y_j)$ the n coordinates of the elements x and y. The geometric distance measures depend exclusively on these coordinates even if they incorporate sample-based estimates.

1. Minkowski L^p metric, $p \geq 1$:

$$d(x,y) \triangleq \left(\sum_{i=1}^{n} |x_i - y_i|^p \right)^{1/p}$$

2. L^2 Euclidean metric:

$$d(x,y) \triangleq \sqrt{\sum_{i=1}^{n} (x_i - y_i)^2}$$

3. L^1 metric:

$$d(x,y) \triangleq \sum_{i=1}^{n} |x_i - y_i|$$

4. Camberra metric:

$$d(x,y) \triangleq \sum_{i=1}^{n} \frac{|x_i - y_i|}{x_i + y_i}$$

5. Chebychev metric:

$$d(x,y) = \max_{i=1,\ldots,n} |x_i - y_i|$$

6. City block distance, with given weights $a_i \geq 0$:

$$d(x,y) \triangleq \sum_{i=1}^{n} a_i |x_i - y_i|$$

7. Quadratic distance, with given weighting matrix Q:

$$d(x,y) \triangleq {}^t(x - y)Q(x - y)$$

8. Mahalanobis distance:

$$d(x,y) \triangleq {}^{t}(x - y)[Cov(x,y)]^{-1}(x - y)\{det[Cov(x,y)]\}^{1/n}$$

where $det[Cov(x,y)]$ is the determinant of the covariance matrix.

9. Chi-square distance with respect to x:

$$d(x,y) \triangleq \sum_{i=1}^{n} \left[\frac{(x_i/\Sigma_{j=1}^{n} x_j) - (y_i/\Sigma_{j=1}^{n} y_j)}{E_x(x)} \right]^2$$

9.3 Separation Measures

The information measures $S(\Omega/Z)$, where $\Omega = \{X,Y\}$ is the set of classes and Z a point in the space, express a measure of separation or discrimination between the classes X and Y at point Z. These information measures also depend on:

i. The a priori probabilities $Pr(X)$, $Pr(Y)$ of the classes X and Y

ii. The conditional probability density functions $f(Z/X)$, $f(Z/Y)$

iii. The a posteriori probabilities $Pr(X/Z)$ and $Pr(Y/Z)$ of the classes, conditional on Z

iv. The combined probability density $f(Z) = Pr(X)f(Z/X) + Pr(Y)f(Z/Y)$

The following is a list of major separation measures:

1. Shannon entropy:

$$S(\Omega/Z) \triangleq E[- Pr(X/Z) \ln Pr(X/Z) - Pr(Y/Z) \ln Pr(Y/Z)]$$

2. Average quadratic entropy:

$$S(\Omega/Z) \triangleq E\{Pr(X/Z)[1 - Pr(X/Z)] + Pr(Y/Z)[1 - Pr(Y/Z)]\}$$

3. Bayesian distance:

$$S(\Omega/Z) \triangleq E[Pr(X/Z)^2 + Pr(Y/Z)^2]$$

4. Kullbach divergence:

$$S(\Omega/Z) \triangleq E\left\{\left[\frac{Pr(X/Z)}{Pr(X)} - \frac{Pr(Y/Z)}{Pr(Y)}\right] \ln\left[\frac{Pr(Y)Pr(X/Z)}{Pr(X)Pr(Y/Z)}\right]\right\}$$

5. Bhattacharyya coefficient:

$$S(\Omega/Z) \triangleq E[\sqrt{Pr(X/Z)Pr(Y/Z)}]$$

6. Chernoff bound for $0 \leq s \leq 1$:

$$S(\Omega/Z) \triangleq E[\Pr(X/Z)^s \Pr(Y/Z)^{1-s}]$$

7. Kolmogoroff variational distance $s > 0$:

$$S(\Omega/Z) \triangleq \frac{1}{2} E[|\Pr(X/Z) - \Pr(Y/Z)|^s]$$

8. Generalized Traubert distance measure:

$$S(\Omega/Z) \triangleq E\left[\frac{\Pr(X/Z)^n + \Pr(Y/Z)^n}{\Pr(X/Z)^{n-1} + \Pr(Y/Z)^{n-1}}\right]$$

Chapter 2

INTRODUCTION TO
FAILURE DIAGNOSIS AND PERFORMANCE MONITORING

In this introductory chapter, the goals are to

    i. Delimit the class of systems for which the techniques described in this book are applicable

    ii. Express failure diagnosis and performance monitoring with respect to related concepts such as reliability, availability, safety, and maintenance

    iii. Demonstrate the impact of good failure diagnosis performance on several operational characteristics of a system, including reconfiguration

1. DEFINITIONS OF THE MAIN COMPONENTS OF THE READINESS CONCEPT

This section serves the purpose of introducing a number of basic concepts used throughout the book and of comparing them. A full list of the definitions used can be found in Appendix 1.

1.1 Basic Events

Failure: A failure is a condition (or state) characterized by the inability of a material, structure, or system to fulfill its intended purpose (task or mission), resulting in its retirement from usable service. Due to priorities among tasks, there may be a priority among failures. Those failures of highest priority will be dealt with in safety analysis; they are called catastrophic failures.

Degradation: A degradation is an event that impairs or deteriorates the system's ability to perform its specified task or mission. This includes improper controls and the effects of the environment.

Malfunction: A malfunction is an inability to operate in the normal
manner or at the expected level of performance. A malfunction may
be intermittent. It can be due to either failures or degradations.
Failure mode: A failure mode is a particular manner in which the
omission of an expected occurrence (or performance of a task) happens. It is thus a combination of failures and degradations. In
the medical field, failure modes are called syndromes.

1.2 Basic Troubleshooting Techniques (see Figure 2-1)
Failure detection: Failure detection is the act of identifying the
presence of an unspecified failure mode in a system, resulting in
an unspecified malfunction.
Failure localization: If the outcome of failure detection is positive, then failure localization designates the materials, structures,
components, or subsystems that have had a malfunction.
Failure diagnosis: Failure diagnosis is the process of identifying
a failure mode (or condition) from an evaluation of its signs and
symptoms (such as performance monitoring measurements). The diagnostic process extends failure detection to the detection of different failure modes.

1.3 Main Components of Readiness
1.3.1 Readiness: For the user, the major concern is the ability
of the system "to carry out a specified task or mission at a specified performance level, without catastrophic failure or interruption,
when activated at any given time." This overall ability is called
readiness; it can be estimated either a priori or a posteriori. Because readiness is a joint event (in probabilistic terms) and is
affected by many factors, readiness analysis is usually accomplished
by examining subevents and analyzing the conditional probability of
each such subevent with respect to one or more factors at a time
(see Chapter 1, Section 3).
1.3.2 Availability at time t: This is the probability of carrying
out a specified task at a specified performance level, without catastrophic failures or interruption, when the system is activated at

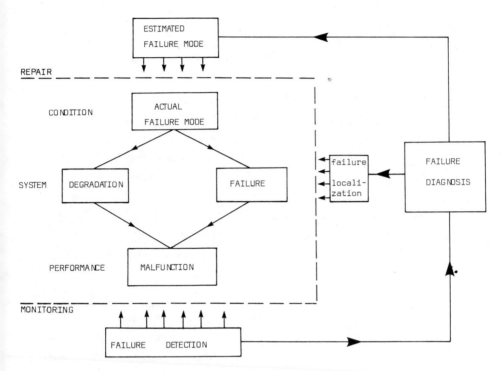

FIGURE 2-1 Basic events and troubleshooting techniques.

time t. The steady-state availability A is the expected value of the
prior availability at time t for a system with infinite lifetime:

$$A = \frac{t_O + t_i}{t_O + t_i + t_m + t_w}$$

where

t_i = idle time (system idle but ready to operate)

t_O = time when the system operates properly

t_m = downtime--when scheduled or unscheduled maintenance is performed

t_w = waiting time for parts, tools, or personnel when the system is down

1.33 Reliability at time t: This is the a priori probability that
the system carries out a specified task at a specified performance

level, without catastrophic failure or interruption, for a specified
period of time after t.

1.3.4 Safety: This is the probability of occurrence of a catastrophic failure during normal operation.

1.3.5 Maintainability at time t: This is the probability that the
specified task can be initiated at some specified time after t,
given the existence of a failure mode at time t.

1.3.6 Credibility at time t: This is the probability of having
detected a failure within a specified period of time after t, given
that it occurred at time t.

1.3.7 Survivability at time t: This is the probability of carrying
out a specified task at a specified performance level, without catastrophic failure or interruption, when the system is active for a
given period of time following the occurrence of a failure at time
t.

    1.4 Technical Performance of a Diagnostic System

    Any diagnostic system can make errors. Each of the following
types of errors can be specified either for a specific failure mode
or (in the expected sense) for the set of all possible failure modes.

1.4.1 Probability of an incorrect diagnosis: This is the probability of diagnosing a failure mode to be different from the actual one.

1.4.2 Probability of a rejection (or miss or nondetection): This
is the probability of not diagnosing or detecting a failure mode
when it is present.

1.4.3 Probability of false alarm: This is the probability of diagnosing that a failure mode is present when no failure has occurred
(the system is in its normal condition).

1.4.4 Probability of correct detection: This is the probability of
correctly detecting a failure mode when it is present. If there is
only one possible failure mode, this is the complement of the probability of a false alarm.

2. APPLICATIONS OF FAILURE DIAGNOSIS AND PERFORMANCE MONITORING

2.1 Assumptions on the System

For systems that are kept in operational readiness and good
repair for performance at high levels, one often faces problems with
the following characteristics:

(a) The systems considered have continuous input and output
signals which are generally nonstationary.

(b) These systems can be remotely monitored either permanently
(possibly with fixed-rate sampling) or during on-condition test sequences; this monitoring is carried out without disassembly.

(c) The number of different failure or degraded modes is low,
from perhaps 4 to 15.

(d) It is possible to observe or identify a statistically significant number of systems of the same design. Some of these must
have the characteristics of each of the failure modes envisaged,
including the mode which corresponds to proper functioning at the
specified performance levels. Such observations make up the learning
data.

(e) The operational readiness and maintenance requirements are
such that it must be possible to take one of the following actions
very rapidly (without prior disassembly) following the detection of
a failure or degradation in the system (see Figure 2-2):

    i.   Alarms or warnings

    ii. Appropriate repairs if the system is accessible

    iii. Reconfiguration if the system cannot be accessed or is
operating in an independent fashion

    iv. Design changes or modified utilization conditions

This diagnosis-induced reconfiguration includes not only hardware
actions (i.e., activation of a standby or spare unit or a redundant
system) but also software tasks (i.e., take a new set of measurements,
modify sampling rates, or activate new sensors).

(f) The diagnostic and monitoring tasks are carried out by a special-purpose hybrid system, processing all measurements in either of the following modes:

    i. On line, real time

   ii. Off line

The diagnostic system is located either off site (which requires a communication link) or as an integral part of the monitored system.

(g) The reliability of the diagnostic system is much greater than that of the operating system.

(h) Multiplexing should be possible in order to monitor several systems at the same time.

2.2 Classes of Diagnostic Measurements

Diagnostic data collected for individual devices fall into the following six categories:

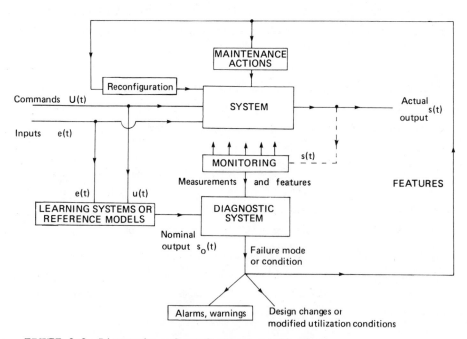

FIGURE 2-2 Diagnosis and performance monitoring.

(a) Design parameters and operational specifications: nominal values of the signals and tolerances as defined for each operational mode

(b) Measurements provided by the monitoring process

(c) Maintenance parameters: maintenance records, mean time between failure (MTBF), mean time between unscheduled repairs, over-hauls

(d) Measurements provided during off-line, nondestructive testing and by automatic test systems

(e) Settings and tunings

(f) Observations and measurements related to individual failures or degradations, including failure mode and effect analysis (FMEA) data

The main phenomena affecting the quality of these measurements are the following:

   i. Measurement errors, lack of sensitivity, improper bandwidth adjustments

   ii. Equipment variability affecting the quality of the learning data

   iii. Condition variability of individual components from test to test and physical memory effects

   iv. Insufficient knowledge of the mission, of the actual environment, and of the controls applied to the equipment

   v. Bad accessibility of some test or measurement points

The diagnostic measurements (a) through (f) used in a specific case should be chosen to comply adequately with the quality requirements (i) through (v). See also Chapters 7 and 11.

2.3 Fields of Application

From conditions (a) and (c) of Section 2.1, we can assume that the systems under study will not be digital systems such as computers for which the signals are essentially binary and have a considerable number of combinatorial states. The equipment of interest will usually consist of mechanical, electrical, electronic, control, thermal, fluidic, microwave, or biological systems, frequently in a control system set-up.

A major source of difficulty in the preceding problems resides
in the nature of the signals used in failure diagnosis. Our point
of view is that the fluctuations in signals, when properly filtered
and selected, may reveal important information regarding the internal
condition of the system, including failures, degradations, and relations to external causes.

It is often important to carry out failure diagnosis without
taking the system apart, carrying out destructive tests, or disturb-
ing its functioning.

Example 1: Consider a rotating machine or a water supply pump which
operates continuously and autonomously. Using a resistive couple in
parallel, one could measure sample values of the rotation speed, the
load, and the electric power consumption in the various parts of the
pump. When an automatic failure diagnosis is made using these measurements, an auxiliary pump is started, and an alarm signals the
maintenance staff regarding the supposed cause of the breakdown.
This enables them to speed up repair work since they are alerted to
their first priority in the fault-finding search. ∎

Example 2: Another typical example is that of an inertial guidance
platform for which one is trying to diagnose deterioration levels
and their effects on drift. ∎

3.   MAINTENANCE POLICIES FOR SYSTEMS
     UNDER CONTINUOUS MONITORING

3.1 Main Maintenance Policies

The four main maintenance policies applying to the systems
defined in Section 2.1 are the following:

Age maintenance policy: Overhaul or replace the whole system when
a predetermined age or number of life cycles is attained.

Block maintenance policy: Overhaul or replace subsystems at equally
spaced points in time independent of the failure history.

Opportunistic maintenance policy: Overhaul or make replacements
either at some well-defined points in time or when some other conditions related to the failure history are fulfilled.

Unscheduled maintenance policy: Overhaul or replace the subsystems only after a failure or degradation has been observed.

3.2 Preventive Maintenance and Condition Maintenance

Preventive maintenance and condition maintenance cover the first three of the preceding policies and aim at reducing high costs due to unscheduled maintenance.

(a) In the case of items which are subject to continuous surveillance so that a failure or degradation is in principle instantaneously detectable, we may wish to replace or overhaul an item before an expected failure in order to prevent the extra costs associated with a random failure, though as a result we then lose the value of the remaining lifetime.

(b) The key issue is then to use all monitoring measurements (see Section 2.2) and to set up rules by which one may decide when to carry out preventive maintenance.

(c) The classical approach is not to use these measurements and to base the timing rule only on an a priori model of the deterioration process. The basic theory for these models is to assume that the transitions between different states of deterioration obey Markovian laws or Poisson distributions.

(d) The modern approach, also called condition maintenance, is to carry out a manual or automatic inspection and diagnosis process in order to discover the actual state of the system and then to decide which maintenance action to take. It is evident that a prerequisite to condition maintenance is a joint performance monitoring and diagnostic capability; failure localization is not always necessary to make the maintenance decision.

3.3 Criteria Applying to Preventive
      and Condition Maintenance Decisions

Any of the following maintenance decision rules can be considered:

(a) Overhaul or replace the system if it is found to be in a state of deterioration exceeding a control limit.

(b) Minimize the cost per service time unit when the cost of replacement or overhaul and the costs of being in the various degraded states are taken into account (including inspection costs).

(c) Maximize the time between replacements or overhauls subject to the assumption that the reliability does not exceed some lower limit.

(d) Minimize the life cycle costs per item, including procurement, testing, maintenance, inspection, and operations.

3.4 Maintenance Model with Markovian Degradations

(a) Systems with wear-out and similar degradation processes as well as systems with different failure modes (requiring different repair actions) can be handled by the following Markov model. Define:

$p_r(n)$: r = 0, 1:   Markov chain transition matrix for no repair (r = 0) and repair (r = $\overline{1}$) decisions, respectively

$p_{ijr}(n)$:   (i,j)th element of $p_r(n)$

m: Number of states (conditions) in the system degradation Markov chain

$a_{ir}(n)$:   Pr(repair action r at time n : given state i at time n)

$x_i(n)$:   Pr(state i at time n)

$b_{ir}(n) \overset{\Delta}{=} x_i(n)a_{ir}(n)$: Pr(repair r and state i at time n)

The transition probabilities here are time dependent, allowing for general degradation distributions. With these definitions,

$$x_i(n + 1) = \sum_{r=0}^{1} \sum_{k=1}^{m} p_{kir}(n)a_{kr}(n)x_k(n) \qquad i = 1, 2, \ldots, m$$

Upon substituting the definition of $b_{ir}(n)$, the linearized transition equations become

$$\sum_{r=0}^{1} b_{ir}(n + 1) = \sum_{r=0}^{1} \sum_{k=1}^{m} p_{kir}(n)b_{kr}(n) \qquad i = 1, 2, \ldots, m$$

where b_{ir} satisfy the constraints

$$b_{ir}(n) \geq 0 \qquad\qquad r = 0, 1; \; n = 0, 1, \ldots, N - 1$$

$$\sum_{r=0}^{1} b_{ir}(n) = x_i(n) \qquad i = 1, 2, \ldots, m; \; n = 0, 1, \ldots, N - 1$$

The total number of such constraints grows only linearly with the number of states.

(b) A close study of this model shows that the equivalence between open- and closed-loop maintenance policies $p_r(n) = \varphi(\{x_i(n)\})$ no longer applies when degradations are considered ($m \geq 2$). For $m = 2$ (only two possible conditions for the system), this equivalence is a consequence of the fact that a two-state system will always be operating immediately after an inspection either because it has not failed or because it was reset by the repair action. In a system with degraded conditions, however, the repair need not be performed immediately following an inspection since several deterioration states may exist in which a repair is neither needed nor advantageous. In contrast to the state of affairs in two-state systems, the state of a system with degradations is, therefore, not necessarily known after an inspection.

4. RELATIONS AMONG RELIABILITY, MAINTENANCE DECISIONS,
    AND THE PROBABILITY OF INCORRECT DIAGNOSIS

Independent of the technique used for failure diagnosis or detection, it is worthwhile illustrating the relationships between the operational availability of a system, maintenance decisions, diagnostic performances, and system reliability. Because of errors in the diagnostic (or detection system) one may also wish to maximize (apart from the availability) the probability of initiating the proper maintenance action when actually needed.

4.1 Assumptions

The system is assumed to operate continuously until one of the following circumstances happens:

(a) A failure, the failure rate being λ

(b) A pulldown, with the following possible diagnostic and maintenance outcomes:

i. The system is found to be in good condition, and the pulldown was therefore unjustified.

ii. The system is found to be in bad condition (failure) and is repaired after a correct diagnosis.

iii. The system is found to be in bad condition (failure) and is repaired after an incorrect diagnosis, keeping it in bad condition.

Define π as the probability of incorrect diagnosis. The criterion J to be minimized is the global probability of either carrying out an unjustified pulldown or performing a bad repair. The equivalent criterion to be maximized is the global probability of carrying out only justified pulldowns and of performing a subsequent good repair. This, in turn, is similar to maximizing availability for a given system reliability level.

At any given time t, the system is in one of the following four states:

S_1 = system in service and in operational status
S_2 = system in operational status but improperly pulled down
S_3 = system with failure and improper repair
S_4 = system with failure and properly repaired

Let $p_i(t)$ be the probability for the system to be in state S_i at time t (i = 1, 2, 3, 4), and define the following transition probabilities:

$$\alpha_1 \, \Delta t = Pr(S_1 \to S_2 \text{ during } [t, \, t + \Delta t] : \text{given } S_1 \text{ at t})$$

$$\alpha_2 \, \Delta t = Pr(S_2 \to S_1 \text{ during } [t, \, t + \Delta t] : \text{given } S_2 \text{ at t})$$

$$\pi\lambda \, \Delta t = Pr(S_1 \to S_3 \text{ during } [t, \, t + \Delta t] : \text{given } S_1 \text{ at t})$$

$$(1 - \pi)\lambda \, \Delta t = Pr(S_1 \to S_4 \text{ during } [t, \, t + \Delta t] : \text{given } S_1 \text{ at t})$$

$$\mu_1 \, \Delta t = Pr(S_3 \to S_4 \text{ during } [t, \, t + \Delta t] : \text{given } S_3 \text{ at t})$$

$$\mu_2 \, \Delta t = Pr(S_4 \to S_1 \text{ during } [t, \, t + \Delta t] : \text{given } S_4 \text{ at t})$$

4.2 Results

It can be shown that the evolution of the $p_i(t)$, $i = 1, \ldots, 4$, are governed by

$$\frac{dp_1}{dt} = -(\alpha_1 + \lambda)p_1 + \alpha_2 p_2 + \mu_2 p_4$$

$$\frac{dp_2}{dt} = \alpha_1 p_1 - \alpha_2 p_2$$

$$\frac{dp_3}{dt} = \pi\lambda p_1 - \mu_1 p_3$$

$$\frac{dp_4}{dt} = (1 - \pi)\lambda p_1 + \mu_1 p_3 - \mu_2 p_4$$

If the system is operational at $t = 0$,

$$p_1(0) = 1 \qquad p_2(0) = p_3(0) = p_4(0) = 0$$

The differential system must fulfill the ergodicity requirement:

$$\lim_{t \to \infty} \left(\frac{dp_i}{dt} \right) = 0 \qquad i = 1, \ldots, 4 \qquad \text{independently of } p_i(0)$$

It is then possible to compute the exact transient solution via Laplace transform techniques. The steady-state solution is the following:

$$p_1 = \frac{1}{a_1 + a_2 + a_3 + 1}$$

$$p_2 = a_1 p_1 \qquad p_3 = a_2 p_1 \qquad p_4 = a_3 p_1$$

$$a_1 \triangleq \frac{\alpha_1}{\alpha_2} \qquad a_2 \triangleq \frac{\pi\lambda}{\mu_1} \qquad a_3 \triangleq \frac{\lambda}{\mu_2}$$

The criterion to be optimized takes the value

$$J \triangleq \Pr[S_2(\infty) \text{ or } S_3(\infty) \;/\; S_1(0)] = \frac{p_2 + p_3}{p_1} = a_1 + a_2$$

$$J = \frac{\alpha_1}{\alpha_2} + \frac{\pi\lambda}{\mu_1}$$

Maximizing the availability (minimizing J) for a given reliability
can thus be achieved by one of the following means:

   i.   Minimizing the number of unjustified pulldowns (reducing α_1)

   ii. Increasing the use of spare systems (increasing α_2)

   iii. Minimizing the probability of incorrect diagnosis (reducing π)

   iv. Increasing the testing and quality control capabilities
after maintenance (increasing μ_1)

A most interesting qualitative result is that the availability
is equally (marginally) sensitive to:

   i.   A change in the rate of unjustified pulldowns or a change
in $\pi\lambda$

   ii. A change in the rate of use of spare systems and in the
rate at which testing and quality control are successful

This demonstrates the importance of efforts aimed at improving diagnostic performance in order to reduce the total maintenance time and
maximize the availability.

5.   ADDED TECHNICAL SPECIFICATIONS
     TO MAKE FAILURE DIAGNOSIS FEASIBLE

Not all systems defined in Section 2.1 can be equipped with a separate failure diagnosis and performance monitoring system of the kind
represented in Figure 2-2. Our purpose in this section is to list
some additional hardware and requirements which have to be fulfilled
to make this possible; actually many more would be welcome.

   5.1 Time Meter or Cycle Counter

   Any subsystem which can be activated separately should be
equipped with a meter or cycle counter. This can be replaced by a
multiplexed meter which periodically tests the operating status of
all subsystems.

   5.2 Accessibility of the Main Test or Measurement Points

   It is necessary to ensure by design the accessibility of all
measurement points selected for those failure modes which are monitored (see Chapter 5). To the largest extent possible, group access

by arrays or clusters should be provided in order to minimize the number of different connectors. In the case of electrical measurements, impedance and bandwidth mismatch should be avoided. All junctions should be packaged for protection against humidity and vibrations, and the connectors should be reliable.

5.3 Measurement Calibration and Filtering

All transducers should be properly calibrated and should ideally allow for automatic testing and calibration. Analog adjustable filtering should be used as much as possible subject to bandwidth requirements and noise constraints.

5.4 Narrow Band Spectral Monitoring of an Analog Signal

In many cases, it is useful to extract and monitor the rms amplitude in some fixed spectral bands (see also narrow band analysis in Chapter 13). Often this can be easily implemented using a set of parallel narrow band analog filters of order 2, 3, or 4 (also called a vocoder). The vocoder outputs, possibly amplified or digitized, should be included in the measurement point panel or connector leads. Protection against 50-Hz and/or 400-Hz parasites should be provided for in the vocoder design.

5.5 Multiplexing and Economic Temporary Data Storage

(a) Whether the system under surveillance is autonomous or not, an analog to digital multiplexing (as well as sample-hold circuits) will often be required before data transmission via cable or radio link.

(b) If the monitoring data acquisition rate is low (a day or more), data transmission may become irrelevant, especially for slowly varying parameters. On-site temporary data storage is a convenient solution; it can use either a memory or a recorder operating as follows:

i. The measurements are multiplexed at adequate rates before recording.

ii. A measurement is recorded only if it exceeds some tolerance; this can be detected by comparison via a small commercial detector circuit (eight 16-bit words).

iii. In the case of actual recording of a measurement, the
value is packed together with the clock and channel readings.

iv. The storage device has a cyclical run, so that one keeps
at most a fixed number of past measurements; this number should be
large enough to observe transients or malfunctions prior to deterioration or failure.

v. The multiplexer and recorder should be protected against
system failure.

5.6 Histogram Estimation

Commercial special-purpose histogram readers can be very useful;
the register contents should be dumped periodically into a read-and-
write, rolling memory.

5.7 Sensor and Transducer Redundancy and Power Supplies

All sensors or transducers should have separate power supplies.
Redundant sensors are recommended for critical measurements. The
diagnostic system must have at all times the prestored calibration
curves of each individual sensor.

5.8 Wear-measuring Sensors

Wear-measuring sensors measure directly the amount and rate of
wear of bearing and friction surfaces (wear: 0 to 3 mm; precision:
1 μm) via a thin film resistor embedded in a plug of material similar to that of the bearing. The design should make provisions for
implementing such sensors when needed.

Chapter 3

DEGRADATION PROCESSES

This chapter is a short introduction to the analysis of degradation processes. Since this area is essentially experimental, each specific system will have to be matched to an appropriate degradation model.

Some classical degradation models are mentioned because of their implications and the possibility of incorporating them in failure diagnosis procedures as a priori information. They are used to compute quantiles of the deterioration distributions; these quantiles represent thresholds for automatic warning procedures. The degradation models considered include the theory of extreme values (or accumulated damage with restoration) for different stress distributions.

1. MAIN CLASSES OF FAILURE MODES

(a) Before any learning data are collected, it is absolutely necessary to carry out a careful failure mode evaluation analysis (FMEA) in order to establish a list of the failure modes and their characteristics. This list must include the following:

i. Major failure modes observed during operational tests after burn-in (categories I, II, and III and delivery tests); these tests should agree with the profiles of typical tasks or missions.

ii. Failure modes identified at the design stage via predictional reliability analysis, safety analysis, event-tree, and fault-tree analysis.

iii. Failure modes identified at the quality control level (mostly due to component variability).

In the case of multicomponent systems, it is essential to remember that there are usually many infrequent failures (occurring in only a few of 100 failure cases).

(b) From general experience, the most typical classes of failures or degradations are the following:

1. Underestimation of the characteristics of the operational environment

2. Improper technical specifications

3. Component and equipment variability

4. Design errors

5. Human errors and misuse

6. Fabrication, testing, or installation errors

7. Packing or casing errors

8. Maintenance errors, including:

    i. Pulling the wrong part

    ii. Pulling a good part from a good system

    iii. Improper installation or adjustment

    iv. Omitting prescribed actions

    v. Applying incorrect material

(c) Because the failure localization procedures used by the maintenance personnel sometimes tend to be inefficient, it is worthwhile to periodically record those failure modes listed in Section 1a which are recalled to have occurred. It is necessary to search for failure modes with a significant probability of occurrence and also for those which tend to be forgotten. In this respect, remember that the short term human memory operates simultaneously with at most three alternate hypotheses, although there may be many more.

(d) When compiling the list of failure modes, it is useful to simultaneously identify the measurements or tests considered to be best suited for detection of the failures or deteriorations (see Table 3-1 for an example).

(e) In the design of a diagnostic system, a critical phase is the selection of a reduced list of failure modes (4 to 15 per system decomposition level) around which the system will be designed. It is wise to restrict them to one or two classes among the eight listed in Section 1b. Another constraint is to select only those failure

TABLE 3-1 Example of a listing of all possible failure modes, with
the corresponding electrical measurements helpful for failure mode
detection; this example is from integrated circuit screening

Failure mode	Electrical measurements for detection
Fixed particles	Change of V_T in MOS-IC; short circuit of p-n junctions
Moving particles	Parameter drift; leak currents; low-frequency noise
Surface particles	Leak currents; capacity-induced breakdown; changes in the frequency bandwidth
Surface impurities	Breakdowns because of pinholes, overdiffusion, etc.; leak currents; bad connections due to corrosion
Bulk failures	Function loss and leak currents; hot spots
Wire bonding failures	Cut connection; lift-off; short circuit; increased resistivity due to oxidation of the bonding surface
Chip bonding failures	Thermal runaway; hot-spot breakdowns
Metallization	Cut connection; corona breakdown; short circuit; leak currents
Masking and bad connections	Breakdown; function loss; short circuit
Corrosion	Cut wire; whisker leak currents
Purple plague	Cut wire; increased resistance
Electron migration	Cut wire
Silver migration	Leak currents
Packaging fracture	Cut wire; thermal transients; bad mark
Parasitic fracture	Cut wire; reduced bandwidths; leak currents
Drift of the parameters	Leak currents

Failure mode distribution: 1. Wiring and bonds, 34%
                            2. Metallization, 23%
                            3. Diffusion and masking, 20%
                            4. Package and die, 19%
                            5. Other, 5%   ∎

modes for which monitoring and nondestructive testing procedures are
efficient (Table 3-2 gives an example of an efficiency evaluation);
measurement selection techniques are discussed in Chapter 5; see
also Table 3-3.

TABLE 3-2 Example giving test and measurement efficiencies for each failure mode. This example is from integrated circuit-screening (see also: MIL-STD-883)

H : High efficiency

M : Medium efficiency

L : Low efficiency

TESTS AND MEASUREMENTS	Surface properties (ions)	Impurities	Oxide pinholes or steps	Metallization, scratches	Bulk	Wire bonding	Chip bonding	Cracks in the chip	Package	Pins (terminals)	Thermal imbalance	Electric stability
External visual inspection									L	H		
Internal visual inspection(pre-cap)			M	H		H	M	H		H		
X-ray examination				L								
Electrical measurements	M	M	M	H		H		M				H
High-temperature tests		M		H		H		H				
Cyclical temperature changes				M		H	M	H	M		H	
Thermal shock						M	M	H		M		
Burn-in	H	H	M	H		H		H			M	H
Stationary humidity				M					H	M		
Cyclical humidity	M			M					H	M		
Centrifugal test						H	M	L	H			
Mechanical shock						M	M	L	M			
Vibrations						L		L	H			
Hermeticity								H	H	L		

(f) Equipment designed to have up to a few hundred hours of mean time between failures should be tested for an accumulated operating life of 20 to 50 times the planned MTBF. Most errors during the early testing stages are due to systematic failures which cannot be predicted by design or reliability analysis. For all these reasons, the reduced list of failure modes should not be selected until after extensive developmental testing, supplemented by results from burn-in testing of some major subsystems.

TABLE 3-3 Families of condition test procedures for each type of mechanical failure mode. For each procedure, a variety of sensors and physical measurements may be considered.

CONDITION TESTS / FAILURE MODE	Position	Size	Particles due to wear	Pressure, speed	Leaks	Temperature	Vibrations	Effect, efficiency	Rupture
Friction						X	X		
Wear	X	X	X	X	X		X		
Rupture	X	X			X		X		
Imbalance	X						X	X	
Corrosion		X			X	X			
Coating		X		X		X		X	
Thermal loading	X	X				X		X	X

2. THEORY OF EXTREMES

2.1 Distribution of the Maximum of a Sequence of Independent Random Variables

(a) When properly utilized, results about the statistics of extreme values can be very useful in failure diagnosis and performance monitoring. The problems for which this approach is relevant are the following:

1. Detection of a change in the shape of the underlying distribution of the measurements (essentially departure from a normal distribution)

2. Setting of alarm or warning thresholds for different degradation levels

3. Detection of strain or stress in materials

(b) Let X_1, ..., X_n be n independent normally distributed random variables, where X_i is $N(\mu_i, \sigma_i^2)$, $i = 1$, ..., n. In other words, the measurements may have different means and variances. Define:

i. $Y_n \overset{\Delta}{=}$ maximum of a particular sample set of X_i, $i = 1$, ..., n

ii. $u_n^* \overset{\Delta}{=}$ the solution of the equation

$$\prod_{i=1}^{n} \Phi\left(\frac{u_n^* - \mu_i}{\sigma_i}\right) = \left(1 - \frac{1}{n}\right)^n$$

iii. $\alpha_n \overset{\Delta}{=} \left(1 - \frac{1}{n}\right) \sum_{i=1}^{n} \frac{1}{\sqrt{2\pi}\,\sigma_i} \exp\left[-\frac{1}{2}\left(\frac{u_n^* - \mu_i}{\sigma_i}\right)^2\right]$$

where

$$\Phi(u) \overset{\Delta}{=} \frac{1}{\sqrt{2\pi}} \int_{-\infty}^{u} \exp\left(-\frac{t^2}{2}\right) dt$$

Then, under certain general restrictions (see Mazumdar [H-8] and Gumbel [A-37]) and provided that the μ_i's and σ_i's are not too different,

$$E(Y_n) \neq u_n^* + \frac{\gamma}{\alpha_n} \qquad \gamma = \text{Euler's constant} = 0.5772$$

$$\mathrm{Var}(Y_n) \neq \frac{\pi^2}{6\alpha_n} \qquad \text{(decreases as n increases)}$$

It should be noted that these formulas still hold if the measurements X_i are weakly correlated.

2.2 Distribution of the Maximum of a Sequence of Dependent or Independent Random Variables

Let X_i, ..., X_n be a sequence of n dependent or independent random variables, and let $F_i(\alpha) \overset{\Delta}{=} \Pr(X_i \leq \alpha)$, $i = 1$, ..., n. Then

$$\Pr(\max\{X_1, \ldots, X_n\} > y) \leq \min\left\{1, \sum_{i=1}^{n} [1 - F_i(y)]\right\}$$

Moreover, there exists a dependent sequence of random variables
having the distributions F_i and achieving the upper bound on the
left-hand side of this inequality.

3. THE WEIBULL DISTRIBUTION AS A DETERIORATION OR FRACTURE PROCESS

The Weibull distribution is frequently used to model failures in
reliability theory (see Ref. C-3). The following derivation of
the Weibull distribution yields a deterioration or fracture model
of wide applicability.

(a) Consider a body of volume V with a uniform stress distribution. That is, at every point the principal stresses s_1, s_2, and
s_3 are equal, and the reduced stress s is hence given by

$$s = s_1 - \nu(s_2 + s_3) = (1 - 2\nu)s_1$$

where ν is Poisson's constant. Suppose that the material of the
body is inhomogeneous and that it contains structural defects which
can be modeled as points, stochastically distributed throughout the
volume of the body. Fracture of the body is initiated if the strength
limit σ of such a structural defect is surpassed by the reduced stress
s at that point.

To investigate this failure model, the following assumptions
are made.

1. The points of structural defects in the body are distributed according to a Poisson distribution over the volume V of the
body; if v is the volume of a part of the body, then the probability
distribution of the number $n(v)$ of structural defects in this part
is given by

$$\Pr[n(v) = k] = \frac{(\lambda v)^k}{k!} e^{-\lambda v} \qquad k = 0, 1, \ldots$$

and for disjoint volumes v_1 and v_2 the stochastic variables $n(v_1)$

and $n(v_2)$ are independent. Here λ is the average number of structural defects per unit volume of the material.

2. The strength limit σ of a structural defect is a stochastic variable with distribution $F(\cdot)$. That is, the probability that the strength limit σ of a structural defect is less than s is given by

$$Pr(\sigma < s) \triangleq F(s)$$

3. The strength limits of different structural defects are independent and identically distributed.

(b) The distribution of the strength limit σ_V of the body may now be derived as follows. If the body contains $n(V)$ structural defects, then the strength limit σ_V of the body is clearly given by

$$\sigma_V = \min\{\sigma_1, \sigma_2, \ \ldots, \ \sigma_{n(V)}\}$$

Hence under the preceding assumptions

$$Pr(\sigma_V < \sigma) = \sum_{k=0}^{\infty} Pr[\sigma_V < \sigma \ / \ n(V) = k] \ Pr[n(V) = k]$$

$$= \sum_{k=0}^{\infty} \{1 - [1 - F(\sigma)]^k\} \frac{(\lambda V)^k}{k!} e^{-\lambda V}$$

$$= 1 - \exp[-\lambda V F(\sigma)] \tag{3.1}$$

Note that

$$Pr(\sigma_V < \infty) = 1 - e^{-\lambda V} \neq 1 \qquad \text{if } \lambda V \text{ is large}$$

Consequently, the probability P that the body fails due to a uniform stress distribution s is given by

$$P(s) = 1 - e^{-\lambda V F(s)}$$

In general,

$$F(\sigma) = 0 \qquad \text{for } \sigma < \sigma_0, \ \sigma_0 > 0$$

and if λV is not too small, then only values of $F(\sigma)$ in the neighborhood of σ_0 are of importance. Hence $F(\sigma)$ can be approximated by

$$F(\sigma) = \begin{cases} 0 & \text{for } \sigma < \sigma_0 \\ c(\sigma - \sigma_0)^{\alpha} & \text{for } \sigma > \sigma_0,\ \alpha > 0,\ c > 0 \end{cases} \tag{3.2}$$

Expression (3.1) may be rewritten as

$$\Pr(\sigma_V < \sigma) = \begin{cases} 1 - \exp[-\lambda Vc(\sigma - \sigma_0)^{\alpha}] & \sigma > \sigma_0 \\ 0 & \sigma < \sigma_0 \end{cases} \tag{3.3}$$

which is the well-known Weibull distribution.

(c) It is now readily seen that if the body consists of m different disjoint volumes V_i (i = 1, 2, ..., m) with λ_i and $F_i(\cdot)$, the average number of structural defects per unit volume and the strength limit distributions in part i, respectively, then the distribution of the strength limit σ_V of the total body is given by

$$\Pr(\sigma_V < \sigma) = 1 - \exp\left[- \sum_{i=1}^{m} \lambda_i V_i F_i(\sigma) \right] \tag{3.4}$$

The formulas (3.1) through (3.4) are now easily extended to bodies in which λ, $F(\cdot)$, and the stress distribution can be represented as functions of the point coordinates in the body. For instance, suppose that λ and $F(\cdot)$ are independent of the coordinates and note s(x,y,z) the reduced stress at point (x,y,z) of the body. Then the probability P that a failure occurs is given by

$$P(s) = 1 - \exp\left\{ -\int_V \lambda F[s(x,y,z)]\ dx\ dy\ dz \right\} \tag{3.5}$$

In formulas (3.4) and (3.5) the same approximations which led to formula (3.3) can be made.

The structure of formula (3.4) immediately reveals the contributions of the various parts of the body to the total strength distribution. The exponent in (3.4) is a weighted probability measure, normalized by $\sum_{i=1}^{m} \lambda_i V_i$.

(d) Formula (3.4) can be used for electronic equipment consisting of m different types of components, each occurring in large quantities, with $\lambda_i V_i$ the average number of weak components of type i and $F_i(\sigma)$ the probability that its breakdown limit is less than σ (assuming that for each type i the number of weak components has a Poisson distribution or can be approximated by a Poisson distribution).

(e) Relations simpler than (3.4) have been proposed to directly relate the failure rate λ (see Section 7 of Chapter 1) to the stress level σ. Stress can have a general meaning:

  i. Power rule model:

$$\frac{1}{\lambda} = \frac{\alpha}{\sigma^\beta}$$

  ii. Arrhenius reaction rate model:

$$\lambda = \exp(\alpha - \frac{\beta}{\sigma})$$

Model i has been applied to capacitors (voltage stress) and ii to semiconductors (thermal stresses). Formula (3.4) leads to yet another failure rate vs. stress model through an application of the definition of failure rate.

4. ACCUMULATED DAMAGE

(a) An important type of system failure is due to fatigue. The system is subjected to damage distributed over time, and when the total amount of damage exceeds the endurance level of the system, it fails. For a general discussion of stochastic fatigue models in mechanical and structural engineering, see Bolotin [C-22].

(b) An interesting and simple model has been considered by Esary et al. [C-23]. They investigate models in which the time instants when damage to the system occurs have a Poisson distribution. Denoting by P_k the probability that the system survives the first k shocks, the probability $H(t)$ that the system survives beyond time t is then given by

$$H(t) = \sum_{k=0}^{\infty} P_k \frac{(\lambda t)^k}{k!} e^{-\lambda t} \qquad t \geq 0$$

$H(t)$ represents the probability that the maximum damage experienced
by the system up to time t is less than x. Their studies concentrate
on the properties of the function $H(t)$ under various assumptions
about the sequence P_k ($k = 0, 1, \ldots$). The wide applicability of
this model is due to the large number of degrees of freedom in the
choice of the P_k sequence. For instance, if $F(x)$ is the distribution function of damage caused by a single shock and if it is assumed
that the damages caused by different shocks are independent identically distributed variables, then

$$P_k = F^k (x)$$

Hence

$$H(t) = e^{-\lambda t[1-F(x)]}$$

Example: This model has been used to study the structural reliability of aircraft wings subject to gust and excitation loads. ∎

   (c) Let us consider a model of accumulated damage to a system
with repair, reconfiguration, or self-restoring possibilities. If
the system has been damaged but not surpassing the endurance limit,
then the effect of damage decreases with time as the system recovers.
Regeneration may be accomplished through repairs or a self-restoring
mechanism; certain metal alloys, after exposure to an electrical or
magnetic field, eventually reobtain their original properties.

   Suppose that at stochastic instants t_1, t_2, $\ldots$, damages of
magnitude τ_1, τ_2, $\ldots$, are experienced by the system and that the
effects of damage decrease linearly with time. The unit for τ is
selected in such a way that it is coherent with time t, after some
scaling. Thus, if the system is initially undamaged and if τ_1 is
less than $(t_2 - t_1)$, the system recovers completely by time $t_1 + \tau_1$.
However, if $\tau_1 > (t_2 - t_1)$, then the magnitude of damage immediately
after t_2 is $\tau_1 - (t_2 - t_1) + \tau_2$ [if magnitudes of damage accumulate
linearly (see Figure 3-1)].

   In Figure 3-1 a possible realization of accumulated damage with
repair is shown. The system recovers completely by time $t_1 + \tau_1 +$
$\tau_2 + \tau_3$. At time t_5 the accumulated damage exceeds the endurance
level K, and the system fails.

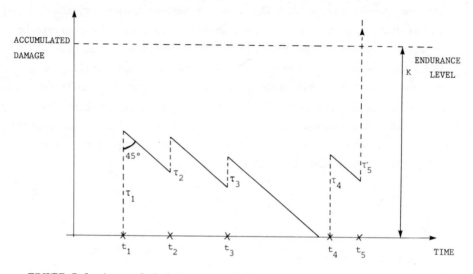

FIGURE 3-1   Accumulated damage model.

The stochastic process in this failure model appears to be identical to that of the virtual waiting-time process of a single-server queuing system. The latter process has been extensively studied. Consequently many results of queuing theory may be given new interpretation as reliability models of accumulated damage with restoration.

5.   NONLINEAR DETERIORATION PROCESSES
     DUE TO RANDOM NORMAL STRESSES

(a)   Let X be a condition parameter that is subject to discrete-time deterioration according to the following process:

$$x_{i+1} - x_i = y_{i+1} h(x_i)   i = 0, \ldots, n; \ x_0 \text{ given}$$

where y_{i+1} is a random stress independent of the current condition and distributed as $N(m, \sigma)$.

(b)   It can then be proved that x_n, the condition after n consecutive stresses, is such that an approximate probability distribution of $g(x_n)$ is $N(nm, \sigma\sqrt{n})$, where the deformation function g is related to h by

$$g(x) = \int_{x_0}^{x} \frac{dy}{h(y)}$$

Examples

i. $h(x) = 1$ $g(x) = x - x_0$ x_n normal

ii. $h(x) = x > 0$ $g(x) = \ln\left(\frac{x}{x_0}\right)$ x_n lognormal

iii. $h(x) = e^{\lambda x} - 1 < 0$ $g(x) = \frac{1}{\lambda} \ln\left(\frac{e^{\lambda x} - 1}{e^{\lambda x_0} - 1}\right)$

(c) This result aids in understanding how nonlinearities in deterioration processes propagate and affect the current condition.

6. BRANCHING POISSON PROCESSES

(a) The basic idea of the branching Poisson model is that recorded failures should be classified into two groups, primary failures and repeated or subsidiary failures.

A primary failure occurs when a component fails for the first time. If this failed component is not immediately detected and replaced, then as soon as the system needs to use it again, a new, repeated failure occurs. So a primary failure may be followed by a random number of repeated failures before the failing component is detected.

(b) The branching Poisson process is a model for the failure pattern just described. It is assumed that primary failures are distributed according to a Poisson process and that the times between successive (repeated) failures are independent, identically distributed variables. The mathematical analysis of this point process has been given by Lewis in Refs. A-35 and A-36.

(c) The branching Poisson process is well suited for modeling failures of electronic systems and for description of error burst patterns occurring in data transmission.

7.   DEGRADATION PROCESSES AND CALIBRATION

The methods and models of the previous sections in this chapter
assume some cumulative effect of time on degradation and that all
pieces of equipment of a given make have uniform capabilities. The
experience is, however, generally that these assumptions are not
justified and that a key issue is the method of calibration; the
classical method of calibration requires a piece of equipment to be
compared with a standard and then adjusted to a nominal value in
order to compensate for degradation (MIL-C-45622A). It is then
found that large proportions of the equipment (e.g., 10 to 15%) are
out of limits in one or more parameters immediately after calibration. The reason for these out-of-calibration events is generally
that some pieces of equipment are chronically drifting or erratic,
thus stressing the previous arguments; for the case of incapable
equipment, the performance is only temporarily improved by recall,
calibration, and bias adjustment: the correct decision would have
been to repair.

Accurate monitoring of equipment performance over time is
essential to detection of defective equipment and to optimum bias
adjustments. While stable equipment fails randomly with time, the
degradation processes of the previous sections may help in detecting
defective equipment at an early stage by a characterization of abnormal drift. These processes may use either simple control limits
(Section 2 and the quality control charts applied to calibration) or
statistical acceptance sampling to detect failed equipment [A-32,
A-45].

Chapter 4

TEST SEQUENCING WITH A PRIORI INFORMATION
FOR FAILURE LOCALIZATION

1. INTRODUCTION

Diagnosis becomes sequential when module inspections and tests are
done in some order. A series of tests or module inspections done in
a predetermined order is called a test sequence. The aim is to determine if the system is operational, and if it is not, to locate
the failed module. A sequential diagnosis uses the results of previous tests in the sequence for each new test. Diagnosis proceeds
via iterative deduction; the test sequence can be represented by a
graph or a test tree.

A tree of tests and inspections should allow one to do the
following:

Requirement A: Find a sequence which minimizes the expected
cost (or the expected time) required to locate a possible
breakdown (see Section 2.5 of Chapter 1).

Requirement B: Select the tests to be made at each stage in
the sequence in accordance with their contribution to the
final diagnosis.

Example

To test the system in Figure 4-1, we examine how information is
transmitted from input E to output S. This test must be done for
each type of input signal under consideration (for example, for
streams of unit steps).

(a) If the system transmits the input signals perfectly, diagnosis is obvious.

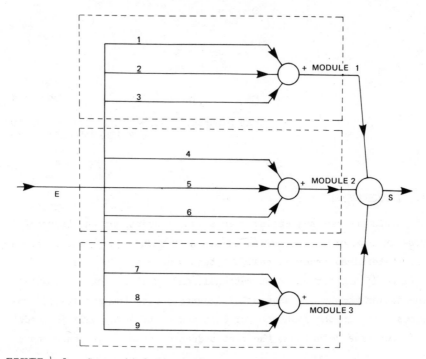

FIGURE 4-1   Sequential diagnosis on a simple device.

(b) If the system does not transmit the input signals, or dis-
torts them, then we must search for the system failure(s). In this
event, there are three possible cases:

1. If we have no a priori knowledge about breakdowns in the
system, then we must test all blocks and lines for faultiness, repairing faulty lines as they are found until the complete system
functions normally.

2. If we know that the system can have only one line cut at a
time, we can test each of the three blocks and repair the block in
which the cut or damaged line is found.

3. If we know that the system can only be in one of N mutually
exclusive conditions, the corresponding line properties for each of
these conditions can be tested for until the true state of the system has been identified.

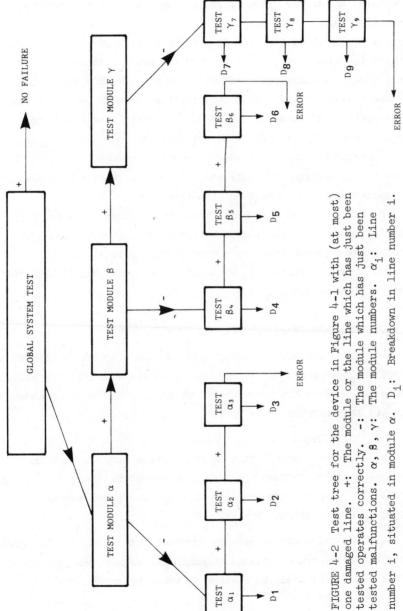

FIGURE 4-2 Test tree for the device in Figure 4-1 with (at most) one damaged line. +: The module or the line which has just been tested operates correctly. -: The module which has just been tested malfunctions. α, β, γ: The module numbers. α_i: Line number i, situated in module α. D_i: Breakdown in line number i.

These three alternatives require increasing amounts of a priori
information and memory. The corresponding test trees become in-
creasingly complex.

Figure 4-2 shows the test tree which corresponds to option 2,
in which the blocks are tested to find out which contains the damaged
line. Note that this tree does not carry any specific designation
of lines and blocks. The test sequencing goals will require a compromise between requirements A and B. The search for this compromise
is dealt with in the following paragraphs. ■

In Sections 5 and 6, we shall stress requirement A, namely the
sequencing of independent tests and inspections so as to minimize
the expected value of a cost or time criterion.

In Sections 3 and 4, we shall combine requirements A and B by
selecting, at each stage, the best test or module while seeking to
minimize the expected value of a cost or time criterion.

But first, in Section 2, we shall deal in more detail with test
trees for failure localization.

2. FAULT AND TEST TREES FOR FAILURE LOCALIZATION

The fault-tree approach is widely used for the computation of systems
reliability. Test and fault trees also provide good representations
of failure localization procedures. We shall first describe these
trees and then discuss their use.

2.1 Fault Trees

(a) Suppose that all test outcomes are binary and that the
states of individual subsystems are represented in binary (operating
or failed). Then many failure localization procedures can be described by a tree without cycles:

i. The nodes are labeled by tests; each node can be interpreted
as a state of ignorance, called an ambiguity subset; the root node,
or full set, corresponds to a state of total ignorance.

ii. The branches are labeled by components or subsystems; all branches that are descendant from a node make up the ambiguity subset of that node.

A test applied at a node serves to partition the associated ambiguity subset, thus reducing the ambiguity of the failure location.

(b) The notation at each node k of the fault tree might be

(test applied)(cost)($\underbrace{\text{subsystems not tested}}_{\text{ambiguity subset}}$)

or

$$T_j(\tau_j)[S(k)]$$

where:

p: Number of components or subsystems among which a failure must be localized.

f_i: A priori unreliability of the subsystem i $(i = 1, \ldots, p)$, or the probability that i had a breakdown just before the failure of the global system was detected. In particular, if the failure distributions of the various subsystems are exponential and if they were all activated simultaneously, then $f_i = 1 - \exp(-\lambda_i T)$, where T = the reading of the hour-meter of the system at the time of the breakdown; this reading is applicable to all subsystems.

T_j: Test j, applied to a set of subsystems or components.

S(k):   Set of those subsystems which have not yet been inspected at stage k in the fault tree; these sets might contain only a single subsystem, including the "no-failure" outcome.

τ_j: Cost of performing test T_j at stage k in the fault tree (or the mean time required for this test); τ_j is given a priori.

2.2 Failure Localization with Cost or Time Minimization

(a) When designing a failure localization procedure which can
be represented as a fault tree, one must simultaneously optimize:

i.   The tree structure in terms of joint tests of several
subsystems at a time

ii. The choice of which tests, among all those possible, are
to be carried out

iii. The test sequence, that is, the order in which the tests
are made

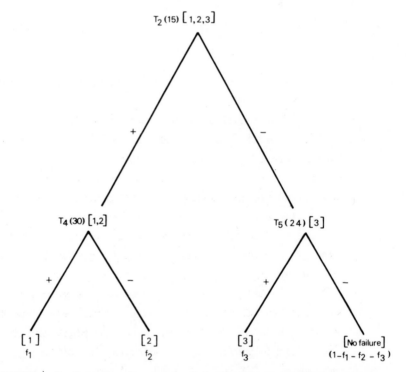

FIGURE 4-3 Example of a general fault-tree representation for
failure localization, to be interpreted as follows: 1: Test [1,
2, 3] by T_2; if outcome is positive, go to T_4; if not, go to T_5.
2: Test [1, 2] by T_4; if the outcome is positive, [1] has failed;
if not, [2] has failed. 3: Test [3] by T_5; if the outcome is positive, [3] has failed; if not, no failure.

In most circumstances, the only possible design approach is to list all feasible procedures and select the one minimizing the expected total cost (or time).

(b) The expected cost of a node is the product of its test costs by the probability of reaching that node (which is simply the sum of the probabilities of all descending branches). The expected cost C of the whole procedure is the sum of all expected costs at the nodes.

Example: See Figure 4-3.

$$C = 30(f_1 + f_2) + 24(1 - f_1 - f_2) + 15 \qquad \blacksquare$$

(c) The expected cost of a path is the sum of all test costs along the path, multiplied by the probability of traversing the path. The expected cost C of the procedure is thus the sum of the expected costs of all paths.

Example: See Figure 4-3.

$$C = f_1(15 + 30) + f_2(15 + 30) + f_3(15 + 24)$$
$$+ (1 - f_1 - f_2 - f_3)(15 + 24)$$

The two quantities C are identical. $\blacksquare$

3. LOCALIZATION OF A SINGLE FAILURE IN MINIMUM MEAN TIME
    OR WITH MINIMUM MEAN COST

(a) When testing subsystems or components individually,

   i. Each test has a cost.

   ii. Each test has an associated probability of passing a failed component.

   iii. Each test outcome depends on the outcomes of all previous tests.

It is advantageous to administer first those tests which are least expensive, thus "weeding out" failures before more expensive tests are needed. It is also desirable to start with tests having the highest discriminatory power, thus minimizing the expected number of tests to be administered. Not surprisingly, there is often a contradiction between these two procedures (as indicated in the introductory example of Section 1).

Determining a test sequence which minimizes the expected time required to locate a single failure or which minimizes the corresponding expected cost can be done rigorously using dynamic programming. This procedure will be described later for a case where subsystems are inspected successively. Dynamic programming and practical experience indicate that the person responsible for system repairs is subject to two conflicting influences when attempting to diagnose a system failure:

i. As more information is obtained regarding the failed system, the risk of formulating an erroneous diagnosis is lowered. Thus a skilled repair person is inclined to perform a large number of tests.

ii. On the other hand, these tests have costs in terms of the time and resources needed to carry them out.

If it is possible to collect the a priori information required, the optimal test sequence for failure location should be given to the repair staff in advance.

We assume that subsystem failures are statistically independent. Let f_i' be the probability of being in state E_i when subsystem i has failed (i = 1, ..., p) but the p - 1 remaining subsystems are still operational. Then:

$$f_i' \triangleq \frac{f_i/(1 - f_i)}{\Sigma_{\ell=1}^p [f_\ell/(1 - f_\ell)]}$$

We can define the state E_i^* of the system by the requirement that subsystem i (i = 1, ..., p) belongs to a set S_i of subsystems which have not yet been inspected and are all assumed to be operating, except for subsystem i. The probability f_i^* of this state E_i^* can be written as

$$f_i^* \triangleq \frac{f_i/(1 - f_i)}{\Sigma_{\ell \in S_i} [f_\ell/(1 - f_\ell)]}$$

We define n_{S_i} as follows:

$$n_{S_i} \triangleq \text{number of subsystems included in the set } S_i$$

For subsystems which have an exponential failure distribution (Section 7.5 of Chapter 1), one has, with the hypotheses given earlier,

$$f_i^* \# \lambda_i \left(\sum_{\ell \in S_i} \lambda_\ell \right)$$

for $\lambda_\ell T$ small (< 0.10).

(b) Suppose that we have to choose the jth subsystem to be inspected; that is, we are at step j of the test sequence ($j = 1$, ..., $p - 1$).

Step j

Suppose E_j^* is the condition of the system:

i. We have already tested $j - 1$ subsystems, and none of them has failed.

ii. S_j designates the subset of those systems not yet inspected; in particular, S_1 contains all the p subsystems.

iii. Select from S_j the subsystem $R(j)$ to be inspected (according to one of the rules ① to ④ that follow). $R(j)$ is the original label of the subsystem assigned the jth position in the suboptimal test sequence.

iv. If subsystem $R(j)$ has failed, the failure has been located, and there is no need to pursue the test sequence; otherwise, continue.

v. Set $S_j \triangleq S_j - R(j)$, increment j to $j + 1$, and repeat the preceding procedure.

(c) The selection rules for choosing which subsystem $R(j)$ is to be inspected are as follows:

$$① \quad \frac{f_{R(j)}^*}{\tau_{R(j)}} = \max_{\ell \in S_j} \frac{f_\ell^*}{\tau_\ell}$$

or its equivalent:

$$\frac{f_{R(j)}}{(1 - f_{R(j)})^{\tau_{R(j)}}} = \max_{\ell \in S_j} \frac{f_\ell}{(1 - f_\ell)^{\tau_\ell}}$$

② $\quad \dfrac{f_{R(j)}}{\tau_{R(j)}} \doteq \max\limits_{\ell \in S_j} \dfrac{f_\ell}{\tau_\ell}$

③ $\quad \dfrac{f^*_{R(j)} \ln(f^*_{R(j)}) + (1 - f^*_{R(j)}) \ln(1 - f^*_{R(j)})}{\tau_{R(j)}}$

$$= \min_{\ell \in S_j} \frac{f^*_\ell \ln(f^*_\ell) + (1 - f^*_\ell) \ln(1 - f^*_\ell)}{\tau_\ell}$$

This rule, based on the neguentropy as a measure of information content, selects the subsystem which maximizes the a priori information concerning the test result relative to the cost of the test (neguentropy is discussed in Chapter 5, and see Section 9.3 of Chapter 1).

Recall that the neguentropy relative to the condition of the subsystem ℓ is, in effect, equal to

- {Pr*(ℓ failed) ln[Pr*(ℓ failed)]

+ Pr*(ℓ in good condition) ln[Pr*(ℓ in good condition)]}

This quantity also represents the expected value of the proportion of possible tests that must be made on subsystem ℓ in order to claim that either ℓ has failed or ℓ is in good condition.

④ Suppose that $f_\ell[r(\ell)]$ is the probability that the subsystem ($\ell = 1, \ldots, p$) fails just before the entire system does, where $r(\ell)$ denotes one of the possible conditions of the subsystem ℓ at this moment; f_ℓ depends on $r(\ell)$ in a known manner. Let $q[r(\ell)]$ be the a priori probability that subsystem ℓ will be in condition $r(\ell)$ when the system fails completely. We may then define

$$\bar{f}_\ell \stackrel{\Delta}{=} \Sigma_r \, q[r(\ell)] f_\ell[r(\ell)] \qquad \ell \in S_i$$

$$f_i^*[r(i)] \triangleq \frac{f_i[r(i)]/\{1 - f_i[r(i)]\}}{\underset{\ell \in S_i}{\Sigma}\ [\overline{f}_\ell/(1 - \overline{f}_\ell)]}$$

$$I_i \triangleq \Sigma_r \left(f_i^*[r(i)] \ln\left\{\frac{f_i^*[r(i)]}{f_i q[r(i)]}\right\} \right.$$

$$\left. + \{1 - f_i^*[r(i)]\} \ln\left\{\frac{1 - f_i^*[r(i)]}{f_i q[r(i)]}\right\} \right)$$

$$\frac{I_{R(j)}}{\tau_{R(j)}} = \underset{\ell \in S_j}{\min}\ \frac{I_\ell}{\tau_\ell}$$

I_ℓ represents the "useful information," in the Shannon sense, of the operator which indicates the condition of subsystem ℓ when the breakdown occurs. It is also the mean mutual information of the two possible states of the complete system and all the conditions of subsystem ℓ, given test results for certain other subsystems. Hence it is conjectured that the preceding test sequencing rule ④ still holds if the test outcomes are dependent.

(d) The preceding procedure, using one of the rules ① to ④, yields test sequences which suboptimize the expected value of the criterion

$$J = \sum_{j=1}^{k} \tau_{R(j)}$$

This sum represents the total cost of failure localization if it is completed at stage k ($1 \le k \le p - 1$). Although these test sequences are only suboptimal, they are much easier to calculate than the optimal sequences determined by dynamic programming.

Example

Table 4-1 contains all the a priori data for 12 independent subsystems of a system with one failed subsystem at most.

Table 4-2 gives the suboptimal test sequences obtained using the selection rules ① to ③. Note that these sequences are different. ■

TABLE 4-1   Intermediate data and results for a suboptimal sequencing problem at the end of step j = 1; the failed subsystem Number 12 is marked by *

I	τ_i	f_i	f_i^*	$f_i/[\tau_i(1-f_i)]$	$-f_i^*\ln f_i^*-(1-f_i^*)\ln(1-f_i^*) \ /\tau_i$	f_i/τ_i
1	13.75	0.0196	0.01	0.0015	0.0041	0.0014
2	18.75	0.0385	0.02	0.0021	0.0052	0.0021
3	5.56	0.0476	0.025	0.009	0.021	0.0086
4	9.47	0.0909	0.05	0.0106	0.021	0.0096
5	4.44	0.1228	0.07	0.0315	0.0571	0.0277
6	7.37	0.1379	0.08	0.0217	0.0378	0.0187
7	12.63	0.1597	0.095	0.015	0.0249	0.0126
8	6.67	0.1803	0.11	0.033	0.052	0.027
9	20.0	0.187	0.115	0.0115	0.0178	0.0093
10	5.26	0.2063	0.13	0.0494	0.0735	0.0392
11	9.47	0.2188	0.14	0.0296	0.0428	0.0231
12	3.16	0.2366	0.155	• 0.0981	* 0.1365	• 0.0749

This example demonstrates some of the practical limitations of these procedures:

i.   If the number of subsystems is large, the rank computation required at each step becomes time-consuming.

ii.   Any computed test sequence must be examined for robustness relative to changes in cost parameter and reliability estimates.

TABLE 4-2   Suboptimal test sequences $R^n(j)$ corresponding to the example given in Table 4-1 and to the rules n = ①, ②, ③

Rank j in the test sequences	1	2	3	4	5	6	7	8	9	10	11	12
Rule ① $R^1(j)$	12	10	8	5	11	6	7	9	4	3	2	1
Rule ② $R^2(j)$	12	10	5	8	11	6	7	4	9	3	2	1
Rule ③ $R^3(j)$	12	10	5	8	11	6	3	7	4	9	1	2

FIRST SUBSYSTEM   LAST SUBSYSTEM
TO BE TESTED   TO BE TESTED

4. COMPARISON OF ALTERNATIVE TEST SEQUENCES

Before implementing a specific test sequence, it is recommended that all the alternative test sequences available be compared. Some of them may be purely experimental, while others might result from design procedures like that in Section 3. This comparison is made using statistical decision theory.

Let $R^n(j)$, $j = 1, \ldots, p$, be the test sequences to be compared, indexed by (n). Recall that $R^n(j)$ is the label of the jth test or subsystem in sequence (n).

We can compute the loss $L(j,n)$ at step j for the sequence resulting from the use of selection rule (n). This loss is the accumulated cost incurred in testing the j modules $R^n(1), \ldots, R^n(j)$:

$$L(j,n) = \sum_{k=1}^{j} R^n(k) \qquad j = 1, \ldots, p - 1$$

The assumption about failure uniqueness implies that at most p - 1 subsystems will be tested. If all these are found to be in good condition, then the pth subsystem must be the failed one. Thus

$$L(p,n) = L(p - 1, n)$$

The resulting table $L(j,n)$, $j = 1, \ldots, p$, is called a loss matrix.

The best test sequence (n)* is selected according to one of the following three classical decision rules:

(a) Min-Max decision:

$$L(\cdot,n^*) = \min_n \max_j L(j,n)$$

(b) Hurwitz α-optimal decision for given α, $0 \leq \alpha \leq 1$:

$$L(\cdot,n^*) = \min_n [\alpha \max_j L(j,n) + (1 - \alpha) \min_j L(j,n)]$$

(c) $$L(\cdot,n^*) = \min_n [\sum_{j=1}^{p} f_{R^n(j)} L(j,n)]$$

Example: In Table 4-3 we give the loss matrix associated with the example given in Table 4-1. Using the definition of $L(j,n)$, we plot

TABLE 4-3 Loss matrix associated with the example given in Tables 4-1 and 4-2 and rules ①, ②, and ③

L(i,n)	①	②	③	f_i
i : 1	102.78	102.78	97.78	0.01
i : 2	102.78	102.78	97.78	0.02
i : 3	84.03	84.03	41.93	0.025
i : 4	78.47	58.47	64.03	0.05
i : 5	19.53	12.86	12.86	0.07
i : 6	36.37	36.37	36.37	0.08
i : 7	49.00	49.00	54.56	0.095
i : 8	15.09	19.53	19.53	0.11
i : 9	69.00	78.47	84.03	0.115
i : 10	8.42	8.42	8.42	0.13
i : 11	29.00	29.00	29.00	0.14
i : 12	3.16	3.16	3.16	0.155
Max L(i,n) i	102.78	102.78	97.78	
Min L(i,n) i	3.16	3.16	3.16	
$\overline{L}(\cdot,n)$	33.28	33.39	33.63	

the accumulated costs incurred in localizing the failed subsystem vs. the number of subsystems inspected.

We look for the best test sequence according to each of the decision rules (a) through (c):

Decision rule	Best rule ⓝ *	$L(\cdot,n^*)$
Min-max	3	97.78
Hurwitz	3	Variable
Bayes	1	33.28

No conclusions can be drawn from this example regarding the respective merits of selection rules ①, ②, ③, and ④. However, in practice, it appears that rules ③ and ④ give the most desirable test sequences.

In terms of cost, rule ① attaches a higher level of priority to subsystem tests than rule ② does. Therefore rule ② tends to be more economical than rule ①. Rules ③ and ④ have the advantage of using previous test results because of dependency between f^*_i and S_i.

It can be shown that rule ① is effectively optimal for an extended class of k/p coherent systems. These are systems which contain p independent subsystems and are operational if and only if at least k of the subsystems are in good condition; thus 1/p denotes a parallel system, and p/p denotes a series system. In the k/p case, testing can be halted as soon as either k - 1 working subsystems or p - k + 1 failed subsystems are found. The optimality of rule ① follows from the assumption the system has failed and that the subsystems fail independently. This rule is not optimal for 2/n systems when there is an upper bound on the total cost (or time spent) for fault finding that is an active constraint.

The decision rules a-c described allow for comparison of testing procedures for individual (or groups of) modules. It should be noted that if the costs of module group tests are high, it is generally preferable to test modules individually.

5. TEST SEQUENCING BY DYNAMIC PROGRAMMING AND SEQUENTIAL TESTING

(a) In many practical situations there is no need to test all the subsystems of a failed system because:

i. The additional information provided by inspection of the remaining subsystems will be negligible in the diagnosis.

ii. It will take too long or be too costly or complicated to test the remaining subsystems.

Another type of maintenance can be used in such situations; consider the example of a device that is moved from a primary maintenance level (such as minor local repair) to a higher level (such as overhaul or return to the manufacturer).

The problem is to identify a group of subsystems for immediate diagnostic testing, given the a priori information available, while taking the time and resource constraints into account. For each stage j of the sequential diagnosis, we evaluate two functions:

1. The first criterion $G(T_j,i)$ is the expected cost of formulating the following diagnosis by the end of stage j: Subsystem $i \in S_{j+1}$ has failed, where S_{j+1} is the set of subsystems which have not yet been tested by the beginning of stage $j + 1$. Thus $G(T_j,i)$ depends on the cost of the j preceding tests; we can then write the following:

$$G(T_j) = \min G(T_j,i) \qquad 0 \le j \le p - 1; \; i \in S_{j+1}$$

$G(T_j)$ is obviously an increasing function of j, the number of tests completed. We call this the stopping cost, since it is the cost of a complete diagnosis at the end of stage j.

2. The second function $H(T_j,i)$ is the expected loss due to omitting the test of subsystem i. This loss depends on any erroneous diagnosis which results; it obviously depends on the outcome of j preceding tests. As before, S_{j+1} denotes the group of subsystems which have not yet been tested at the beginning of stage $j + 1$. One can then write the following:

$$H(T_j) = \min H(T_j,i) \qquad 0 \le j \le p - 1; \; i \in S_{j+1}$$

$H(T_j)$ is a function which decreases with j; since the loss envisaged is linked to an erroneous diagnosis from lack of information, we call this the cost-to-go.

At each stage j, a comparison rule between criteria $G(T_j)$ and $H(T_j)$ is used to decide whether to stop the test sequence and make a diagnosis or to test some more subsystems. This rule is commonly called the stopping rule.

Stopping rules are frequently of the following types:

Stopping rule A: Stop the test sequence as soon as the cost-
to-go $H(T_j)$ becomes less than the stopping
cost $G(T_j)$, that is, when $H(T_j) < G(T_j)$.

Stopping rule B: Stop the sequence as soon as the following
two conditions are satisfied: $H(T_j) \le h$ and
$G(T_j) \le g$.

Stopping rules of type B are useful if one anticipates that
the stopping cost and cost-to-go will have greatly different orders
of magnitude.

(b) All the possible test sequences of length p can be represented as a test tree. The search principle in this tree, based on
dynamic programming, is as follows: if it is possible to place upper and lower bounds on the costs H and G along each branch of the
test tree, one need only follow the branch which, for each step, has
the most favorable cost bounds.

A priori we can specify the following:

f_i: The a priori probability that subsystem 1, i = 1,
..., p, has broken down just before failure occurs
for the complete system

τ_i: The inspection cost of subsystem i, i = 1, ..., p,
or the mean time required for inspection

$C(k,i)$: The cost associated with a diagnosis of failure for
subsystem k when in fact subsystem i has failed

$P(i/T_j)$: The a priori probability that subsystem i $\in S_{j+1}$ has
failed, given the results T_j of the previous tests.

From these definitions, we derive the following formulas:

$$G(T_j,k) = \sum_{i \in S_{j+1}} C(k,i)P(i/T_j) \qquad j = 0, \ldots, p - 1; \; k \in S_{j+1}$$

$$H(T_j,k) = \tau_k + [1 - P(k/T_j)]H(T_{j+1}) \qquad \begin{aligned} &j = 0, \ldots, p - 1 \\ &k \in S_{j+1} \end{aligned}$$

$P(i/T_j)$ is often unknown; we then use the following approximation:

$$P(i/T_j) \# \frac{f_i}{\sum_{k \in S_{j+1}} f_k} \qquad j = 0, \ldots, p - 1$$

The decision rules

$$G(T_j) = \min_{i \in S_{j+1}} G(T_j, i) \qquad j = 0, \ldots, p - 1$$

$$H(T_j) = \min_{i \in S_{j+1}} H(T_j, i)$$

are Bayesian decision rules and are closely related to the optimality condition of dynamic programming.

(c) We can now generate the optimal test sequence.

① Take $H(T_{p-1}, k)$ = the cost or time needed to replace subsystem k or to carry out effective repair ($k = 1, \ldots, p$).

② Using ①, go back up the branches of the test tree, from the bottom to the top, and compute for each successive step the cost-to-go $H(T_j)$, $j = 0, \ldots, p - 1$, following at each step the branches which minimize $H(T_j, k)$ for all $k \in S_{j+1}$, depending on the starting point chosen at stage $j = p$.

③ Take $P(i/T_0) = f_i$, and from this compute $G(T_0, k)$ for $i = 1, \ldots, p$ and $k = 1, \ldots, p$.

④ Using ③, come back down the branches of the test tree, from top to bottom, and compute the stopping cost $G(T_j)$ at each step j; at each step, follow the branches which minimize $H(T_j, k)$ for all $k \in S_j$. Continue to move from top to bottom until the stopping rule interrupts the tests and thus identifies an optimal test sequence. The optimal test sequence then has length m, where $m < p$.

⑤ Finally, use this optimal test sequence as follows:

i. If the fault is located after at most m tests, then the failure diagnosis has been made.

ii. If these m tests do not discover any fault condition, either replace the equipment entirely or replace the (p - m) modules which were not tested.

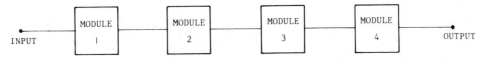

FIGURE 4-4 Series device to be tested sequentially.

Example

Consider the series device in Figure 4-4; it consists of four independent modules. We know that there can be only one failed module each time a system failure occurs. There is an inspection and test procedure for each module. In this example, we ignore repair or replacement costs for the faulty module.

Module	1	2	3	4
f_i	1/6	1/4	1/4	1/3
τ_i	2	3	4	5
C(1,i)	0	18	16	14
C(2,i)	20	0	16	14
C(3,i)	20	18	0	14
C(4,i)	20	18	16	0

Let us calculate the cost-to-go along a branch which passes through modules 1, 2, and 3 and terminates at module 4 in the test tree shown in Figure 4-5. We move from bottom to top. With the preceding hypotheses, we need only test a maximum of three modules (out of 1, 2, 3, 4) in order to locate the failure:

$$H(T_3,k) = H(T_3) = 0 \qquad k = 1, \ldots, 4$$

Thus:

1. $H(T_2) = \min(\tau_3 + 0, \tau_4 + 0) = \tau_3 = 4$

2. $H(T_1) = \min\limits_{k \in S_2} \left[\tau_k + \left(1 - \dfrac{f_k}{\Sigma_{i \in S_2} f_i} \right) \times 4 \right]$ $S_2 = \{2,3,4\}$,

$H(T_1)$ minimum for k = 2

$$H(T_1) = 3 + \left(1 - \dfrac{1/4}{1/4 + 1/4 + 1/3} \right) \times 4 = 5.8$$

3. $H(T_0) = \min\limits_{k \in S_1} \left[\tau_k + \left(1 - \dfrac{f_k}{\Sigma_{i \in S_1} f_i} \right) \times 5.8 \right]$

$S_1 = \{1,2,3,4\}$, $H(T_0)$ minimum for k = 1

$$H(T_0) = 2 + \frac{5}{6}(5.8) = 6.83$$

which yields the following optimum sequence, terminating with module
4: 1-2-3-(4). Consider now the two sequences

    1-2-3-(4)   or   2-1-3-(4)

Compute the stopping costs for both these sequences but
proceeding this time from the top toward the bottom. The costs
attached to localization decisions taken without inspecting any
subsystem, but based solely on a priori information, can be written
as follows:

$$G(T_0,1) = \tfrac{1}{6} \times 0 + \tfrac{1}{4} \times 18 + \tfrac{1}{4} \times 16 + \tfrac{1}{3} \times 14 = 13.17$$

$$G(T_0,2) = \tfrac{1}{6} \times 20 + \tfrac{1}{4} \times 0 + \tfrac{1}{4} \times 16 + \tfrac{1}{3} \times 14 = 12.0$$

$$G(T_0,3) = \tfrac{1}{6} \times 20 + \tfrac{1}{4} \times 18 + \tfrac{1}{4} \times 0 + \tfrac{1}{3} \times 14 = 12.67$$

$$G(T_0,4) = \tfrac{1}{6} \times 20 + \tfrac{1}{4} \times 18 + \tfrac{1}{4} \times 16 + \tfrac{1}{3} \times 0 = 11.83$$

$$G(T_0) = G(T_0,4) = 11.83$$

The successive values of $G(T_j)$, j = 0, 1, ..., p - 1, are shown
in Figure 4-5, together with $H(T_j)$. Because all stopping costs are
greater than the costs-to-go at all steps (j = 0, 1, 2, 3), stopping
rule A leads us to choose a test sequence of maximum length (3).
Thus we must test until the failed module is found, inspecting at

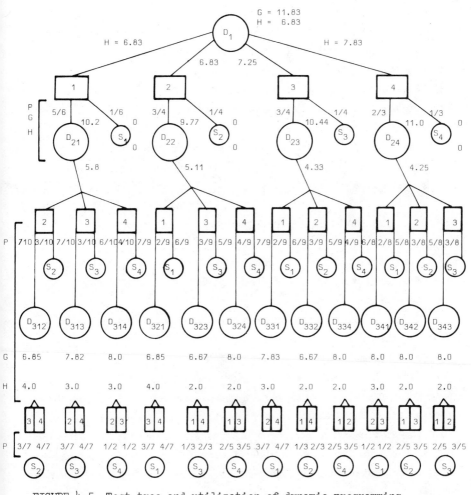

FIGURE 4-5 Test tree and utilization of dynamic programming.
P: transition probability $\triangleq 1 - P(i/T_j)$; C: the stopping cost [in
this case for an erroneous diagnosis only, since $C(i,i) = 0$]; H:
cost-to-go; $\boxed{i}$: test of module i; $\left(S_i\right)$: end of the sequence, the
failure having been identified in module i; $\left(D\right)$: choice of the following module to be tested; D_{ijk}: k is the last module to be tested.

most three modules. We can verify that the optimal test sequence
is the one given earlier, terminating with module $j = 4$, which has
the highest cost of failure detection.

The fact that the test sequence is of maximum length, $p - 1 = 3$,
can be easily understood. The $C(i,j)$ are an order of magnitude
greater than the τ_j's. Thus numerous tests are made, since the cost
τ_j of making a test is so low relative to the penalty for not detecting a failure. We shall obtain test sequences of length 2 or
less by considering penalties $C(i,j)$ that are three or seven times
lower, with some of the C values smaller than some τ values. ■

6.   THE GAMMA PROCEDURE FOR DETERMINING
     A SUBOPTIMAL TEST SEQUENCE

Frequently the number of subsystems is very high, which makes the
use of dynamic programming very costly and complex. The test tree
is then enormous.

We noted that dynamic programming requires bottom-up computations in the tree, starting with the lowest level. The gamma procedure is a simplification of the computational procedure for the
costs-to-go $H(T_j)$; one need only look from top to bottom in the
tree for a predetermined number of stages, instead of going to the
very bottom. The evaluation of costs-to-go can then be carried out
in a top-down manner, using previous results concerning the stopping
costs of the predetermined number of stages. This greatly simpli-
fies the computations, but the sequences which are found are suboptimal.

Example

Consider the example of Section 5 with a gamma procedure that
looks one stage ahead. In other words, we operate as if looking
for the test sequence that specifies at most one test for failure
localization. At any step, the stopping rule will tell us whether
the test sequence ought to be interrupted or not.

At any step, the following test will be the test which minimizes the expected cost-to-go; the corresponding stopping cost will
have been evaluated previously (see Figure 4-5):

Step $j = 1$: $S_1 = \{1,2,3,4\}$.

$$H(T_0) = \min_{k \in S_1} \left[\tau_k + \left(1 - \frac{f_k}{\Sigma_{i \in S_1} f_i} \right) G(T_1, k) \right]$$

$k = 1 \Rightarrow H(T_0) = 2 + \frac{5}{6}(10.2) = 10.5$

Step $j = 2$: $S_2 = \{2,3,4\} = S_1 - \{1\}$.

$$H(T_1) = \min_{k \in S_2} \left[\tau_k + \left(1 - \frac{f_k}{\Sigma_{i \in S_2} f_i} \right) G(T_2, k) \right]$$

$k = 2 \Rightarrow H(T_1) = 3 + \frac{7}{10}(6.85) = 7.8$

Step $j = 4$: $S_3 = \{3,4\} = S_2 - \{2\}$.

$$H(T_2) = \min_{k \in S_3} \left[\tau_k + \left(1 - \frac{f_k}{\Sigma_{i \in S_3} f_i} \right) G(T_3, k) \right] \quad \text{minimum for } k = 4$$

$k = 4 \Rightarrow H(T_2) = 5 + \frac{3}{7}(16.0) = 11.85$

Thus if the stopping rule is disregarded, the suboptimal sequence is 1-2-4-(3). ∎

7. IMPLEMENTATION OF SEQUENTIAL TESTING

(a) Sequential diagnosis, with proper utilization of a priori information, enables us to avoid some of the major drawbacks of logical diagnosis. The approach described in this chapter requires an evaluation of the probabilities f_i and $P(i/T_j)$ as well as the costs τ_i and $C(k,i)$. Often this can be done only with a high level of uncertainty. This uncertainty is also encountered when estimating the operational reliability of a system or the interdependence among failure modes of a subsystem and the observations which characterize them.

Baily and Spire [B-27] proposed approximations for these probabilities on the basis of small samples and the normality hypothesis.

Some authors have studied the dependence between observations carried out during inspection of a damaged subsystem, particularly for medical systems. Pashkovskiy [D-12] stresses that the number of test sequences that can be envisaged is low compared with the number of possible breakdown conditions for the system. Thus these suboptimal test sequences have the advantage, not of minimizing the cost or the duration of inspection, but of providing a good compromise among the various constraints to be satisfied.

It is important to emphasize that it is usually difficult to obtain f_i and $P(i/T_j)$ as functions of the past history of the system or of its operational condition before the failure occurred.

(b) It is always recommended that the size of test trees be reduced by looking for a procedure which limits the number of subsystems and the number of tests to be carried out per subsystem. In particular, one must eliminate redundant tests by identifying these through principal component or correspondence analysis (see Chapters 7 and 8).

(c) Also, it should be remembered that, wherever possible, it is desirable to test the subsystems individually, under conditions which are close to the operational environment and with controls that comply with operational specifications.

(d) The inspection of a subsystem can give rise to a quasi-optimal test sequence at that level.

One must be careful:

1. To determine a test sequence for each operational mode; tests which are not effective and modules which are not operational should be excluded.

2. To establish, for each operational mode, a list of the nominal inputs and outputs for the subsystem.

3. To set up the complete test tree for the subsystem under study for each operational mode.

Then the localization of failures in the system is being carried out on two different levels:

    i. Localization of the failed subsystem

    ii. Search within the failed subsystem for the failed part(s).

    In such a two-level sequential procedure, it is often appro-
priate to determine at the first level if the cost τ_ℓ of inspecting
the subsystem ℓ ($\ell = 1, \ldots, p$) is indeed the sum of the cost of
detecting a failure in that subsystem and the average costs of detection and repair (or replacement) of a damaged module in the subsystem.

    (e) Finally, it may prove useful to take the following phe-
nomenon into consideration. The test (or repair person) for sub-
system ℓ ($\ell = 1, \ldots, p$) will generally have only a probability δ_ℓ
< 1 of identifying correctly that the subsystem is operational.
Consequently there is a probability $1 - \delta_\ell > 0$ of classifying it as
having failed when it is actually operational. Assume that the
automatic test system (or the repair person) operates as follows:
if the failure of a given subsystem ℓ is not detected, the test
sequence is carried out to its end, and the last subsystem is thus
tested. Then the whole system is tested again until subsystem ℓ
is reexamined and finally identified as having failed. The extra
cost associated with testing all the subsystems is

$$\theta = \sum_{k=1}^{p} \tau_k$$

The average cost associated with repeating the test for all
subsystems due to a fault in the automatic test system (or of the
repair person in charge of the subsystem ℓ) is therefore $(1 - \delta_\ell)\theta$.

    If $\delta_\ell < 1$, it is appropriate to replace the cost τ_ℓ throughout
the present chapter by

$$\tau'_\ell = \tau_\ell + (1 - \delta_\ell)\theta \qquad \ell = 1, \ldots, p$$

This correction is applicable both to the first level (subsystems)
and to the second level (modules) of the localization procedure
(with different data, of course).

Chapter 5

COMPARATIVE EVALUATION OF TESTS

1. INTRODUCTION

In this chapter we shall consider a single system in which we wish
to diagnose the possible conditions E_i, $i = 1, \ldots, n$, n finite.
We have a certain number of test procedures available, designated
by the common symbol T. Test T applied to this system can have only
K (a finite number of) results, which are denoted by $T(k)$, $k = 1,$
$\ldots, K.$

Example

Test T is a voltage measurement with at most 10 possible values
$(0, 0.1, \ldots, 0.9)$ when the scale graduation and the system characteristics are considered. ∎

Suppose we must choose between system measurements of greatly
differing nature. We would like to be able to assess the relative
merits of these measurements in order to select those which both

    i. Maximize the probability of correct diagnosis

   ii. Minimize the error probability

Such measurements will be referred to as useful tests.

In these circumstances a golden rule is as follows: the useful
tests will most likely be those which characterize the physical processes involved or which govern the operation of the system in its
n possible conditions. In other words, the manufacturer or user
must know the system well enough to provide a list of tests in which
possible failures are reflected by changes in measured quantities
which depend on the conditions E_i, $i = 1, \ldots, n$.

Once the measurements are selected, it quite commonly happens that the resulting list is rather long, because of the natural tendency to include test procedures whose diagnostic performance is not well known.

We shall describe some methods for comparing the test procedures in this list. The comparisons are based on the evaluation of T using a utility function. With each test T we associate a number; the bigger the number, the better the test. This utility is equivalent to the evaluation function used to measure the value of an operator T in the field of artificial intelligence.

Later we shall propose other methods which are helpful in test selection (Chapters 7 and 8).

2.   GENERALIZED NEGUENTROPY

With each of the K possible values of the test T, we associate the following conditional distributions for $i = 1, \ldots, n$ and $k = 1, \ldots, K$:

$P[E_i, T(k)]$:   The a posteriori probability that test T will give the result $T(k)$ when the system is in the failed state E_i

$P_m[E_i, T(k)]$:   The estimate of $P[E_i, T(k)]$ after $m \geq 0$ inspections only of the system under study

$P(E_i, T), P_m(E_i, T)$:   K-dimensional vectors of the aforementioned quantities

$P(E_i)$:   The a priori probability that the system is in the failed state E_i

$P[T(k)]$:   The probability of measuring the result $T(k)$

By using the preceding data, the Bayes formula gives the posterior probability that the failed system is in failure mode E_i, $i = 1, \ldots, n$, given outcome $T(k)$; this is the conditional probability (see Chapter 1, Section 3):

$$P_m[E_i/T(k)] = P(E_i) \frac{P_m[E_i, T(k)]}{\sum_{\ell=1}^{n} P(E_\ell)P[E_\ell, T(k)]}$$

Let $V(x,y)$ be a known utility function, where y is the estimated value of a random variable having a true value of x.

We designate by $U(P_m(E_i,T),P(E_i,T))$ the utility function giving
a numerical value to the discrepancy between the estimated probability distribution $P_m(E_i,T)$ and its true value $P(E_i,T)$. Clearly the
utility functions V and U are related. We can make the following
assumptions:

   ① $\forall$ x, y, $V(x,x) \geq V(x,y)$.

   ②   If we add a constant to the value of $V(P(E_i,T(k))$,
$P_m(E_i,T(k)))$, k = 1, ..., K, then $U(P_m(E_i,T),P(E_i,T))$ increases by
the same amount.

   ③ $U(P_m(E_i,T),P(E_i,T))$ is an additive function of K, the
number of possible results for the test T.

   ④ $U(P_m(E_i,T),P(E_i,T))$ is invariant if the condition E_i is
divided into two disconnected conditions E_i', E_i'' such that

$$P_m(E_i',T) = \lambda P_m(E_i,T)$$

$$P(E_i',T) = \lambda P(E_i,T)$$

$$P_m(E_i'',T) = (1 - \lambda)P_m(E_i,T)$$

$$P(E_i'',T) = (1 - \lambda)P(E_i,T)$$

where $0 < \lambda < 1$.

A utility function $U_{a,b}$ which satisfies these four conditions
is

$$U_{a,b}(P_m(E_i,T),P(E_i,T)) \triangleq \frac{1}{b} \ln\left\{ \sum_{k=1}^{K} P[E_i,T(k)]\left[\sum_{\ell=1}^{K} P_m[E_i,T(\ell)] \right.\right.$$
$$\left.\left. \times \exp(V\{P_m[E_i,T(\ell)],P[E_i,T(\ell)]\}) \right]^{b/a} \right\}$$

Let us analyze this quantity as a function of the number of
applications m of test procedure T to the system under study. Since
an evaluation of T requires reference to a priori information, we
take $P_0[E_i,T(k)]$ as given.

If some of these probabilities $P_0[E_i, T(k)]$ are very low, it is recommended that their values be set to zero so as to avoid certain errors.

For $m \geq 1$, we can determine relative values of the utilities $U_{a,b}[P_m(E_i,T), P(E_i,T)]$ with respect to the origin $U_{a,b}[P_0(E_i,T), P(E_i,T)]$. $\{U_{a,b}[P_m(E_i,T), P(E_i,T)] - U_{a,b}[P_0(E_i,T), P(E_i,T)]\}$ then represents a distance measure between $P_m(E_i,T)$ and $P_0(E_i,T)$, given $P(E_i,T)$ (see Section 9 of Chapter 1).

A source of difficulty lies in the fact that $P(E_i,T)$ is unknown. We want to find the best approximate value for this distribution in order to evaluate the utility $U_{a,b}[P(E_i,T), P(E_i,T)]$ of test procedure T for the diagnosis of E_i. We can therefore define $U'_{a,b}[P_m(E_i,T), P_0(E_i,T)]$ be replacing $P(E_i,T)$ by $P_m(E_i,T)$ in the distance measure defined previously:

$$U'_{a,b}[P_m(E_i,T), P_0(E_i,T)] \triangleq U_{a,b}[P_m(E_i,T), P_m(E_i,T)]$$
$$- U_{a,b}[P_0(E_i,T), P_m(E_i,T)]$$

It can be shown that by appropriately choosing V, a, and b the relative utility $U'_{a,b}$ can be identified with the expected neguentropy:

$$U'_{a,b}[P_m(E_i,T), P_0(E_i,T)] = H(E_i,T,m)$$

where

$$H(E_i,T,m) \triangleq - \sum_{k=1}^{K} P_m[E_i,T(k)] \ln \frac{P_m[E_i,T(k)]}{P_0[E_i,T(k)]}$$

This constitutes a new distance measure between $P_m(E_i,T)$ and $P_0(E_i,T)$.

Neguentropy $H(E_i,T,m)$ represents the lack of homogeneity of the distribution $P_m(E_i,T)$ with respect to the reference distribution $P_0(E_i,T)$. If the latter is uniform, then (to the nearest constant) we can find entropy $S(E_i,T,m)$, which is an absolute measure of the uniformity of the distribution $P_m(E_i,T)$:

$$S(E_i,T,m) \triangleq - \sum_{k=1}^{K} P_m[E_i,T(k)] \ln[P_m[E_i,T(k)]] \geq 0$$

The greater this value, the more the various measurements resulting from T contribute to the diagnosis of E_i. One must avoid situations where the entropy is too large for the conditions E_i, i = 1, ..., n, since then the test procedure T cannot contribute to differentiation among these failure modes.

Example

Suppose that the number of possible failure modes n is equal to K, the number of possible results for T. Then it would be ideal for some permutation of the index values k to have

$$P_m[E_i,T(k)] = \begin{cases} 1 & \text{if } i = k, \ i = 1, \ ..., \ n \\ 0 & \text{if } i \neq k, \ k = 1, \ ..., \ n \end{cases}$$

where m = 0, ...

In this case, a measurement T enables a diagnosis to be made with certainty.

For any m we then have

$$H(E_i,T,m) = S(E_i,T,m) = 0 \qquad \blacksquare$$

3. MUTUAL INFORMATION BETWEEN A TEST
   AND AN EQUIPMENT CONDITION

Because the notion of entropy has cropped up in Section 2, we can imagine representing an automatic diagnosis or repair procedure as an information channel between the system and the devices used for the test T.

Using communication theory, we can define the following for two propositions A and B (see Figure 5-1):

$$I(A,B) \triangleq \ln \frac{P(A \cup B)}{P(A)P(B)} = \ln \frac{P(A/B)}{P(A)} = I(B,A)$$

which represents the mutual information between A and B, or the logarithm of the association ratio between A and B. We can define I(A,B/C) by conditioning all these probabilities on C.

FIGURE 5-1 Diagnosis as a communication channel between the failed
system and the test system.

For example, define.:

A: The system has failed and is in condition E_i.

B: The result of the test procedure T is T(k).

C: The system has been inspected only m times.

Then we have

$$I[E_i,T(k)/m] = \ln \frac{P_m[E_i,T(k)]}{P(E_i)P[T(k)]}$$

The expectation of $I[E_i,T(k)/m]$ over all K possible results of
T is

$$I[E_i,T/m] = \sum_{k=1}^{K} P_m[E_i,T(k)]I[E_i,T(k)/m]$$

which represents the mutual information, in the Shannon sense, between T and E_i. Finally, we define the mutual information between
T and the failed system as

$$I(system,T/m) = \sum_{i=1}^{n} I(E_i,T/m) \geq 0$$

This quantity can be designated as follows: the useful information
provided by test procedure T for identifying the condition of the
system under study.

The system entropy S,

$$S(system) = - \sum_{i=1}^{n} P(E_i) \ln(P(E_i))$$

represents, in accordance with questionnaire theory, the minimum of

the expected number of tests that must be made in order to classify
the system as being in condition E_i with probability 1 for i = 1,
..., n.

We then have the following:

$$0 \le I(system,T/m) \le S(system)$$

If the test identifies the system condition with absolute certainty, then $I(system,T/m) = S(system)$.

Define the conditional entropy of the system, given that $T(k)$
is the result of test procedure T, as

$$S(system/T(k)/m) \overset{\Delta}{=} - \sum_{i=1}^{n} P_m[E_i/T(k)] \ln[P_m[E_i/T(k)]]$$

Then

$$I[E_i,T(k)/m] = S(system) - S[system/T(k)/m]$$

If the probability of an erroneous diagnosis (denoted as ϵ)
is low, then as a first approximation

$$S[system/T(k)/m] \# \epsilon_{km} \ln \epsilon_{km}$$

4. COMPOSITION OF SERIES AND PARALLEL TESTS

It is possible to have different test operators (say T_1 and T_2) in
series or in parallel (see Figures 5-2 and 5-3).

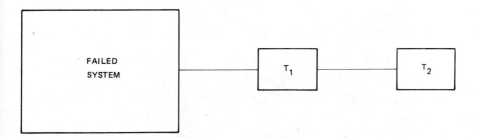

FIGURE 5-2 Series tests.

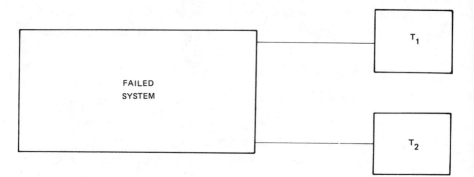

FIGURE 5-3 Parallel tests.

(a) If T_1 is connected to the system and T_2 is in series with T_1, then T_2 tests the various values of the measurements prescribed by T_1. We can then show that the mutual information between the failed system and T_1 is greater than or equal to the mutual information between the failed system and the T_2 output.

(b) If T_1 and T_2 are connected in parallel to the system, we can define the composite test (T_1,T_2) formed by all pairs of measurements provided by T_1 and T_2. It can be shown that

$$I[\text{system},(T_1,T_2)/m] \geq I(\text{system},T_1/m)$$

$$I[\text{system},(T_1,T_2)/m] \geq I(\text{system},T_2/m)$$

$$I[\text{system},(T_1,T_2)/m] \geq I(\text{system},T_1/m) + I(\text{system},T_2/m)$$
$$- I(T_1,T_2/m)$$

5.   COMPARISON OF TESTS

Let us return to the problem of choosing useful tests from a list dictated by practical considerations.

From the preceding discussion, after m inspections of the system we might select tests T which:

① Maximize the average value, over all conditions E_i, of the relative utility $U'_{a,b}[P_m(E_i,T),P_0(E_i,T)]$

② Maximize the average value, over all conditions E_i, of the neguentropy $H(E_i,T,m)$

③ Minimize the average value, over all conditions E_i, of the entropy $S(E_i,T,m)$

④ Maximize the useful information $I(system,T/m)$ provided by the test T

These rules are neither comparable nor optimal, because of the approximation used in Section 2.

6. APPLICATIONS TO SEQUENTIAL AND INTERACTIVE TEST SELECTION

Suppose that we have chosen $I(system,T/m)$ in order to compare tests. In a sequential approach (see Section 5 of Chapter 4), the repair-person tries to select a test sequence $(T_{R(j)})$ that maximizes the probability for correct diagnosis, knowing the results of the j tests. Suppose that τ_j represents the cost (or testing duration) of test T_j; $R(j)$ is defined as in Section 3 of Chapter 4.

Using comparison criterion ① from Section 5 and one of the sequencing rules described in Section 3 of Chapter 4, we can determine a _quasi-optimal_ test sequence using the rule α:

$$\alpha: \quad \frac{I(system,T_{R(1)}/1)}{\tau_{R(1)}} \geq \frac{I(system,T_{R(2)}/2)}{\tau_{R(2)}} \quad \cdot$$

$$\geq \ldots \geq \frac{I(system,T_{R(j)}/j)}{\tau_{R(j)}}$$

Justification for such a sequencing rule is found in the theory of pseudoquestionnaires as well as in some equivalent rules (cf. Chapter 4). In particular, it can be shown that if the tests are all independent and if the useful information from test $T_{R(j)}$ is such that

$$I(system,T_{R(j)}/j) \geq (1 - \rho) \sup_{\ell \in S_j} I(system,T_\ell/j) \qquad 0 \leq \rho \leq 1$$

where S_j is the subset of the remaining tests, then

$$\lim_{j \to +\infty} I(system,T_{R(j)}/j) = S(system)$$

If $P_j(\text{system}) \triangleq [P_j(E_1), \ldots, P_j(E_n)]$ is the vector of estimated probabilities $P_j(E_i)$, $i = 1, \ldots, n$, of the system having fault E_i, then with knowledge of the results of the j preceding tests in the optimal sequence we have

$$\lim_{j \to \infty} P_j(\text{system}) = [P(E_1), \ldots, P(E_n)]$$

and we can designate $P_j(\text{system})$ to be the diagnosis vector. It is appropriate, moreover, to replace the probabilities $P(E_i)$, $i = 1, \ldots, n$, by their current estimates.

If the tests $T_{R(j)}$ are independent and each has one single outcome $k_{R(j)}$, then $P_j(E_i)$ may be estimated using the Bayes formula:

$$P_j(E_i) = 1 - \prod_{\ell=1}^{j} \{1 - P_\ell[E_i | T_{R(\ell)}(k_{R(\ell)})]\}$$

$$P_\ell[E_i / T_{R(\ell)}(k_{R(\ell)})] = P_{\ell-1}(E_i) \frac{P_\ell[E_i, T_{R(\ell)}(k_{R(\ell)})]}{\sum_{m=1}^{n} P_{\ell-1}(E_m) P_\ell[E_m, T_{R(\ell)}(k_{R(\ell)})]}$$

$$i = 1, \ldots, n$$

Note that the estimated utilities of those tests not yet performed do vary from step to step; this is basically due to the fact that the useful information brought by each of them depends on the outcomes of all previous tests.

This is in keeping with what happens in test trees based on dynamic programming, where all the conditional probabilities have to be given in advance. It is natural that a repair person may not understand the objectives of a given, predetermined test sequence. In this situation, he or she can assess the developing quality of the diagnosis [by means of vector $P_j(\text{system})$] and approve (or reject) new tests as they are proposed by the sequencing rule indicated earlier.

We can then envisage the selection and sequencing of the tests using an interactive or conversational system, as previously implemented by the author.

Step j:

   ①   j - 1 tests have already been carried out on the failed system, and the resulting diagnosis vector is P_{j-1}(system).

   ② S_j is the set of those tests not yet carried out.

   ③   By using rule α (or an equivalent rule), the test $T_{R(j)}$ is selected from among S_j:

      i.   P(system) is estimated by P_{j-1}(system).

     ii.   The costs τ_1 have been previously stored in memory.

    iii.   The transition probabilities $P_j[E_i, T_\ell(k)]$ for $\ell \in S_j$ are entered by the repair person into the computer through an alphanumeric keyboard display (where i = 1, ..., n and k = 1, ..., K_ℓ).

   ④   The results of the selection procedure, namely $T_{R(j)}$ and also tests $\ell \in S_j$ with the same (utility/cost) ratio, are displayed.

   ⑤   The repair person then confirms the choice of test $T_{R(j)}$ or chooses a comparable test from S_j.

   ⑥   Resulting measurement of the test selected in ⑤.

   ⑦   Update the diagnosis vector P_j(system), and display it.

   ⑧   If P_j(system) allows for a diagnosis with low rejection and error risks, stop the procedure and carry out the repair; if not, increment j and return to ①.

The main advantage of this interactive system is to provide the repair person with the possibility of assessing the probabilities $P_j[E_i, T_{R(j)}(k)]$ which cannot be statistically estimated with a sufficient degree of confidence. These probabilities depend on both the nature and quality of the tests.

To further facilitate repair tasks, only a few probability updates in ③ need be made. New estimated values can either replace former estimates or be averaged out with them.

Another advantage is that repair personnel need only bear in mind the utilities of tests and not their costs or the durations (these two parameters are incorporated in the selection of the lists of good tests displayed during step ④). Thus frequent errors of judgment that repair people make regarding the costs of repair actions can be avoided. We can also inhibit the natural tendency to request additional tests so as to postpone dealing with the problem.

On occasion, we have seen the utilization of such a system, by personnel with the appropriate training, enable correct diagnosis on the basis of only 60% (±20%) of the usual number of tests. The time savings were generally somewhat higher [30% (±10%)], because these selection procedures tend to leave out long or costly tests and those which prove relatively useless. The applications observed involved complex mechanical and electromechanical equipment with degradation states $(E_i, i = 1, \ldots, n)$ which were well differentiated.

7. APPLICATION TO PERFORMANCE MONITORING AND SEQUENTIAL DIAGNOSIS OF CONTROL SYSTEMS

In this case, the test T is the process of measuring the K coordinates of a stochastic process at time m (see Chapter 15 and Section 4, Chapter 1); for diagnostic purposes, this stochastic process (including noise) will be modeled in some way, thus allowing for analytical expressions of $P_m[E_i, T(k)]$. These expressions will include decision thresholds whereby the equipment conditions E_i, i = 1, ..., n, are to be discriminated; they will typically be values of k-variate normal distributions.   ∎

The theories of this chapter are directly applicable to performance monitoring and sequential diagnosis of control systems; they are the key to solutions of the following problems:

i. Optimize the decision thresholds for sequential diagnosis of control systems; the optimization is carried out by any of the rules of Section 5.

ii. Suboptimal test sequencing, in the event that not all K coordinates can be processed at the time for diagnostic purposes; the sequencing rules of Chapter 4 and Section 6 indicate how to screen periodically the K process coordinates.

Chapter 6

RELIABILITY AND MAINTENANCE DATA BANKS

1. INTRODUCTION

One of the aims of any diagnostic procedure is to identify a failure
or joint set of failures (also called a syndrome) on the basis of
the following:

(a) Information regarding the past history of the equipment,
including maintenance operations already carried out, and its operational utilization. Such information provides learning data which
are generally stored in a reliability and maintenance data bank and
are updated periodically.

(b) Information regarding the circumstances of degradations
and failures, visual inspections of the equipment, and the results
of nondestructive tests. Such information composes the coordinates
of a description vector called the feature vector.

When the system fails, a search for correlations between the
symptoms described by the feature vector and the learning data will
hopefully enable it to be classified as being in one of the possible
failure modes (which are assumed to be in a finite number: see
Section 2.2 of Chapter 2). The final classification decision will
be made using a predesigned decision rule.

Because of the important part played in such a diagnostic procedure by a priori information (here called learning data), it is
important to state several general rules for compiling data about
the maintenance and reliability of a family of similar devices.

2. PRELIMINARY DESIGN STUDY

The first important step is to study any reliability and maintenance documentation which might be available from public agencies, enterprises, and users of the system being investigated. It is also essential to collect data describing the operating characteristics and conditions arising when failure or degradation occurs for each type of equipment.

   The objective of such a study is to obtain a large data base which represents present and past experience with each type of equipment, independent of support systems and elementary components. A list of foreseeable failure and degradation modes should also be compiled. If possible, this list should detail the specific failure modes of each subsystem and component; this will facilitate later analysis or more detailed data collection.

3. CHOICE OF THE SUBSYSTEMS, COMPONENTS, AND PARAMETERS
    TO BE MONITORED BY THE DATA COLLECTION SYSTEM

   (a) It is recommended that the largest possible number of the following be considered as candidates:

      i. Subsystems or components appearing on users' inventory lists or for which some workshop has received the maintenance responsibility

      ii. Parameters that are accessible using the existing sensors or are likely to be recorded if they play a significant role in the physical behavior of the system

   This will enable later selection, for each specific case, of those subsystems, components, and parameters which offer the best potential for diagnosis, given operational or economic constraints and other priorities.

   (b) Subsystems, components, and parameters should then be grouped by general mission categories or operational functions. This enables later classification of failure-related information and comparison of equipment under similar operating conditions even

if specific mission profiles vary within each category. We can then
tabulate all the information within each category without further
study of the equipment providing it.

(c) If other systems use similar components or subsystems under
equivalent conditions, this information can be included. Users of
similar systems or subsystems can exchange information and compare
relevant operational and maintenance characteristics. We should
consider a wide range of operating durations; in particular, data
on early failures should be accumulated.

However, prototypes and systems existing only in small numbers
will have to be dealt with separately.

(d) If the selection process is motivated by customer or user
complaints, it should be remembered that this information alone is
insufficient; on the whole, a customer complains only when he or she
has reached a certain level of frustration.

4. THE DATA SOURCES

An effort should be made to combine all the information available
about failures and maintenance of a system of interest to several
organizations for the purpose of carrying out a statistical analysis. Even if it is not felt advisable to bring all such information
together in the form of a data bank, it should still be possible to
communicate by telephone or mail.

Great care and the most stringent measures must be taken to
protect the data bank and control access to it. Usually each data
supplier should have access only to his or her own data and to fully
aggregated numerical values. Within the organization responsible
for the data bank, special care must be taken to avoid indiscretions
with respect to outside inquiries.

Experience has shown that it is often very difficult to obtain
complete and detailed information about a particular failure even
if one addresses the organizations responsible for such inquiries
or those which propose technical solutions. Therefore it is often
necessary to include a team of experts having experience in the

design, maintenance, and use of the equipment within the services
responsible for managing the data bank and providing its data.
These teams of experts should be authorized to carry out the inves-
tigations required for proper utilization of available data. This
may lead to psychological difficulties, but it is often necessary
to improve data quality and to make information-supplying organizations aware of their collective and individual responsibilities.
Moreover, since these experts will have direct relationships with
users, it can be hoped that they will increase user interest beyond
the level of tedious acceptance corresponding to the strict periodical encoding of anonymous follow-through data cards. Experts
located in design offices should check that failure reports from
the data bank are actually received and used.

5. THE CONTENTS OF THE VARIOUS FOLLOW-THROUGH CARDS

(a) Efforts in data collection must be oriented in two main
directions:

1. Data related to failures of equipment in normal operation
and under maintenance; this study leads to general statistical analysis.

2. Detailed documentation of operations, failures, and maintenance of subsystems or components chosen for specific analysis.

The accuracy and data requirements for these two cases are
distinctly different.

(b) Information useful for general statistical analysis is
stored in the main data bank as standardized cards or report files.
Such information and corresponding analyses are used to identify
the most interesting subsystems or components from the reliability,
diagnosis, or maintenance viewpoints. These subsystems and components are then specifically analyzed. The main data bank contains
information about all subsystems and components, lists of which were
compiled in Section 3 under mission- or function-oriented categories.
For each failure or degradation mode occurring in a listed subsystem
or component, a file card containing information similar to that in
Table 6-1 should be supplied.

TABLE 6-1 Contents of a subsystem or component follow-through card
in the main data bank, following failure, degradation, or repair
intervention

---

1. System description

    1.1 Designation

    1.2 Model/type, users' codes

    1.3 Nomenclature, item number

    1.4 Number of operating hours between inspections and dates
        of the inspections or general/partial overhauls

    1.5 Nominal operational specifications for the mission under
        consideration

    1.6 Designation of the workshop carrying out repairs and names
        of the persons responsible for repair work and editing of
        the report

2. Identification of the subsystem or component

    2.1 Part name and location

    2.2 Part number and main adjustments (numerical values)

    2.3 Function

    2.4 Readings on the hour-meter of the subsystem and of the
        cycle meter (power on, aircraft landings, etc.)

    2.5 Modifications, previous treatments

    2.6 Description of all previous maintenance operations carried
        out on the part (preventive, corrective) and corresponding
        durations

3. Description of the failure or degradation

    3.1 Origin of the part or subsystem and its history up to the
        time that the system failure was noted

    3.2 Current settings

    3.3 Accurate designation and values of measurement points

    3.4 Diagnosis: failure or degradation mode and supposed cause
        as determined after necessary corrective action has been
        carried out, the duration required for diagnosis, whether
        further intervention is justified or not, whether the
        failure cause lies in the equipment or not

TABLE 6-1   (Continued)

  3.5 Recent operating parameters and the operational environment

  3.6 Actions taken: repair, replacement, adjustment, modification, forwarding to the specialized maintenance unit, etc; corresponding durations; possible zero resetting of the hour-meter; newly evaluated potential life span

4. Comments, visual observations: recounted clearly

5. Administrative information

  5.1 Date and hour of repair intervention

  5.2 Date of file encoding

  5.3 Billing of equipment and parts used for repairs; management of the spare parts used

  5.4 Maintenance manual used

  5.5 Organization requesting the intervention

  5.6 The number of the preceding follow-through file card.

The formats and codes used enable selective and detailed retrieval to be made of information with a special interest. All associated comments should be written as accurately as possible; they are retrievable only by the data bank experts. General statistical analysis is carried out periodically and sent to all subscribers contributing to the main data bank. General statistical analysis should also be available upon request in the shortest possible time.

   (c) Information which is useful for certain special analyses can be extracted from different files available in design departments, user departments, and maintenance workshops and compiled in a secondary data bank. Of particular interest are complete reports on breakdowns, expert analyses of damage, test results, and descriptions of the circumstances under which the failure or degradation is observed (see Table 6-2 for an example).

TABLE 6-2 Checklist for detailed failure mode analysis and data collection of structural failures in aircraft; these data are to be stored in the secondary data bank

---

I. Component description

    A. Size, shape, dimensions

    B. Part photographs and/or drawings

II. Component manufacturing processes

    A. Forged, cast, machined, spun, rolled, combination, fabrication

    B. Joining method (welded, brazed, bolted, bonded, etc.)

    C. Surface treatment

        1. Shot peening and other deliberate compressive surface stresses to component

        2. Manufacture-induced residual stresses

            (a) In a large section (thermal or transformation)

            (b) Due to welds

        3. Pickling or other cleaning treatments

        4. Cadmium plating and/or other hydrogen charging process

III. Component metallurgy

    A. Component material

        Alloy compositional variations within specifications

        1. Interstitial content (titanium alloys)

        2. Carbon, phosphorus, and sulfur content (steels)

        3. Other tramp elements in alloys

    B. Melting practice and ingot breakdown

        1. Techniques to improve purity (vacuum degassing, electric melting, etc.)

        2. Cross rolling or unidirectional rolling

    C. Heat treatment

        With hardness, mechanical property tests, and metallographic sections, attempt to answer the following:

        1. Was tempering temperature correct (steels)?

        2. Was aging temperature correct (Al and Ti alloys)?

        3. Was 500 and $800°$ F embrittlement present (steels)?

TABLE 6-2 (Continued)

 D. Microstructure

  1. Mechanical fibering and banding from chemical segregation

  2. Grain size and shape

   (a) Elongated with respect to stress axis

   (b) Grain run-out in machined forgings

 E. Anisotropy

  If possible, with available material determine K_{IC}, K, yield strength and elongation with respect to critical flaw orientation

IV. Stress state for component

 A. Type of stresses

  1. Magnitude of stress levels (design stress)

  2. Type of stress (e.g., mode I, II, or III, or combinations)

  3. Presence of stress gradients

  4. Magnitude or possibility of fit-up stresses

 B. State of stress: plane strain vs. plane stress

  1. From fracture surface appearance (shearlip percent)

  2. From calculations of estimated plastic zone/thickness ratio

 C. Effect of load variation (time and loading frequency)

  1. Hours of flying time

  2. Flight profiles

  3. Cyclic loads

  4. Single or multiple overloads (wind gusts and landings)

  5. Random loading

V. Macro- and microscopic examination of fracture surface

 A. Critical flaw leading to fracture

  1. Location of critical flow by macroscopic examination

  2. Critical flaw size, shape, and orientation before instability

TABLE 6-2 (Continued)

---

    3. Macro- or microevidence of fatigue and/or corrosive attack (e.g., rust, beach marks, etc.)

    4. Surface or embedded flaw (evidence of fretting)

    5. Direction of crack propagation (chevron markings, beach marks)

  B. Manufacturing flaws

    1. Scratches

    2. Undercuts

    3. Weld defects (geometrical, hot or cold cracks)

    4. Misfit components

  C. Metallurgical flaws

    1. Inclusions

    2. Large second-class particles

    3. Entrapped slag

    4. Voids

    5. Weak internal interfaces

  D. Fractographic observations

    Mechanism(s) of failure (dimpled rupture, cleavage, quasi-cleavage, intercrystalline fracture, fatigue striations)

VI. Service information

  A. Aircraft location and conditions

    1. Weather experience (home base or en route)

    2. Cold weather de-icing chemicals

    3. Water or saltwater environment

    4. Oils and fuel

  B. Overhaul information

    1. Cleaning fluids

    2. Refurbishing procedures

It is generally difficult to find a common format and coding. Therefore all the information is often stored on magnetic tape, organized in chronological order on the basis of breakdowns and degradations.

Recall that the breakdowns and degradations requiring special analysis are chosen as in Section 5b, because their frequency of occurrence is too high or because of a desire to study the failure mechanism in detail. For each subsystem or component chosen, manufacturers must provide a list of detailed information to be collected and of measurements to be made.

Periodically, the list of subsystems or components designated for detailed analysis should be updated, with the agreement of all parties concerned. Those in charge of the secondary data bank must be able to continue requesting information from all the possible sources if a majority of these consider it to be necessary.

6. FORMATS OF FOLLOW-THROUGH CARDS

To minimize costs due to the variation in the presentation of information, one should either:

(a) Require all subscribers to the data bank to use the same follow-through cards, codes, dates, and collection procedures (this may require significant financial resources which the data bank might contribute toward on a pro rata basis).

(b) Allow each subscriber to process and compile his or her own data; the subscribers then need to agree upon a common format for presentation of intermediate aggregated results. Follow-through cards assigned to the secondary data bank must be added if the need arises.

Combined coding and maintenance instruction manuals must also be published in large numbers and updated.

7. RESULTS OF GENERAL STATISTICAL ANALYSES

Based on the needs of data bank subscribers, general statistical analyses will require the following:

i. Standard statistical programs

ii. Estimation programs for the reliability, failure, or hazard rates (properly defined), with calculations of the corresponding confidence intervals (see Sections 7.1, 7.2, and 7.10 of Chapter 1)

   iii.   Selective sorting and retrieval programs

   iv.   Tabulation programs for dealing with component-by-component analyses, or with subsystems and components considered to be critical and designated for later special analysis

   Overall results include the following:

   1.   The number of breakdowns per subsystem or component in the latest period under consideration as a function of time and as related to the cumulated operating hours.

   2.   The number of breakdowns per mission category and its distribution as a function of time relative to the number of cumulative operating hours for missions of this type.

   3.   Evolution of the equipment fleet by subsystem or component number.

   4.   The proportion of breakdowns and interventions of each type which have given rise to outage of the system or to cancellation of the mission.

   5.   The failure rates with confidence intervals, and the predicted and nominal failure rates; these parameters are calculated at the system and major subsystem levels (see Section 7.9 of Chapter 1).

   6.   Classification of systems by failure rates in operation.

   7.   Classification of systems by maintenance load per hour of operation, e.g., by the number of interventions per hour of operation.

   8.   Classification of systems by the proportion of interventions which require the unit to be sent back to the manufacturer or to a specialized workshop.

   9.   Estimates of the mean time between failure per system, subsystem, or component after selection of those breakdowns which specifically arise from the equipment.

   10.   Estimates of conditional failure or degradation probabilities of the various subsystems which are used in diagnostic proce-

dures; for quantity measured by T with value T(k), one must estimate the probabilities $P[E_i/T(k)]$ that the subsystem can be identified as being in condition E_i, given T(k).

The conclusions of such general statistical analyses are sent to those subscribers authorized to receive them. They must then study them and indicate those corrective actions which have been implemented and those specific analyses which might be useful. The data bank department should ask manufacturers, repair workshops, and users whether critical failures have motivated design changes or modifications in utilization and maintenance procedures.

The exploitation of general and specific analyses should be organized and carried out in compliance with all relevant standards, specifications, or governmental instructions, such as the following: standards CCT 190, NFX-06-501/502/022, AIR 2008, MIL-STD-785 B/C, MIL-STD-756, MIL-STD-757, MIL-STD-1472, MIL-STD-781, MIL-STD-721-B, DOD-TR-7, and contractual incentive reliability plans (see also Chapter 7).

All presentations of results should account for variations in the number of systems in service.

8. A PRACTICAL PROCEDURE FOR THE ESTIMATION
    OF TIME-DEPENDENT FAILURE RATES OF
    A GIVEN FAMILY OF EQUIPMENT

(a) Specification of the data: On a given calendar date T (i.e., January 1, 1978) we retrieve from the main data bank the following data pertaining to all equipment of a given type:

   i.   The accumulated operating hours H at T

   ii. The successive operating hours h before the first intervention or since the last one, and the nature of past interventions

All interventions can be divided into four classes:

   i.   Repair actions

   ii.   Withdrawals from active duty

   iii. Modifications (whether implemented or not)

   iv.   Overhauls (following a major failure or for preventive reasons

(b) Data format: The preceding data are displayed on a Gantt diagram (see Figure 6-1). It is essential to include in the caption of the diagram the date T, symbol explanations, and the type of equipment.

(c) Data analysis: The data defined in Section 8a are analyzed as follows. First, the time axis is divided into intervals (i) of equal duration, i.e., $\Delta t = 100$ hr. Next, within any such interval (i.e., from 100 to 199 hr), we count the following:

n_i: The number of interventions in the interval (i) due to the actual equipment; n_i is thus the total number of:

   i. Repair actions

  ii. Withdrawals

 iii. Modifications following a repair

 iv. Overhauls following a failure

    in the interval (i) (according to the h values).

N_i: The number of different devices that reached or passed the start of the interval (i), according to their h values.

(d) Displaying failure rate variations: At date T we set up a table of n_i and N_i vs. the time intervals (i). The instantaneous failure rate or hazard rate (see Sections 7.2 and 7.3 of Chapter 1) is estimated by

$$\lambda_i \triangleq \frac{n_i}{N_i \, \Delta t} \qquad (\text{hours})^{-1}$$

and is displayed graphically as a function of the number of operating hours h. The abscissa of the point representing λ_i is the middle point of the interval (i) (see Figure 6-2).

The intervention category symbols also appear on the failure rate curve (Figure 6-2) for the following categories:

   i. Overhaul for preventive reasons

  ii. Modifications actually implemented (the modification number also appears)

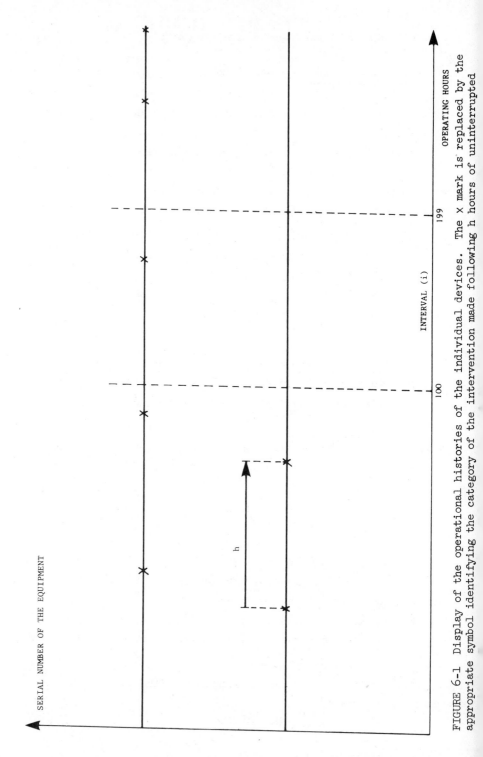

FIGURE 6-1 Display of the operational histories of the individual devices. The x mark is replaced by the appropriate symbol identifying the category of the intervention made following h hours of uninterrupted

116

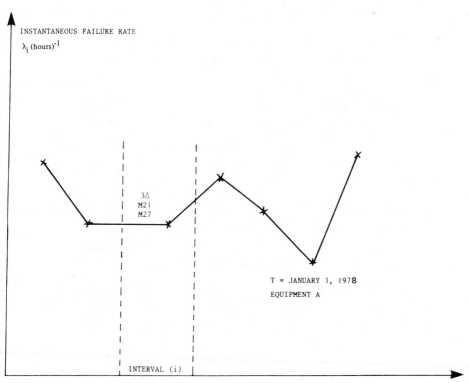

FIGURE 6.2 Time-dependent variation of the instantaneous failure rate in the operations of all type A equipment. M: Modification, followed by the number; Δ: preventive overhaul, preceded by the number of such interventions in the interval considered.

(e) Estimation of the reliability function in operations: At a given date T, the lifetime of a piece of equipment of a certain type is the time interval t_j, defined as follows:

Beginning of t_j	End of t_j

Introduction into operational duty
 	
 OR
 	
 Intervention due to equipment failure prior to T
	Earliest event among the following three, occurring after the beginning of t_j:
	
	   i. Intervention due to equipment failure prior to T
	  ii. Withdrawal before T
	 iii. Crossing the date T with the equipment still operational

With this we can determine the following:

N: Number of lifetimes retrieved from the data bank

N_i: Number of lifetimes of duration t_j $(j = 1, \ldots, N)$
     or equal to t_i $(t_j \geq t_i \geq 0)$

We may then estimate the operational equipment reliability R(t) regardless of when it is put into active duty (see Section 7.1 of Chapter 1 and Figure 6-3):

$$R(t_i) \triangleq \frac{N_i}{N}$$

Note that erroneous estimators of R(t) are found if one forgets about lifetimes terminating at date T with the equipment still operational. Such erroneous estimators are always pessimistic, and their deviations from R(t) increase rapidly with t for given T.

(f) Estimation of the operational mean time M between interventions due to the equipment itself: Following the results of Section 7.4 of Chapter 1,

$$M = \text{mean value } (t_j) = \int_0^{+\infty} R(t) \, dt$$

which is computed from the graph of R(t) (Figure 6-3). M is called the mean length of active duty at date T.

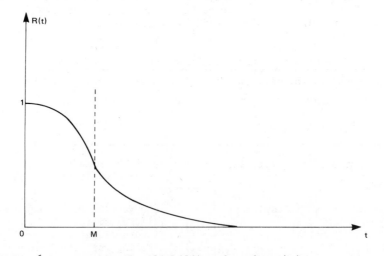

FIGURE 6-3 Operational reliability of equipment A.

(g) Numerical example:

(1)	(2)	(3)	(4)	(5)	(6)	(7)
Time intervals (i) (hours)	Number n_i of interventions in (i)	Number of devices without intervention in (i)	Cumulated number of interventions [(2) bottom up]	Cumulated number of lives [(3) bottom up]	Number N_i of devices having reached t $N_i = (4) + (5)$	Interventions + lives having reached t $(4)_o + (5)$
0-100	29	1	87	60	147	147
100-200	12	2	58	59	117	146
200-300	5	3	46	57	103	144
300-400	5	4	41	54	95	141
400-500	4	6	36	50	86	137
500-600	4	2	32	44	76	131
600-700	4	3	28	42	70	129
700-800	3	5	24	39	63	126
800-900	4	5	21	34	55	121
900-1000	2	6	17	29	46	116
1000-1100	5	7	15	23	38	110
1100-1200	4	9	10	16	26	103
1200-1300	3	6	6	7	13	94
1300-1400	3	1	3	1	4	88

$$\lambda_i = (2)/(6) \qquad\qquad R(t_i) = (6)/147 \ .$$

t_i (hours)	instantaneous failure rate λ_i (in 10^{-3}h)	Reliability $R(t_i)$
0	1.97	1
100	1.03	0.802
200	0.49	0.715
300	0.53	0.646
400	0.47	0.585
500	0.53	0.517
600	0.57	0.476
700	0.48	0.429
800	0.73	0.374
900	0.44	0.313
1000	1.32	0.259
1100	1.54	0.177
1200	2.31	0.089
1300	7.50	0.027

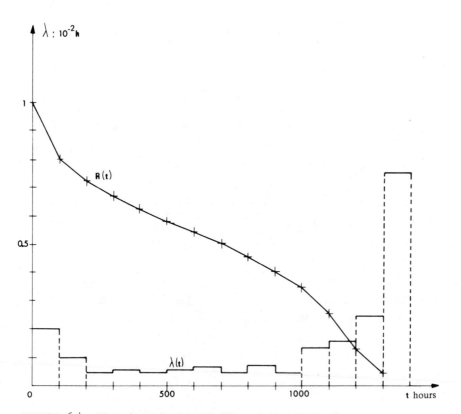

FIGURE 6-4   Time dependent variation of the instantaneous failure rate λ and reliability for the example of Section 8g.   ∎

9.   IMPLEMENTATION PROBLEMS OF RELIABILITY
AND MAINTENANCE DATA BANKS

A number of practical implementation problems which affect the accuracy and the validity of statistical analyses are often encountered.

Some failure modes appear only intermittently in follow-through reports; this may induce later diagnostic errors.

The monitoring equipment for each system should be as permanent as possible. It is important that all subsystems be equipped with individual hour-meters, especially if they do not operate simultaneously.

Special instructions may require the pulldown, inspection, and removal of a certain subsystem from a fleet of systems. Special mention of this should be made in the follow-through cards to avoid identifying such events as regular maintenance interventions.

The evolution of a given system over time due to configuration changes, new standards, modifications, special treatment, and substitution of nonstandard components must be described. To do this, follow-through card collection must be rapid both from subscribers and within the data bank organization.

Sometimes a certain subsystem or component failure results in the production of several follow-through cards for the data banks; for example, one at the pulldown and inspection level, a second for repair, and a third for a component change. The coding system used must allow for reconstruction of the entire sequence of events without confusion; this is accounted for in Table 6-1 (point 5.6).

It is essential that coding and maintenance instruction manuals be written very clearly. A good practical rule is to always question the contents of the reporting cards and other reports, because coding errors happen and because an arbitrary code may be recorded to avoid spending time to find the appropriate one.

Cards are frequently filled out very poorly, excessively, or in an inconsistent manner. This may be due to psychological factors or because insufficient time is set aside to fill out the cards.

A major problem in diagnosis is the frequent absence of complete or pertinent information about the failure or deterioration mechanisms. Specification of the important measurements to be gathered and entered in expertise or maintenance reports is often neglected, simply because of the higher priorities assigned to actual repairs than to understanding fault mechanisms. A related difficulty lies in the fact that the evolution of operating characteristics prior to the failure instant is very often not available. There is also no knowledge about the stagewise growth of deterioration (see Chapter 3) and about the initial equipment condition when the deterioration first occurs. To obtain some of the missing information about a specific failure mode, it may be useful to contact persons elsewhere who have looked at the problem. This task can be accomplished by representatives of the manufacturer.

An amazing phenomenon is the great skill used to describe the first occurrence of a specific failure mode compared to the reporting of later appearances of the same event. The Royal Navy has admitted that only 30% of failures result in filled-out failure reports, usually for those failures that maintenance "likes" and knows something about. This is equivalent to assuming that the deterioration mechanism remains forever the same, which is highly unlikely given the modifications made to remedy a recurrent failure.

It is useless to stress that information about a failure will be evaluated in terms of the technical training and experience of the persons doing the reporting. Finally, geographical or organizational changes make it difficult to consistently interpret information. Data collection and retrieval systems should be structured so that comparative evaluation of such aspects is possible (see Table 6-1).

All the preceding difficulties are encountered during both the establishment and operation of a data bank. They are constraints on failure analysis or diagnosis methods using all stored data. However, data bases have definite advantages. For example, if a foreman quits, portions of his experience can be used by his successor; previously, most of this experience was lost. This lengthened the training period of a new maintenance foreman. Failure diagnosis methods can contribute to speeding this training by providing advice about choices to be made from data available to the data bank (see Chapters 7 and 9).

There remains the difficult problem of intermittent failures. We consider it necessary to use performance monitoring (Chapters 2 and 11) to deal with such cases. This also holds for failures which cannot be reproduced in the laboratory, because they happen only in an operational environment.

10. EXAMPLES OF RELIABILITY AND MAINTENANCE DATA BANKS

(a) Reliability and maintenance data banks can be found among users of the following:

1. Aerospace components or systems.

2. Electronic and microelectronic components.

3. Telephone systems: The information is the performance data in logbooks maintained by telephone exchanges or for carrier telephone systems; the importance of such a data bank can be realized by considering some component counts for a typical electromechanical telephone exchange: 70,000 resistors, 42,000 diodes, 9000 capacitors, 12,000 transistors, 4500 coils and transformers, 4500 relays, 150 rotary selectors, and 550,000 soldered joints (see Borg [E-20]).

4. Mechanical systems and components.

5. Nuclear power plants and other energy systems.

6. Pneumatic systems and parts.

7. Hydraulic systems and parts.

8. Military vehicles: The records include total mileage, durability in kilometers, excess accelerations, engine hours, engine overhauls, idle hours, starter-engagement times, brake application times, communication times, number of immersions, drivers' hours, traverse gear actuation times, rounds fired, MTBF, and MTTR (workhours). The major subsystems considered are the power pack (engine, gearbox), the electrical system, and the generator (see Ullman [E-21]).

(b) There are also general-purpose systems for data exchange and failure rate estimation; examples include GIDEP, FARADA, and ALERT in the United States; FORWARD (Royal electrical and mechanical engineers) in the United Kingdom; and CEA and CNET in France (see Adnot et al. [E-23]).

Chapter 7

FAILURE AND MAINTENANCE DATA ANALYSIS

1. LINKS BETWEEN DATA ANALYSIS AND FAILURE DIAGNOSIS

Confronted with a set of overlapping and highly correlated data, a sociologist or reliability expert may call upon a statistician for help and will usually have some hypothesis or ready-made theory about the data, whereas the statistician will have none. Statistical methodology alone is inadequate for fact-finding in such a situation. The study of breakdowns by varying one parameter at a time is often impossible because the time and means to produce all such trials are lacking.

Through the synthesis of a fair number of elementary facts, the basic notions of a model can be developed from a set of data and causal relationships determined. Models should not be based solely on a priori axioms and fragmentary measurements, however. Moreover, the human mind alone is incapable of constructing such models without making arbitrary choices that can render the result devoid of meaning.

To address these questions, methods of data analysis have been developed to process different kinds of statistical information containing a great number of correlations. These methods are especially intended to reveal the causal relations and parametric structures best explaining observed phenomena. Analysis is used to determine independent stochastic variables (or causal factors) which express the information structure in a condensed way. Most of the causal relations can then be interpreted. The validity of these

interpretations depends on the sample size. Data analysis also makes
possible quantitative assessment of the relative importance of factors. Suppose that the observed data are known to arise from one of
a class of models. Factors extracted from the data may allow for
identification of the appropriate model and calculation of its most
likely parameter values. In this way, data analysis methods gener-
alize regression analysis.

These methods may greatly assist the specialist since they help
to form an accurate picture of the causal relations present in learning data. These tools compensate to some extent for an analyst's
lack of memory and experience by preventing recent or frequent breakdowns from being overly influential.

Finally, data analysis can achieve the following objectives:

    i. Elimination of most redundant observations or tests.

    ii. Selection of tests and observations giving the best pos-
sible discrimination between failure causes and determination of
equipment condition.

    iii. Simplification of follow-through cards and reports for
users and repair people, thus saving time.

    iv. Elimination of imprecise symptoms and minor breakdowns.

    v. Accurate and effective display of compressed learning
data for diagnostic purposes; these methods may aid in the simultaneous display of observed syndromes, the corresponding breakdowns,
operational conditions, and maintenance actions.

    vi. Easy updating of the learning data, so that data gathered
during recent interventions are considered.

All of this means reduced costs in the gathering and processing
of information and improved equipment availability resulting from
the higher probability of correct diagnosis (see Chapter 2).

Another advantage is the considerable benefits derived by manufacturers who can thus get an overall view of the operational behavior of their equipment.

There is nothing to prevent the sequential use of data analysis methods (see Chapter 4 and Section 11 in this chapter); at each
step, all the available learning data can be compressed in a sequential diagnostic process. For automated sequential diagnosis, the
formula for observation compression at each stage should be stored
in advance for retrieval as the diagnosis progresses.

In this chapter we shall describe three important data analysis
methods:

    i. Normalized principal components analysis (Pearson, Ho-
telling) (Section 6)

    ii. Discriminant analysis (Section 8)

    iii. Canonical analysis (Section 9)

But first, in Sections 2, 3, 4, and 5 we shall deal specifically
with prerequisite data manipulations.

2. SET, STATISTICAL, AND PROBABILITY CORRESPONDENCES

Our object in this section is to describe the different types of
data which are used in data analysis methods.

A random phenomenon linking two sets I, J (or more) can be inferred only to the extent that relations between elements of these
sets are known. These relations may be of the following types:

2.1 Correspondence Between Sets

A correspondence between sets is characterized by a relation r
taking one of two possible values for any pair $(i,j) \in I \times J$.

Example 1
_____

I = consonants of the spoken language, and J = vowels of the
spoken language:

$$
r(i,j) = \begin{cases}
1 & \text{if and only if the consonant } j \text{ can be found} \\
  & \text{immediately behind the vowel } i \\
\\
0 & \text{if the consonant } j \text{ can never be found} \\
  & \text{immediately behind the vowel } i
\end{cases}
$$

2.2 Statistical Correspondence

A statistical correspondence is defined by the set of occurrences $k(i,j)$ of the pair $(i,j) \in I \times J$.

Example 2

I = sample of passengers questioned about a flight on an airline, and J = set of questions asked [degree of satisfaction (coded 1 to 20), use of airlines, answers yes/no, etc.]:

$k(i,j)$ = the mark given by passenger i in answer to question j

2.3 Random Correspondence

A random correspondence is defined by a discrete probability measure p on $I \times J$.

Example 3

I = successive periods of operation (lives) of a given piece of equipment, and J = catalogue of damages (overall damage, component damage, and/or maintenance operations):

$p(i,j)$ = probability of damage j or maintenance operation j
occurring during a life i

2.4 Transforming a Set or Statistical Correspondence into a Random Correspondence

A set correspondence r between I and J (r with nonnegative values) can be associated with the random correspondence p_r over $I \times J$:

$$\forall\, (i,j) \in I \times J \qquad p_r(i,j) \triangleq \frac{r(i,j)}{\displaystyle\sum_{(\ell,k) \in I \times J} r(\ell,k)}$$

With the statistical correspondence k over $I \times J$ (k with nonnegative values) can be associated the random correspondence p_k over $I \times J$:

$$\forall\, (i,j) \in I \times J \qquad p_k(i,j) \triangleq \frac{k(i,j)}{\displaystyle\sum_{(\ell,m) \in I \times J} k(\ell,m)}$$

3. CONTINGENCY TABLE ASSOCIATED WITH
A RANDOM CORRESPONDENCE

(a) Suppose we are given the discrete probability measure p
over the set product I x J:

$$p(i,j) \triangleq \Pr(X = x_i \text{ and } Y = y_j)$$

where X and Y are two random discrete variables taking, respectively,
the values x_1, x_2, $\dots$, $x_{Card(I)}$ and y_1, y_2, $\dots$, $y_{Card(J)}$ in finite
number.

Card ($\cdot$) represents the number of elements of the argument set.

The table of numbers $p(i,j)$ defining the random correspondence
under study is called a contingency table (Table 7-1).

(b) The probabilities relative to X and Y alone are then

$$\forall \; i \in I \qquad p(i,\cdot) \triangleq \sum_{j \in J} p(i,j)$$

and

$$\forall \; j \in J \qquad p(\cdot,j) \triangleq \sum_{i \in I} p(i,j)$$

where

$$\sum_{(i,j) \in I \times J} p(i,j) = \sum_{i \in I} p(i,\cdot) = \sum_{j \in J} p(\cdot,j) = 1$$

The sum $p(\cdot,j)$ of the numbers $p(i,j) \geq 0$ in column $j \in J$ is
called the marginal probability of occurrence of the measurement y_j
from Y; a similar definition holds for $p(i,\cdot)$, and

$$p(\cdot,j) = \Pr(Y = y_j)$$
$$p(i,\cdot) = \Pr(X = x_i)$$

Column j defines a discrete distribution over the values of X
and contains the probabilities of X-values corresponding to given
values y_j of Y (see Section 2.3 of Chapter 1).

(c) The probability of $Y = y_j$, when it is known that $X = x_i$,
is supplied by the theorem about conditional probabilities:

$I \times J$	J (Y)				$p(I,\cdot)$
I (X)	y_1	$y_2 \cdots$	$y_j \cdots$	$y_{Card(J)}$	
x_1					$p(1,\cdot)$
x_2					$p(2,\cdot)$
$\cdots$ x_i			$p(i,j)$		$p(i,\cdot)$
$\cdots$					$\cdots$
$x_{Card(I)}$					$p(\bar{i},\cdot)$
$p(\cdot,J)$	$p(\cdot,1)$ $p(\cdot,2) \cdots$	$p(\cdot,j) \cdots$	$p(\cdot,Card\ (J))$		1

TABLE 7-1 Contingency table of the random correspondence $p(I,J)$

$$Pr(Y = y_j/X = x_i) \overset{\Delta}{=} Pr(j/i) = \frac{p(i,j)}{p(i,\cdot)}$$

For a fixed value of i, the quantities $Pr(j/i)$ are proportional to $p(i,j)$, and their sum equals 1:

$$\sum_{j \in J} Pr(j/i) = 1$$

$Pr(j/i)$ is the probability of y_j conditioned on x_i.

4. EXPLICIT FORMAT FOR THE DATA REPRESENTATION k(I,J)

Assume that all data $i \in I$ collected at any intervention $j \in J$ on systems of a given type or standard originate from one of the following three sources:

(a) A primary or secondary data bank as discussed in Chapter 6; this information comes from follow-through cards and visual inspections, possibly including diagnostic codes from the interventions.

(b) A sampled-data performance monitoring system, recording system parameters as well as some characteristics of the operating mode and operational environment.

(c) Outputs from built-in test equipment (BITE) and from other nondestructive test instruments, all recorded after the occurrence of the failure leading to intervention j.

Notice that some of these data are binary [(a) and (c)], while some have essentially continuous values [(a) and (b)]. All data $i \in I$ about one specific intervention j are called explicit data; the set of explicit data about intervention j is denoted by $\{k(i,j)$; $i \in I] \overset{\Delta}{=} k(I,j)$.

Whatever the condition of the system when intervention j is initiated, we assume that the explicit data $k(I,j)$ include the hour-meter or cycle-meter reading t_j (since the last intervention on the same equipment). From a sample set of t_j readings, it is possible to estimate the operational reliability function $R(t)$ for the given type of system at a given calendar date (see Section 8 of Chapter 6).

The learning data at a given calendar date is the table $k(I,J)$ covering all interventions $j \in J$ up to that time.

$k(i,j)$ / J	I	VIBRATIONS $=1$	FAILURE A $=1$	POSITION OF THE EQUIPMENT ON THE AIRCRAFT			LIFE LENGTH t_j	OIL FLOW cm^3/s
				P_1	P_2	P_3		
INTERVENTION OR LIFE (j)		1	0	0	1	0	352 h	8.2

(a)

$n(i,j^*)$ / j^*	I	VIBRATIONS $=1$	FAILURE A $=1$	POSITION OF THE EQUIPMENT ON THE AIRCRAFT			OIL FLOW cm^3/s < 10	OIL FLOW cm^3/s $\geqslant 10$
				P_1	P_2	P_3		
LIFE INTERVAL j*: 100-200 h		32	68	256	612	132	415	585

(b)

$k^*(i,j^*)$ / j^*	I	VIBRATIONS $=1$	FAILURE A $=1$	POSITION OF THE EQUIPMENT ON THE AIRCRAFT			OIL FLOW cm^3/s < 10	OIL FLOW cm^3/s $\geqslant 10$
				P_1	P_2	P_3		
LIFE INTERVAL j*: 100-200 h		32	68	$\frac{256}{1000}$	$\frac{612}{1000}$	$\frac{132}{1000}$	$\frac{415}{1000}$	$\frac{585}{1000}$

(c)

TABLE 7-2 Learning data $k(I,J)$: explicit and implicit formats k, n, k^*

Due to the nature and coding of the explicit data i ∈ I, usually only p independent measurements can be found in any record {k(i,j), i ∈ I}, because some measurements [m] ⊂ I have a finite number of exclusive alternatives i ∈ [m].

Example: A command switch can be in three possible positions: $k(i_1,j)$, $k(i_2,j)$, $k(i_3,j)$ are three binary digits indicating that the switch is in position 1, 2, or 3 (respectively) when the digit is equal to 1. Consequently, one and only one of these three numbers is nonzero at intervention j; i_1, i_2, and i_3 are three alternatives of the measurement [m] $\triangleq$ switch position. We put [m] = $\{i_1,i_2,i_3\}$ ⊂ I. See Table 7-2. ■

5. IMPLICIT FORMAT FOR THE DATA REPRESENTATION k*(I,J*)

(a) The implicit format is another representation of the learning data k(I,J), derived from measurements i ∈ I on interventions j ∈ J. This representation is implicit because it does not reveal information pertaining to specific interventions j ∈ J. All occurrences j ∈ J are ordered according to values of a continuous measurement, such as the lifetime length t_j. The interventions are then sorted into t_j intervals, and a similar procedure is applied to the corresponding measurements.

One purpose of such an aggregation is to attempt to compensate for some types of data coding errors, especially for isolated missing data.

It should be remembered that:

i. The explicit format is required for diagnostic purposes and each time a new record k(I,j) is compared with the learning set.

ii. The implicit format is preferable for overall analysis of the operational behavior of a fleet of similar devices; this analysis is carried out periodically.

(b) Design of the implicit table

① Rank all interventions j ∈ J by increasing values of t_j (the length of the corresponding life) and define $\bar{t} \triangleq \max\{t_j : j \in J\}$.

Had $[0,\bar{t}]$ been partitioned into intervals $j^* \in J^*$ of equal length,
then the number of interventions j assigned to any one such interval
j^* would probably decrease with t_{j^*}, because the survivial probability $R(t)$ is nonincreasing and because

$$t_{j^*} \overset{\Delta}{=} \text{mean value of all lifetimes } t_j, \text{ restricted to those}$$
$$\text{interventions } j \in J \text{ where } t_j \text{ belongs to the } j^* \text{ in-}$$
$$\text{terval}$$

If so, the confidence interval for any probability estimated õn
interval j^* would widen when t_{j^*} increases, which is a serious
drawback to this uniform sampling scheme.

Instead, we partition $[0,\bar{t}]$ by letting the length of any partitioned interval $j^* \in J^*$ be approximately proportional to $[1/r(t_{j^*})]$,
where $r(t) = (dR/dt)(t)$ is the estimated lifetime probability density
function. This is justified in detail in Section 5 of Chapter 9.

② (a) It may happen that some boxes in follow-through cards
have not been filled out; some of the $k(I,j)$ data are then missing.
To reconstruct some of the missing information when designing the
implicit table $k^*(I,J^*)$, we use the coding dependence of the data.

Define

$$n(i,j^*) \overset{\Delta}{=} \begin{cases} \begin{array}{ll} \text{mean value of } k(i,j) & \text{if the class } [m] \text{ is} \\ \text{for all } t_j \in j^* & \text{restricted to that} \\ & \text{single measurement } i \\ \\ \text{number of cases such} & \text{if the measurement } i \\ \text{that } t_j \in j^* \text{ and} & \text{belongs to a class } [m] \\ k(i,j) \neq 0 & \text{having more than one} \\ & \text{alternative measurement} \end{array} \end{cases}$$

where

$$i \in [m] \subset I \qquad j^* \in J^* \qquad [m] = 1, \ldots, M$$

(b) If measurement i belongs to a class $[m]$ with at least two
independent alternatives, then $n(i,j^*)$ is replaced by the relative
frequency $k^*(i,j^*)$ of that occurrence within the $[m]$ class; if $i =$
$[m]$ has no alternative, keep $n(i,j^*)$. In both these circumstances,
estimation of mean values or relative frequencies is done using all
observations of i available in the learning set $k(I,J)$.

$$k^*(i,j^*) \triangleq \begin{cases} \text{i has no alternative} & k^*(i,j^*) \triangleq n(i,j^*) \\ \text{measurement} & \\ \text{i has independent} & k^*(i,j^*) \triangleq \dfrac{n(i,j^*)}{\sum\limits_{\ell \in [m]} n(\ell,j^*)} \\ \text{alternatives within} & \\ \text{the class [m]} & \end{cases}$$

where

$$i \in [m] \qquad j^* \in J^* \qquad [m] = 1, \ldots, M$$

③ Implicit tables are derived from $k(I,J)$ by considering rankings other than by life lengths t_j. Any continuous measurement recorded at each intervention will do (i.e., flow values, voltages, frequency range).

(c) For the technique described in Chapter 8, attempts are made to avoid the implicit format. The format considered there is of the explicit type, retaining the raw t_j measurements; in most examples investigated with this format, the following remarks are applicable:

i. Because of the high marginal probability of the t_j column, all interventions j tend to cluster around the overall center of gravity (see Section 5 of Chapter 8); this makes diagnosis virtually impossible because of the lack of discrimination between failure-mode-labeled interventions.

ii. The proportion τ_1 of discriminant information carried by the first axis is too high (50 to 80%) (see Section 5 of Chapter 8).

iii. The time dependence of specific failure modes does not appear when the lifetimes t_j are represented by a single point rather than by several points as in the implicit format.

(d) Small sample effects for some classes: In the case where the follow-through cards are indexed by a failure diagnosis condition $d(i)$, $i \in I$ (see Sections 3 and 5.1 of Chapter 10), it may well happen that for some of these classes $d(i)$ only few cards will have been collected. If this is the case, one should assign to each class a weight related to the number of samples of each; this weight will be accounted for in the feature extraction (see Section 3 of Chapter 8).

6. NORMALIZED PRINCIPAL COMPONENTS ANALYSIS

(a) The random correspondence $X(I,J)$ is supposed to be zero mean, made up of the $n \triangleq \mathrm{Card}(I)$ sample vectors $X(i,\cdot)$. In each row vector $X(i,\cdot)$, there are $p \triangleq \mathrm{Card}(J)$ observations.

The covariance matrix of the n sample vectors is estimated by

$$C = [c_{\ell j}] = \frac{1}{n-1} \sum_{i=1}^{n} {}^{t}X(i,\cdot)X(i,\cdot) = \frac{1}{n-1} {}^{t}X(I,J)X(I,J)$$

$$\mathrm{Rank}(C) = m \leq p \qquad \dim(C) = \begin{pmatrix} p \\ p \end{pmatrix} \qquad \dim(X(i,\cdot)) = \begin{pmatrix} 1 \\ p \end{pmatrix}$$

$$E(X(i,\cdot)) = 0$$

If $m < p$, there are $p - m$ linear relations linking observations in the correspondence under study, so that the total variance may be expressed by m independent variables representing features. If p and n are large, it is difficult to determine the correspondences between observations. If $m < p$, we therefore seek to decrease the number of observations in each sample by realizing a transformation on the p original observations, thus producing $m < p$ independent features.

(b) More precisely, let this transformation be represented by an orthonormal matrix A corresponding to a rotation of the axes $j \in J$:

$$Y(i,\cdot) = X(i,\cdot)A \qquad A^{-1} = {}^{t}A \qquad {}^{t}AA = I$$

$$i \in I \qquad \dim(Y(i,\cdot)) = \begin{pmatrix} 1 \\ p \end{pmatrix} \qquad \dim(A) = \begin{pmatrix} p \\ p \end{pmatrix}$$

$$E(X(i,\cdot)) = E(Y(i,\cdot)) = 0$$

An attempt is made to adjust the rotation A so as to achieve the maximum expected variance for the feature $Y(i,\cdot)$, given any sample $X(i,\cdot)$:

$$\mathrm{Var}_{X}[Y(i,\cdot)] = \frac{1}{p} E_{X}(Y(i,\cdot){}^{t}Y(i,\cdot)) = \frac{1}{p} E_{X}[X(i,\cdot)A{}^{t}A{}^{t}X(i,\cdot)]$$

It is known that the necessary and sufficient condition for this to hold is that the columns of matrix A be proportional to the eigenvectors u_j of the n-sample covariance matrix C, with the normalization $A^{-1} = {}^t A$. The covariance matrix S of the n transformed samples $Y(i, \cdot)$ is then the following diagonal matrix:

$$S = \frac{1}{n-1} \sum_{i=1}^{n} {}^t Y(i, \cdot) Y(i, \cdot) = \begin{bmatrix} \lambda_1 & & \\ & \ddots & \\ & & \lambda_p \end{bmatrix}$$

where $\det(S) = \det(C) = \lambda_1 \cdots \lambda_p$ and λ_j is the variance of the jth eigenvector of C.

These eigenvectors are ranked in decreasing order:

$$\lambda_1 \geq \lambda_2 \geq \cdots \geq \lambda_p \geq 0$$

and

$$A = \begin{bmatrix} u_1 & \vdots & \cdots & \vdots & u_j & \vdots & \cdots & \vdots & u_p \end{bmatrix} \qquad \dim(u_j) = \binom{p}{1}$$

$$u_j \triangleq [u_{\ell_j} : \ell = 1, \ldots, p]$$

λ_j represents (up to a coefficient) the proportion of the total variance of the transformed samples $Y(I,J)$ restored by the eigenvector u_j. By definition, u_j is the jth principal component of the table $X(I,J)$ in the space of the original observations. The first principal component is the direction in which the variance is highest.

(c) Note that A does not alter the total variance of the $X(I,J)$, which is equal to the total variance of the transformed samples. Indeed,

$$Var[X(I,J)] = Trace(C) = Trace(S) = \sum_{i=1}^{p} \lambda_i$$

The preceding reasoning leads to the identification of the eigenvectors and spectra of A and C (within a reordering). It takes for granted that $Rank(C) = p$; that is, that matrix C is regular. However, the result may be extended to the case where $Rank(C) < p$.

It is also possible to adjust the rotation A so that the entropy

$$- \sum_{j=1}^{p} Y(i,j) \ln(Y(i,j))$$

of any transformed sample $Y(i,\cdot)$ has minimum expected value. The corresponding matrix A has columns which are again the principal components of $X(I,J)$.

Principal components analysis solves the problem of feature selection. Often the first few principal components contain a considerable proportion of the total variance of $X(I,J)$, and it suffices to use only the first few principal components, which are statistically independent, and to express any new sample vector in terms of them.

More specifically, let $x \triangleq [x_j : j = 1, \ldots, p]$ be a p-dimensional sample, with coordinates ordered according to the representation adopted for the principal components. Let $y \triangleq [y_j : j = 1, \ldots, p]$ be the transformed sample:

$$y = xA$$

where

$$y_j = \sum_{\ell=1}^{p} x_\ell u_{\ell_j} \qquad j = 1, \ldots, p$$

If only the m first principal components are retained, A is replaced by a matrix A^m made up of the m first principal components, and y is replaced by the m-dimensional vector y^m:

$$y^m = xA^m$$

where

$$y_j^m = \sum_{\ell=1}^{p} x_\ell u_{\ell_j} \qquad j = 1, \ldots, m$$

and

$$A^m = \left[u_1 \; \vdots \; \cdots \; \vdots \; u_m \right] \qquad \dim(A^m) = \binom{p}{m}$$

Principal components analysis allows us to see the "real dimension" m of a sample $X(I,J)$ and the relative weights λ_j of the features y_j $(j = 1, \ldots, m)$ for the first principal components and to represent any new sample x in a space of lower dimension m. This space contains the proportion

$$\tau_j \triangleq \frac{\Sigma_{j=1}^m \lambda_j}{\text{Trace}(C)}$$

of the total variance $X(I,J)$, or $Y(I,J)$.

(d) One disadvantage of this method is the strong dependence implied between the measuring units for the observations. Therefore it is sometimes desirable to use normalized principal components analysis with measurement vectors X' that have been standardized beforehand by the following nonsymmetrical transformation (with respect to I and J):

$$x_{ij} = \frac{x'_{ij} - \bar{x}'_j}{\sigma'_j} + K$$

where

$$\bar{x}'_j = E[x'(i,j), \; i \in I] = \frac{1}{n} \sum_{i=1}^{n} x'(i,j)$$

σ'_j = standard deviation of $x'(\cdot,j)$

$$= \frac{1}{\sqrt{n-1}} \sqrt{\sum_{i=1}^{n} [x'(i,j) - \bar{x}'_j]^2}$$

K = constant added to make all the quantities $x_{ij} \geq 0$ if needed

(e) Another variant is to use the matrix of the correlation
coefficients instead of the covariance matrix $C = [c_{\ell j}]$. That is,
the columns of A (the principal components) are then the eigenvectors of ρ:

$$\rho = [\rho_{\ell j} : \ell = 1, \ldots, p; j = 1, \ldots, p] \qquad \text{symmetrical}$$

where

$$\rho_{\ell j} = \frac{c_{\ell j}}{\sigma_\ell \sigma_j} \qquad \ell = 1, \ldots, p; j = 1, \ldots, p$$

σ_ℓ = standard deviation of $X(\cdot, \ell)$

(f) The most useful variant of principal components analysis
is used as circumstances warrant.

Note that principal components analysis cannot discover causal
relationships between observations and samples; it can only do so
among samples or among observations. Thus, from an explicit table,
no diagnosis can be made about a sample device from the observations
on it.

Computer programs for principal components analysis often work
sequentially, using a growing number of observations. They rank
samples by increasing abscissa values along each principal component.

7. EXAMPLE: AN APPLICATION OF PRINCIPAL COMPONENTS
    ANALYSIS TO POTENTIOMETER TESTS

Consider an explicit table representing environmental tests of 29
types of adjustable electric potentiometers spanning the following
technologies: coiled wire, carbon film, cermet, and metal film.
The primary aim is to distinguish among these potentiometers according to operating conditions. See Table 7-3.

There are two variants of each potentiometer; one has a high
electrical resistance (10 to 100 kΩ) and the other one a low resistance (100 Ω). Fifteen high-resistance and 11 low-resistance measurements are made. There are 5 additional observations, giving a
total of 31 measurements for each type of potentiometer (see Table
7-4):

TABLE 7-3 The 29 types of potentiometers (from different manufacturers)

Technology	Number	Code
Carbon film	1	A01 to A04
Cermet	2	B11 to B28
Coiled wire	3	C31 to C36
Metal film	4	D41

$X(i,j) \triangleq$ measurement i on potentiometer j

Two principal components analyses can be made:

(a) One from measurements I on the potentiometers J (as in Section 6)

(b) One concerning the varieties J of potentiometers [by transposing the tableau $X(I,J)$]

The following percentage values were obtained for the relative variances of the principal components:

$\lambda_i/\mathrm{Trace}(C)$ i	1	2	3
Measurements on potentiometers	21%	13%	11%
Types of potentiometers	27%	23%	11%

It seems that redundancy among the measurements is quite low and that these can hardly be reduced in number. On the other hand, a smaller number of measurements is sufficient to represent the various types of potentiometers and discriminate among them. In particular, it is possible to represent them using the first two principal components, which contain 50% of the total measurement variance. A glance at Figure 7-1 reveals a grouping (clustering of the different types of potentiometers) that it more precise than one resulting solely from knowledge of the technologies used. Tech-

TABLE 7-4 Measurements on potentiometers

Number	Code	Observation
1	FA	Type of technology, by number
2	FB	Maximum power
3	FC	Maximum voltage
4	FD	Maximum rotation angle
5	FE	Price
	Prefix L:	Low resistance variant (100 Ω)
	Prefix H:	High resistance variant (10 or 100 kΩ)
6, 21	LA, HA	Duration of life test: resistance variation
7, 22	LB, HB	Resistance to static humidity (manufacturer)
8, 23	LC, HC	Temperature factor at 25 to 70° C
9, 24	LD, HD	Temperature factor at 25 to -25° C
10, 25	LE, HE	Life span: test 1 on contact noise
11, 26	LF, HF	Life span: test 2 on contact noise
12, 27	LG, HG	Exposure 1 to static humidity: contact noise
13, 28	LH, HH	Exposure 2 to static humidity: contact noise
14	LJ	Life span: test 1 on contact resistance
15	LK	Life span: test 2 on contact resistance
16	LL	Exposure 1 to static humidity: contact resistance
17	LM	Exposure 2 to static humidity: contact resistance
18, 29	LN, HI	Vibration test: resistance variation
19, 30	LP, HJ	Shock test: resistance variation
20, 31	LQ, HK	Chemical bath test: resistance variation

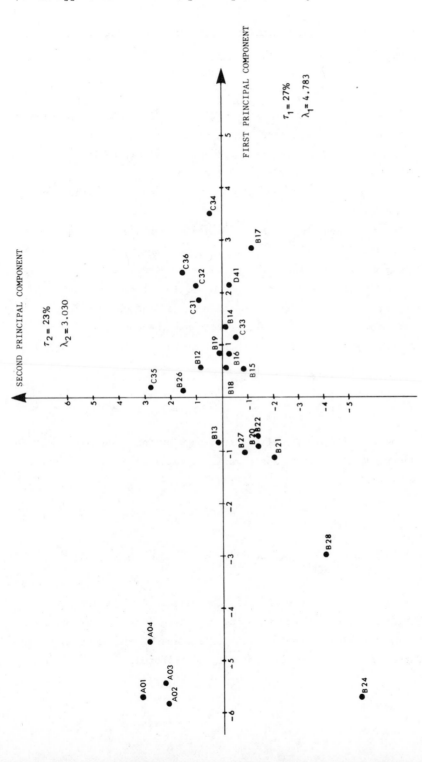

FIGURE 7-1 Principal components analysis of the potentiometers.

nologies B and C, though sometimes similar, are nonetheless distin-
guishable.

8. DISCRIMINANT ANALYSIS

(a) Discriminant analysis is directly linked to the problem
of automated diagnosis, since it involves a reclassification of the
learning data as a whole (displayed as an explicit table).

Define the tableau $X \triangleq [x_\ell : \ell = 1, \ldots, L]$, where x_ℓ is the
p-dimensional row vector containing the p observations made during
the intervention ℓ, $\ell = 1, \ldots, L$.

It is assumed that we have a given number n of classes, denoting
possible conditions E_i, $i = 1, \ldots, n$, of the equipment at the interventions recorded in the explicit table. These conditions are known,
since each intervention on a piece of equipment results in a diagnosis, that is, a classification into one of the classes E_i.

To simplify calculations, assume that the cost $C(i_1, i_2)$ of
classifying a device into E_{i_2} when it is in fact in E_{i_1} is defined by

$$C(i_1, i_2) \triangleq \begin{cases} 1 & i_1 \neq i_2 & i_1 = 1, \ldots, n \\ 0 & i_1 = i_2 & i_2 = 1, \ldots, n \end{cases}$$

The mean p-dimensional observation m_i within each class E_i and
the corresponding intraclass covariance matrices S_i are estimated
as follows:

$$m_i \triangleq \frac{1}{n_i} \sum_{\ell \in E_i} x_\ell \qquad n_i = \text{Card}\{\ell \in E_i ; \ell = 1, \ldots, L\}$$

$$S_i \triangleq \frac{1}{n_i - 1} \sum_{\ell \in E_i} {}^t(x_\ell - m_i)(x_\ell - m_i) \qquad \dim(S_i) = \binom{p}{p}$$

(b) The aim of discriminant analysis is thus to determine
discriminant functions so that the resulting decision rule minimizes
the expected classification costs of a piece of equipment under the
hypothesis that samples are normally distributed.

Let q_i, $i = 1, \ldots, n$, be the a priori probability that the equipment is found in condition E_i before an intervention.

For the case of $n = 2$ classes, the classification rules are the following:

Classification rule i: $S_1 \neq S_2$:

$$V_{12}(x) = -\frac{1}{2}(x - m_1) S_1^{-1} {}^t(x - m_1) + \frac{1}{2}(x - m_2) S_2^{-1} {}^t(x - m_2)$$

$$+ \frac{1}{2} \ln \frac{|S_2|}{|S_1|} + \ln \frac{q_1}{q_2}$$

$$\dim(x) = \binom{1}{p} \qquad i = 1, \ldots, n; \; j = 1, \ldots, n$$

$$V_{12}(x) \begin{cases} > 0 : & x \in E_1 \\ \leq 0 : & x \in E_2 \end{cases}$$

Classification rule ii: $S_1 = S_2$:

$$S \triangleq \left(\frac{n_1 - 1}{n_1 + n_2 - 2} \right) S_1 + \left(\frac{n_2 - 1}{n_1 + n_2 - 2} \right) S_2$$

$$V_{12}(x) = [x - \frac{1}{2}(m_1 + m_2)] S^{-1} {}^t(m_1 - m_2)$$

$$V_{12}(x) \begin{cases} > 0 : & x \in E_1 \\ \leq 0 : & x \in E_2 \end{cases} .$$

In all the preceding, it is assumed that samples of size n_i from class E_i are large enough to ensure that the estimates m_i, S_i are acceptable.

Note that discriminant functions partition the p-dimensional observation space by means of hyperplanes. A diagnosis can be made for equipment x at the time of an intervention, after collection of all p measurements, by calculating the values of the $n(n - 1)/2$ quantities $V_{ij}(x)$.

In practice, the linearity of discriminant functions may prove to be a major handicap, since the classes E_i might not be separable by hyperplanes.

Example 1: Potentiometers (see also Section 7): The data bank used
in Section 7 also supplied an overall quality mark (graded from 1 to
5) for each of the 29 types of potentiometers. These marks were
provided by test personnel based solely, in principle, on the tests.
In fact, we shall see that this was not the case.

Five classes E_i, i = 1, ..., 5, were defined accordingly, and
discriminant analyses were done with a variable number of measurements for each type of potentiometer. For checking purposes, an
attempt was then made to reclassify these observations using the 10
discriminant functions already calculated. It turned out that 29
types were reclassified correctly if at most 6 measurements were
used on each type; these were the 6 observations closest to the 6
first principal components in Section 7.

For a larger number or another choice of measurements, the
probability of good reclassification dropped to 42% for a maximum
of 31 measurements. ∎

The conclusion to be drawn from this example is not that discriminant analysis is a poor method but rather that the criteria
guiding classification of the potentiometers into five classes do
not correspond to the natural discrimination criterion used in the
discriminant analysis.

Example 2: Discriminant analysis has been considered for quality
control, specifically for the screening of defective components
and selection of high-reliability components produced by a stable
production line. It has also been applied to acceptance control
of components by lots.

The classification rule uses pre-burn-in tests, and the learning samples are for classes resisting or failing during such tests.

To achieve stable classification results, it is recommended
that the number of learning samples for each class E_i be 5 to 10
times larger than the number of measurements on each item.

Similar work has been done in the Soviet Union on cathode-ray
tubes and planar transistors with 5000 hr as the MTBF. ∎

9. CANONICAL ANALYSIS

   (a) Canonical analysis combines discriminant and principal
components analysis and is used for classification. Canonical
analysis seeks p directions such that the variances between the n
condition classes E_i are maximal; in contrast, principal components
analysis looked for the p directions of global maximum variance in
the measurement space. What is wanted here is an orthogonal linear
transformation of the sample vector x:

$$y = xC$$

$$t_C = C^{-1} \qquad \dim(C) = \begin{pmatrix} p \\ p \end{pmatrix}$$

$$\dim(x) = \dim(y) = \begin{pmatrix} 1 \\ p \end{pmatrix}$$

which maximizes the interclass variance. The p directions resulting
are called canonical axes or directions.

   (b) We shall examine two models:

   i. Model ω considers all the L samples constituting X.

   ii. Model Ω considers the n classes E_i, each represented by
n_i samples.

i. Model ω

   Let V_ω be the p-dimensional vector of averaged measurements in
X; S_ω is the corresponding covariance matrix of these p measurements:

$$V_\omega = \frac{1}{L} \sum_{\ell=1}^{L} x_\ell \qquad\qquad \dim(V_\omega) = \begin{pmatrix} 1 \\ p \end{pmatrix}$$

$$S_\omega = \frac{1}{L-1} \sum_{\ell=1}^{L} {}^t(x_\ell - V_\omega)(x_\ell - V_\omega) \qquad \dim(S_\omega) = \begin{pmatrix} p \\ p \end{pmatrix}$$

ii. Model Ω

   It is assumed that the intraclass covariance matrices of the
n classes E_i are the same and equal to S_Ω:

$$S_\Omega = \frac{1}{L-p} \sum_{i=1}^{n} \sum_{x_\ell \in E_i} {}^t(x_\ell - m_i)(x_\ell - m_i)$$

(c) It is then possible to express the interclass covariance matrix describing the difference between models ω and Ω, or between the n classes E_i, as follows:

$$\overline{\overline{\quad}} \triangleq \frac{(L - 1)S_\omega - (L - p)S_\Omega}{p - 1}$$

Reasoning similar to that used in principal components analysis leads us to maximize the interclass covariance matrix $^tC \overline{\quad} C$ of the transformed samples on the basis of the argument outlined in Section 9a. This maximization must be made subject to the constraint

$$^tCS_\Omega C = I$$

Let us take

$$F \triangleq S_\Omega^{1/2}C \qquad \dim(F) = \binom{p}{p}$$

Then the preceding problem is equivalent to the following:

$$\text{Maximum } {}^tF(S_\Omega^{-1/2} \overline{\quad} S_\Omega^{-1/2})F$$

$$^tFF = I$$

as studied in principal components analysis.

(d) The result is the following: the canonical direction W_j, 1, ..., p, is the jth eigenvector of the matrix $S_\Omega^{-1/2} \overline{\quad} S_\Omega^{-1/2}$, where the eigenvectors are ranked by decreasing eigenvalues:

$$C = \left[W_1 \; \vdots \; \cdots \; \vdots \; W_p \right] \qquad \dim(W_j) = \binom{p}{p} \qquad j = 1, \ldots, p$$

If n = 2, the first canonical direction is parallel to the axis joining the mean vectors m_1 and m_2 of the two classes; the second direction is perpendicular to the first and points in the direction of maximum interclass residual variance.

The search for the m < p most useful feature measurements and for the representation of a new sample vector in the canonical space

TABLE 7-5 Canonical analysis of potentiometers: five classes in
addition to the group U of potentiometers which were not classified
(the unspecified class); X and Y are the coordinates on the first
and second canonical axes, respectively

GROUP	.	1	.	MEAN COORDINATES	222.584		− 27.986

	X	Y	
1	223.601	− 29.070	B 12
2	221.567	− 26.901	B 22

GROUP	2	MEAN COORDINATES	− 148.483		− 63.673

	X	Y	
1	− 148.409	− 63.679	B 21
2	− 148.498	− 63.668	B 28

GROUP	3	MEAN COORDINATES	− 37.901		+ 24.143

	X	Y	
1	− 37.891	+ 23.634	B 27
2	− 36.802	+ 25.010	C 32
3	− 38.638	+ 24.405	C 34
4	− 38.273	+ 23.522	C 36

GROUP	4	MEAN COORDINATES	56.588		+ 0.355

	X	Y	
1	56.931	+ 1.145	B 14
2	55.025	− 0.352	B 19
3	57.806	+ 0.272	B 25

GROUP	5	MEAN COORDINATES	− 33.272		+ 17.136

	X	Y	
1	− 33.523	+ 18.985	B 15
2	− 32.142	+ 16.228	B 16
3	− 34.381	+ 15.821	B 26
4	− 32.700	+ 17.246	C 31
5	− 33.616	+ 17.401	C 33

GROUP	U	MEAN COORDINATES	12.091		+ 10.813

	X	Y	
1	− 6.290	+ 19.392	B 13
2	− 30.644	+ 17.898	B 17
3	− 10.552	+ 15.150	B 18
4	+ 201.762	− 33.946	B 20
5	− 38.593	+ 20.281	B 24
6	− 25.535	+ 19.279	C 35
7	− 10.414	+ 16.285	D 41

is done in the same way as in principal components analysis, with W_j playing the role of u_j.

For a new sample, classification and diagnosis are carried out as in discriminant analysis; it is worthwhile to use a feature vector basis made up of canonical axes or vectors, originating in V_ω and parallel to the canonical directions W_j, $j = 1, \ldots, p$. With such a reference system, it may be possible to consider only the m first dimensions for classification.

Canonical analysis again has the disadvantage of ignoring the causal relations between sample equipment and measurements. For this reason the next chapters are devoted to correspondence analysis, which makes such diagnoses possible.

Example: Potentiometers (see Sections 7 and 8): Return to the data of Section 7; we studied the 24 types of potentiometers B12 to D41, distributed among five classes E_i, $i = 1, \ldots, 5$ (see Table 7-4), with seven types not taken into account in the canonical analysis.

It can be seen from Table 7-5 that this analysis succeeds in clearly discriminating class E_1 from E_2 and that E_3, E_4, and E_5 are practically identified. This is confirmed by the principal components analysis of Section 7.

Six of the seven remaining U types (not yet classified) are automatically assigned to E_5, and the last one to E_1, when more than two canonical coordinates are considered.

Here again, we stress the considerable importance of the initial classification of the learning samples, which is taken into account when calculating the canonical axes and associated discriminant functions.

10. DYNAMIC CLUSTERS METHOD

The dynamic clusters method is another unsupervised clustering procedure. It performs no data compression, like those described in Sections 6, 8, and 9. Although computationally slow, it has some practical appeal because of its simplicity.

10.1 Assumptions and Principles

(a) The dynamic clusters algorithm operates on N n-dimensional samples X_j belonging to K possible classes, where K is a given constant. The other parameters of the procedure are the following:

i. An integer m such that $mK \leq N$, $m \geq 1$

ii. A metric D between subsets of points in $\mathbb{R}^n$ (see Section 9.1 of Chapter 1)

iii. A metric d between points in $\mathbb{R}^n$ (see Section 9.2 of Chapter 1), which helps to define D

There is a condition on K, n, D, and d to guarantee convergence of the algorithm in terms of the minimization of a linear combination of the final interclass D distances (see Diday [B-6]).

(b) The algorithm recursively updates the following subsets of the sample set:

i. The clusters P_k (k = 1, ..., K), which partition the sample set $\{X_j : j = 1, ..., N\}$ into K classes at each iteration

ii. The kernels λ_k, which are K disjoint subsets of the sample set, all having m elements; the kernel λ_k is assumed to be a "good" representation of the cluster P_k in terms of the metrics d and D

10.2 The Dynamic Clusters Algorithm

The dynamic clusters algorithm involves the recursive grouping of samples into clusters around a smaller number of samples (the kernels); the end result is a partition into K clusters which minimizes a linear combination of the interclass D distances. The steps of the algorithm are as follows (see Figure 7-2):

① Define λ_1^0, ..., λ_K^0 as K subsets of m samples, each drawn at random from the N samples; $i \triangleq 1$.

② Step i

(a) Define the K clusters P_1^i, ..., P_K^i by assigning each of the N samples X_j to the class represented by the D-closest kernel:

$$X_j \in P_\ell^i \Leftrightarrow D(\{X_j\}, \lambda_\ell^{i-1}) = \underset{k=1,...,K}{\text{Min}} \; D(\{X_j\}, \lambda_k^{i-1})$$

(b) Update the kernels λ_k^{i-1}, k = 1, ..., K, by defining λ_k^i to be the m points of P_k^i which are D-closest to P_k^i.

③ Set i $\overset{\Delta}{=}$ i + 1, and return to ② unless $P_k^i = P_k^{i-1}$ for k = 1, ..., K; if so, end.

10.3 Application to Component Acceptance Control
      (see Ref. E-19)

Given quality control measurements and production monitoring measurements on all components in a lot of size N (i.e., condensators

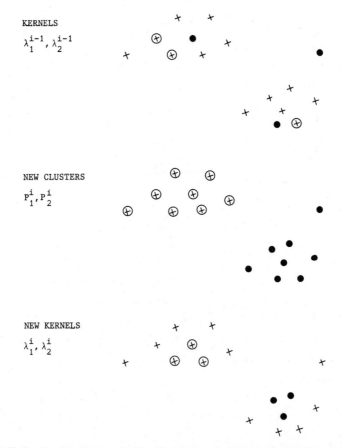

KERNELS
$\lambda_1^{i-1}, \lambda_2^{i-1}$

NEW CLUSTERS
P_1^i, P_2^i

NEW KERNELS
λ_1^i, λ_2^i

FIGURE 7-2 Basic steps of the dynamic clusters algorithm for K = 2 classes and m = 3; the class k = 1 is represented by ○ and the class k = 2 by ●.

each described by n = 8 measurements), we try to detect any clustering effect among them.   If the algorithm reveals K nonempty clusters,
then components from each such cluster should be analyzed more closely
(e.g., the kernel components) to find out whether these clusters are
due to defects or reveal latent stresses which burn-in tests would
eliminate.   The diagnosis first helps isolate bad components otherwise accepted by standard quality control; the diagnosis also makes
it possible to eliminate components without having to carry out
burn-in tests.   This approach can be very useful for high-cost components produced in small series numbers, such as in space or nuclear
applications.

11.   SEQUENTIAL USE OF DATA ANALYSIS METHODS
FOR DIAGNOSTIC PURPOSES

It is thoroughly recommended that data analysis methods be used at
each stage of a sequential diagnosis (Chapter 4) if a growing number
of observations are considered (see also Section 1).

It is then possible not only to choose useful feature observations at each stage but also to follow the variations of the relative
variances of the principal components, canonical axes, or factorial
axes (in correspondence analysis).   Let m be the number of features
selected at a given stage.   It is necessary to check that the sum
of the m largest relative variances is above some confidence threshold (for instance, 60%).   If not, these m observations cannot be
accepted as satisfactory for formulation of a preliminary diagnosis
at this stage.

If the appropriate confidence test is met, then the conditional
failure probabilities (Chapters 4 and 5) can be updated on the basis
of these m observations only, instead of using them all.

As the number of completed stages increases, a drop in the
highest relative variance is observed.   Eventually these variances
stabilize, as the additional observations used at each stage are
redundant in relation to former ones.   It is then time to stop and
make a final diagnosis, since further iterations are useless (provided the process is stationary).

Chapter 8

CORRESPONDENCE ANALYSIS FOR FAILURE ANALYSIS

1. INTRODUCTION

Correspondence analysis (canonical analysis of contingency tables)
is another unsupervised data analysis procedure. It has a number
of theoretical and practical advantages which make it well adapted
for failure diagnosis. Many examples will be given in Chapter 9.
It is especially useful for the joint analysis of failure, test, and
maintenance data which are organized as an incidence table $k(I,J)$ or
as a contingency table $p(I,J)$ (see Chapter 7).

(a) Application to data compression

Correspondence analysis is best suited for failure diagnosis
when the smallest dimension of $k(I,J)$ or $p(I,J)$ is fairly high (e.g.,
dimension larger than or equal to 15), that is, when multivariate
regression becomes inefficient.

The dimension r of the feature space (after compression) can
be optimized by a classical χ^2 test (see Section 6.1 of this chapter).

Considered as a data compression operator, correspondence analysis may be parameterized by replacing the marginal distributions
[i.e., $p(I,\cdot)$] by a specified distribution $h(I)$ [B-18].

The asymptotic distribution of the r-dimensional features can
be estimated for increasing sample sizes.

(b) Application to learning

By generalizing the classical partition of a contingency table
by a χ^2 test (Pearson), correspondence analysis yields natural clus-

ters (a set of rows and columns) which form a natural group; these
clusters are also called nodums. They are based on geometrical
proximities between rows (i ε I) and columns (j ε J) in the feature
space. This clustering is unsupervised and is based on all interactions between row and column measurements.

The compression operator can be parameterized in an optimal
way (for a given dimension of the feature space) in order to maximize the separation between these clusters and thereby facilitate
failure diagnosis.

The rows and the columns of $p(I,J)$ or $k(I,J)$ can be displayed
on maps spanned by pairs of feature basis vectors (factor axes).
These maps are a valuable tool for the visual clustering of the
clusters and for diagnosing causality relations between measurements
and failure nodes. This will be discussed later.

By construction, the effects of dependent rows and columns
such that

$$p(i,j) = p(i,\cdot)p(\cdot,j)$$

will be removed.

If, for all i ∈ I, two measurements or attributes j_1 and j_2 are
redundant, they are immediately identified as having the same representation in the feature space (and thus on the maps). A procedure
exists for the removal of redundant measurements from $p(I,J)$ or
$k(I,J)$ without perturbing the other features.

(c) Application to failure diagnosis

Assume that the data are presented as an explicit tableau (see
Section 4 of Chapter 7) $k(I,J) \geq 0$. The cluster (or nodum) will
group together in the feature space devices i ∈ I and measurements
j ∈ J. Statistical dependency considerations and the corresponding
proximity relations on the maps may then be interpreted as causality
relations between these devices and measurements.

In addition, labels can be added to the display maps representing the failure mode $d(i)$ of each device i ∈ I. Failure diagnosis

can then be inferred from proximity relations between devices (or measurements) and equipment conditions $d(i)$, $i \in I$. Because it is an unsupervised procedure, correspondence analysis allows for the computation of the r feature measurements derived from observations $j \in J$ on any new device by straightforward use of the linear compression operator. The failure mode of this new equipment can be determined by proximity analysis of neighboring learning devices, whose failure modes might then be attributed to the new device.

(d) Conclusion: Correspondence analysis is an unsupervised data analysis and compression procedure applicable to incidence as well as contingency tables. It is well suited for the identification of causality relations among rows and columns if they are assumed to be correlated.

As a data compression operator, it also computes independent basis vectors in the feature space (factor axis) such that any vector $i \in I$ or $j \in J$ can be expressed in this basis.

The interpretation of the results is facilitated by display maps spanned by pairs of factor axes. Proximity analysis among rows $i \in I$ and measurements $j \in J$ helps to identify clusters or nodums that have diagnostic meaning.

2. DESCRIPTIVE PRESENTATION OF CORRESPONDENCE ANALYSIS

In this section we shall provide an informal geometrical presentation of correspondence analysis. A formal probabilistic and algorithmic treatment may be found in Section 4.

2.1 Data Selection Phase

(a) A given two-dimensional incidence table $k(I,J)$ of nonnegative numbers may be transformed into a contingency table $p(I,J)$, as explained in Section 3 of Chapter 7. The rows $i \in I$ are called individuals, and the columns $j \in J$ are measurements, which are made on each individual. See Figure 8-1.

(b) $k(I,J)$ specifies the joint occurrences of discrete random variables X and Y (having ranges I and J, respectively). Let $Z \triangleq (X,Y)$

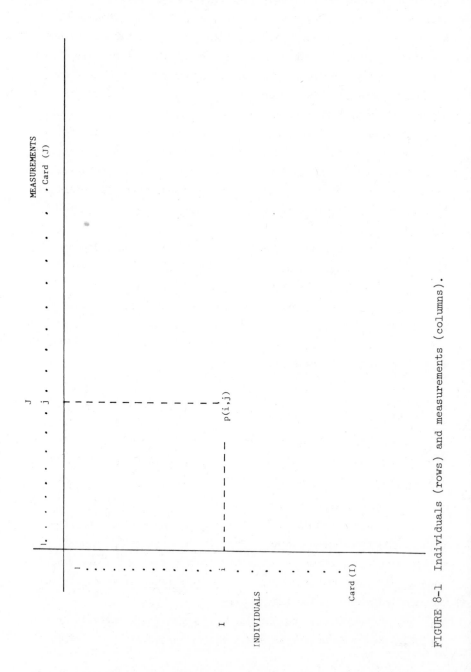

FIGURE 8-1 Individuals (rows) and measurements (columns).

be the bivariate random variable specifying the outcome of each individual observation from which the incidence table $k(I,J)$ is assembled. The counts $k(i,j)$, and thus $p(i,j)$, are proportional to the number of times that the random variable Z assumes the value (i,j) in the observed sample within the ranges of X and Y.

Example
___

   Define:

   X: Operating hours

   Y: Maintenance operations

$k(i,j)$ is the number of maintenance operations of type $j \in J$ observed during the operating hours interval $i \in I$ in the observed sample of Z realizations within the ranges and quantizations of X and Y. ∎

   (c) The same data can be represented by a typological incidence
matrix $T(k)$ in which the occurrences of the random variable $Z = (X,Y)$ are individually registered by two binary codes in each column (one for $i \in I$ and the other for $j \in J$).

Example
___

$$k(I,J) \triangleq \begin{bmatrix} 1 & 1 & 0 \\ 0 & 1 & 3 \end{bmatrix} I$$

$$J$$

$$T[k(I,J)] \triangleq \begin{bmatrix} 1 & 1 & 0 & 0 & 0 & 0 \\ 0 & 0 & 1 & 1 & 1 & 1 \\ & & \cdots & & & \\ 1 & 0 & 0 & 0 & 0 & 0 \\ 0 & 1 & 1 & 0 & 0 & 0 \\ 0 & 0 & 0 & 1 & 1 & 1 \end{bmatrix} \begin{matrix} I \\ \\ \\ J \end{matrix} \qquad \text{values of } Z = (X,Y)$$

$$1 \quad 2 \quad \cdots \quad m$$

$$\xrightarrow{\hspace{4cm}}$$

Realizations of $Z = (X,Y)$

The sum of all numbers appearing in the same column of $T[k(I,J)]$ is equal to 2. ∎

   (d) Instead of applying correspondence analysis to the inci-
dence table $k(I,J) \geq 0$, it may be better to apply a transformation u and to use the incidence table $u_o k(I,J)$. The typological incidence

matrix transformation T is an example of such a transformation. The purpose of u may be any of the following:

   i.   To disperse some individuals or measurements

   ii.   To increase the proximity of some individuals or measurements

   iii.   To compensate for intrinsic relations between individuals and measurements

   iv.   To process in a different way selected measurements [B-18]

   2.2 Data Compression Phase

2.2.1 Cluster $N(I)$: To each individual $i \in I$, we associate a weighting point M_i in the space of dimension $Card(J)$ having mass $p(i, \cdot)$ equal to its marginal probability in the contingency table. The coordinates of $i \in I$ are defined by

$$x(i,j) = \frac{p(i,j)}{p(i,\cdot)p(\cdot,j)} - 1 = \frac{Pr(Y = j/X = i)}{p(\cdot,j)} - 1$$

   The set of weighting points comprises a cluster $N(I) = \{[M_i, p(i,\cdot)]\ ;\ i \in I\}$ (cluster of all individuals) in the measurement space J. The center of mass of this cluster is the origin since

$$\forall\ j \in J \qquad \sum_{i \in I} p(i,\cdot)x(i,j) = \sum_{i \in I} \frac{p(i,j)}{p(\cdot,j)} - \sum_{i \in I} p(i,\cdot)$$

$$= 1 - 1 = 0$$

   We can also define the cluster $N(J)$ of all measurements $j \in J$ in the space of the individuals I. This space has "dual" properties to those of $N(I)$, because the $x(i,j)$ formula remains invariant under transposition of I and J.

2.2.2 Individual profile

   (a) This notion is intended to characterize all possible behaviors of an individual on the basis of observations; scale factors should not alter this profile:

$$f_i(J) \triangleq \{Pr(Y = j/X = i)\ ;\ j \in J\}$$

   (b) It is essential to remember the following property of correspondence analysis: any two individuals i_1, $i_2 \in I$ having the same profile ,

$$f_{i_1}(J) = f_{i_2}(J)$$

are assigned the same coordinates $x(i_1,j)$, $x(i_2,j)$. By definition, $N(I)$ identifies individuals which have the same profile (independent of any scale).

(c) Suppose that two random variables X and Y are statistically independent; that is,

$$\forall\ (i,j) \in I \times J \qquad p(i,j) = p(i,\cdot)p(\cdot,j) \Leftrightarrow p(I,J) = p(I,\cdot) \otimes p(\cdot,J)$$

The cluster $N(I)$ is then reduced to the origin. Consequently, correspondence analysis is of interest only if there is some dependence between X and Y, e.g., between equipment failure modes and the measurements.

Example

The cluster $N(I)$ associated with the incidence table $k(I,J)$ is as follows:

TABLE $k(I,J)$

Passengers I ╲ Questions J	Drinks	Seat comfort	Movie	Food
A	16	14	10	12
B	6	14	4	15
C	12	10.5	7.5	9

TABLE $x(I,J)$

Passengers I ╲ Questions J	Drinks	Seat comfort	Movie	Food
A	0.17	-0.09	0.19	-0.16
B	-0.41	0.20	-0.37	0.29
C	0.17	-0.09	0.19	-0.16

Although passenger C is much more reserved in these judgments than
A, both have the same profile; in other words, A and C nuance their
judgments in the same way.   ■

2.2.3 χ^2 metric and proximity analysis

(a) The measurement space containing N(I) has a distance measure, called the χ^2 metric, which is discussed in Section 3:

$$d^2(M_i, M_\ell) \triangleq \sum_{j \in J} p(\cdot,j)[x(\ell,j) - x(i,j)]^2$$

$$= \sum_{j \in J} \frac{[Pr(Y = j/X = \ell) - Pr(Y = j/X = i)]^2}{p(\cdot,j)}$$

(b) By using this metric, the inertia of a weighting point M_i
of N(I) with respect to an axis (moment of inertia) can be computed
as the product of the mass $p(i,\cdot)$ and the square of the χ^2 distance
to the axis. The inertia of the whole cluster N(I) is the sum of
the inertia of all points with respect to the orthonormal basis axes.

(c) In correspondence analysis, any geometric proximity analysis for clustering into clusters will be inferred from the values of
the χ^2 distance measure.

2.2.4 Data compression and computation of the factor axes

(a) Correspondence analysis computes the best fits of $N_r(I)$,
$N_r(J)$ to the clusters N(I), N(J) in a feature subspace of given
dimension r such that:

i. The inertias of $N_r(I)$ and $N_r(J)$ in this subspace are min-
imal, and, by definition, the r coordinate axes of this subspace are
the factor axes.

ii. $N_r(I)$, $N_r(J)$ are the projections of N(I), N(J) into the
subspace in terms of the χ^2 metric.

The data compression becomes more efficient as the dimension r
of the feature subspace becomes smaller than the dimension Card(I),
Card(J) of N(J), N(I), respectively.

(b) In an analogy from mechanics, where N(I), N(J) are treated
as solids made of discrete weighting points, the basis vectors in
the r-dimensional feature space are identical to the r first (principal) axes of inertia of these solids. These basis vectors are

called factor axes and are ranked by increasing order of their corresponding moments of inertia. Recall that minimizing the moment of
inertia of a solid with respect to a specified axis and maximizing
the variance of the cluster along this axis are equivalent. Consequently, the factor axes are also ranked by decreasing variances
along these directions. See Figure 8-2.

(c) It should be noted that the vector basis minimizing the
inertia of $N_r(I)$ (criterion $\underline{i}$) is identical to the basis minimizing
the inertia of $N_r(J)$ (see Refs. A-3 and A-15). This homomorphism
requires changes of scale in the coordinates $x(i,j)$, $(i,j) \in I \times J$,
depending on whether $N(I)$ or $N(J)$ is being analyzed.

Example

The following is an example illustrating the ideas just presented.

Consider a cluster of points of mass unity in E^3, shaped as an
ellipsoid of center O. The direction of maximum elongation is the one having the smallest moment of inertia.
Now vary the dimension r of the feature space after data
compression:

i. $\underline{r = 1}$: The unique factor axis is identical with the
axis of maximum elongation. $N_1(I)$ is reduced to that
portion of this axis which intersects with $N(I)$.

ii. $\underline{r = 2}$: The first factor axis is the first axis of
inertia; the second factor axis is the second axis
of inertia [the main axis of the elliptic section
of $N(I)$ by the plane orthogonal to the first factor
axis in the origin O]. $N_2(I)$ is composed of all
projections of points from the ellipsoid $N(I)$ onto
the plane spanned by the two first factor axes; thus
the outer contour of $N_2(I)$ is the ellipse in which
$N(I)$ intersects this plane.

iii. $\underline{r = 3}$: $N_3(I)$ is identical to $N(I)$, and there is no
data compression.

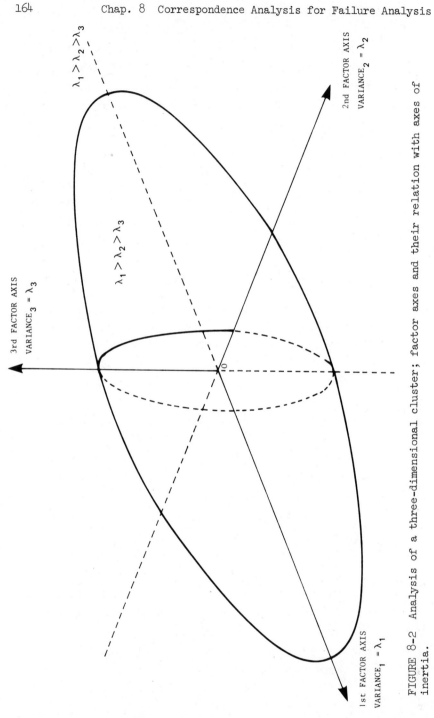

FIGURE 8-2 Analysis of a three-dimensional cluster; factor axes and their relation with axes of inertia.

If, however, $N(I)$ can be approximated by a spherical bowl, it
is impossible to compute unique factor axes. This corresponds to the case where the data reveal dependence between
X and Y and hence a lack of causality structure.   ∎

2.3 Feature Extraction Phase

Each of the r factor axes is characterized by the equation of
any such line in the original Card(J)- or Card(I)-dimensional space.
These equations describe how feature measurements along each factor
axis can be expressed as functions of the original measurements in
J or I. These feature measurements are synthetic measurements which
allow for data compression and proximity analysis (see Chapter 10).

2.4 Display Phase and Interpretation

2.4.1 Display: The interpretation requires a number of two-dimensional displays of those portions of the r-dimensional feature space
occupied by all individuals $i \in I$ and measurements $j \in J$. These
displays (maps) are defined as follows and are ranked by increasing
total inertias:

    i. First factor map: spanned by the first and second factor
axes

    ii. Second factor map: spanned by the first and third factor
axes

    iii. Third factor map: spanned by the second and third factor
axes

We define, as computed in Section 4.3,

$G(i,n)$: coordinate of the individual $i \in I$ on the nth factor
    axis

$F(j,n)$: coordinate of the measurement $j \in J$ on the nth factor
    axis

2.4.2 Proximity analysis

Geometrical proximity analysis may be carried out on each factor
map, following a procedure to be described in Sections 3 and 5.

In the following, we assume that our results arise from the
correspondence analysis of $N(I)$.

(a) Center of inertia: It can be shown that any individual
$i \in I$ is located at the center of inertia of all measurement points

$j \in J$ having the weights $Pr(Y = j/X = i)$. However, $j \in J$ is <u>not</u> at the center of inertia of all individuals $i \in I$ assigned with these same weights.

(b) Probability of association: Geometrical proximity analysis is based on a number of theoretical results, of which the following is essential: <u>If two individuals or measurements have similar profiles in terms of the χ^2 metric, then their probability of association π (defined below) will be high, and their projections onto factor maps will be close.</u>

Conversely, if two individuals or measurements are close on the factor maps, then it is likely that their profiles are similar; this conclusion needs to fulfill certain validity tests, however, e.g., by the probability of association.

It is therefore useful to first identify, by visual or algorithmic clustering (see Sections 4.2 and 5.1), those subsets of individuals or measurements which build up groups (clusters) of their own. This can be done by computing the following Euclidean distances between their representations in the feature space:

$$D^2(i_1,i_2) \triangleq \sum_{n=1}^{r} [F(i_1,n) - F(i_2,n)]^2$$

$$D^2(i,j) \triangleq \sum_{n=1}^{r} [F(i,n) - G(j,n)]^2$$

$$D^2(j_1,j_2) \triangleq \sum_{n=1}^{r} [G(j_1,n) - G(j_2,n)]^2$$

The asymptotic distributions of these statistics for large $Card(I) \times Card(J)$ are the same χ^2 distribution, with $[Card(I) - 1] \times [Card(J) - 1]$ degrees of freedom. This allows the following definition of the <u>probability of association</u> between two individuals or measurements: $\pi(i_1,i_2)$, $\pi(i,j)$, $\pi(j_1,j_2)$ are the probability levels of this asymptotic χ^2 distribution corresponding to the fractiles $D(i_1,i_2)$, $D(i,j)$, $D(j_1,j_2)$, respectively.

The probability of association is (in addition to geometrical proximity on the factor maps) a second criterion for clustering the individuals or measurements, thus inferring <u>causality relations</u> among them. However, it is essential to point out that correspondence analysis alone does not reveal how such causality operates. Additional (usually not quantifiable) technical information is needed to conclude whether i ∈ I acts on j ∈ J or the opposite occurs (see the following example).

<u>Example</u> (Figure 8-3)

From the results of the correspondence analysis, we get, after scaling,

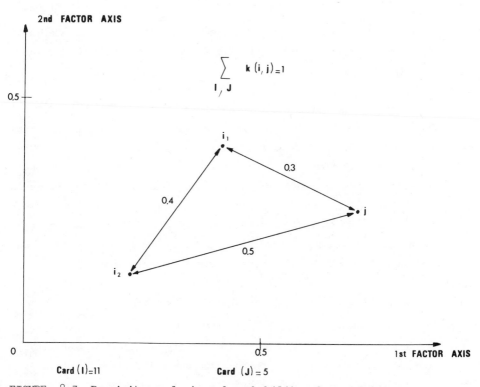

FIGURE 8-3 Proximity analysis and probability of association.

$$D(i_1, i_2) = 0.4 \qquad D(i_1, j) = 0.3 \qquad D(i_2, j) = 0.5$$

The χ^2 statistical table yields, for $[Card(I) - 1][Card(J) - 1] = 40$ degrees of freedom, the following probabilities of association:

$$\pi(i_1, i_2) = 81\% \qquad \pi(i_1, j) = 99\% \qquad \pi(i_2, j) = 42\%$$

As a consequence,

i. The profiles of measurement j and individual i_1 are almost identical. We shall say that j and i_1 are very strongly associated and that the measurement j is the main cause of the characteristics of the individual i_1 (or conversely).

ii. The profiles of individuals i_1 and i_2 are relatively close; i_1 and i_2 are considered to be associated, and their characteristics are often the same.

iii. The profiles of measurement j and individual i_2 are quite far apart; j and i_2 are only weakly associated and will rarely influence each other. ∎

Example

Consider failures due to temperature stress. Two mechanical pieces A and B, attached together, are heated until one of them, say A, cracks. Assume that the temperatures of A and B are not measurable. It is obvious that there exists a causality relation between A and B, but it is impossible to conclude from the sole failure event whether A broke because of A alone, because of B, because of A and B, or for a fourth possible reason. Moreover, it is impossible to predict or verify that a later failure of B is due to B alone or to the delayed effects of A being heated (memory effect). ∎

3. THE χ^2 METRIC AND DISTRIBUTIONAL EQUIVALENCE

3.1 General χ^2 Metric

(a) Let f, g, h be three elements of the set of probability density functions (p.d.f.) on the discrete set J, assuming that h is essential [for all $j \in J$, $h(j) > 0$]. A generalization of the χ^2

metric of center h, between the p.d.f. f and g, can be defined as
follows:

$$d_h^2(f,g) = \sum_{j \in J} \frac{[f(j) - g(j)]^2}{h(j)}$$

d_h is a distance measure, because the three basic axioms are
fulfilled, in addition to the two axioms of distributional equivalence (see Section 3.2 below):

    i. $d_h^2(f,g) = d_h^2(g,f) \geq 0$.

    ii. $d_h^2(f,f) = 0$.

    iii. $d_h^2(f,g) \leq d_h^2(f,e) + d_h^2(e,g)$.

The metric $d(\cdot,\cdot)$ defined in Section 2.2.3 is a special case
of the preceding.

    (b) Note that the Pearson statistic by which a p.d.f. estimate
$\hat{f}$ is compared to the true p.d.f. f is equal to the product $md_{\hat{f}}^2(f,\hat{f})$
of the sample size m and the squared χ^2 distance of center f between
f and $\hat{f}$. If the Pearson theorem holds, then $md_{\hat{f}}^2(f,\hat{f})$ is asymptotically distributed as a χ^2 statistic with $Card(J) - 1$ degrees of freedom.

3.2 Distributional Equivalence

The two properties embodied in this concept are extensively
used at the interpretation stage of correspondence analysis; $h(J)$ is
again assumed to be an essential probability density function on J.

    (a) <u>Axiom I</u>: The χ^2 distances $d_h(i_1, i_2)$ will be zero if the
individuals i_1, i_2 have the same profiles with respect to J:

$$f_{i_1}(J) = f_{i_2}(J) \Leftrightarrow d_h(i_1, i_2) = 0$$
$$\Leftrightarrow \forall \ j \in J, \ Pr(Y = j/X = i_1) = Pr(Y = j/X = i_2)$$

Observe that the χ^2 distance is scale independent.

    (b) <u>Axiom II</u>: If two measurements j_1, $j_2 \in J$ have the same
profiles with respect to I and if they are replaced by a single
measurement j_0 such that:

i. $\forall\ i \in I,\ p(i,j_0) = p(i,j_1) + p(i,j_2)$

ii. $\dfrac{p(\cdot,j_0)^2}{h(j_0)} = \dfrac{p(\cdot,j_1)^2}{h(j_1)} + \dfrac{p(\cdot,j_2)^2}{h(j_2)}$

then all the d_h distances between elements in I remain unchanged despite this replacement.

This is the property allowing the elimination of redundant measurements.

3.3 χ^2 Metric in Correspondence Analysis
      (See Section 2.2.3)

(a) The χ^2 metric used in correspondence analysis between individuals in I uses the marginal p.d.f. $p(\cdot,J)$ as a center.

(b) As a consequence, if a measurement $j \in J$ yields high conditional probabilities $Pr(Y = j/X = i)$ for all $i \in I$, the possibly large contribution of $[Pr(Y = j/X = i_1) - Pr(Y = j/X = i_2)]^2$ to the expression of $d^2(M_{i_1},M_{i_2})$ is compensated for by the factor $1/p(\cdot,j)$. In other words, correspondence analysis does not allow for discrimination among individuals based only on the scaled values of the incidence data $k(I,J)$. The correction factor $1/p(\cdot,j)$ compensates for cases where one measurement is usually much larger or smaller than the others in J.

(c) It has been shown [B-18] that correspondence analysis may be carried out with the general χ^2 metric d_h, where the p.d.f. $h(J)$ is not necessarily data dependent.

It then becomes a parameter, which may be chosen to improve cluster separability for diagnostic purposes or to assign weights $h(j)$ proportional to the reliability or accuracy of the sensor delivering this measurement $j \in J$.

4.   THEORY OF CORRESPONDENCE ANALYSIS

In this section we shall summarize the main theoretical aspects and properties of correspondence analysis; it is left to the reader to seek additional information in the literature [A-3, A-15, A-46, B-18]. One approach might be to detail the reasoning sustaining

the descriptive presentation in Section 2, which closely parallels
principal components analysis (see Section 7 of Chapter 7) except
for transformed coordinates derived from the contingency table.
However, it is preferable to give a more concise theoretical presentation which is more fruitful and original.

4.1 Definition of Correspondence Analysis $C_0[k(I,J)]$

(a) Correspondence analysis (which is also called Fisher's
canonical analysis of contingency tables) involves looking for vec-
tors $F = {}^t[F(1), \ldots, F[\text{Card}(J)]]$ and $G = {}^t[G(1), \ldots, G[\text{Card}(I)]]$
such that the correlation between the random variables $f(Y)$ and $g(X)$
is maximal, where the functions f, g of the random variables $(Y,X) =$
(j,i) are defined by the relations

$$f(Y) = F(j) \qquad g(X) = G(i)$$

Correspondence analysis applies to nonnegative incidence tables
$k(I,J)$ as well as to contingency tables $p(I,J)$; the former will be
considered below.

(b) Let $k(I,\cdot)$ and $k(\cdot,J)$ be the __diagonal__ matrices of row and
column totals, assuming that none are zero. The sequence of operations

$$F^{(1)} = [k(\cdot,J)]^{-1}{}^t k(I,J)G^{(1)}$$

$$G^{(2)} = [k(I,\cdot)]^{-1} k(I,J)F^{(1)}$$

$$F^{(2)} = [k(\cdot,J)]^{-1}{}^t k(I,J)G^{(2)} \qquad \text{etc.}$$

in which new vectors $F^{(m)}$, $G^{(m)}$ are successively derived from an
initial vector $F^{(1)}$ is referred to as the $C_0[k(I,J)]$ algorithm corresponding to the tableau $k(I,J)$.

(c) Its eigenvectors, as defined below, are the solutions of
the correspondence analysis problem. The coordinates of the individuals and measurements in the feature space are simply

$$F(j,n) = F_n^*(j) \qquad G(i,n) = G_n^*(i)$$

where $n = 1, \ldots,$ Min$\{$Card(I),Card$(J)\}$ and F_n^*, G_n^* are the eigenvectors of rank n of the algorithm $C_0[k(I,J)]$ ranked by decreasing eigenvalues λ_n.

(d) Each triple (ρ, F^*, G^*) is an eigensolution if

$$\rho G^* = [k(I,\cdot)]^{-1}k(I,J)F^*$$

$$\rho F^* = [k(\cdot,J)]^{-1}{}^t k(I,J)G^*$$

where $\rho \overset{\Delta}{=} \sqrt{\lambda}$.

ρ is then the correlation of F^* and G^* with respect to the tableau $k(I,J)$. Proposition 1 in Section 4.2.1 gives a constructive solution to this problem.

4.2 Basic Properties of Correspondence Analysis

4.2.1 Proposition 1: The correspondence analysis problem is equivalent to a singular value decomposition problem and is therefore solved by extracting the eigenvectors of the semidefinite matrix $\{[k(I,\cdot)]^{-1/2}k(I,J)[k(\cdot,J)]^{-1/2}\} \cdot {}^t\{[k(I,\cdot)]^{-1/2}k(I,J)[k(\cdot,J)]^{-1/2}\}$ which represents the inertia matrix of the cluster $N(I)$. ∎

Proof: (ρ, F^*, G^*) is a solution of $C_0[k(I,J)]$ if and only if

$$\rho\{[k(I,\cdot)]^{1/2}G^*\} = \{[k(I,\cdot)]^{-1/2}k(I,J)[k(\cdot,J)]^{-1/2}\}[k(\cdot,J)]^{1/2}F^*$$

$$\rho\{[k(\cdot,J)]^{1/2}F^*\} = \{[k(I,\cdot)]^{-1/2}k(I,J)[k(\cdot,J)]^{-1/2}\}[k(I,\cdot)]^{1/2}G^*$$

This establishes that the solutions are equivalent to a singular value decomposition. We see that

$$\rho^2[k(I,\cdot)]^{1/2}G^* = \{[k(I,\cdot)]^{-1/2}k(I,J)[k(\cdot,J)]^{-1/2}\}$$
$$\cdot {}^t\{[k(I,\cdot)]^{-1/2}k(I,J)[k(\cdot,J)]^{-1/2}\}$$
$$\cdot [k(I,\cdot)]^{1/2}G^*$$

The matrix preceding $[k(I,\cdot)]^{1/2}G^*$ on the right-hand side is of the form B^tB and is therefore semidefinite; $\lambda \overset{\Delta}{=} \rho^2$ is the eigenvalue of the solution, and the factor axes are (as eigenvectors) taken to be ordered by decreasing eigenvalues λ. Note that after all eigenvectors G_n^* have been computed via the last equation, the corresponding eigenvectors F_n^* can easily be derived as linear combinations of them.

4.2.2 Proposition 2: The maximal solution of the correspondence analysis problem $C_0[k(I,J)]$ is $\rho = \lambda = 1$, $F^* = {}^t1$, $G^* = {}^t1$, where ${}^t1$ is the column vector of ones. ∎

As a consequence, there is always a trivial first factorial axis, which is actually assigned the rank $n = 0$ and disregarded.

4.2.3 Proposition 3: Solutions of rank $n \neq 0$ satisfy the relation

$$\sum_{i \in I} k(i,\cdot)G(i,n) = \sum_{j \in J} k(\cdot,j)F(j,n)$$ ∎

This shows that the feature coordinates are centered so as to have a weighted mean of zero.

4.2.4 Proposition 4: If the sequence $F^{(m)}$, $G^{(m)}$ of Section 4.1b is orthogonalized with respect to the trivial factor axis $n = 0$ in accordance with Propositions 2 and 3, then it will eventually converge to the maximal nontrivial solution F_1^*, G_1^*. By repeating the process with this new starting point, we thus obtain a sequential solution algorithm. ∎

4.2.5 Proposition 5:

(a) A triple (ρ, F^*, G^*) is a solution of $C_1[k(I,J)]$, the first-order correspondence analysis of $k(I,J)$, if it is a solution of $C_0\{T[k(I,J)]\}$, where $T[k(I,J)]$ is the typological incidence matrix derived from $k(I,J)$ (see Section 2.1) and is used for simultaneous multidimensional scaling of the individuals and measurements.

(b) The factor axes defined by the two problems are the same, although the eigenvalues differ. ∎

The practical significance of this result is that correspondence analysis can be considered to be equivalent to simultaneous multi-dimensional scaling $C_1[k(I,J)]$ of individuals and measurements, thus establishing causality relations among them.

Moreover, and this is essential for diagnostic applications (see Section 4 of Chapter 7), it validates the present method of analysis of multidimensional data with mixed discrete and continuous measurements. This reduces continuous measurements to discrete variates by division of the ranges into intervals. The analysis C_1 can then be applied directly.

4.2.6 Proposition 6: The analyses C_0 and C_1 are equivalent to each other and to canonical correlation analysis (see Ref. A-49). C_1 analysis is also equivalent to principal components analysis in which the measurements are rescaled. However, only C_0 and C_1 allow for the joint treatment of the individuals and measurements. ∎

4.2.7 Proposition 7: The correspondence analysis $C_0[k(I,J)]$ maximizes the χ^2 norm $\mu_k \overset{\Delta}{=} ||k(I,J) - k(I,\cdot) \otimes k(\cdot,J)||_{\chi^2}$ as well as its restriction to any r-dimensional feature space. ∎

In other words, correspondence analysis maximizes the difference between the incidence table and one having the same marginals but based on the independence of I and J. It is clear that the latter table is useless for diagnostic purposes.

4.3 Computational Formulas and Data Compression

The computational formulas needed for computer implementation of the correspondence analysis $C_0[p(I,J)]$ are summarized below. This is the nonsequential algorithm (see also Proposition 4).

Step (1) Define the dimension $1 \leq r \leq \inf\{Card(I), Card(J)\}$ of the feature space after data compression.

Step (2)

(a) G_n^* and $\lambda_n = \rho_n^2$ are, respectively, the $(n + 1)$st column eigenvector and associated eigenvalue of the symmetrical semidefinite matrix $S = [s_{j\ell}]$:

$$s_{j\ell} = \sum_{i \in I} \frac{p(i,j)p(i,\ell)}{p(i,\cdot)\sqrt{p(\cdot,j)p(\cdot,\ell)}} \qquad j,\ell \in J$$

which has $\lambda_0 = 1$ as the largest eigenvalue with all coordinates of G_0^* equal.

(b) These eigenvectors $G_n^* = [G_n^*(i) : i = 1, \ldots, Card(I)]$ are ranked by decreasing eigenvalues $1 \geq \lambda_1 \geq \cdots \geq \lambda_r > 0$. They are the factor axes of $N(I)$.

Step (3) The factor axes F_n^* of $N(J)$ are associated with the same eigenvalues λ_n, and

$$F_n^* = \frac{1}{\sqrt{\lambda_n}} \cdot [p(\cdot,J)]^{-1 t}p(I,J)G_n^*$$

$$[p(\cdot,J)]^{-1t}p(I,J) = \frac{p(j,i)}{p(\cdot,j)} \qquad i = \text{row},\ j = \text{column}$$

Step 4

(a)   The coordinate $G(i,n)$ $(n = 1, \ldots, r)$ of individual $i \in I$ on the factor axis G_n^* is $G_n^*(i)$.

(b)   The coordinate $F(j,n)$ $(n = 1, \ldots, r)$ of measurement $j \in J$ on the factor axis F_n^* is $F_n^*(j)$.

(c)   Both individuals $i \in I$ and measurements $j \in J$ may then be displayed in the same r-dimensional feature space, with basis vectors G_n^*, $n = 1, \ldots, r$.

(d) $G(i,n) = (1/\sqrt{\lambda_n})[1/p(i,\cdot)] \sum\limits_{j \in J} p(i,j)F(j,n)$, where $i \in I$ and $n = 1, \ldots, r$.

Step (5)   Data reconstruction formula:

$$p(i,j) = p(i,\cdot)p(\cdot,j) \cdot [1 + \sum_{n=1}^{r} \sqrt{\lambda_n}\, F(j,n)G(i,n)]$$

5.   INTERPRETATION PROCEDURE

This section supplements the basic rules of Sections 1 and 2 for interpreting the results of correspondence analysis. The validity tests are summarized in Section 6.

5.1   Clustering

(a)   As pointed out in Section 2.4, proximity analysis and clustering into clusters are essential steps of the interpretation phase. Clustering is an unsupervised nonhierarchical process in which nearby individuals and/or measurements are classified into groups (clusters). This process is visual if map displays only are used, and it is algorithmic if a procedure like cluster analysis is used (see Section 10 of Chapter 7). Whereas the final verbal interpretation of all possible causality relations rests with the user of the equipment under study, proximity analysis and clustering ought to remain the responsibility of specialists who are skilled in applying data analysis: their task is to provide lists of all possible causality relations derived from the results to the user, with an

indication of their validity. The equipment users and maintenance
management must then try to provide a rational explanation for each
such causality relation or demonstrate that it is meaningless.

In the case of overlap between clusters, correspondence analysis $C_1[k(I,J)]$ should be applied to the typological incidence data
$T[k(I,J)]$. followed by clustering.

Example

This example serves the sole purpose of showing how visual
clustering may be carried out. It should be remembered that it is
not always possible to obtain disjoint clusters. In the case of
overlaps, it is recommended that additional information be used to
obtain improved discrimination or that each cluster be restricted
by introducing borders (having some appropriate thickness) in which
nothing can be inferred without validity tests. See Figure 8-4.

(b) Certain special shapes of clusters $N(I)$ or $N(J)$, when
displayed on a factor map, are frequently encountered:

i. Disjoint subsets: $I = (\cup I_n)(\cap I_n) \neq \phi$ (null set) and
there is a similar decomposition of J; in this case, the incidence
table $k(I,J)$ is likely to be partitioned into square submatrices k_i:

$$k(I,J) = \begin{bmatrix} k_1 & 0 & 0 \\ 0 & k_2 \cdot \cdot \cdot & \\ 0 & & k_m \end{bmatrix} \quad J$$

$$\qquad\qquad I_1 \quad I_2 \quad I_m$$

If such a partition exists, then there are m clusters corresponding,
respectively, to the individuals and measurements in each submatrix
k_i, $i = 1, \ldots, m$. The eigenvalue λ_1 of the factor axis corresponding to the partition (the axis between clusters) is equal to 1.
Some symmetry of all feature points and clusters with respect to
origin will usually be apparent.

ii. Quadratic clusters (see Figure 8-5): In this case, if the
feature vectors [e g., $N(I)$] form an approximately quadratic cloud,
it is likely that the data $p(I,J)$ are a good approximation to a
multivariate normal distribution with all individuals i $\in$ I equally

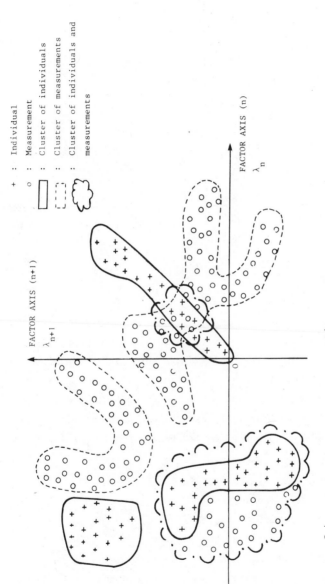

FIGURE 8-4 Clusters of individuals and/or measurements.

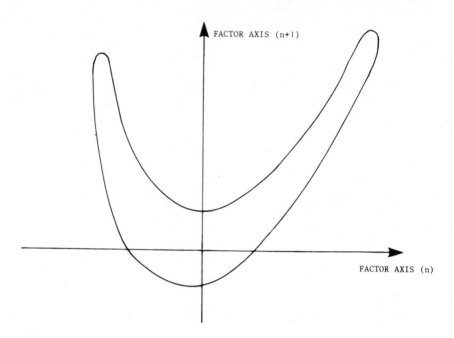

FIGURE 8-5 Quadratic cluster.

correlated. This effect also occurs for disjoint subsets of I (or
J) and for subsets of normally distributed individuals each uncorrelated with all others.

The existence of such a quadratic relation is a frequent source
of surprise to data analysis experts who assume that the second factor axis (polynomial axis) should be independent of the first.

5.2 Types of Factor Axes

(a) The factor axes fall into three broad shape categories:

i. Axes of seriation

ii. Polynomial axes

iii. Axes between clusters

The last two types have already been discussed.

For axes of seriation, individuals and measurements are not
clustered into clusters but are distributed along such axes from
one end to the other. Seriation axes commonly arise in correspondence

analysis $C_1[k(I,J)]$; this suggests underlying trends in the data
rather than dichotomies.

(b) In addition to shape categories, two different classes of
factor axes are defined at the interpretation stage:
Class 1: The factor axes can be directly interpreted as basic
feature measurements. Axes of seriation are often (but not always)
in this class.

i. Class 1: The factor axes can be directly interpreted as
basic feature measurements. Axes of seriation are often (but not
always) in this class.

ii. Class 2: The factor axes essentially fulfill the role of
separating two or more clusters; the natures of the corresponding
basic feature measurements cannot be verbally interpreted by themselves.

Example 1 (see Section 2.1 of Chapter 7)

This interpretation reveals factor axes of class 1: sound
level, vowel-consonant harmony. Correspondence analysis permits
differentiation between spoken languages (e.g., Italian and German)
due to different configurations of the clusters with respect to
these factor axes. ∎

Example 2 (see Section 2.2 of Chapter 7)

Correspondence analysis of the cluster $N(I)$ of all interviewed
passengers allows discrimination between occasional passengers and
frequent travelers. Although the first factor axis is of class 1
(because it indicates the frequency of air travel), the second factor axis is of class 2 since it compares types of services preferred
by each of these two classes of passengers. ∎

Example 3 (see Section 2.3 of Chapter 7)

Correspondence analysis isolates components suffering from
either early incipient failures or drift failures and identifies
inadequate maintenance procedures: the factor axes are both of
class 1 and class 2. ∎

5.3 Sequential Analysis of the Factor Maps

Frequently the interpretation of a given factor map (defined
in Section 2.4) can be defined by consideration of significant factor maps of higher rank. Therefore if a specified causality relation or factor axis interpretation has been inferred from the first
factor map (axes 1 and 2), it is advisable to look for it in the

second factor map (axes 1 and 3) as well, especially if the information carried on factor axis 3 is significant (as identified in Section 5.5).

5.4 Dependence Ratio Between an
     Individual and a Measurement

This notion, the dependence ratio between an individual and a measurement, supplements the concept of probability of association (Section 2.4.2b). An individual $i \in I$ and a measurement $j \in J$ may have a low distance $D(i,j)$ in the feature space and thus a high probability of association $\pi(i,j)$ without necessarily having a high dependence ratio:

$$\mu(i,j) \triangleq \frac{p(i,j)}{p(i,\cdot)p(\cdot,j)}$$

Possible reasons for this are the following:

i. The location of individual i in the feature space is determined not only by $p(i,j)$ but by all joint frequencies $p(i,\ell)$, $\ell \in J$. Thus $i \in I$ may be D-close to $j \in J$, because it is highly dependent on other measurements $\ell \in J$ for which $\mu(i,\ell)$ is close to 1.

ii. In the data reconstruction formula (Section 4.3.5), the contribution to $\mu(i,j)$ of positive products $F(j,n)G(i,n)$ may be largely compensated for by negative products of the same type, derived from factor axes n (n = 1, ..., r) which have not been accounted for by visual proximity analysis.

In general, a high probability of association $\pi(i,j)$ will reveal high dependence ratios $\mu(i,j)$, although it is necessary to verify this in each specific case.

5.5 Analysis of Contributions and
     Interpretation of the Factor Axes

On a factor map, the squared Euclidean distance D between individuals and/or measurements has the same value as the χ^2 distance between the corresponding profiles and

$$\lambda_n = \sum_{j \in J} p(\cdot,j)[F(j,n)]^2 = \sum_{i \in I} p(i,\cdot)[G(i,n)]^2 \qquad n = 1, ..., r$$

This justifies the following definitions:

i. $p(i,\cdot)[G(i,n)]^2 \cdot Sign[G(i,n)]$ is the contribution of the individual $i \in I$ to the factor axis n of inertia λ_n.

ii. $p(\cdot,j)[F(j,n)]^2 \cdot Sign[F(j,n)]$ is the contribution of the measurement $j \in J$ to the factor axis n of inertia λ_n.

The rule is then to interpret the factor axis n (see Section 5.2) only in terms of those individuals and measurements which have the largest (or smallest) contributions to that axis and which explain "most" (e.g., 80%) of the λ_n.

If a single individual or measurement contributes to more than, for example, 25% of λ_n, then a residual correspondence analysis should be carried out in which this element has been removed.

Often higher-rank factor axes can be interpreted from only a few elements i or j. Because λ_n may be small for large n, these elements can be better identified through the relative contributions

$$\frac{G(i,n)}{D(i,0)} \qquad and \qquad \frac{F(j,n)}{D(j,0)}$$

where 0 is the origin in the r-dimensional feature space.

6. TESTS OF VALIDITY

The purpose of tests of validity is to establish the validity of results derived from correspondence analysis.

6.1 Test on the Dimension r of the Feature Space

(a) The total inertia (defined in Section 2.2.1) of the cluster $N(I)$ with respect to origin is

$$\mu_p = ||p(I,J) - p(I,\cdot) \otimes p(\cdot,J)||^2$$

$$= \sum_{I,J} \frac{[p(i,j) - p(i,\cdot)p(\cdot,j)]^2}{p(i,\cdot)p(\cdot,j)}$$

Let m be the total number of independent sample events by which the incidence table $k(I,J)$ leading to $p(I,J)$ has been derived. If the outcomes (i,j) of (X,Y) are binary, then m is equal to the number of columns of $T[k(I,J)]$. If the outcomes are continuous, then all the sample events (i,j) must be added together.

(b) It is not significant to extract more than r feature dimensions when the statistic $t_1(r)$, representing the residual inertia in the higher-dimensional feature space given by

$$t_1(r) \triangleq m(\mu_p - \lambda_1 - \lambda_2 - \cdots - \lambda_r)$$

is less than the 95% quantile of a standard χ^2 distribution with $[\text{Card}(I) - 1][\text{Card}(J) - 1]$ degrees of freedom.

(c) As an approximation to this threshold value, one may take the expected value of this χ^2 distribution. The dimension r must satisfy

$$t_1(r) \geq [\text{Card}(I) - 1][\text{Card}(J) - 1]$$

6.2 Test on the Location of a Point in the Feature Space

(a) The estimate $p(i,j)$ derived from $k(I,J)$ (see Section 2 of Chapter 7) becomes inaccurate when one of the marginal distributions $k(I,\cdot)$, $k(\cdot,J)$ has elements $k(i,\cdot)\, k(\cdot,j) \geq 0$ which are very small. It is necessary to eliminate such individuals or characters if they do not meet the following test.

(b) This test defines a confidence zone for the location of an individual $i \in I$. For a given confidence level α, this confidence zone is the interior of the sphere centered at O with radius $\sqrt{\chi^2(\alpha)/k(i,\cdot)}$, where $\chi^2(\alpha)$ is the quantile of a χ^2 distribution with $\text{Card}(I) - 1$ degrees of freedom at the probability level α. If the point representing $i \in I$ in $N_r(I)$ is outside this sphere, then i should be rejected.

6.3 Fraction of the Inertia μ_k Explained by a Set of Factor Axes

(a) As explained in Section 2.2.4, the determination of the dimension r of the feature space (after data compression) results from a compromise. This is also true of the interpretation stage (based on the factor maps).

(b) Define the fraction τ_n of the inertia μ_k explained by the factor axis of rank n by

$$\tau_n \triangleq \frac{\lambda_n}{\Sigma\,\lambda_i} = \frac{\rho_n^2}{\Sigma\,\rho_i^2}$$

$\lambda_n = \rho_n^2$ is the variance of the cluster in the direction of factor axis n, n = 1, ..., $\inf\{\mathrm{Card}(I),\mathrm{Card}(J)\}$. The fraction τ_n, expressed as a percentage, will always be shown on the factor maps next to the corresponding factor axis.

(c) Define the fraction τ_{n_1,n_2} of the inertia μ_k explained by the factor map consisting of the independent factor axes of ranks n_1 and n_2 by

$$\tau_{n_1,n_2} = \tau_{n_1} + \tau_{n_2}$$

τ_{n_1,n_2} can be interpreted as the fraction of the dependence between (X,Y), or I and J, displayed in that factor map. It should be noted that the factor maps are (by definition) ranked by decreasing values of τ_{n_1,n_2} (see Section 2.4.1). <u>The sequential analysis of the factor maps during the interpretation (see Section 5.3) ought to be carried out for decreasing values of τ_{n_1,n_2}</u>.

(d) No valid interpretation can be derived from factor axes or factor maps representing extremely small fractions τ_n or τ_{n_1,n_2} of the total intertia μ_k. Even if the test on r from Section 6.1 shows a factor axis to be significant, it should be disregarded if it is too small (e.g., less than 5%).

6.4 <u>Variations of λ_n, τ_n with the Dimensions of the Problem</u>

(a) Interesting conclusions may be derived from a careful analysis of the sequence of values τ_n. First, τ_n is always a decreasing function of $\inf\{\mathrm{Card}(I),\mathrm{Card}(J)\}$ and is fairly independent of

$$t_2 \triangleq \frac{\underset{I,J}{\Sigma}\ k(i,j)}{[\mathrm{Inf}(\mathrm{Card}(I),\ \mathrm{Card}(J))]^2}$$

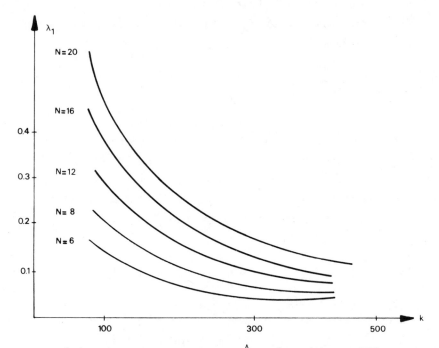

FIGURE 8-6 Variations of λ_1 with $N \triangleq \inf\{\text{Card}(I),\text{Card}(J)\}$ and
$\Sigma_{I,J} k(i,j)$; these are only simulation results.

However, λ_n varies with respect to t_2 as well as with respect to $\inf\{\text{Card}(I),\text{Card}(J)\}$ (e.g., see Figures 8-6 and 8-7 for the typical variations of λ_1, which assume the data to be Gaussian).

(b) Deviations of λ_n, τ_n can be analyzed with respect to such normal variations. Clearly, if the first factor axis has a $\tau_1 \geq 50\%$, it is always significant. If there is a large jump between τ_n and τ_{n+1}, then the factor axis n ought to have a clear interpretation. If τ_1, τ_2 are close and about 20 to 30%, interesting relations can be derived between feature measurements.

If $\lambda_1 > 0.6$ or $\tau_1 > 60\%$, there is likely to be a dichotomy in the data or some points which are isolated from the remainder of the cluster [see Section 5.1b(i)].

6.5 Computational Constraints

Computationally, correspondence analysis is an eigenvalue problem (see Section 4). Since only the factor axis of largest variance

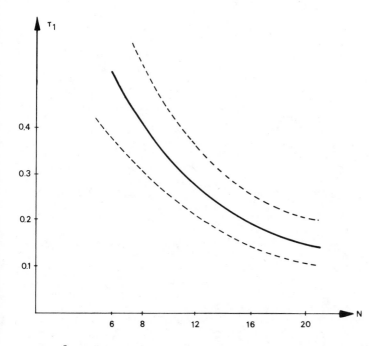

FIGURE 8-7   Variations of τ_1 with N; these are only simulation results.

λ_1 is needed, it is always better to use sequential algorithms that compute the eigenvectors in order of decreasing eigenvalues.

If analysis $C_0[k(I,J)]$ is used, the smallest dimension of $k(I,J)$ ought to be less than 400 (with no limitation on the other dimension).

If $C_1[k(I,J)]$ is used, the representation $T[k(I,J)]$ will be sparse, and great storage savings can be achieved by the use of direct iteration algorithms, such as those based on the results of Section 4.1, Propositions 4 and 5. The data should be accessed sequentially.

Consequently, there is generally no limit to the size of the problem which can be tackled if suitable sequential storage or block access is available, which allows for easy implementation on microprocessors and small minicomputers. Problems may arise only if the data are degenerate in some sense or if r is large (e.g., more than 10).

Chapter 9

APPLICATIONS OF
FAILURE ANALYSIS METHODS: EXAMPLES

1. FAILURE ANALYSIS AND DIAGNOSIS
   FROM STATISTICAL INFORMATION

1.1 Fields of Application

Failure analysis and diagnosis usually concern a population of
identical systems that are observed, a posteriori, through a systematic compilation of all kinds of information (see Chapter 6). Digital diagnosis and testing are very different since they involve individual systems on which binary localization tests are carried out,
without the use of a priori statistical information.

Experience shows that users are rarely organized to use the
many reports and studies which contain information about equipment
performance, maintenance, and changes following corrective interventions. Users should control incentive reliability contracts and
contractual maintenance on the basis of equipment histories. If
equipment performance and maintenance are unsatisfactory, the user
should become aware of these facts as rapidly as possible, since it
is in the interest of both the supplier and repairer to delay any
possible penalty.

To meet the preceding needs the author has adapted some data
analysis methods (Chapters 7 and 8), especially correspondence analysis, so as to attain the following results from automated follow-
up cards (of damages and repairs) retrieved from data banks (Chapter 6):

(a) Direct plotting of reliability curves per component, sub-system, or device (with a restriction relating to the available sample sizes).

(b) Location of functional zones or operational conditions that threaten to cause breakdowns due to design or manufacturing errors (throughout the entire operational lifetime of the device or during certain intervals).

(c) Identification of systematic anomalies in the coding of failures or maintenance operations; updating the contents of the maintenance manual.

(d) Critical evaluation of certain maintenance operations and their scheduling.

(e) Incorporation of an increased number of etiological parameters [for example, parameters recorded in flight or outputs of an automatic test system (ATS)].

(f) Elimination of all redundant tests and measurements through selection of those giving the best discrimination among failure causes; it must be remembered that there will always be external factors reducing the effects of process redundancies (such as fluids, maintenance actions, human factors, and the environment).

(g) More precise study of the five common types of maintenance errors:

   i. Removing and repairing parts not responsible for the breakdown

   ii. Removing and repairing a good part in a device in working condition

   iii. Erroneous setup or adjustments

   iv. Neglecting some reactivation actions

   v. Using incorrect material (wrong oil, etc.)

(h) Invariance of computations and interpretation procedures with regard to the equipment under study.

(i) Easy updating of learning data.

(j) Implementation of diagnostic procedures by nonexpert personnel.

The interpretation procedure for factorial maps (Section 5 of Chapter 8) is relatively easy to understand. It can be implemented in maintenance workshops and at managerial levels to monitor equipment and the repair work.

(k) Design reviews and modification proposals.

(l) Display of all causal relations, to be confirmed (if needed) by statistical tests; each time a causal relation is brought forward, such as between a pressure measurement and a maintenance operation, the maintenance department must either demonstrate that the relation is meaningless or provide technical explanations and corrective measures.

It is important to stress that this approach is of limited interest when solving diagnostic problems for equipment having internal conditions that can be identified through binary tests. Failure analysis and diagnosis using statistical information have only limited diagnostic efficiency in purely digital or logical systems. However, they remain indispensable for the following:

i. Acquiring systematic understanding of poorly characterized degradation processes.

ii. Effectively diagnosing damages in mechanical, electronic, control, and other types of systems whose conditions are characterized by continuous random parameters; it is assumed that the number of breakdown and deterioration modes is relatively limited (15 at most; see Section 2.1 of Chapter 2).

In these two cases, statistical failure analysis and diagnosis yield results which are actually used in operational conditions.

1.2 Review of Applicable Methods (Chapters 7 and 8)

It is assumed that from coded follow-up cards about a given equipment type, a set of learning data can be compiled in one of the following forms:

i. An explicit table, where each intervention is described by measurements, including hour-meter readings (see Section 4 of Chapter 7)

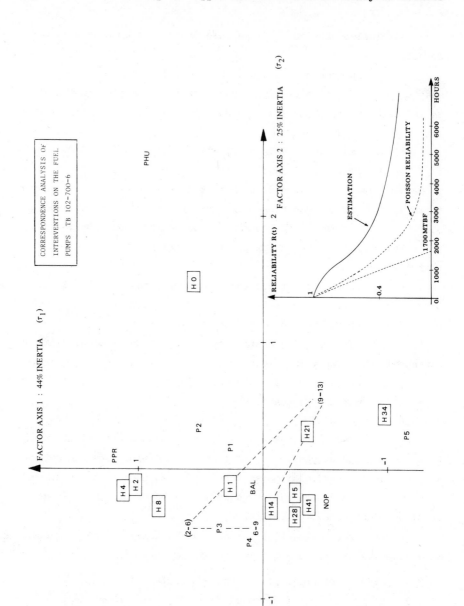

FIGURE 9-1 Fuel pumps. Correspondence analysis of interventions on fuel pumps TB 102-700-6. Axis 1: 44% inertia (τ_1); axis 2: 25% inertia (τ_2).

p: Smallest number following n in the list n = 0, 0.5, 1, 2, 4, 8, 14, 21, 28, 34, 41
Hn: Interval of operating hours starting at 100 × n hr and ending at 100 × p hr
NOP: No breakdown (NOP = 1)
PPR: Pressure drop (PPR = 1)
PHU: Oil leakage (PHU = 1)
Pi: Position occupied on the plane by the removed pump i = 1, 2, 3, 4, 5 (Pi = 1)
BAL: Single, individual length of brushes at pulldown, in mm
2-6:   Brush length at pulldown: between 2 and 6 mm
6-9:   Brush length at pulldown: between 6 and 9 mm
9-13:   Brush length at pulldown: between 9 and 13 mm

ii. An <u>implicit</u> table, where the events are sorted out into
successive intervals between removals (the removal stage remaining
to be defined) (Section 5 of Chapter 7)

A data analysis method (Chapters 7 and 8) is then applied to
these learning data; usually correspondence analysis is used. Analysis of proximities between individuals, through comparison of
corresponding distributional profiles, leads to the formulation of
causal relations that are supported by the computation of associated
probabilities of association.

1.3 Examples

In this chapter we shall give a number of concrete applications.
Most involve correspondence analysis. In each case, it is left to
the reader to complete the interpretation in question. We intend,
above all, to suggest other applications of these methods.

That such interpretations are possible demonstrates that failure
analysis and diagnosis are valuable tools for the use of accumulated
experience, serving, for example, despite personnel changes.

2. FUEL PUMP FAILURES: DIAGNOSIS AND MODIFICATIONS

Let us interpret a few of the associations among failure modes,
measurements, and life intervals in Figure 9-1, pertaining to a type
of airborne fuel pump. The learning data form an implicit table,
with $R(t) = \exp(-\lambda t)$; $1/\lambda = 1700$ hr.

The relationship between pressure drop PPR and brush lengths
is in inverse ratio to the latter; in particular, severe wear (2 to
6 mm) is closely associated with pressure drops, happening most
frequently in positions P3 and P4.

Let us next analyze the associations between operating hour
intervals and failure modes. Note the following:

i. Brush wear is severe between 200 and 800 hr, and weak or
moderate up to 4500 hr (mainly in the case of no breakdown).

ii. Oil-leak breakdowns are explicitly separated, being the
most frequent early failures (between 0 and 50 hr).

iii. Pressure drops mostly take place between 200 and 500 hr, and rarely around 100 or 1500 hr, together with severe brush wear.

Thus the potential life of the pumps could probably be doubled by means of technical rememdies to avoid pressure drops.

3. RADIO COMPASS: EQUIPMENT AVAILABILITY AND
    CODING OF MAINTENANCE FOLLOW-THROUGH CARDS

Let us interpret a few of the associations in Figure 9-2 pertaining to electromechanical radio compass RNA-26-C. The learning data form an implicit table. We shall analyze the coding of follow-up cards.

Individuals in category 1 (physical causes of breakdowns) are (with two exceptions) aligned on the first factorial axis in the following order (Figure 9-3), which appears likely from a technical standpoint:

i. Electromechanical failures are halfway between electrical and passive component failures.

ii. Electrical breakdowns are on one end of the chain and mechanical failures on the other.

Failures of active electronic components are sharply dissociated; that is, these components suffer breakdowns from very specific causes, and these specific breakdowns are the most frequent causes of degradation in active components.

Miscellaneous breakdowns are very sharply dissociated from active component breakdowns. Thus there should be no amiguity in the minds of those classifying and coding active component breakdowns. Failures which result from active component breakdowns will not be found under the heading "miscellaneous breakdowns."

The breakdowns 1 TE, 1 EM, and 1 ME are approximately equidistant from 1 DV. In other words, there is a similar tendency to classify these three types of breakdowns as miscellaneous ones. These breakdowns are relatively dissociated from miscellaneous breakdowns, however, and cases of ambiguity are therefore infrequent.

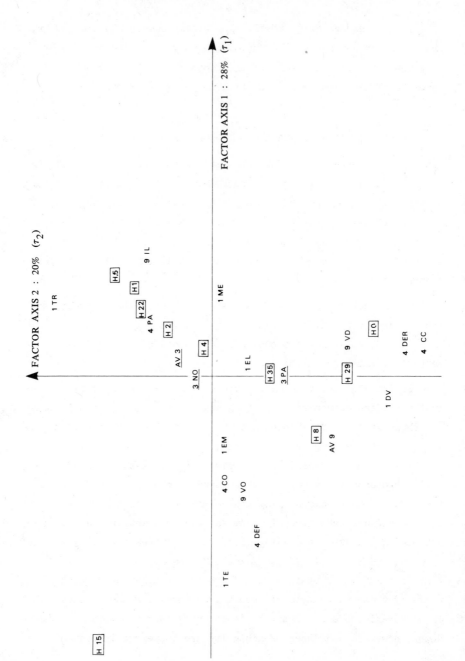

FIGURE 9-2 Analysis of interventions on the RNA-26C (VOR-LOC) radiocompass.

[c]: Information class	i ∈ [c]: Al-ternatives	
AV (equipment-carrying aircraft type)	AV 3	Caravelle
	AV 9	Fokker friendship
H (length of time between removals)	Hj*	Hj* is the duration of the interval j* ∈ J* between the last and the present removal. H 400 represents the interval j* ∈ J* starting at 400 hr; the next starts at 800 hr.
1 (nature of component implicated)	1 EL	Passive electronic component breakdowns (resistances, etc.)
	1 TR	Active electronic component breakdowns (transistors)
	1 EM	Electromechanical component breakdowns (relays, etc.)
	1 ME	Mechanical part breakdowns
	1 TE	Power feed breakdowns
	1 DV	Unidentified miscellaneous breakdowns
3 (nature of inter-vention)	3 PA	Justified maintenance operation: actual component breakdown
	3 NO	Other maintenance operations: no intervention, inspec-tion, adjustments, etc.)
4 (diagnosis)	4 DEF	Defective component to be changed
	4 DER	Component out of tolerance
	4 CO	Bad contact
	4 CC	Short circuit
5 (sequel of inter-vention)	9 VO	Intervention needed on VOR receiver
	9 VD	VOR receiver out of order
	9 IL	Intervention needed on ILS receiver

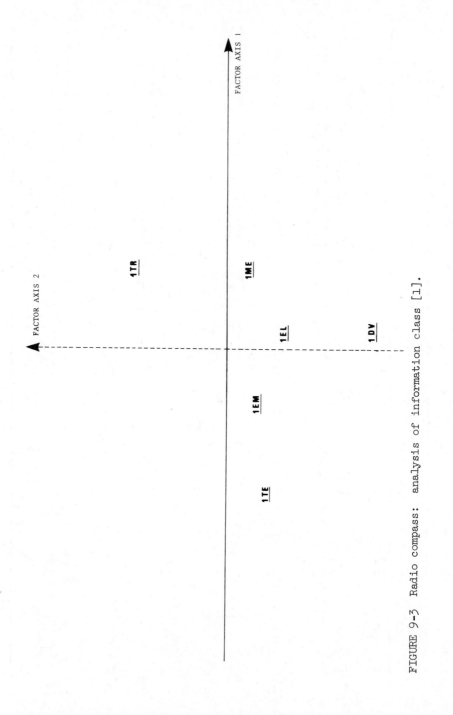

FIGURE 9-3 Radio compass: analysis of information class [1].

On the other hand, passive component breakdowns are associated
with miscellaneous breakdowns at a medium level; thus miscellaneous
breakdowns are often actually failures of passive components. There
seems to be a frequently recurring ambiguity at the coding stage or
before. Consequently, the representative point 1 EL is attracted
by 1 DV. The reverse is equally possible: breakdowns which are in
fact "miscellaneous" may be classified under the heading "passive
component breakdowns."

To improve the coding, the maintenance manual was modified to
avoid coding ambiguities between 1 TE, 1 EM, or 1 EL vs. 1 DV. This
corrective action was effective.

Note that 1 EL and 1 EM are the deterioration conditions which
should be remedied first, so as to extend the average life span to
hopefully 400 to 800 hr.

4. COMMUNICATIONS SYSTEMS: DIFFERENTIAL ANALYSIS
    OF THE MAINTENANCE OF THE VARIOUS SUBSYSTEMS

Correspondence analysis is applied here to the maintenance data bank
of an airborne communications system made of 63 components (see
Figure 9-4). Data are placed into an explicit table; the individuals
are components characterized by their successive removals, and the
measurements are sets of information relating to component maintenance and life spans [E-8].

Each component is represented by a four-digit code: the three
first digits represent the subsystem and the last one the number of
the component in this subsystem. Thus 8211 and 8212 stand, respectively, for a transmitter-receiver and the control box connected
with it in the VHF communications subsystem (821).

The aim here is to see if components can really be grouped by
subsystems or equivalent sets [such as the so-called "least repairable units" (LRUs)]. If this is not the case, the reason lies in
different life spans and maintenance procedures for components within
the actual subsystem or LRU.

Differentiated maintenance procedures should then be established
with different intervals between preventive overhauls. If components

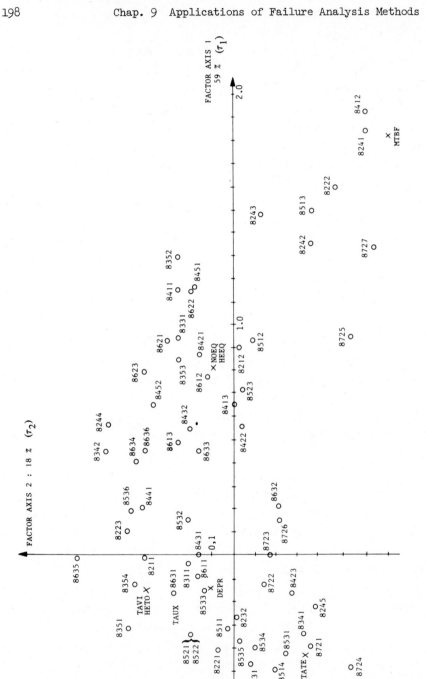

FIGURE 9-4 Communications system.

Symbol abcd	Interpretation a, b, c, d integers: component d of subsystem number abc
1. TAVI	Cumulative length of intervention on aircraft (removal, reinstallation)
2. TATE	Cumulative duration of maintenance in workshop
3. DEPR	Number of removals during the period under study
4. HETO	Cumulative operating hours at the time of the last removal
5. NOEQ	Number of abcd components per aircraft in the fleet
6. HEEQ	= NOEQ × (cumulative fleet flight hours during the period under study)
7. TAUX	= DEPR/HEEQ is an evaluation of a frequency of removals per flight hour
8. MTHF	= HEEQ/(number of justified removals - removals for systematic overhaul) is a form of mean flight time between failure-caused justified removals

cluster in the factorial maps, in conformity with their functional
or organic relationships, inspections (either preventive or on-
condition) can be envisaged for complete subsystems or LRU blocks.

For example, all components of the meteorological radar (853),
as well as those of the anemometer (862), are clustered.

On the other hand, component profiles for the VHF radio (821)
and UHF radio (822) are clearly differentiated. In the radio-altim-
eter (852), the transmitter-receiver (8521) and amplifier (8522)
are close, while the indicator (8523) is far from them.

It would be justified to simultaneously study the maintenance
characteristics of the computer (8632) and control box (8726) of the
automatic pilot.

Components 8211, 8354, 8631, and 8351 are apparently closely
associated with the duration of maintenance operations on the aircraft. Some exploration of this fact is needed.

Note that the learning data constitute an explicit table, with
each component abcd described by the above-mentioned eight measurements, all from the previous 6 months.

Note that the present study could well have been carried out
using principal components analysis if the purpose had been only
the one described earlier.

5. APPROXIMATE PLOTTING OF THE RELIABILITY CURVE
    OF A DEVICE BASED ON CORRESPONDENCE ANALYSIS
    OF AN IMPLICIT TABLE

Assuming that we have learning data relating to operational failures
of a given type of equipment, we shall, successively,

(a) Justify the sampling of operating time in intervals having
lengths inversely related to equipment failure probability density,
as described in Section 5 of Chapter 7 in connection with the design
of the implicit table

(b) Define a new class of measurements, in addition to the [m]
classes in the implicit table of Section 5 of Chapter 7

(c) Provide a graphical process for construction of an approximate operational reliability curve, plotting the survival probability
vs. operating time since the last overhaul.

5.1 Sampling of Operating Time Intervals

(a) In the statistical relationship $k(I,J)$, J denotes the operating period and I the observation. In this section, a <u>removal</u> refers to a recall from operational service, either because of a failure or because of scheduled preventive maintenance; the recall is followed by calibration or repair and full restoration of the working condition. Time sampling is characterized by an increasing sequence $\{t_j\}$, $j \in \mathbb{N}$, with first element $t_0 = 0$. The operating period associated with character $j \in J$ is defined to be the interval $[t_{j-1}, t_j)$ of length $(t_j - t_{j-1})$.

Suppose that the preceding sampling has been realized by taking a constant step $(t_j - t_{j-1})$ for any $j \in J$. There is then a $j_0 \in J$ beyond which the sample sizes of:

    i. Devices surviving after t_{j-1} operating hours

    ii. Events $i \in I$ noted within period $[t_{j-1}, t_j)$

become very small. These small statistical samples will fail to meet confidence tests; hence observations of rank greater than j_0 must unfortunately be suppressed.

This motivates taking a step size $(t_j - t_{j-1})$ that is an increasing function of $j \in J$, so that the sample sizes of events $i \in I$ observed in each consecutive interval remain fairly constant. This assumes a fixed fleet size, that is, a constant population of N_0 devices.

Let us assume that the removal rate δ is time-invariant. The probability distribution $\Delta(t)$ of the number of devices not yet removed is then Poisson (if a few regularity conditions on Δ are satisfied ;   see Figure 9-5):

$$\Delta(t) \ \# \ N_0 \ exp(-\delta t) \qquad t \geq 0 \qquad discretized$$

where $N_0 \triangleq$ initial number of devices in the population under study.

The removal rate δ can be estimated by

$$\delta_j = \frac{n_j}{N_j(t_j - t_{j-1})} \ \# \ constant$$

where

$n_j \overset{\Delta}{=}$ number of removals in interval $[t_{j-1}, t_j)$

$N_j \overset{\Delta}{=}$ number of devices not yet removed after t_{j-1} operating
  hours (or surviving until t_{j-1})

The condition $n_j \#$ constant for all j, on the number of removals
in each interval, is therefore satisfied if $1/(t_j - t_{j-1})$ is propor-
tional to the discretized probability density $|\Delta'(t)|$ of the number
of devices not yet removed:

$$\Delta'(t) = \delta N_0 \exp(-\delta t)$$

Hence we obtain the approximation

$$t_j - t_{j-1} \# (t_1 - t_0) \exp(\delta t_{j-1}) \qquad t_1 > 0 \text{ given}$$

(b) For any $t \geq 0$, we have the following given quantities:
have the following given quantities:

$\Delta(t)$ = assumed probability distribution of the number of
   devices not yet removed (see Figure 9-5)

$\Delta'(t)$ = corresponding probability density function

$\delta(t)$ $= -\dfrac{\Delta'(t)}{\Delta(t)}$ removal rate associated with Δ

Consider a sample of finite initial size N_0 having Δ as its
underlying reliability distribution. Define the positive nondecreasing sequence $\{t_j\}$ as follows:

$$t_0 = 0 \qquad\qquad T > 0$$

$$t_j - t_{j-1} = T \left| \frac{\Delta'(0)}{\Delta'(t_{j-1})} \right| \qquad \forall\ j \geq 1 \text{ and } j \in J$$

Then, under certain conditions of regularity on Δ and T, the
quantity φN_0 given by

$$\varphi N_0(t_{j-1}) \overset{\Delta}{=} N_j(t_j - t_{j-1}) \left| \frac{\Delta'(t_{j-1})}{\Delta(t_{j-1})} \right|$$

converges uniformly, with respect to $t > 0$, toward a finite constant
when $N_0 \to +\infty$. This limit is equal to the number of removals in the
period $[t_{j-1}, t_j)$.

(c) In practice, assuming that the probability distribution
of the sample is close to a given distribution $\Delta(t)$, we construct
the sequence $\{t_j\}$ as indicated. T is determined using a confidence
test in the first interval, with the confidence level one of the
preset parameters. For high values of t_j and j, the temporal localization of an event i $\in$ I with respect to an interval j will be
imprecise. However, it at least exists and is correct to within a
confidence level comparable with the one expected from the sample
$k(I,J)$ in $[t_0, t_1)$.

Note that in the preceding a Poisson reliability function is
not required; the sampling formula in Section 5.1b makes this possible.

It should be noted that this variable step sampling affects
the confidence levels expected in the location testing of a given
individual or measurement on a factorial map (Section 6.2 of Chapter 8).

5.2 Definition of a New Class of Observations

(a) Assume that $k(I,J)$ is such that the set I of characters
is split into q categories, denoted by [m] (see Section 5 of Chapter
7).

Example: Recall the example of the radio compass and its data bank
(cf. Section 3 and Figure 9-2).

An equipment follow-up card contains (for each removal) at most
10 observations, corresponding to q = 8 measurement categories. It
may very well happen that an observation is left out of such a card
in one of the following categories (see Figure 9-2):

[1]: Nature of component implicated
[2]: Reason for removal without failure
[3]: Nature of intervention
[4]: Diagnosis

[5]: Test and control operations (sequel of intervention)

[6]: Type of modification

[7]: Repaired, tested, or modified functional subsets

[8]: Component adjustments or trimmings   ∎

(b) Define a category [q + 1] made of two rows/individuals (I + 1, I + 2) corresponding respectively to the failures and non-failures of the equipment (or subsystem, or component) under study, defined by

$k(I + 1, j)$ = number of actual independent failures in time interval $j \in J$, based on all indications [1], ..., [q]

$k(I + 2, j)$ = number of devices, subsystems, or components that survived until t_{j-1}, and which had neither a failure nor an intervention in $[t_{j-1}, t_j)$, based on all indications [1], ..., [q]

(c) Example (continued; see also Section 3 and Figure 9-2): After t_1 = 100 operating hours, there were N_2 = 40 devices in good working condition. In interval j = 2, the following were observed:

Category [1]: k(1,2) = 8 active component failures

k(2,2) = 2 electromechanical failures

k(3,2) = 3 miscellaneous failures

Other categories = 0 intervention

Therefore,

$k(I + 1, j) = 8 + 2 + 3 = 13$

$k(I + 2, j) = N_2 - k(I + 1, j) = 40 - 13 = 27$ ∎

5.3 Approximate Plot of the Operational Reliability Curve (Poisson Case)

(a) Call $D_0(I + 2, j)$ the numerical value of the Euclidean distance (measured with a ruler) between the individual (I + 2) and the character $j \in J$ in the first factorial map; the units are the same as those of the factorial axes 1 and 2. According to Section 2.4 of Chapter 8, $D^2(I + 2, j)$ has a χ^2 probability distribution χ_2^2 with 2 degrees of freedom. Consequently, by reading the χ_2^2 table backwards,

$$Pr[D^2(I + 2, j) > D_0^2(I + 2, j)] = (\chi_2^2)^{-1}[D_0^2(I + 2, j)]$$

In conformity with the interpretation procedure (cf. Section 2.4.2 of Chapter 8), we define the probability of association $\pi(I + 2, j)$ between the individual nonfailure $i = I + 2$ and a time interval j as the minimum reliability $\Delta(t_j)/N_0$ in $[t_{j-1}, t_j)$.

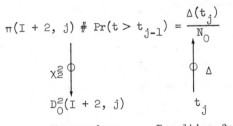

Measured on   Resulting from
the factorial map   Δ and from the
                     sampling of J

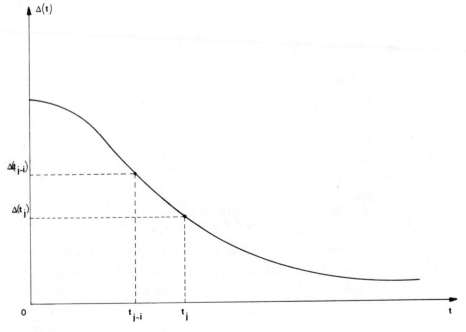

FIGURE 9-5

Now, if Δ is a Poisson law, it coincides with a χ^2 having precisely 2 degrees of freedom (from the definition of the χ^2 distribution).

Given the approximations, it can be stated that the reference process Δ has the following property:

$$\forall_j \in J \; \frac{t_j}{D_0^2(I + 2, j)} = \frac{\Delta^{-1}[\pi(I + 2, j)]}{N_0 \cdot \chi_2^2[\pi(I + 2, j)]} \overset{\Delta}{=} u(t_j) \neq \text{constant}$$

where the left-hand side results merely from reading the simultaneous map representation of all individuals and measurements.

By examining the extent to which the former relation is verified by measurement points $j \in J$, it is possible to discern differences between the real failure process and the Poisson reference process Δ.

(b) Example (continued): Figure 9-6 displays the following:

1. The Poisson reliability curve $\Delta(t)/N_0$ (taken as reference) with an MTBR in the region of 1200 hr.

2. The reliability curve directly estimated from the sample by

$$\frac{\Delta(t_j)}{N_0} = \frac{N_j}{N_j + n_j}$$

(see Section 8 of Chapter 6).

3. The reliability curve deduced from the results of correspondence analysis. The reader is invited to obtain it using the factorial map included in Figure 9-2 taking $(I + 2) = 3N_0$. Note the high value of $D_0(I + 2, j)$ for $[t_{j-1}, t_j] = [1500 \text{ hr}, 2000 \text{ hr}]$. ∎

6. EXPERIMENTAL STUDY OF THE EXISTENCE OF A STATISTICAL
    DEPENDENCE BETWEEN THE FAILURES OF SEPARATE DEVICES:
    APPLICATION TO AIRCRAFT SAFETY STUDIES [F-20, F-45]

(a) Modern concepts of aircraft safety and the development of technical specifications for aircraft certification require a knowledge of the estimated and experiemntal reliability of major aircraft

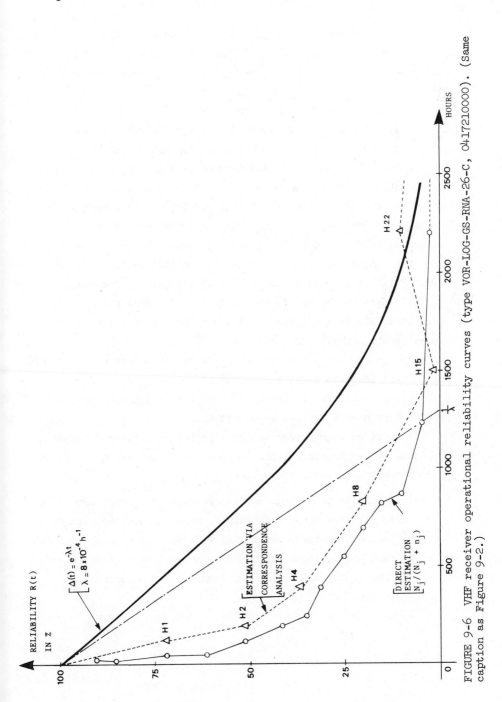

FIGURE 9-6 VHF receiver operational reliability curves (type VOR-LOG-GS-RNA-26-C, 0417210000). (Same caption as Figure 9-2.)

systems (such as navigation, guidance, propulsion). This knowledge must cover cases of multiple, simultaneous, or possible delayed failures. It is clear that these failure probabilities are difficult to estimate with adequate confidence, due to the hypothesis of failure independence on which most reliability estimation procedures are based. Simple common sense tells us that failures of some devices carrying out similar functions are in fact dependent.

Certain deviations observed between experimental and estimated reliabilities (taking into account confidence intervals) might be attributed to the nonvalidity of this independence assumption. The problem consists, then, in confirming or denying the existence of a dependence among failures of separate devices performing similar functions. As a corollary, efforts will be made to determine a measure of this dependence and to reveal its principal consequences.

This problem can be approached by a theoretical simulation based on an aircraft mission model and on the fault and event trees of the function under scrutiny.

(b) We consider, however, that statistical diagnosis, in making use of data analysis methods, has the advantage of developing a more realistic and truthful representation of this dependence phenomenon from available experimental measurements.

It suffices to consider and process the data files obtained by combining (in an implicit table) all available measurements of correspondence among the following sets:

I: Catalogue of various devices carrying out some part of the function studied (for example, piloting) and (possibly) of random parameters associated with the operational environment and the past history of such equipment (such as turbulence, altitude, vibrations, number of overhauls, former MTBR)

J: Successive intervals of operation of this equipment, or adjacent intervals of variation of parameters associated with the environment

$k(i,j)$: Number of occurrences of observation i in the period j, $i \in I$, $j \in J$

The results obtained are the transition probabilities connected with the different utilization phases of the function when considering successive time intervals $j \in J$.

(c) The probability of association $\pi(i_1,i_2)$ between two devices i_1 and $i_2 \in I$ ($i_1 \neq i_2$) gives a measure of the similarity of the distributional failure profiles of these two devices with respect to operating hours (see Section 2.4.2 of Chapter 8).

i. If $\pi(i_1,i_2) = 1$, one of the following holds:

α. Either i_1, i_2 have identical designs

β. Or i_1, i_2 have different designs, and the failures of i_1 and i_2 are statistically dependent with a correlation coefficient equal to 1. This property is independent of the lifetime sampling used, provided sample sizes are adequate.

ii. If $\pi(i_1,i_2)$ is small and close to the sum of statistical hazards (due to the sample size and the number of extracted factors; see Sections 6.1 and 6.4 of Chapter 8) it is impossible to make any conclusion.

iii. If $\pi(i_1,i_2)$ is less than 1 but clearly greater than the statistical hazards, the diagnosis must be one of the following alternatives:

α. Either i_1, i_2 have similar designs, possibly with common components

β. Or i_1, i_2 do not have similar designs, and their failures are statistically dependent with a correlation coefficient strictly between 0 and 1

γ. Or i_1, i_2 satisfy both of the preceding simultaneously

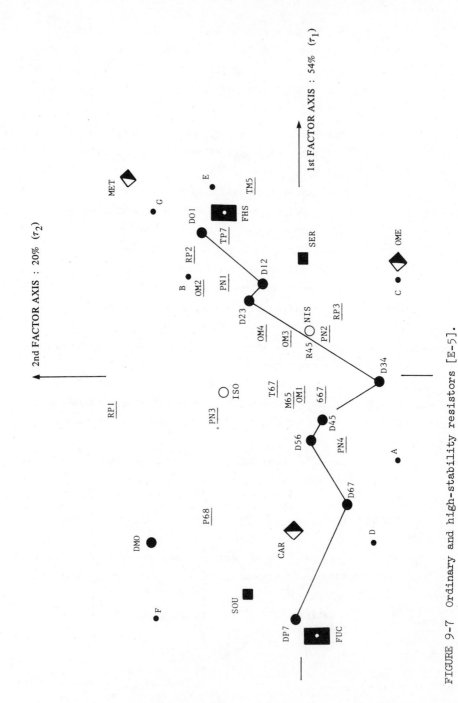

FIGURE 9-7 Ordinary and high-stability resistors [E-5].

DMO: Negative drift of electrical resistance at 1000 hr

D01, D12, D23, D34, D45, D56, D67, DP7:   Dmn indicates a positive drift of the resistance at 1000 hr, included between m and n% of the nominal resistance

FHS, FUC: High-stability and common resistors, respectively

CAR, MET, OME: Carbon, metal, and metal oxide resistive layers, respectively

ISO, NIS: Insulated or noninsulated layer

SOU, SER: Soldered or crimped connector

A-G: Symbols of firms manufacturing the resistors of both types under study

M65, 667, P68:   Resistances manufactured before 1965, in 1966 or 1967, or after 1968

PN1, PN2, PN3, PN4:   Rated nominal power, limited by 250, 500, and 1000 mW

OM1, OM2, OM3, OM4:   Rated nominal resistances, limited by 35 Ω and 100 and 300 kΩ

TM5, T67, TP7:   Test temperatures, limited by 50 and 75° C

RP1, RP2, RP3, RP45:   Ratio of real to nominal power, limited to 25, 50, and 75%

Given successive measurements, the conditional probabilities
of an equipment failure can be expressed using the coordinates of
the distributional profiles under consideration. Approximately determined probabilities of association (by means of χ^2) constitute
an overall dependence measure, similar to the dependence ratio (see
Section 5.4 of Chapter 8).

It should be noted that the present approach has been applied
in practice, confirming statistical dependencies which were in
agreement with known technical characteristics.

7. ORDINARY AND HIGH-STABILITY RESISTORS:
    COMPONENT TESTS AND MANUFACTURER SELECTION

(a) An implicit table is scrutinized to analyze relations between the resistance drift parameter and other characteristics obtained during tests [E-5]. See Figure 9-7.

It is seen that the factorial axis f_1 ranks the drifts by decreasing values in such a way that all other measurements are arranged
in terms of the resistance drift. Thus FHS "high-stability" and FUC
"ordinary" resistors are diametrically opposed in the f_1 direction,
and their absolute contributions to f_1 are high. Resistors with a
metallic resisting layer behave better than those with an oxide film
and much better than those with a carbon film.

DMO negative drifts are satisfactorily explained by the second
factorial axis and by the manufacturer F of carbon film resistances
with strong negative drifts. However, F is not the only manufacturer
of carbon film resistors, and material choice (or "technology")
alone cannot explain this situation. Manufacturer E is in a desirable position with respect to the first two factorial axes, even
though he produces both metallic and carbon layer resistors with
greatly differing drifts. It seems that other factors, such as
quality control by the manufacturers, are required to interpret
cases E and F; technology is not the sole factor implicated here.

(b) A similar study has been made of capacitor drifts after
1000 hr of test (see Ref. E-5). By applying the technique of Chapter
8, a minimum set of five test measurements is selected, having the

additional property of reducing perturbations due to additional data on the capacitors.

8.   CRACK ANALYSIS AND STRUCTURAL RELIABILITY: OTHER APPLICATIONS IN METALLURGY

(a) Progress in the field of structural stress calculations demands a better understanding of how materials behave. This understanding has largely been prevented by the increased complexity of structures, their use under widely differing operating conditions, and demands for longer lifetimes. At the same time, prototype testing has increased our knowledge of the operational environment and real stresses on modern aircraft.

For these reasons, analytical methods should be considered for improved definition and (if possible) estimation of the potential life of aircraft structures. It is difficult to refrain from mentioning the considerable maintenance costs due to fissures and cracks in these structures. Appearance of a crack does not necessarily lead to the replacement of the part, but it apparently does tend to predetermine the remaining life span (as observed when in-flight loads and material characteristics can be measured).

Data analysis should facilitate the correlation of certain characteristics of structural defects and lead to the discovery of conditions (of the materials and loads) favoring the occurrence of cracks.

The analysis of fractures during operations, supplemented by both destructive tests (stereomicroscope, electron microscope, fractography, chemical analysis) and laboratory tests, presents extremely interesting possibilities.

(b) In the study of solid crystals, powerful methods have been tried since 1973. Defects in solid crystals are simulated on a computer to provide "learning" micrographs for each class of defects.

When a fracture or a defect is observed, it is compared (visually or automatically) with these learning micrographs. This is a pattern recognition task (Chapter 10); it is applicable for isolated

or simple dislocations, independent of the degree of elastic anisotropy in the cubic, tetragonal, or hexagonal crystal under study.

Data compression is applied here to the information found in
the directional intensity profiles (measured by electronic microg-
raphy) and in the calculation of Burger dislocation vectors for
anisotropic materials.

9.   OTHER APPLICATIONS TO FAILURE ANALYSIS

Data analysis methods (Chapters 7 and 8) for the diagnosis and in-
ference of causality relations were experimentally used in France
as early as 1969; the first implementation dates from 1970. Since
then, a number of quite diversified applications have been found
which have given rise to research and wider use.

9.1   Analysis of Errors in a Gyroscopic Platform (1971) [F-12]

A linear relation between the calibration measurements and
errors in a gyroscopic platform was estimated and then inverted
using principal components analysis and the pseudoinverse notion
(Section 1.6 of Chapter 1). A difficulty lies in the fact that the
number of errors (21) is larger than that of the possible measurements (12). This analysis served to develop a guidance system calibration model.

9.2   Analysis of Failure Modes
of a Thermal Generating Plant

The multilevel structure of a thermal generating plant and
the complex physicochemical processes involved make it extremely
difficult to find an identifiable model of such a plant. Similarly,
variations of the few control parameters are very slow, and time
constants in the region of a few hours affect the output. Finally,
the internal functioning of the plant core is not well known. A
statistical diagnosis of the plant deterioration modes from learning
data, extracted from some 50 possible measurement points in the core,
has been carried out. Some observation syndromes most suitable for
diagnosis have been identified.

9.3 Component Failures in Analog or Digital Circuits

A number of experiments tend to demonstrate that statistical diagnosis is <u>not</u> applicable to components in analog or digital circuits for the following reasons:

(a) The learning data samples are too small for individual circuit component failures.

(b) The number of possible defects or failure modes is generally very high (two to three times the number of discrete components); in particular, more than half of the anomalies observed during tests on a complete circuit may be caused by faulty soldering or assembly.

(c) The implementation of automated testing or diagnosis procedures will, in general, require notable improvement in the quality control of individual components and modules and in the manufacturing assembly processes.

(d) The difficulty in selecting internal measurement points to discriminate among failure modes.

(e) The inaccessibility of these measurement points (problems of space occupation and connectors).

(f) The noises affecting certain measurements.

(g) The importance of feedback in the electrical design, with the result that certain outputs or measurements are completely insensitive to breakdowns of certain important components; this is the case with counterreaction amplifiers and feedback in general.

(h) The variability of individual component parameters, and corresponding difficulties in specifying margins for individual measurements, within which the whole circuit operates correctly.

(i) The training of personnel for card encoding.

(j) The administrative burden associated with the coding of follow-through cards and other human problems.

It is believed that automatic test systems may be useful, provided the number of types of defects can be greatly reduced.

Recall that statistical diagnosis is most useful in the analysis of mechanical or electromechanical equipment. It is hoped,

TABLE 9-1   Quality control of analog measuring instruments, lots of 800 instruments: failure detection and localization times

		% of lot size
Number of defects noted	710	89%
Component failures	395	49%
Soldering, assembly defects	315	39%
Cumulated search time for failure detection (hr)	257 hr	
Component defects	115 hr	
Soldering, assembly defects, or wiring faults	142 hr	
Search time for defect localization in a failed circuit (hr)	0.36 hr	
Component defect	0.29 hr	
Faulty soldering, assembly	0.45 hr	
Search time for a possible defect per controlled circuit (hr)	0.32 hr	
Component defect	0.14 hr	
Faulty soldering, assembly, or wiring	0.17 hr	
Average number of defects per circuit	0.89	
Number of circuits with one defect	254	32%
Number of circuits with two or more defects	184	23%
Number of circuits without defect	362	45%

however, that difficulties (a) through (j) do not constitute an obstruction to specific experiments with discrete analog and digital circuits. See Table 9-1.

9.4   Failures of Electromechanical Registers, Relays, and Contacts

The failure of electromechanical registers, relays, and contacts constitutes an area of great concern because of the importance of such components in control systems.

9.5 Failures of Spark Plug Systems [E-18] and Other Igniters

By applying the technique of Chapter 8, causality relations can be established from field data decomposed into failure rate intervals, among vibration level, engine revolutions per minute, diameter of the axis, engine volume, compression ratio, temperature profile, etc.

A similar procedure has been applied to rocket igniters [F-65].

9.6 Selection of Nondestructive Test Measurements for Aircraft Engine Condition Monitoring

Many nondestructive tests can be used for engine on-condition monitoring, in addition to those methods described in Chapters 13 through 15:

  i.   Spectrometric oil analysis program (SOAP)

  ii. Paper chromatography

  iii. Oil capacitance measurements

  iv. Metal concentrations in crankcase oil

Here again, a major goal is to reduce the number of tests needed.

9.7 Aircraft Engine Component Health Monitoring Programs

A representation of the health of the engine is made by assigning a "grade" to each of the three major subsystems: the compressor, the combustor, and the turbine sections. These grades correspond to a component condition evaluation and are assigned after general inspection; each subsystem is assigned the grade of its worst component. The grade vectors are then compressed and eventually classified into overall engine health classes. Learning is carried out using engine cells.

9.8 Acceptance Quality Control of Components

(a) Assume that a number of measurements k_i $(i = 1, \ldots, n)$ is made on each lot of p components, $n \geq p$, and that data analysis can be applied to map the k-vector into a lower-dimensional feature vector $g = (g_j; j = 1, \ldots, r)$.

(b) Periodic production quality control then operates as
follows:

    i. Map each lot description vector k into the r-dimensional
space (in Figure 9-8, r = 2).

    ii. Draw the time-dependent trajectory followed by the points
describing the consecutive lots produced (see Figure 9-8 and Refs.
F-28 and B-18).

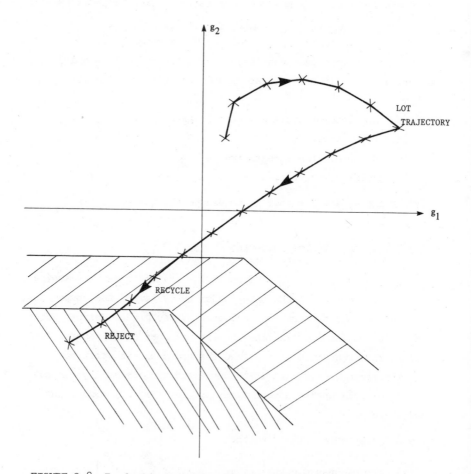

FIGURE 9-8 Production quality control of component lots.

iii. Make one of the following decisions:

(1) Recycle the lot into the production line.

(2) Reject the lot.

(3) Transfer the lot to final acceptance quality control, depending on whether the lot trajectory intersects or not with the regions characterizing (1), (2), or (3).

(c) Such a procedure removes production line variability, allowing the capability of recycling a lot before expensive acceptance control or burn-in tests.

9.9 Measurement Selection for Lot Production Quality Control of ICs

The production process contemplated involves integrated circuits. At each stand P_n ($n = 1, \ldots, 7$) there is a test including the following:

(a) Visual inspection (100%)

(b) Electrical testing, leading to acceptance or rejection with four possible reject causes

(c) Recycling the components to an upstream stand if rejected

The goal is to raise the total productivity, as evaluated at the end of the assembly line, by recycling parts within the line instead of waiting for a final acceptance control.

The analysis uses the following measurements: $k(i,j)$ = rejection percentage in lot i during the test at stand $n = [\mathcal{I}(j/4) + 1]$ ($n = 1, \ldots, 7$). The rejection is due to cause $\ell = j - n + 1$ ($\ell = 1, \ldots, 4$). $\mathcal{I}(\cdot)$ here represents the integer part of a rational number.

By using correspondence analysis, it is possible to discover the causal relations between rejection causes and production stands and to deduce from them a recycling policy.

This policy is implemented, naturally, at the cost of notable modifications in the manufacturing process. Its advantages should be estimated over a sufficiently large number of lots.

9.10   Prototype Tests for
       Modifications (1972)
       [E-12, E-13]

Statistical diagnosis can also be applied to the analysis of
the Card(I) removals of a single physical prototype for which Card(J)
measurements are recorded.   Interest then lies in matching the analysis results based on the implicit table of the prototype with the
corresponding factorial maps produced in operation.

It is thus possible to estimate the consequences of design
changes using modifications carried out only on the prototype.

Applications can be found in reliability studies of equipment
manufactured in small quantities, with a single prototype (for example, certain nuclear components having very high testing or manufacturing costs or risks).   The volume of learning data taken into
account is increased and updated sequentially by the sequential
selection of the best observation tests (cf. Chapters 4 and 5).

9.11   Degradation Process Modeling (Chapter 3)

The development of a degradation process model, based on regression or identification techniques, is of interest for certain
electronic or mechanical components.   Statistical diagnosis techniques can be applied, to some extent, to analyze the residual
deviations between real breakdown processes (tests on stands and
experimental data) and the degradation model.

9.12   Selection of Spectral Features (Chapter 13)

Assume that a short-term or stationary spectrum or cepstrum is
extracted from a signal, and digitized by frequency bands.   Not all
spectrum or cepstrum bands are good features for failure detection
and diagnosis.   Data analysis applied to the digitized spectrum or
cepstrum yields good spectral bands.

Chapter 10

AUTOMATED FAILURE DIAGNOSIS
BY PATTERN RECOGNITION

1. PRINCIPLES OF AUTOMATED DIAGNOSIS FROM STATIC MEASUREMENTS

It is conceivable that medical diagnoses could sometimes be based exclusively on the analysis of patients' answers to certain questionnaires without a systematic clinical examination requiring a physician.

Similarly, we can envisage, in an engineering application, failure diagnoses based on the statistical analysis of available information about a system's operations and environment prior to the time of failure. This statistical analysis could be automated, with dismantlement of the equipment used only as a last resort in identifying the failure cause. If the failure cause is determined without dismantlement, it may also be possible to determine which subsystems are damaged.

Only when the automatically determined failure causes do not include the actual cause is a clinical examination or dismantlement necessary for diagnostic and maintenance purposes.

In medical applications, automated processing of questionnaires requires a large, general-purpose computer.

In engineering applications, automated failure diagnosis (for a given device) can be carried out using a special-purpose processor with a stored fixed program or an arithmetical unit running in the time sharing mode.

We define automated statistical diagnosis to be the recognition of possible failure causes from observed symptoms and previous operating history. An extreme example is classification by simple association of symptoms to an illness or failure cause; in this case a

simple <u>symptom-failure matrix</u> is used. If these symptoms are into
a measurement vector, this vector is a <u>pattern</u>, in the terminology
of pattern recognition.

In this case, an automated diagnosis is the automatic recognition of a symptom pattern from the set of all observable patterns
(divided into failure mode or illness cause classes).

Recall that recognition assumes preliminary learning, with or
without compression of observed patterns, to speed up diagnosis formulation. We might consider correspondence analysis (Chapter 8) or
other data analysis methods (Chapter 7) for learning with data compression.

It is important to understand that the goal of automated statistical diagnosis in medical or engineering applications is not
the localization of the damaged elements. On the contrary, the objective is to determine the most probable failure causes (or modes),
given the observations. Causes might be internal or external to
the equipment: this is why a symptom-failure table is inadequate.
Such a selection among possible causes allows a reduction in maintenance costs and a shortening of equipment unavailability times.

Automated statistical diagnosis is particularly suitable for
complex failure situations, involving wear, multiple failures, and
the consequences of external working conditions. This approach is
useful when direct measurements and logical tests prove inadequate,
but it demands numerous preliminary equipment tests to obtain learning data about all possible equipment conditions. These data can
be obtained in part when the equipment is damaged during operations.
Automated statistical diagnosis has been used successfully in engineering applications. However, there have been only limited results in automated medical diagnosis: an explanation involves the
notion of incurred risk. In medical applications this risk is
enormous and unacceptable; in technical applications it is generally
well defined and less costly.

Besides logical and statistical diagnosis, there is a third
approach to the problem. This involves developing an analytical
and physical understanding of the relations among the condition of

a piece of equipment, the parameter variations governing it, and the degradation processes (see Chapter 3).

Knowing the relations between symptoms and failures, it is possible to anticipate breakdowns and to ensure the best possible choice of adequate measurements. This approach is not contradictory to statistical diagnosis; on the contrary, it can be considered an indispensable tool for improvement of the learning data, through a reduction in the number of preliminary trials required and a selection of condition variables closely linked to actual equipment breakdowns and degradation.

We shall introduce in a more precise manner the concepts of pattern recognition before proceeding to discuss methods of automated failure diagnosis.

2. BASIC NOTIONS IN PATTERN RECOGNITION

The patterns contemplated for automated diagnosis are vectors, with coordinates composed of measurements describing breakdowns, previous history, and the environment of the equipment.

2.1 Pattern

We define a pattern to be a uniformly observable element in the set spanned by these vectors. A pattern is either static or dynamic and can be "described" (i.e., communicated from human to machine or from machine to machine).

Example: A television image with discrete resolution.   ■

Counterexample: A "beautiful" painting and "nice patterns" in it. A pattern presents itself as it is; processing only gives it a structure or an informative character.   ■

2.2 Object Space

The object (or measurement) space is a specified subspace of the physical world; an object has a meaning only within this space, via its physical appearance. The object space is often a vector space, characterized by the unitary vectors associated with each physical measurement and with each coordinate (continuous or discrete)

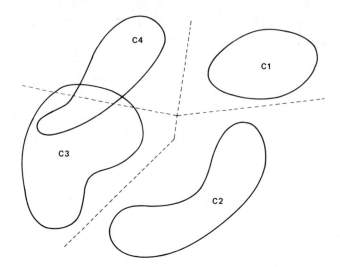

FIGURE 10-1 Discrimination among four pattern classes, two of which
are overlapping (C3 and C4).

of the pattern vectors. It should be stressed that the object space
is only partially known in practice.

Example

    Consider the first n formants of a sound; the object space is $\mathbb{R}^n$,
but frequencies are measured only in a certain bounded subset of $\mathbb{R}^n$. ∎

    2.3 Concepts, Classes, and Clusters

    Pattern recognition and learning presume the existence of an
abstract concept; the pattern constitutes its physicomathematical
realization. The concept symbolizes all the "appearance modes" of
a pattern in the object space under consideration.

Example

    M and m have nothing in common, but together they pertain to
the same concept, which is "the letter m." ∎

    This concept is the model, established by a human or machine, for
objects in space having certain common properties. Although a single
pattern reduces a concept in the object space into a physical observation of this sole pattern, it is generally assumed that a concept
may have several different representations. If this is so, a repre-

sentation of the concept obtained from its partition is called a
class (or cluster, when no such partitions are available, except
sample patterns). See Figure 10-1.

Example

    Concept: Damaged bicycle chain

    Classes: Each chain link forms a class (good or bad)

    Cluster: Sample of bad links which are all too narrow ■

2.4 Learning

Recognition implies a complete and precise description of each
class in the object space. This operation, the materializing of a
concept in the object space, is called learning.

When the pattern recognizor is human, learning results from
knowledge of the appropriate concept by a human mind. When recognition is carried out by machine, learning involves a memorization of
the concept through a partitioning of the object space.

We mention in passing that knowledge of a concept can rarely
be complete, because learning is achieved via only a limited number
of patterns belonging to a class the learner is cognizant of.
"Knowledge" is thus complete only in a subspace of the object space,
which is called the feature space.

2.5 Classification

Suppose that we have preliminary information or important experience about each class in numerical form. These a priori data
are called the learning data. To recognize a pattern produced by a
sensor is to place it in the pattern class having representative
patterns that are the "most similar" to it.

Example

    Consider an electronic circuit with N discrete components, each
in good (1) or bad (0) condition:

    i. The object space is isomorphic to $\{(0,1)\}^N$.

    ii. A pattern is a vector with N coordinates equal to the
respective conditions of each of these N components; there are 2^N
patterns in the object space under study.

iii.   The concept is that of a failed circuit.

iv.   The classes are the individual conditions of the components; each failure is defined by the corresponding damaged components.

v.   Recognizing a pattern means deciding that the damaged components of the circuit are isomorphic with a particular class (due to a specific cause).   ∎

The recognition of a pattern involves the risk of placing it in the wrong class and the risk of rejecting it if it is sufficiently dissimilar to all the classes.   For a given class, the probability that a pattern belonging to it will be correctly classified is called the rate of (correct) recognition.   When the number of classes is finite, it is possible to construct a square confusion matrix, where each element (line ℓ, column k) is the probability of classifying a pattern of class k as being in class ℓ.   These performance measurements are of capital importance in a pattern recognition system. See Table 10-1.

3.   THE PROCESSING OF LEARNING PATTERNS
     AND DATA COMPRESSION

The learning data generally consist of a large number of patterns, termed learning patterns.   Two circumstances can arise:

i.   These learning patterns have previously been assigned to learning classes; this is supervised learning (with a teacher).

ii.   They have not been classified previously; this is unsupervised learning (without a teacher).

Supervised learning can be limited to selected representatives of each class, sometimes called strong patterns, for instance, the average of the class learning patterns or the extreme patterns. Discriminant analysis (Section 8 of Chapter 7) is frequently used to find the hyperplanes that best limit the volume containing patterns of a single class at a given time.   It may happen that a class defined a priori contains empty parts; then it is necessary to seek well-defined subclasses.

In the case of unsupervised learning, taxonomy algorithms must be utilized. Some of these are also called clustering methods. Using no preliminary hypothesis other than a similarity measure, these algorithms group or cluster together the "most similar" patterns, sequentially constructing a set of natural classes; then the problem becomes one of supervised learning (see Section 10 of Chapter 7). Clustering or taxonomy algorithms use similarity functions (Section 9 of Chapter 1) expressed solely in terms of pattern coordinates. They generally require an evaluation of the maximum number of natural classes. In contrast, correspondence, principal components, and correlation analyses use statistical tests with approximately known performances to measure the similarity between patterns.

In the preceding, the dimension of the learning patterns is identical to that of the observed patterns (supplied by the sensors). This is generally high. Hence the capacity required to store all strong learning patterns in a read-only memory is often enormous. For this reason, a fundamental aspect of pattern recognition is the compression of observed patterns into patterns of smaller dimension. Instead of storing (strong) learning patterns, only previously compressed (strong) learning patterns are stored. Similarly, instead of classifying observed patterns on the basis of the complete learning patterns, compressed observed patterns are classified on the basis of compressed (strong) learning patterns.

The performances of a data compression method are measured by the following characteristics:

i. Real-time operations on any observed pattern.

ii. Elimination of pattern redundancy or, in probability terms, minimization of the stochastic dependencies between the pattern coordinates.

iii. Ability to discriminate the patterns belonging to all different classes, that is, to preserve a maximum of the discriminatory information; techniques for achieving this particular property are called feature extraction methods.

TABLE 10-1 Confusion matrix

		CLASSES LEARNED			
	%	E_0	E_1	E_2	E_3
	E_0	81	26	30	0
	E_1	4	42	0	0
	E_2	0	10	55	0
	E_3	15	22	15	100
	N_i Number of learning patterns of class E_i	15	20	20	10
	n_i Number of test patterns of class E_i	50	50	50	50
	π_i A priori probability of belonging to class E_i	0.12	0.16	0.32	0.40

CLASSES RECOGNIZED

RECOGNITION RATE = EXPECTED VALUE OF DIAGONAL TERMS
$$=(50 \cdot 81 + 50 \cdot 42 + 50 \cdot 55 + 50 \cdot 100)/(50+50+50+50) = 69.5\ \%$$

Numerous compression methods have been published that comply with these three requirements. The great majority of these methods are empirical, making use of a thorough experimental knowledge of the phenomenon to be analyzed. Hence they tend to be very sensitive to the size of the learning sample used.

A special-purpose operational system generally cannot compress the learning data; this task is usually given to a large, general computer. Only the transformation formulas are stored in the special-purpose processor. To this end, it is important to have an idea of the required number of learning patterns. It has been shown that if n classes are separable by hyperplanes, the required number of learning patterns is approximately $\nu \triangleq n[1 + (1/P)]$, where P is the maximum tolerable error probability. Thus $P = 10^{-3}$ gives ν in the neighborhood of 1000n.

4. CLASSIFICATION METHODS IN PATTERN RECOGNITION

After learning is completed and a compression method is chosen, the recognition process divides into several phases (Figure 10-2):

    i. <u>Discrimination</u>, which is the choice of a similarity measure between a compressed pattern and a learning class (see Section 9 of Chapter 1); difficulties arise because strong learning patterns, representing a certain class, constitute a cluster that is generally not disconnected from the clusters representing the other classes in the N-dimensional space; such a situation is illustrated in Figure 10-1.

    ii. <u>Decision</u>, which involves assigning the observed pattern to one of the learning classes or rejecting it on the basis of previously calculated similarities.

    iii. <u>Diagnosis</u>, which may include display and control of a process; standby equipment might be put into service or the failed device disconnected (both operations are part of an overall system reconfiguration).

We shall mention briefly the discrimination and decision techniques involved.

4.1 Partition of the Feature Space

The ideal situation is when the clusters associated with various classes are disjoint in the N-dimensional space. These clusters can then be separated by means of discriminant surfaces (hyperplanes, quadratic surfaces, prisms). Recall that at most $n(n - 1)/2$ planes are needed to separate n linearly separable classes. Potential methods, which assimilate a discriminant surface with an isopotential surface, are applicable when the strong patterns are treated as punctual electric charges, generating a potential field. A decision is made by finding the region in the feature space to which the pattern belongs.

Example

The best discriminant functions (which are quadratic) are derived, in the class of Gaussian patterns, from weighted Euclidean

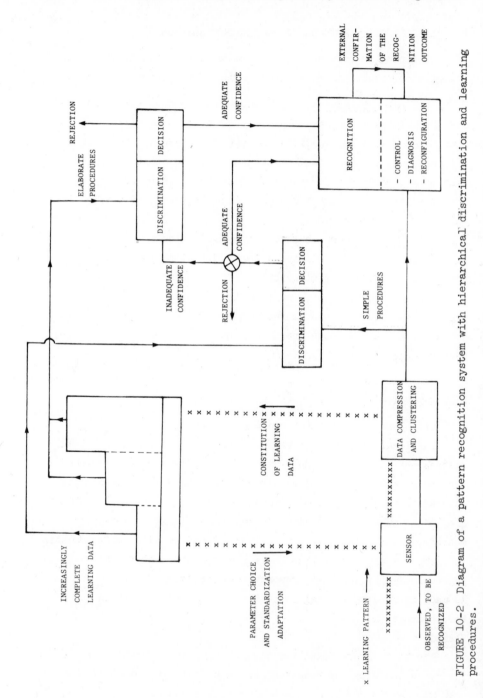

FIGURE 10-2 Diagram of a pattern recognition system with hierarchical discrimination and learning procedures.

distances between the pattern X and the mean patterns μ_i for each
of the classes E_i (i = 1, ..., n):

$$d^2(X,E_i) = {}^t(X - \mu_i)\Sigma_i^{-1}(X - \mu_i)$$

where

> μ_i: The mean $E(Y ; Y \in E_i)$ of all patterns $Y \in E_i$, or the mean
> of all learning patterns belonging to E_i
>
> Σ_i: The covariance matrix of all patterns $Y \in E_i$ as estimated
> by learning

The decision rule involves calculating the distances $d(X,E_i)$
between the feature X and each class E_i (i = 1, ..., n) and selecting the class for which this distance is the smallest. ∎

Overlaps are frequent. Discriminant surfaces of a more general
nature are then sought. One example is to minimize the classification error probability via linear discriminant analysis; hence the
number of misclassified samples is minimized. The decision principle
remains the same except that confidence margins can be used. The
discriminant surface approach is not really satisfactory in practice
(except for problems having few classes and low dimension) because
its implementation is too dependent on learning techniques and because nonlinear transformations, which are hard to adjust [B-20],
may be required to improve class separation. It should be noted,
however, that hardware implementation of polynomial discriminants
is now possible using appropriate LSI and MSI circuits.

4.2 Bayesian Decision Through the Estimation of the Class Conditional Probabilities

Assuming there exist classes E_k (k = 1, ..., n) and that the
coordinates x_i (i = 1, ..., N) of each pattern X are independently
drawn variables, then

$$f(E_k/X) = \frac{f(E_k)}{f(X)} \prod_{i=1}^{N} f(x_i/E_k)$$

where $f(x_i/E_k)$ is the a priori probability of observing parameter x_i

when X belongs to E_k (calculated by learning), $f(E_k/X)$ is the conditional a posteriori probability density of class E_k in X, and $f(X)$ is independent of the classes.

Let $a_{k\ell}$ be the cost associated with the classification of a pattern from class E_k into class E_ℓ (where a_{kk} is the cost of a correct assignment of the pattern). The minimum risk Bayes rule will assign X to class E_k, so that

$$\sum_{\ell=1}^{n} a_{k\ell} f(E_k/X) = \min_{1 \le j \le n} \{ \sum_{\ell=1}^{n} a_{j\ell} f(E_j/X) \}$$

In a diagnosis, $a_{k\ell}$ ($k \neq \ell$) might be, for example, the replacement cost of a good component and a_{kk} the repair cost for component k.

This approach allows some flexibility in the choice of estimators for the a priori probability densities $f(x_j | E_k)$; for example, local probability densities, a nearest neighbor rule, or an approximation of a density by Gaussian sums might be used (Figure 10-3). Recall that these statistical methods are largely independent of the learning data distributions; this often facilitates optimization of the recognition system [B-20]. However, these advantages are obtained via a large number of learning patterns and considerable computations.

4.3 Similarity Measures (Section 9 of Chapter 1)

Similarity measures can be functions as simple as the Euclidean distance from the center of gravity of each class (strong pattern) or homogeneity and rank tests and more complex distances. Since a discriminant surface is defined by fixing the value of a similarity function, this approach is similar to partitioning. The principal advantage is the short computation time required for decision; the isotropy of these functions sometimes contradicts the complex shapes of different learning clusters.

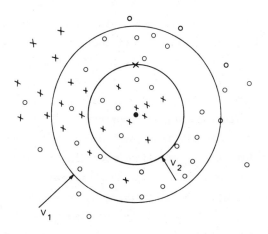

Class E_k	Class E_1 (symbol O)	Class E_2 (symbol x)
n_k	28	9
π_k	β	$1 - \beta$
N_k	38	25
V_k	2.50	0.529
$\dfrac{n_k \pi_k}{(N_k + 1)V_k}$	0.287β	$0.654(1 - \beta)$

The observed pattern $\bar{i}$ = ● belongs to class

$-E_1 = d(\bar{i})$ if $\beta > 0.692$

$-E_2 = d(\bar{i})$ if $\beta \leq 0.692$

FIGURE 10-3 Automated diagnosis by means of the n_k-nearest neighbor rule. The neighborhoods under consideration are in the sense of the Euclidean L^2 metric.

4.4 Syntactic and Quasi-topological Algorithms

Consider the visual process of reading; it involves the decomposition of an unknown physical pattern into smaller elements (letters → trees → bars) and comparison of the number, connectivity, and relative positions of these elements using classification rules.

This might involve formal comparison with symbolic reference sentences (using the formal languages of Chomsky, Backus, Web, and others) or with reference graphs characterizing the pattern.   In doing this, the syntactic rules of the grammar in question are used, along with distance measurements (such as the Hamming distance in coding theory). The statistical properties of such algorithms are evidently unknown. Despite their cumbersomeness, these algorithms are quite suitable for the off-line processing of simple patterns (for example, the waveforms arising in performance monitoring and diagnosis). This approach has motivated a great number of studies in the last 3 or 4 years. A major accomplishment would be the ability to evaluate the properties of stochastic grammars which can describe noisy patterns.

If such procedures are developed, and their individual performances can be evaluated, it would be desirable to rate them on the basis of their ratios of (total recognition time)/(probability of correct recognition). A costly procedure (having a large ratio) should be avoided if a less costly one can make decisions with a suitable level of confidence.

5. AUTOMATED DIAGNOSIS BY THE NEAREST NEIGHBOR
    CLASSIFICATION RULE

An automated diagnosis involves:

(a) Obtaining a list of failure or deterioration modes, ranked by order of decreasing probabilities

(b) Displaying the causal relations relating symptoms and failure or deterioration modes

(c) Minimizing the probability of false recognition (which is identical here to the probability of incorrect diagnosis; see Section 1.4.1 of Chapter 2)

The following automated diagnosis procedure includes an initial learning phase, an (optional) phase of data compression, and a final recognition phase, where a compressed pattern of dimension N is compared with the compressed learning data.

5.1 Learning Phase

Learning data, in the form of an explicit table $k(I,J) = \{k(i,j) \geq 0 ; i \in I, j \in J\}$, are obtained by collecting all measurements $(j \in J)$ during successive removals $(i \in I)$ of similar devices. At each removal, it is assumed that the failure or deterioration mode $d(i)$ for learning pattern i is found.

We assume that the number n of failure modes E_k $(k = 1, \ldots, n)$ is small in comparison with the total number $Card(I)$ of removals.

It is also assumed that the a priori probabilities $\{\pi_k : k = 1, \ldots, n; \pi_k > 0; \Sigma_k \pi_k = 1\}$ of the failure modes have been evaluated from learning data or otherwise specified.

The compressed learning patterns used for recognition diagnosis are images of the patterns $(i \in I)$ in a space of dimension $N \leq \inf [Card(I), Card(J)]$. We assume that correspondence analysis is used for data compression.

5.2 Compression of Any Removal Pattern Requiring Diagnosis

A failure discovered in one member of a fleet of similar equipment gives rise to a removal $\bar{i}$ after collection of all the measurements $\{k(\bar{i},j) ; j \in J\}$ related to $\bar{i}$.

$\bar{i}$ can be considered as an additional learning pattern, belonging to an unknown class $d(\bar{i})$; that is, $d(\bar{i})$ is the failure or deterioration mode causing removal $\bar{i}$.

However, the data compression (by, e.g., correspondence analysis) applied to $k(I,J)$ does not take into account $d(I)$, which is called the vector of learning diagnoses. If $\bar{i}$ does not significantly alter the learning data, this equipment can be represented in the feature space by the formula (cf. Section 4.2 of Chapter 8)

$$G(\bar{i},\ell) = f_\ell \cdot [Pr(j/\bar{i}), j \in J]$$

where

$$Pr(j/\bar{i}) = \frac{k(\bar{i},j)}{\sum_{\ell \in J} k(\bar{i},\ell)} \qquad \ell = 1, \ldots, n$$

and $G(\bar{i},\ell)$ is the coordinate of $\bar{i}$ on the axis f_ℓ.

Next we examine the factorial maps and associations of $\bar{i}$ with learning removals ($i \in I$) when $d(i)$ is known and/or when measurements ($j \in J$) are available.

This motivates, in large part, the formulation in Section 5.3 of experimental hypotheses about the appearance of failure or deterioration $d(\bar{i})$.

5.3 Diagnosis and Classification

(a) A Bayesian decision rule is used, with the class conditional probability densities estimated by the generalized neighbor rule (in the N-dimensional space of all compressed learning patterns). $\bar{i}$ is assigned to the most likely class unless the corresponding class conditional probability is below a given threshold; if this occurs, then $\bar{i}$ is rejected, and no automated diagnosis is made. That is,

i. $\bar{i}$ in the failure mode $\Leftrightarrow \dfrac{n_{d(\bar{i})} \pi_{d(\bar{i})}}{[N_{d(\bar{i})} + 1]V_{d(\bar{i})}} = \displaystyle\max_{k=1,\ldots,n} \left\{ \dfrac{n_k \pi_k}{[N_k + 1]V_k} \right\}$

$$\text{and} \quad \frac{n_{d(\bar{i})}}{[N_{d(\bar{i})} + 1]V_{d(\bar{i})}} \geq \alpha > 0$$

$$d(\bar{i}) \in (E_1, E_2, \ldots, E_n)$$

ii. No diagnosis can be made for $\bar{i}$ iff

$$\max_{k=1,\ldots,n} \left\{ \frac{n_k}{[N_k + 1]V_k} \right\} < \alpha$$

Here,

> k or E_k = class of failure mode
>
> N_k = number of learning patterns ($i \in I$) belonging to class E_k
>
> π_k = a priori estimate of the probability of failure E_k occurring (see Section 5.1)
>
> n_k = an integer parameter, fixed for each class E_k, such that

$$\lim n_k = +\infty \qquad \text{and} \qquad \lim(n_k/N_k) = 0 \text{ when } N_k \rightarrow +\infty$$

α = confidence threshold for a class

V_k = volume of the smallest neighborhood of $\bar{i}$ (in the compressed N-dimensional space) such that $(n_k - 1)$ learning patterns of class E_k are inside it, while only a single learning pattern is on its border

An ϵ neighborhood of $\bar{i}$ is defined as follows (in the compressed N-dimensional space):

$$V(\epsilon,\bar{i}) \triangleq \{i \in I : \sum_{\ell=1}^{N} |G(i,\ell) - G(\bar{i},\ell)| < \epsilon\}$$

These neighborhoods are defined using the L^1 metric instead of L^2 (Section 9 of Chapter 1); the author has shown that this modification reduces the classification time while providing recognition scores at least as good as those obtained with the L^2 metric [B-20].

(b) The following is a brief explanation of this classification procedure: $\varphi_k \triangleq n_k/(N_k + 1)V_k$ represents a nonparametric estimate (asymptotically unbiased) of the probability density of class E_k using learning patterns from E_k in the N-dimensional space. By the definition of V_k, this estimate is made at the point representing $\bar{i}$ in this space (see Section 5.2). The parameter n_k is adjusted to maximize the probability of correct classification in the confusion matrix. Thus if $n_k = 1$ and N_k is constant, φ_k is clearly a density measure for class E_k at $\bar{i}$; as $\bar{i}$ approaches a learning pattern from E_k, V_k decreases, and φ_k increases.

By using the Bayes rule, removal $\bar{i}$ is classified (if possible) into the failure mode class E_k maximizing the a posteriori probability $(\pi_k\varphi_k)$.

(c) A closely related classification rule is the (r,r'), $r' < r$, nearest neighbor rule with a reject option (see Ref. B-1). This rule looks at the r nearest neighbors of $\bar{i}$ (regardless of the classes to which they belong). No diagnosis is made if less than r of these neighbors are from the same class; if some classes have at least r' learning samples among these r nearest neighbors, a decision is made by maximizing $(\pi_k \varphi_k)$ or maximizing the number of learning samples present among the r nearest neighbors.

(d) $d(\bar{i})$ is the most probable diagnosis. An alternative diagnosis $d^1(\bar{i})$ maximizes $(\pi_k \varphi_k)$ over all classes E_k except $d(\bar{i})$; this process can be repeated, producing a list of diagnoses having decreasing likelihoods.

Repairs are carried out at first as if $d(\bar{i})$ is the correct diagnosis; if this is not true, then a search is made for damaged components related to failure mode $d^1(\bar{i})$, and so forth.

If the actual failure is not included in the original list, another set of failure modes and a larger volume of learning data must be used.

Recall that if a list of alternate diagnoses is on hand, only the few components associated with the most probable diagnoses need to be pulled down and repaired. Thus diagnosis automation allows for the following sort of application: consider a system on a mobile platform equipped with monitoring, communication, and diagnostic subsystems; the list of most likely diagnoses is known before this platform is brought to a standstill; maintenance is thus faster and more efficient.

5.4 Remark on the Probability Density Estimate φ_k

This density estimate has several other applications, due to the observations for which it is evaluated. By using an appropriate choice of learning data, it can serve to evaluate transition probabilities in cases with small samples and nonnormality assumptions (e.g., in safety research; see Section 6 of Chapter 9).

5.5 Remark on the Nearest Neighbor Classification
      Rule for Binary Features

This rule can also be extended to the case of binary feature measurements, in which case the city block or Hamming distances (see Section 9.2 of Chapter 1) should replace the L^2 metric. One such

example is the classification of the logical states of digital cir-
cuitry by comparing the binary feature vector with learning features
in a symptom-fault table [G-35].

6. APPLICATION OF AUTOMATED DIAGNOSIS TO QUALITY CONTROL IN A DISCRETE PARTS MANUFACTURING LINE USING PROCESS MEASUREMENTS

6.1 Monitoring a Manufacturing Process

The use of automated machine tools is developing for increasing
productivity in discrete parts manufacturing. It is of particular
interest in the automobile industry and in other industries utilizing
comparable metal processing.

Monitoring and diagnostic systems seem to be especially useful
for comparatively long manufacturing lines, such as in cutting,
welding, milling, and assembly. The multiple interactions between
machines make it very difficult to diagnose the cause of a drop in
production rate or of systematic parts defects. Such defects may
be the result of cumulative minor degradations, originating in different machine tools, but small enough to be unnoticed separately.
Diagnosis of these should allow increased production rates and increased availability of the production line. It is too costly to
halt the whole manufacturing line to inspect all the machines.

Making use of our statistical diagnostic methods, it is possible
to isolate and identify the effects of "wear and tear" of tools on
faulty parts. In this way, improved replacement policies can be
developed for these tools, and removal delays can be shortened.

An assembly line monitoring system has other uses as well, such
as stock management, scrap control, and productivity calculations.

The main sensors used on each machine tool are pneumatic valves,
tachometers, flow gauges, thermometers, pressure gauges, etc. Measurements are taken either continuously or only on request. Other
data are entered manually through alphanumeric keyboards. All these
observations are transmitted to the monitoring system or recorded in
the control units of the largest machines.

Other hardware elements include the following:

(a) Control logic for the machine tools: relays or programmable.

(b) Process computer, with interface and buffer memory ensuring the processing of digitized measurements.

(c) Hardwired multiplexer, generally connected to 20 to 30 machines and including programmable clocks for sequencing the production process and the transmission of measurements.

(d) Data concentrators, the most advanced of which are sometimes actual channel computers; they control the production cycles and fill out condition or observation logbooks. (See Figure 10-6.)

There are two very different system architectures:

(a) Parallel architecture (Figure 10-4): The same central processing unit is shared by programmable controls and data concentrators. The essential practical problem here is to ensure that the other hardware elements are compatible with computers available on the market. In this case, it is not necessary to change concentrators each time a new control logic is implemented.

(b) Serial architecture (Figure 10-5): Transmissions are sequenced by an adapter on the data bus linking the computer with the 30 to 50 concentrators, each coping with up to 16,000 measurement points (in this example). The main concentrators are programmable and are generally part of the computer. Alphanumeric keyboards or displays are also connected to the data bus; they supply or receive information regarding the production process.

6.2 Diagnosis in a Manufacturing Line
     for Discrete Parts

Diagnosis is always made at the computer level.

For systems available at the end of 1973, only a rather limited "diagnostic" process was achieved. These systems only checked that the line underwent a good start-off (good initial positions of tools with respect to the parts). They produced statistical reports about items such as parts counts, measurements of tool utilization times, maintenance, and unavailability periods, and they warned when a

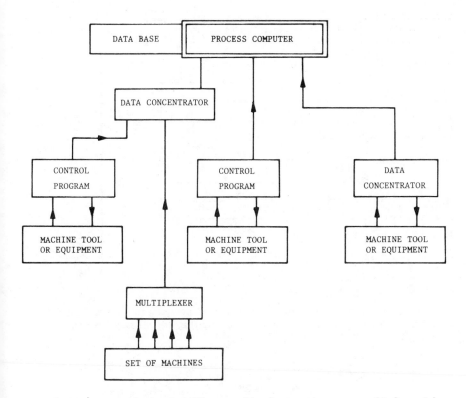

FIGURE 10-4 Manufacturing line monitoring system: parallel architecture.

tool's potential lifetime was exceeded. A few systems could also
tell at what stage of its cycle a given machine tool stopped and
could signal slowdowns. When a slowdown occurred, a message was
displayed, specifying the workshop, machine tool, head number, cycle
stage, and cumulative delay.

   Exaggerated talk, motivated by essentially commercial ends,
declared these elementary operations to be "diagnosis." However,
in a couple of systems developed since 1972, the control logics of
the machine tools are presented in a tabular form, making possible
real diagnosis, provided that a symptom-fault table can be set up
and appropriate sensors installed. In certain cases, such tables
enable the failure to be localized.

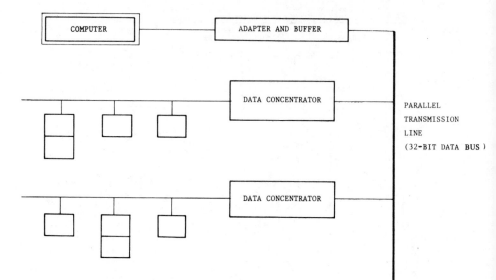

FIGURE 10-5 Manufacturing line monitoring system: serial architecture. Empty boxes are machine controls, which may be connected
to alphanumeric keyboards.

6.3 Examples of Partially Automated Quality Control
[A-45, F-26, F-27, F-28]

The problem faced by the author concerned a manufacturing line
of electromechanical parts, with strict specifications and very
small-dimensional tolerances. Production of such parts required
several milling and superimposed wire spooling operations. For each
part (i $\in$ I), N = 82 measurements were made: some came from the
materials acceptance quality control, but most measurements were
made about the machine tools processing the part (tool settings,
cumulative operating time, elapsed time since last overhaul, tool
type, cooling air flow, temperatures, oil flows, rotation speeds,
technicians operating the machines, etc.). Among the n = 21 classes
of defects, the class E_0 contained all parts which were later accepted
by the final quality control. In the present framework, this quality
control department played the role of a "teacher" (see Section 3).

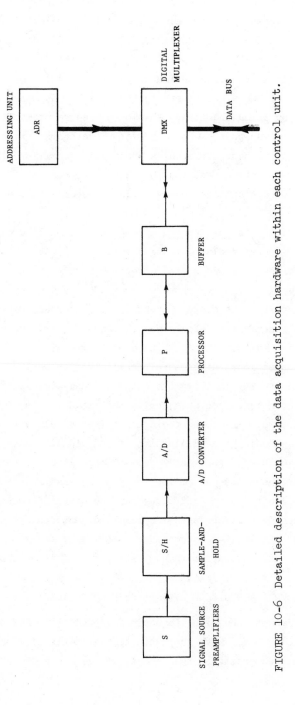

FIGURE 10-6 Detailed description of the data acquisition hardware within each control unit.

(a) Learning phase: Learning data were collected on Card(I) =
2000 parts (20 days of production), of which 800 had defects identified as belonging to 20 classes. These learning data were compressed
into an explicit table on an IBM computer 370-65 (12-mn CPU); the
computation of the eigenvectors f_ℓ ($\ell = 1, \ldots, N$) posed some numeric
problems. By using the interpretation procedure of Section 5 of
Chapter 8, it was possible to discover those characteristics of the
manufacturing process having high probabilities of association with
various defect categories. In this case, the control of oil flow
was found to be a critical characteristic leading to a number of
defects.

(b) Diagnosis test phase: Using the automated diagnosis of
Section 5, a correct classification rate of 92% was achieved in
class E_0 during a second period of approximately 20 days, during
which the quality control tests were made on each automatically
classified part. The average probability of correct diagnosis for
the 20 classes of real defects was 81% when $N = 10$; the diagnosis
time per part was 0.46 sec CPU (on a minicomputer).

(c) Operational diagnostic phase: This phase involved placing
into service (early in 1974) the complete real-time monitoring system,
with 82 measurements per part, collected gradually in the course of
its manufacture. The correct diagnosis rate in class E_0 remained
above 90%, allowing the elimination of individual quality control
testing of each good part as it came off the line. Personnel were
thus freed to operate the monitoring system, analyze the quality
control implicit tables, and study manufacturing process modifications. Considerable savings were realized, especially in productivity and through final acceptance sampling of the good parts
classified into E_0, rather than 100% control of each part.

7. AUTOMATED DIAGNOSIS OF OVERALL SHIP CONDITIONS

7.1 System Condition Diagnosis from Condition Ratings

Section 6 dealt with the automated diagnosis of manufacturing
defects, corresponding to the concept of failure mode diagnosis.

In logistics, with readiness requirements in mind, there exists a very important diagnosis problem related to the <u>classification of deterioration conditions of a system</u>. The system is expected to be without failures affecting its operational performance. On the basis of an inspection of all subsystems and components, one wishes to know whether the complete system can fulfill some new mission with an adequate probability of success. It might happen that initial wear at the mission start is such that a breakdown will occur after a short time, leading to mission cancellation.

7.2 Overall Ship Condition Diagnosis [E-14, G-3]

The ship is assumed to have a monitoring system for certain on-board parameters, in particular those relating to propulsion. In addition, the ship is periodically inspected by a team of experts for 1 to 2 weeks every 1 to 2 years. The ship comprises a set of major systems, a set of functions for each system, and a set of parts for each function. There are, for example, 12 systems with an average of 5 functions per system and 8 parts per function. The entire ship is described by a large number of independent parts, in this case 480. During inspection, each part is evaluated according to its condition (Table 10-2 below).

Ratings

TABLE 10-2 Condition ratings
_____

(a) New or recent equipment, operating in accordance with specifications, well connected to other equipment, and furnished with all necessary additional facilities (including spare units).

(b) Equipment in good condition, generally operating in accordance with specifications without excessive maintenance, and provided with essential additional facilities.

(c) Equipment in acceptable condition, generally satisfying the requirements for a typical mission. The probability that this equipment condition will cause the interruption of a 3-month mission of the ship is low.

(d) Equipment in unsatisfactory condition and of inadequate efficiency.

(e) Equipment in poor working condition, useless, unreliable, or dangerous.
_____

On the basis of these 480 marks, and with available learning data for this class of ships, one wishes to diagnose the overall ship condition as either "satisfactory" or "unsatisfactory." If the overall condition is judged to be satisfactory, then a certain number of missions can be accomplished by the ship without a new overall inspection.

The manner in which this mark is usually given is not clearly understood. It depends on the actual condition of the parts and on a priority ranking of the various parts. In other words, this overall mark might be calculated as a weighted sum of the individual marks.

However, this approach has three important deficiencies:

1. The weighting is too subjective.

2. By using the monitoring system, it should be possible to supply frequent diagnoses of the overall ship condition (more often than once a year).

3. It is necessary to monitor the conditions of all similar parts in a fleet vs. time and to transmit this information to the commanding unit.

The following method has been adopted:

(a) Use all vectors describing past inspections ($i \in I$) of a certain type of ship as patterns belonging to one of the following classes:

E_0: Mission without loss of operational performances

E_1: Mission with at most "a" failures

E_2: Mission with between "a + 1" and "2a" failures, and so forth.

$d(i)$ (for $i \in I$) is obtained after each mission, following an inspection by experts, and the outputs of the shipborne monitoring system.

(b) Use the automated diagnostic procedure of Section 5 to classify a ship, before it departs on its mission, into one of the classes E_i. Departure permission depends on this diagnosis and its confirmation.

Experiments have demonstrated that this method of condition diagnosis is more reliable (and less subjective) than one making use of only the weighted ratings.

There remain problems associated with the acquisition of description vector coordinates. In particular, it should be possible to test equipment during operation; test signals should be applied in a manner that does not disturb the operations.

A standard exists (MIL-STD-1326 (Navy), 15th January 1968) that specifies the monitoring systems of equipment on board ships, particularly the measurements to be made and the characteristics of interfaces.

Even if a vessel is equipped with a central computer, difficulties exist in the costs of sensors and interfaces needed for a monitoring system; these may prove to be excessive in comparison with the savings and improved performances they bring (for example, in the case of tankers).

8. APPLICATION OF AUTOMATED DIAGNOSIS
   TO ACCELERATED LIFE TESTING

(a) Sometimes estimates of parameters can be achieved only through the use of a very limited number of similar devices. The problem then lies in the achievement of the estimates in minimum time or with minimum cost.

The most widely used methods are the following:

i. Utilization of forced operating conditions; this approach has the advantage of accelerating deterioration and causing breakdowns not generally encountered in stationary operations. However, it is difficult to test the system adequately.

ii. Extrapolations from previous measurements; these predictions hold only for short time periods; eventually, complete tests must be undergone.

The following palliative may be tried for the preceding problem: Try to gradually increase (in terms of the cumulative operating time) the number (m) of measurements on each device which must be considered for the estimation of those parameters needed to determine the system's condition.

(b) Following a cumulative operating time of t, the description vectors [$X^s(t)$] are available for devices [s = 1, ..., S(t)] which run until breakdown and are repaired before t. These S(t) description vectors are of dimension m.

The maximum cumulative operating time (T) of the tests and the number of measurements to be taken for estimation purposes (m) are given.

Call the learning data accumulated in $\tau > 0$ operating hours the set of description vectors $X^s(\tau)$ [s = 1, ..., S(τ); $0 \le \tau < t$]. The initial learning data $X^s(0)$ [s = 1, ..., S(0)] are determined before actual prototype tests from predicted reliability parameters and the results of previous experiments on similar equipment.

After t hours of operation, two prototype classes are defined:

Class A: Those devices operating until t, or failing earlier, with all the m parameters remaining within specified tolerances

Class B: Those devices running until t, or failing earlier, but having at least one of the m parameters exceeding the tolerances between 0 and t

It is assumed that a classification algorithm is available for the successive description vectors $X^s(t)$ [s = 1, ..., S(t)] based on the learning data available (t being excluded) but ignoring all preset tolerances.

The testing is stopped after T* hours of cumulative operating time; T* is the first value of t such that the algorithm classifies the description vectors $X^s(T^*)$ [s = 1, ..., S(T*)] into Class A or Class B with a probability of error below a predetermined threshold. The description vectors (up to and including T*) are all taken to have dimension m. Besides the interruption of accelerated testing, this process specifies the number S(T*) of prototypes which must be tested. In practice, as soon as the cumulative operating time T* is reached, the activation of new test prototypes will cease. See Figure 10-7.

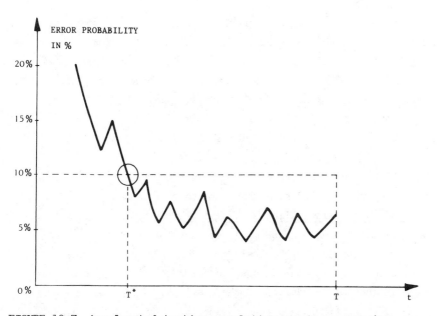

FIGURE 10-7 Accelerated testing; evolution vs. the cumulative operating time t, of the probability of erroneous classification. This is the probability of classifying into A a description vector $X^s(t)$ from B [and into B a vector $X^s(t)$ from A] on the basis of learning data available at time t.

(c) To determine with respect to time which of the m measurements are usable for parameter estimation, the following procedure may be used. After t hours of cumulative operation, a classification test is made using the description vectors, including an additional measurement chosen from those not yet selected. The selected measurement is the one leading to the smallest probability of error in the previous classification test (b) at time t. For other test selection methods, refer to Chapter 5.

(d) If a degradation model is available for the system being tested, simulation using the Monte Carlo method is recommended in order to study the sensitivities of various quantities.

(e) The preceding method is of a special interest for the accelerated testing of nuclear equipment and spaceborne prototypes.

(f) To ensure that diagnosis outcomes are suggestive and read-
able, they may be displayed in the form of a histogram of classes
(A, B, and rejection). As new information comes in, the probability
distribution of these outcomes changes. At each stage, the most informative test carried out is also displayed.

9. OTHER APPLICATIONS OF AUTOMATED DIAGNOSIS
    FROM STATIC MEASUREMENTS

Since 1968, research results have been published which supplement
the experiments described in the preceding sections.

1. Jet engine failures (1968) [B-3, F-24]: From a spectral
analysis of the noise generated by a jet engine during run-up and
the extraction of the spectral rays, Becker classified the jet engine condition into three possible classes: normal operation, defect in the nozzle, defect of the bearings.

2. Car, truck, and tank engine failures (1970) [F-5, F-6]

(a) Four-cylinder internal combustion engines M-151, provided
with strapped down piezoelectric accelerometers to measure vibrations, are studied here. Three hundred measurements per cycle are
recorded and normalized and their spectrum calculated over a 5-kHz
bandwidth. Eighty spectral rays constitute the pattern describing
an engine cycle. The probabilities of incorrect diagnosis for six
classes of defects are found to be below 5%. These defects are all
related to various ball or needle bearings and valves. The aim
pursued is to equip each truck or tank with a circuit making diagnoses by means of prewired discriminant functions so as to speed up
maintenance and make on-the-spot repairs possible anywhere.

(b) Early in 1974, a system was marketed in the United States
for computerized troubleshooting of car engines and printing out the
action required to fix problems. Learning data (called vehicle
service data) are available on 5.2-megabit standard tape cassettes,
each capable of storing information for a manufacturer's entire
line of recent models.

3. <u>Diagnosis of metal sample defects (1971) [F-16]</u>: Spatial
Fourier transformations of the transparency of titanium samples
taken from different points of an aircraft structure are calculated.
These samples are then classified into 11 possible classes according
to overheating and stress suffered by the aircraft in flight and to
earlier surface treatments. The average rate of correct diagnosis
is 64%.

4. <u>Klystron power amplifiers</u>

5. <u>Valves</u>

6. <u>Shipborne equipment</u>: Automatic diagnosis is needed on
board ships for the supervision and control of the main propulsion
machinery (alarm, safety, control), auxiliary machinery, and the
boiler.

7. <u>Nuclear power plants</u>: The measurements used are the neu-
tronic power, input and output core and coolant temperatures, control bar temperatures and positions, etc. Diagnosis has been tested
either to verify the position of the control bars via their short-
term effects or to identify operating malfunctions [F-68, F-69].

Chapter 11

AUTOMATED DIAGNOSIS FROM
TIME-DEPENDENT MEASUREMENTS

1. METHODOLOGIES FOR AUTOMATED DIAGNOSIS
    AND SIGNATURE ANALYSIS

(a) We shall discuss the main approaches to failure diagnosis
using time-dependent measurements; the static case (Chapter 10) will
be considered as a special case.

The systems (S) under consideration are represented by a transfer operator H, which transforms the multidimensional input signal
e(t) into a multidimensional output signal s(t). The corresponding
time functions [denoted by e($\cdot$) and s($\cdot$)] are stochastic processes
in the dynamic case or random variables in the static case. It is
assumed that e($\cdot$) is independent of s($\cdot$); that is, there is no feedback loop injecting s(t) into the input of (S). It is assumed that
systems having such a feedback loop are transformed into an open-
loop form (S) whenever possible. See Figure 11-1.

We also assume that the input e(t) and output s(t) are observable and measurable at all times, using appropriate sensors which

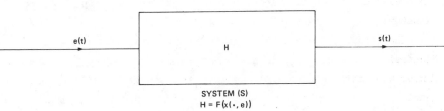

SYSTEM (S)
$H = F(x(\cdot, e))$

FIGURE 11-1 System (S) in open-loop form; the internal condition
is x($\cdot$,e).

may be noisy. It may be necessary to build an appropriate number
of specific sensors around each component or subsystem.

(b) Any pair $[e(\cdot), s(\cdot)]$ where $s(\cdot)$ is the output produced
by (S) given $e(\cdot)$ is called a <u>signature of (S)</u>. Let us then define
on the sets of functions $e(\cdot)$ and $s(\cdot)$, respectively, two quasi-
distances d_e and d_s, that is, two distance measures with nonzero
kernels (see Section 9 of Chapter 1):

$$\exists\, e_1(\cdot),\; e_2(\cdot) \qquad e_1(\cdot) \neq e_2(\cdot) \qquad d_e(e_1, e_2) = 0$$

$$\exists\, s_1(\cdot),\; s_2(\cdot) \qquad s_1(\cdot) \neq s_2(\cdot) \qquad d_s(s_1, s_2) = 0$$

Specify a set of different signatures $\{[e_k(\cdot), s_k(\cdot)] : k = 0,$
$\ldots, n - 1\}$ characterizing n possible conditions E_k of a system (S)
that has a given design and fixed initial standard. Each of these
pairs represents a failure or degradation mode E_k of (S).

A system (S) is said to have failure or degradation E_k, $k = 0$,
$\ldots, n - 1$, if and only if its input $e(\cdot)$ and corresponding output
$s(\cdot)$ simultaneously satisfy

$$d_e(e, e_k) = 0 \qquad \text{and} \qquad d_s(s, s_k) = 0$$

This definition assumes the initial condition $x(0, e)$ at $t = 0$
to be the same for all possible inputs $e(\cdot)$.

In many circumstances where $e(\cdot)$ is fixed, the signature $[e(\cdot),$
$s(\cdot)]$ is reduced to $s(\cdot)$, and thus only d_s is needed in the previous
definition of the failure mode E_k.

Among the n possible conditions of a system (S) is condition E_0,
the so-called "good operating" condition; it satisfies all technical
and operational specifications. Condition E_0 is represented by the
signature $[e_0(\cdot), s_0(\cdot)]$.

The techniques discussed in this book generally do not allow
diagnosis of systems like those in Section 2.1 of Chapter 2 if the
number n of different possible conditions is above 15; at the very
least, it is difficult to guarantee adequate probabilities of correct diagnosis. However, if n is less than 4 or 5, there are often

more effective diagnostic processes which are less complicated or
costly than the methods under discussion.

(c) The meaning of the preceding formalism for failure diagnosis is that this problem is equivalent to the classification of
the internal conditions $x(t,e)$ of (S). A more precise formulation
should call on the notion of observability of (S). The condition
$x(t,e)$ is said to be observable if and only if it can be calculated
at time τ from the knowledge of $[e(t),s(t)]$ for $t > \tau$. If one of
the internal conditions $x_k(\cdot,e)$ is not observable, then the failure
mode E_k cannot be diagnosed automatically. We therefore assume that
the conditions E_k characterizing failures and degradations of (S)
are all related to observable internal conditions $x_k(\cdot,e)$.

It is then formally equivalent to characterize a failure or
degradation E_k, $k = 0, \ldots, n - 1$, by the signatures $[e_k(\cdot),s_k(\cdot)]$,
by the corresponding internal condition $x_k(\cdot,e_k)$, or by the transfer
operator $f[x_k(\cdot,e_k)]$ [depending on $x_k(\cdot,e_k)$]. From the quasi-dis-
tances d_e and d_s one can infer a quasi-distance d_x between the internal conditions of (S), called the structural distance. In particular, (S) is said to have the failure E_c if and only if

$$d_x[x(\cdot,e),x_c(\cdot,e)] = 0 \qquad \text{for all inputs } e(\cdot) \qquad (1.1)$$

2. DIAGNOSTIC PROCEDURES: EXTERNAL AND INTERNAL DIAGNOSIS

The failure or degradation modes E_k can be diagnosed in two different
ways, given the foregoing hypotheses.

2.1 External Diagnosis

External diagnosis makes use of the signature $[e(\cdot),s(\cdot)]$
without any explicit observation, measurement, or direct estimation
of the parameters characterizing the internal condition of the system (S). External diagnosis requires external learning information,
such as signatures $[e_k(\cdot),s_k(\cdot)]$ and semidistances d_e and d_s; it
often uses signal transients analysis for diagnostic purposes.

However, a substantial proportion of all practical failure diagnosis problems can be solved simply by detecting whether some
measurements exceed thresholds or whether a sensor output is satu-
rated. As mentioned in the introduction, in this book we deal mostly
with more subtle cases.

2.2   Internal Diagnosis

The internal diagnosis approach uses $[e(\cdot),s(\cdot)]$ to observe,
measure, or estimate parameters characterizing the internal state
$x(\cdot,e)$ of the system $s(\cdot) = H_x[e(\cdot)]$, where $H_x = f[x(\cdot,e)]$. Internal diagnosis is similar to the identification problem and requires
internal learning information, that is, transfer operators H_k or
internal conditions $x_k(\cdot,e)$, $k = 0, \ldots, n - 1$, and a semidistance
d_x. Since equipment dismantling and any interruption of operations
is forbidden, internal diagnosis is achieved as follows:

   i.   By direct identification methods, with a deconvolution
between input and output in order to find $H = f[x(\cdot,e)]$.

   ii.   By the model method, in which a parametric model (M) of
(S) is recursively adjusted in order to minimize a distance d_s between the output $s(\cdot)$ of (S) and the output $\hat{s}_M(\cdot)$ of model (M),
characterized by an estimated condition $\hat{x}_M(\cdot,e)$. Diagnosis is then
carried out by classifying the estimated internal condition $\hat{x}_M(\cdot,e)$
in one of the classes E_k, $k = 0, \ldots, n - 1$, by comparison with the
learning conditions $x_k(\cdot,e)$ using d_x [see equation (1.1) of Section
1]. See Figure 11-2.

2.3   Implementation

It should be noted that it is often difficult to distinguish
between internal and external diagnosis. In both methods, an important factor is the nature and quantity of information used and
the time interval during which $[e(t),s(t)]$ is observed (with or
without comparison to learning signatures $[e_k(t),s_k(t)]$, $k = 0, \ldots,$
$n - 1$). We shall distinguish two cases.

   (a)   Diagnosis by tests: A known input $e(\cdot)$ is applied to (S),
and diagnosis is carried out only after a period T has gone by. The

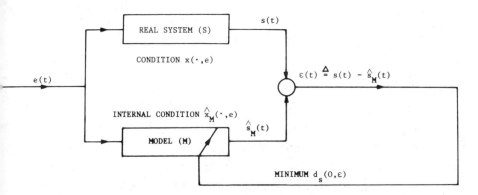

FIGURE 11-2   Internal diagnosis of (S) by identification of the (M) model.

data recorded for failure classification are $\{[e(t),s(t)] : t \in [0, T]\}$; this testing generally requires the interruption of normal operations.

(b) Adaptive diagnosis: This diagnosis can be made at any time $t \geq 0$; its chief function is to detect sudden variations of the internal condition of the system (S) or degradations beyond predetermined thresholds. The data for failure classification at time $t \geq 0$ are $\{[e(\tau),s(\tau)] : \tau \in [0,t)\}$.

In both cases, failure localization is assumed to follow failure diagnosis, the latter guiding the search for failed components (see Chapters 4 and 5).

3. EXAMPLE: INTERNAL DIAGNOSIS OF AN
    ELECTRICAL dc MOTOR

In this section we shall briefly study a system having the characteristics specified in Section 1 and in Chapter 2. Our goal is to indicate the difficulties met in the application of the assumptions and of the definition of observable failure modes.

Speed fluctuations and the transient rotation speed of a dc motor are governed by the differential equation

$$C_m[N(t)] - C_r[N(t)] = 2\pi J_T \frac{dN}{dt} = C_i(t) \tag{3.1}$$

where

$$J_T = J + MR^2$$

and in which

$N(t)$ = rotation speed in rpm
$C_i(t)$ = inertia torque
$C_m(\cdot)$ = driving torque, given by its characteristic curve
$C_r(\cdot)$ = resistant torque, given by its characteristic curve
R = gyration radius with respect to the axis of the force
J = moment of inertia of all rotating parts
M = mass animated by translation

For locomotive engines, $J(dN/dt)$ is small in comparison to $MR^2(dN/dt)$. On the other hand, in a rolling mill the inertia of the moving mass (metal bars) is low in comparison to the inertia of the rotating parts (armature, inertia wheel, and cylinders). In a machine tool (drill) there are no translation parts, and J is relatively low.

From the structure of equation (3.1), it follows that it is impossible to separately determine J, M, and R solely from the measurement of the rotation speed $N(t)$. It is therefore necessary to measure other variables to identify the internal condition: in this case, to evaluate J and M for the purpose of discriminating between failure modes. If the current $I(t)$ in the inductor can be measured and if it is known that

$$\frac{dI}{dt} = f(I,N,J,M,R) \tag{3.2}$$

then the failure mode and a good operating mode can be defined on the basis of conformance to the relation obtained by eliminating one of the unknowns J and M between equations (3.1) and (3.2):

E_0: $g(N,dN/dt,dI/dt,J,R) = 0$

E_1: $g(N,dN/dt,I,dI/dt,J,R) \neq 0$

E_1 then corresponds to a failure linked to a variation of J, the inertia of all the rotating parts.

More generally, the coefficients in the transfer equation
$s(\cdot) = H_x[e(\cdot)]$ are aggregate parameters specific to the physical
components of the system. In an electrical R-C circuit, the time
constant RC is an example of such an aggregated parameter. If internal diagnosis is possible, it will only supply the values of the
aggregated parameters, which will generally not be specific enough
to allow for the localization of faulty parts. As a result, it may
be difficult to interpret the failure modes in the estimated analytical condition $\hat{x}_M(\cdot, e)$ from the aggregated parameters.

Note that equation (3.1) is a nonlinear equation due to the
nonlinearity of the characteristics. However, most identification
methods are effective only for linear or linearized systems.

Consequently, methods for internal diagnosis will certainly
not enable us to diagnose difficult cases such as engine failures
during takeoff. Such failures will require external diagnosis unless the system (S) can be linearized over a wide range of operating
and internal condition parameters.

4. HARDWARE REQUIREMENTS FOR AUTOMATED DIAGNOSIS FROM DYNAMIC MEASUREMENTS

Whether diagnosis by tests or adaptive diagnosis is considered, the
time dependence of all measurements and stimuli produce the hardware
requirements previously mentioned in Section 5 of Chapter 2. A generalization is that diagnostic systems which are able to account for
this time dependence will almost always be based on a special-purpose
digital processor or logic similar to that used in automatic test
systems (ATSs) (see Ref. C-5).

4.1 Stimuli Control Unit

The stimuli control unit must be able to control and sequence
digital and analog stimuli. It is thus generally a programmable
function generator with associated A/D or D/A converters.

4.2 Coupler

The coupler, a sequential unit, adapts the data flow and test
output rates to the measurement characteristics. It also includes
decoding circuits to direct data flows to the stimuli control units.

4.3 Adapters

If the same diagnostic system hardware is used to monitor different systems, an adaptation unit must provide a flexible connector compatibility, making the loading of specific software programs as easy as possible.

4.4 Sensor Error Compensation

(a) For time-dependent measurements, it is essential to carry out adequate calibration of each sensor separately, in addition to specific measurement corrections. Sensor failures will have to be detected separately, e.g., with one of the methods of this book.

(b) Moreover, for all the methods described in the following chapters, we recommend introduction of a weighting matrix containing the conditional probabilities of providing an accurate and reliable sensor output vs. the sensor sensitivity. This helps to improve failure mode diagnosis performance in terms of sensor characteristics and environmental interferences.

4.5 Temporary Storage

Temporary storage is required to keep track of all controls, stimuli, and monitoring measurements until the diagnostic decision has been computed and confirmed.

It is especially important to have the capability of retrieving the list of all components and subsystems detected to be failure-free up to the current time. This capability can be used by the maintenance team if none of the suggested diagnoses are actually correct.

5. CLOSED-LOOP CALIBRATION OF STIMULI SIGNALS

It is essential for reliable operation of a diagnostic or test system that each source instrument of stimuli $e_i(t)$, i = 1, ..., n_e, has first been commanded to the correct calibrated signal and that a second procedure has verified that the source instrument is, in fact, providing the desired signal. Closed-loop calibration of stimuli signals is made even more crucial considering nonlinearities and drift of the signal source together with errors of the A/D or D/A converters used in the diagnostic system.

Define the following:

u(t):   Calibration control applied to the signal generator

$\Delta t = 1$:   Sampling period

$e_0(t)$:   Desired reference stimulus signal

e(t):   Actual stimulus signal, applied to the unit under
           test; this signal has to be calibrated

K_0:   Assumed signal generator transfer function or gain

K(t):   Current gain of the calibrated signal generator

A closed-loop calibration procedure applied to the signal generator which minimizes the steady-state calibration error for step
inputs is

$$K(0) = K_0$$

$$e(t) = K(t)u(t)$$

$$u(t) = u(t - 1) + \frac{e_0(t) - e(t - 1)}{K(t)}$$

$$K(t) \triangleq \frac{e(t - 1) - e(t - 2)}{u(t - 1) - u(t - 2)}$$

If u(0) is the initial calibration control applied to the signal generator, this procedure computes the sequence of values of u(t)
such that the calibration error $[e_0(t) - e(t)]$ is minimized as fast
as possible.

Chapter 12

EXTERNAL DIAGNOSIS FOR
CONTROL SYSTEMS AND OTHER EQUIPMENT

1. EXPERIMENTAL METHODS OF EXTERNAL DIAGNOSIS: USE OF THE FREQUENCY RESPONSE

1.1 Graphical Representations of the Transfer Function

If the system (S) is linear with a one-dimensional input and output, the transfer function $H(p)$ can be defined and represented in various ways in terms of the frequency f, the gain $A(f)$, and the phase $\varphi(f)$:

(a) Black's diagram (A, φ), with graduation in frequency

(b) Nyquist or Bode's diagram $[\text{Re}(H(p)), \text{Im}(H(p))]$, with graduation in frequency (where $p \triangleq 2\pi jf$ and $j \triangleq \sqrt{-1}$)

For diagnostic purposes, consider the transfer loci T_k corresponding to E_k and $(e_k(\cdot), s_k(\cdot))$ (for $k = 0, \ldots, n - 1$). These loci are generally obtained by simulating the failures of a prototype system and performing a frequency analysis for each using one of the preceding graphic representations. The frequency bands and test signals ensuring the best discrimination between transfer loci are generally determined experimentally.

If a system (S) has broken down, first its frequency response and then the corresponding transfer locus T are determined.

An ex post facto diagnosis is then achieved by comparing this transfer locus T with the loci T_k that characterize the failure modes E_k (using a distance measure D to compare curves; see Section 3). (S) is said to have failure E_k if the transfer locus characterizing E_k is the closest to T (and is sufficiently close). With this method, the best discrimination is generally achieved with Black's representation.

The frequency response of (S) is obtained by conventional testing methods such as the following:

(a) Sinusoidal test signals $e(t)$ = sin $2\pi ft$, with frequency interpolation

(b) Step test signals $e(t)$ and harmonic analysis of the response, with frequency interpolation when required

(c) Test signals $e(t)$ which are pseudorandom and are eventually superimposed upon the nominal controls applied to (S)

1.2 Bilinear Transformation of the Transfer Function

If the system (S) is linear and has an explicitly known transfer function, it is possible to improve the preceding method. The idea is to apply a fixed transformation to the output $s(\cdot)$ such that the transfer loci T_k of (S) in the conditions E_k can be better discriminated. See Figure 12-1.

Example

The transfer function of an electric circuit is often a homographic function of each circuit component parameter x_i:

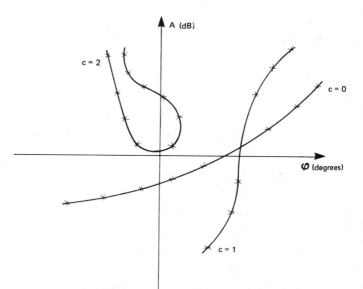

FIGURE 12-1 Discrimination between Black's transfer loci.

$$H_i(p) = \frac{\alpha_i(p)x_i + \beta_i(p)}{\gamma_i(p)x_i + \delta_i(p)} \qquad \alpha_i\delta_i - \beta_i\gamma_i \neq 0, \; x_i > 0$$

For given $p = 2\pi jf$, the locus T_i of $H_i(p)$ is either an infinite half line or an arc, both graduated in x_i with the other parameters x_j ($j \neq i$) having nominal values. These n transfer loci T_i (i = 1, ..., n) intersect at a point A such that the graduation values in A on each locus are the nominal parameter values (cf. Figure 12-2).

We now consider a system (S) of the preceding type that is assumed to be damaged.

(a) If H(p) is at the point A, (S) is in condition E_0, as related to the nominal values x_i (i = 1, ..., n).

(b) If H(p) is on one of the T_i curves, the component i is damaged, and the corresponding value of x_i can be read on T_i.

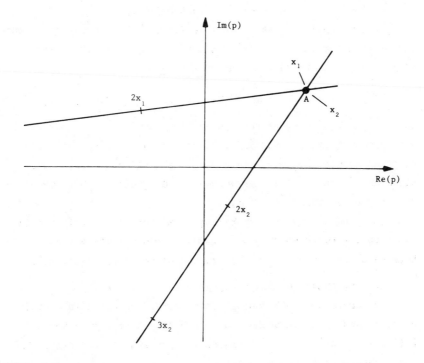

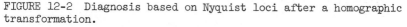
FIGURE 12-2 Diagnosis based on Nyquist loci after a homographic transformation.

(c) If $H(p)$ is not on any of the T_i curves, at least two components are damaged, and a very simple procedure will identify them.

This procedure is repeated for different test frequencies. This technique is effective for at most a dozen distinct components x_i. See Figure 12-2.   ∎

1.3 Multivariate Nyquist Diagram of a Perturbated Closed-loop System (S)

Let $H(p)$ be the multivariate open-loop square transfer matrix and $L(p)$ a square perturbation matrix, nominally zero, which represents the additive deviation of $H(p)$ from the true plant equation due to failure and/or mismatch. It is essential, to estimate the robustness of the corresponding feedback system, to determine the magnitude of the perturbation $L(p)$ which may be tolerated without instability. Only stable perturbations are considered, since a failure would be characterized by instability.

If $\det(H(p)) \neq 0$ and if $L(p)$ is stable, the closed-loop system (S) of transfer function $G(p) = H(p)[I + H(p)]^{-1}$ remains stable if additively perturbed in such a way that [H-74]

$$\lambda_{inf}(I + H(p)) > \lambda_{sup}L(p)$$

where λ_{inf}, λ_{sup} are, respectively, the singular values of lowest and largest norms of $G(p)$ and p belongs to a right half-plane semicircular Nyquist contour extended on the imaginary axis. These singular values are the eigenvalues of $[G^*(p)G(p)]$, where $G^*(p)$ is the conjugate transpose of $G(p)$.

Applying the Nyquist stability criterion [A-51] (right half-plane poles) to the previous inequality, one obtains a test to determine the stability of the perturbed closed-loop system (S).

1.4 Spectral and Phase Signatures

The above concepts, and the procedures described in Sections 2, 3, 4, and 5, remain unchanged if the time-dependent signature $[e(\cdot), s(\cdot), z(\cdot)]$ is made frequency dependent (f replaces t) or phase dependent (φ replaces t).

2. SIGNATURE ANALYSIS

The method of signature analysis for direct analysis of the signals
$e(\cdot)$, $s(\cdot)$, is appropriate if it proves too difficult or time-consuming to determine the frequency responses of (S). It is indispensable for equipment in which operating failures appear as fluctuations with respect to the signature $(e_0(\cdot), s_0(\cdot))$. For example,
in an interlocking gear, mechanical vibrations and sounds must be
measured throughout the operating cycle, especially at the moment
of engagement or disengagement, and must be compared to a prestored
signature.

2.1 Signal Preprocessing

The signals $e(\cdot)$, $s(\cdot)$, being noisy, have to be preprocessed in
a way such that both periodic fluctuations and slow variations related to degradation modes are preserved. See Figure 12-3. To
these signals apply the following operations in batch or in parallel:

(a) Analog or digital filtering; for example, use a Hamming
window (see Section 6.1 of Chapter 1).

(b) Envelope detection, with adjustable cutoff frequencies.
(See Figure 12-4.)

(c) Time averaging (see Chapter 8).

2.2 Signature Compression

In mechanical devices having many closely connected moving
parts, sensors provide measurements resulting from combinations of
component conditions. In signature analysis it is necessary to
eliminate redundancies among various parallel measurements and to
select those measurements best able to characterize the condition
of each part separately for diagnostic purposes.

It is imperative to analyze the autocorrelation and cross-
correlation functions of the various stochastic processes under
study, that is, of the signatures $(e(\cdot),\ s(\cdot))$ and $(e_k(\cdot),\ s_k(\cdot))$
(see Sections 6.4 and 6.6 of Chapter 1).

Autocorrelation and cross-correlation are precisely the foundations of principal components analysis and discriminant analysis,
respectively. Data analysis methods must be implemented in the time

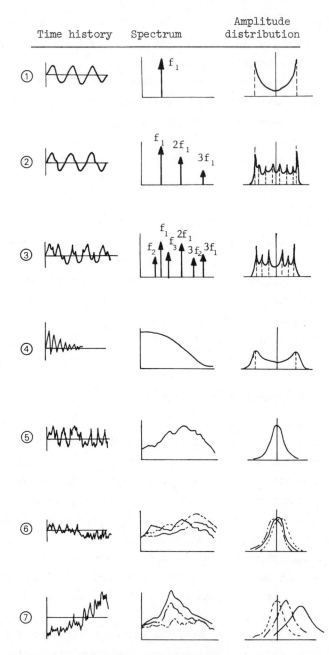

FIGURE 12-3 Classification of time-history signatures.

	Remarks	Possible sources
①	One frequency, synchronous or asynchronous Repeatable	Resonances Unbalance
②	Harmonically related frequencies Repeatable spectrum	Gear noise, fan noise, etc.
③	Mixture of harmonically related and unrelated frequencies Repeatable spectrum Infinite peaks on distributor	Common to rotating machines
④	Decaying sinusoid-type wave	Shock excited vibrations, e.g., piston slap
⑤	No obvious harmonic relationships Repeatable spectrum	Fluid dynamic effects
⑥	Nonrepeatable spectra No distinctive changes taking place	Slight variations in machine load/speed, etc. Measurement errors
⑦	Nonrepeatable spectra Distinctive changes occurring	Indicative of major change taking place, possibly failure

FIGURE 12-3 (Continued)

domain for signals $e(t)$ and $s(t)$ that are assumed to be sampled with a period τ. Define the following:

n_e: Number of coordinates $e_i(t)$ of $e(t)$, $i = 1, \ldots, n_e$

n_s: Number of coordinates $s_i(t)$ of $s(t)$, $i = 1, \ldots, n_s$

n_z: Number of coordinates $z_i(t)$ of $z(t)$, $i = 1, \ldots, n_z$

$z(t)$: Vector of the external operating conditions and/or disturbances applied to (S), $i = 1, \ldots, n_z$; for example, conditions of other systems, surrounding temperature, etc., but also noise; $Z(t)$ is included in the signature of (S)

I: Time samples of $e(t)$, $s(t)$, and $z(t)$ needed for the diagnosis of a single system (S) and describing (S) over the test period of duration $\tau \times \text{Card}(I)$

J: Record of the $n_e + n_s + n_z$ measured values $e(t)$, $s(t)$, $z(t)$

The explicit table $k_s(I,J) \triangleq [e(i\tau), s(i\tau), z(i\tau)]$, $i = 1, \ldots,$ $\text{Card}(I)$, of dimensions $\text{Card}(I) \times \text{Card}(J)$ is obtained by aggregating the vectors representing the signatures of (S) at successive sampling times. The application of an unsupervised data analysis method to this statistical correspondence k_s (Chapters 7 and 8) provides, in a fixed N-dimensional space, $N \leq \inf\{\text{Card}(I), \text{Card}(J)\}$, a representative point i for each sample vector $[e(i\tau), s(i\tau), z(i\tau)]$ of the signature (cf. the equations of Section 2.5 of Chapter 8). The time-ordered sequence of $\text{Card}(I)$ sample vectors will give a sequence of points in an N-dimensional space which is ordered in terms of the sampling times $i\tau$, $i = 1, \ldots, \text{Card}(I)$. When these points are connected in time order, each signature $[e(\cdot), s(\cdot), z(\cdot)]$ of (S) can be represented as a polygonal line pattern vs. time [F-28].

2.3 Line Pattern Classification and Automated Diagnosis [F-28]

After preprocessing, the diagnostic procedure is as follows:

(1) Represent in the N-dimensional space the learning signatures $[e_k(\cdot), s_k(\cdot), z_k(\cdot)]$ by line patterns T_k, $k = 0, \ldots, n - 1$, one for each failure mode E_k.

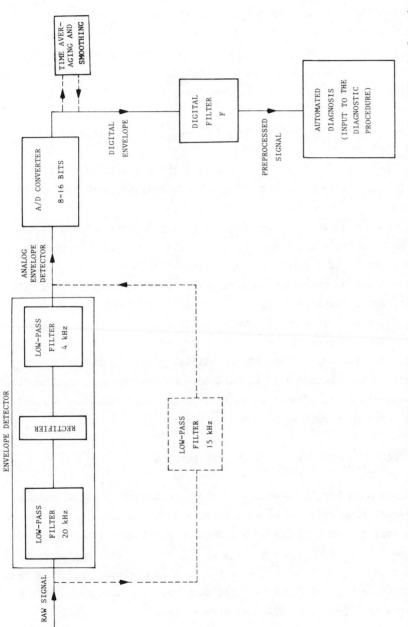

FIGURE 12-4 Preprocessing of signature signals for diagnostic purposes: case of a mechanical system. The envelope detector may be replaced by the 15-kHz low-pass filter; the output of F is an orientated line pattern (see Sections 2.2 and 2.3).

(2) Observe a system (S) to be diagnosed for the duration of a test. Record and preprocess its signature $[e(\cdot),s(\cdot),z(\cdot)]$, and compress these signals in order to represent them in the N-dimensional space of the learning signatures (1) by a line pattern T_S.

(3) Calculate the distances $D(T_S,T_k)$, $k = 0, \ldots, n - 1$, between line patterns; the distance measure D is discussed in Section 3.

(4) Find the failure mode $d(S)$ such that $D(T_S,T_{d(S)}) = \min D(T_S,T_k)$, $k = 0, \ldots, n - 1$.

(5) If $D(T_S,T_{d(S)}) \leq \gamma$, then (S) is in the failure mode $d(S)$. If $D(T_S,T_{d(S)}) > \gamma$, then no diagnosis is possible with high confidence.

γ is a confidence threshold depending on noise, the dimension N, and the desired correct diagnosis rate. To find a compromise value for γ, if a model of (S) is available, Monte Carlo simulation methods can be applied. In particular, the cumulative effect of component tolerances in (S) on the stability of the line patterns T_S, T_k, $k = 0, \ldots, n - 1$, can be studied.

The advantage of the preceding method is that it leads to failure and degradation diagnosis by utilizing fully all signal transients. This method also applies to nonlinear systems if appropriate measurements are selected. In Ref. F-30 , an example of a speed regulator with switching relays is described.

3. DISTANCE MEASURE D BETWEEN LINE PATTERNS
    REPRESENTING SIGNATURES

We have seen how diagnosis by spectral responses or signature-based external diagnosis can be reduced to a classification task based on the computation of a distance D between multidimensional line patterns $T = \{x_i \in \mathbb{R}^N ; i = 1, \ldots, r\}$. T stands for either a transfer locus (N = 2) or a signature of (S) in N dimensions. Defining such a distance D is difficult and has only recently become the object of research [B-17, B-33]. See Figure 12-5.

The definitions of two such distances which will be adequate in a great number of practical cases are given below.

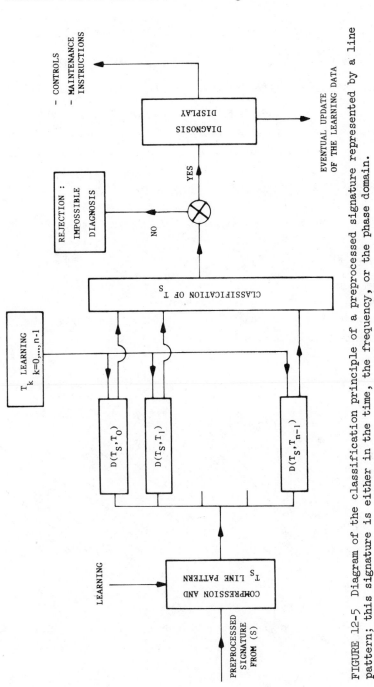

FIGURE 12-5 Diagram of the classification principle of a preprocessed signature represented by a line pattern; this signature is either in the time, the frequency, or the phase domain.

(a) Distance based on the separating surface

$\ell_1 \overset{\Delta}{=}$ length of line pattern T_1 in $\mathbb{R}^N$, with r_1 points

$\ell_2 \overset{\Delta}{=}$ length of line pattern T_2 in $\mathbb{R}^N$, with r_2 points

$S_{12} \overset{\Delta}{=}$ conic surface in $\mathbb{R}^N$ of minimum area bounded by T_1
      on one side, and T_2 on the other

Then

$$D(T_1,T_2) \overset{\Delta}{=} \frac{2S_{12}}{\ell_1 + \ell_2} \qquad (\text{see Figure 12.6})$$

(b) Distance of the mean chord: If $r_1 \leq r_2$, then

$$d(T_1,T_2) = \frac{1}{r_2}\left(\sum_{i=1}^{r_1} \| x_i^1 - x_i^2 \| + \sum_{i=r_1+1}^{r_2} \| x_{r_1}^1 - x_i^2 \| \right)$$

where $\| \cdot \|$ designates the norm used in $\mathbb{R}^N$.

A more general distance measure applying to oriented line patterns is studied in Ref. B-33. See Figure 12-7.

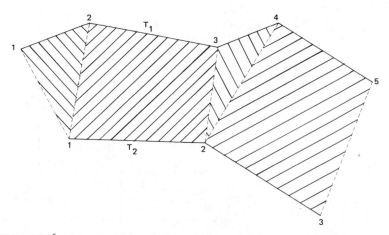

FIGURE 12-6 Computation of the minimum surface S_{12} included between T_1 and T_2 in $\mathbb{R}^2$.

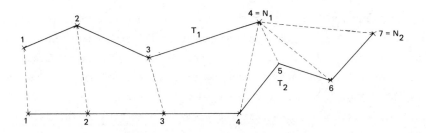

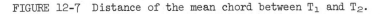

FIGURE 12-7   Distance of the mean chord between T_1 and T_2.

4.   CLASSIFICATION OF RESPONSES s(·) TO TEST SIGNALS e(·)

For systems with signals which are not very noisy and where identical input signals e(·) hold for different failure modes E_k, signature classification is reduced to the classification of the output signal s(·) over time horizons equal to the test window T.   As a matter of fact, we have e(·) = e_k(·) for k = 0, ..., n - 1.

Let $f_i(t)$ be the zero-mean probability density of the measurement $s_i(t)$, i = 1, ..., n_s.   Let us define the following:

$$\epsilon_{ik} \overset{\Delta}{=} d_i(s,s_k) = \frac{1}{T}\{\int_0^T [s_i(t) - s_{ik}(t)]^2 f_i(t) \, dt\}^{1/2}$$

where

$$i = 1, ..., n_s$$
$$k = 0, ..., n - 1$$
$$s \overset{\Delta}{=} (s_1, ..., s_i, ..., s_{n_s})$$
$$s_k \overset{\Delta}{=} (s_{1k}, ..., s_{n_s k})$$

and where ϵ_{ik} is the expected standard deviation between the ith coordinates of s(·) and the signature s_k(·) characterizing failure E_k.   From this, a vector $\bar{e}_k = [\epsilon_{1k}, ..., \epsilon_{n_s k}]$ is obtained for each failure mode E_k, k = 0, ..., n - 1.

The task of diagnosing the system (S) which produced the test output signal s(·) given e(·) is thus reduced to a simple pattern recognition problem. It suffices to apply a decision rule to the vectors $\bar{\epsilon}_k$, resulting in the assignment of (S) into one of the failure classes E_k, k = 0, ..., n - 1 (see Chapter 10). The simplest of these rules consists of deciding that (S) has failure E_c if $\bar{\epsilon}_c$ is the vector $\bar{\epsilon}_k$ which is closest to zero in norm, c = 0, ..., n - 1.

This method applies satisfactorily to electrical circuits and to small mechanical devices which run iteratively with the same control e(·) during relatively short periods of time.

5. ADAPTIVE DEGRADATION DIAGNOSIS VIA
    HISTOGRAMS OF THE FLUCTUATIONS OF THE (e(·),s(·)) SIGNATURES

(a) We assume that catastrophic failures are excluded from the following discussion, and we deal only with those deteriorations of (S) as they may be revealed by fluctuations of the signature (e(·),s(·)) in relation to $(e_0(·),s_0(·))$. Instead of studying the mean value of $(e(·) - e_0(·),s(·) - s_0(·))$, as in Section 4, we diagnose degraded conditions E_k by comparing the statistical distributions of $(e(·) - e_0(·),\ s(·) - s_0(·))$ with known distributions of $(e_k(·) - e_0(·),\ s_k(·) - s_0(·))$ for k = 0, ..., n - 1.

For practical reasons, these signatures are assumed to be quantized at the step size Δx. Consequently, the preceding probability distributions are represented by histograms H^i of the n_s measurement coordinates, i = 1, ..., n_s:

$$\hat{h}_i(x) \overset{\Delta}{=} \text{estimated frequency of a measurement } \epsilon_i(t) = s_i(t) - s_{i0}(t)$$

   belonging to the interval $\delta x \overset{\Delta}{=} [x - \Delta x/2,\ x + \Delta x/2]$,

   i = 1, ..., n_s.

(b) Each such histogram H^i is a polygonal line pattern. For diagnostic purposes, H^i is compared with the line patterns H^i_k, k = 0, ..., n - 1, i = 1, ..., n_s.

However, because H^i and H^i_k are both estimated from finite samples of $\epsilon_i(·)$, it is wrong to compare these line patterns by the procedure outlined in Section 2.3. The correct way of comparing them is to consider confidence bands around each histogram and to

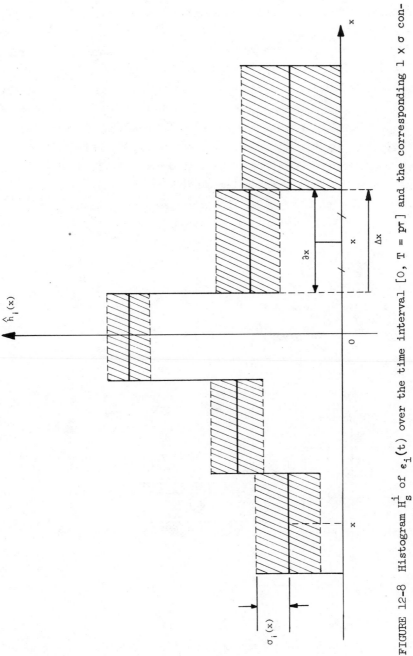

FIGURE 12-8 Histogram H_s^i of $\epsilon_i(t)$ over the time interval $[0, T = pr]$ and the corresponding $1 \times \sigma$ confidence band.

introduce a distance measure between histograms [H-45]. See Figure
12-8.

Let $\sigma_i(x)$ be an estimate of the standard deviation of the esti-
mator $\hat{h}_i(x)$ (see Appendix 3). The confidence band $H_i(x)$ around $\hat{h}_i(\cdot)$
at level 1 x σ is the surface between two lines, each 1 x $\sigma_i(x)$ from
$\hat{h}_i(x)$.

(c) Similarity measure between scalar histograms: Let $h_1(x)$
and $h_2(x)$ be two histograms of the same scalar random variable x
over the time interval [0,pτ] with a step size Δx. We denote by
$H_1(x)$ and $H_2(x)$ the corresponding confidence bands at the level
A x σ. Following Figure 12-9, the similarity d_H between H^1 and H^2
is given by

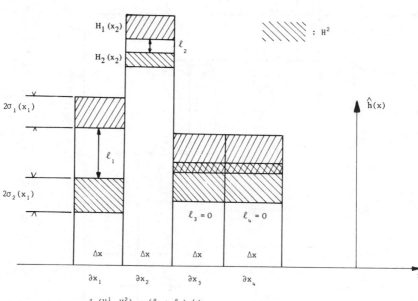

$$d_H(H^1, H^2) = (\ell_1 + \ell_2) / 4$$

FIGURE 12-9 Similarity measure d_H between histograms of a scalar
random variable x.

$$d_H(H^1, H^2) \triangleq \frac{\sum_i \ell_i(H_1(x_i), H_2(x_i))}{\omega_{12}}$$

where

x_i: center of an interval δx_i where at least one of the estimates $h_1(x_i)$, $h_2(x_i)$ is nonzero

ℓ_i: 0 iff $H_1(x_i)$, $H_2(x_i)$ intersect each other in δx_i; if not, ℓ_i is equal to the smallest distance between the closest boundaries of $H_1(x_i)$ and $H_2(x_i)$ in δx_i

ω_{12}: number of intervals of length Δx where at least one of the estimates $h_1(\cdot)$, $h_2(\cdot)$ is nonzero

If one of the frequencies h_1 or h_2 is zero, then ℓ_i is equal to the ordinate of the lower boundary of the nonzero histogram. This rule leads to the comparison of histograms of random variables having different mean values (Figure 12-10).

(d) Similarity measure between n_s-dimensional histograms H: Using the previous definition, we can compute a similarity measure between n_s-dimensional histograms H^1 and H^2 with confidence bands

$$d_s(s_1, s_2) \triangleq \sum_{j=1}^{n_s} r_j d_H(H^{1j}, H^{2j}) \qquad r_j \geq 0 \qquad H^{\ell j} = \text{j-th co-ordinate of } H^\ell$$

where

r_j = nonnegative weighting factor, proportional to the probability of $d_H(H^{1j}, H^{2j})$ being measured correctly

Two processes $s_1(\cdot)$ and $s_2(\cdot)$ are identical at the A x σ confidence level iff $d(s_1, s_2) = 0$.

(e) The resulting diagnostic procedure is then the following:

i. Alarm case: This is the problem of two classes E_0 and E_1. The alarm is sounded as soon as fluctuations of the observed signature $(e(\cdot), s(\cdot))$ produce a line-pattern-histogram H^i moving more than one threshold $\delta^i > 0$ away from H^0, where δ^i is an alarm threshold, $i = 1, \ldots, n_s$.

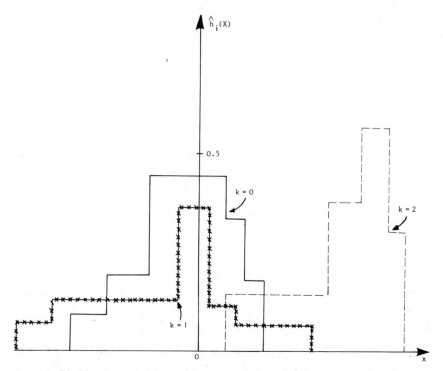

FIGURE 12-10   Degradations diagnosis by comparing an observed histogram of $\epsilon_i(x)$ to learning histograms associated with failure modes
E_k, $k = 0, \ldots, n - 1$.

    ii. Case of deterioration mode diagnosis: Diagnosis is made
through computation of the distances $d_s(s, s_k)$, $k = 0, \ldots, n - 1$.
Classification is achieved by minimization of this quantity over
all possible degradation modes E_k.

    (f) An application to automated quality control of paper pro-
duced by a rotating mill is reported in Ref. H-45.

6. ON-LINE EXTERNAL DIAGNOSIS OF SOME CONTROL SYSTEMS

As shown in Chapter 11, many control systems are such that on-line
diagnosis cannot be carried out without breaking feedback loops

(Chapter 15) or estimation loops (Chapter 14). However, for some special linear systems, external diagnosis is possible in the time domain, provided that the signals are not too noisy. Moreover, external diagnosis is also feasible for a category of nonlinear control systems of low accuracy and having few failure modes.

One of the major difficulties of external diagnosis is to preserve a sufficient stability margin before and also after the failure has been detected (see Section 1.3).

6.1 Special Linear Systems

(a) These special-structure linear control systems are assumed to consist of r single-input/single-output independent filters having transfer functions $H_i(p)$, $i = 1, \ldots, r$, of the following type:

$$H_i(p) = \frac{a_{mi}H^m(p) + \ldots + a_{1i}H(p) + a_{0i}}{b_{mi}H^m(p) + \ldots + b_{1i}H(p) + b_{0i}} \qquad i = 1, \ldots, r$$

$$\det \begin{vmatrix} a_{1i} & a_{0i} \\ b_{1i} & b_{0i} \end{vmatrix} \neq 0$$

This means that all units of the original control system can be obtained by connecting the outputs of modules having the same transfer function $H(p)$. The global control system has n failure modes E_k, $k = 0, \ldots, n - 1$.

(b) The basic structure of the diagnostic system is:

i. To monitor on-line the r inputs $x_i(t)$ and outputs $y_i(t)$ of the r basic units. Laplace transforms are denoted by $X_i(p)$, $Y_i(p)$.

ii. To add to the original control system, for each failure mode E_k, an additional circuit Λ_k combining the r + n measurements $y_i(t)$, $i = 1, \ldots, r$; the output of this is $y_{r+k+1}(t)$.

iii. To carry out the diagnosis using as features n linear combinations Δ_k of $y_i(t)$ and $y_{r+k+1}(t)$, $k = 0, \ldots, n - 1$; the classification logic may range from threshold tests to more elaborate procedures (Chapters 9 and 15).

(c) The n linear combinations Λ_k are defined in the p domain by

$$Y_{r+k+1}(p) = \sum_{i=1}^{r} [\alpha_{0i}^{k} X_i(p) + \beta_{0i}^{k} Y_i(p)]$$

$$+ H(p) \sum_{i=1}^{r} [\alpha_{1i}^{k} X_i(p) + \beta_{1i}^{k} Y_i(p)] + \cdots$$

$$+ H^m(p) \sum_{i=1}^{r} [\alpha_{mi}^{k} X_i(p) + \beta_{mi}^{k} Y_i(p)] \qquad (6.1)$$

In equation (6.1) some of the X_i and Y_i values are equal because of interconnections (the output of one module may be the input to another module).

(d) The n linear combinations Δ_k are defined as follows in the time domain:

$$\Delta_k(t) = \sum_{i=1}^{r+n} d_{ik} y_i(t) \qquad k = 0, \ldots, n - 1$$

where d_{ik} are parameters.

One possible diagnostic system design is to require that all $\Delta_k(t)$ ($k \neq 0$) outputs be identical to zero for any input $x_i(t)$, $i = 1, \ldots, r$, if the linear system is failure-free; the failure mode E_0 corresponds to normal operating conditions. The appearance of a nonzero $\Delta_k(t)$ indicates that the failure mode E_k has appeared in the system:

$$\Delta_k(t) = 0 \qquad \text{failure mode } E_k \text{ absent}$$
$$\Delta_k(t) \neq 0 \qquad \text{failure mode } E_k \text{ present} \qquad (6.2)$$

where $k = 0, \ldots, n - 1$.

The linear circuits Λ_k are designed to satisfy $\Delta_k(t) \equiv 0$ for all possible inputs and no E_k failures:

$$\alpha_{0i}^{k} = -d_{ik} a_{0i} \qquad \beta_{0i}^{k} = d_{ik} b_{0i} - d_{ik}/d_{(r+1)k}$$
$$\alpha_{ji}^{k} = -d_{ik} a_{ji} \qquad \beta_{ji}^{k} = d_{ik} b_{ji} \qquad (6.3)$$

where $i = 1, \ldots, r$, $j = 1, \ldots, m$, and $k = 0, \ldots, n - 1$ and where d_{ik} are given weight factors, optimized in order to fulfill the diagnostic conditions (6.2).

6.2 Example: Third-order Linear Control System

(a) Let us consider the system represented in Figure 12-11 (notice the interconnections):

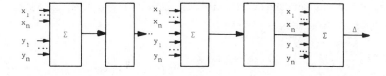

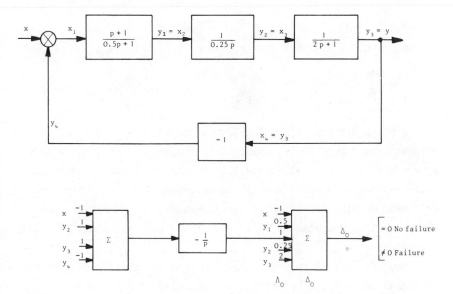

FIGURE 12-11 On-line diagnosis of a third-order linear control system.

$$H_1(p) = \frac{p+1}{0.5p+1} = \frac{Y_1}{X_1} \qquad H_2(p) = \frac{1}{0.25p} = \frac{Y_2}{X_2} \; .$$

$$H_3(p) = \frac{1}{2p+1} = \frac{Y_3}{X_3} \qquad H_4(p) = -1 = \frac{Y_4}{X_4} \qquad H_0(p) = \frac{1}{p}$$

Input: x or X(p)

Output: $y = y_3$ or $Y_3(p)$

(b) For failure detection (n = 2), we introduce the no-failure detection condition:

$$\Delta_0(t) = y_1(t) + y_2(t) + y_3(t) + y_4(t) + y_5(t) = 0 \qquad (6.4)$$

The equation for the auxiliary signal $y_5(t)$ provided by Λ_0 is sought in the form (6.1):

$$Y_5 = \sum_{i=1}^{4} (\alpha_{0i}X_i + \beta_{0i}Y_i) + \frac{1}{p} \sum_{i=1}^{4} (\alpha_{1i}X_i + \beta_{1i}Y_i) \qquad (6.5)$$

The equation $\Delta_0(t) = 0$ will be satisfied identically iff [equation (6.3)]

$$\alpha_{01} = -1 \qquad a_{02} = \alpha_{03} = 0 \qquad \alpha_{04} = 1$$

$$\beta_{01} = 0.5 - 1 = -0.5 \qquad \beta_{02} = -0.75 \qquad \beta_{03} = 1 \qquad \beta_{04} = 0$$

$$\alpha_{11} = \alpha_{12} = \alpha_{13} = -1 \qquad \alpha_{14} = 0$$

$$\beta_{11} = \beta_{13} = 1 \qquad \beta_{12} = \beta_{14} = 0$$

A block diagram of the Λ_0 circuit providing y_5 and of Δ_0 is presented in Figure 12-11, taking into account $x_1 = x + y_4$, $x_2 = y_1$, $x_3 = y_2$, $x_4 = y_3$. If all units of the original control system are failure-free, then $\Delta_0(t)$ must be zero for any input x(t) and any mode of operation (transient or steady state). A failure in the system will be detected by $\Delta_0(t) \neq 0$ if the test threshold is fairly noise-insensitive.

(c) For actual failure diagnosis (n > 2), it is necessary to introduce other Λ_k, Δ_k circuits; for example, if k = 1 and

$$\Delta_1(t) = y_1(t) + 2y_2(t) + 3y_3(t) + 4y_4(t) + y_6(t)$$

then one can show that failure localization of the failed module
(four possible failures) can be achieved by linear classification
(Chapter 7) of the two-dimensional $[\Delta_0(t), \Delta_1(t)]$ vector.   ∎

6.3 Linear Closed-loop Control Systems (S)

(a) Assume that the actual system (S) can be represented by
the following linear model (see Section 5 of Chapter 1):
System (S):

    i.   State equation: $\dot{x}_S(t) = A_S(t)x_S(t) + B_S(t)u(t) + v_S(t)$

    ii. Observed equation: $y_S(t) = C_S x_S(t) + w_S(t)$

    iii. Control: $u(t)$

    iv. Noises: $v_S(t)$, $w_S(t)$

Using a monitoring control system of similar nature to (S), we
want first to extract signatures accounting for the closed-loop
structure that are efficient for failure mode detection and next to
apply one of the previous external diagnosis procedures to these
signatures. The state of this monitoring system is $x(t)$, and the
control $u(t)$ is the same as for (S).

(b) The idea is to have a linear feedback [with gain $D(t)$] of
the modeling error signal or measurement residual,

$$\varepsilon(t) \triangleq y(t) - y_S(t)$$

into the state equation for $x(t)$. The output of this feedback loop
is interpreted as a perturbation of the monitoring control action
$B(t)u(t)$ (see Figure 12-12):
Monitoring:

    i.   State equation: $\dot{x}(t) = A(t)x(t) + B(t)u(t) + D(t)\varepsilon(t)$

    ii. Observation equation: $y(t) = Cx(t)$

    iii. Control: $u(t)$

Within this framework,

    i. An autonomous system failure corresponds to a change
$\Delta A_S(t)$.

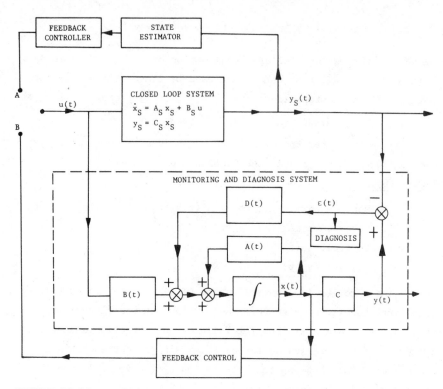

FIGURE 12-12 On-line external failure diagnosis of a closed-loop
system with associated monitoring and diagnosis system. The feedback control u(t) can be provided: case A: either using a separate
state estimator on the actual system (S); case B: or using the
state estimator from the monitoring system [x(t) accessible].

   ii. An actuator failure corresponds to a change $\Delta B_S(t)$.

   iii. A sensor failure corresponds to a change $\Delta C_S(t)$.

   iv. A failure in the control loop $u(t) = F[x_S(t)]$ corresponds
to a change in F.

   v. A failure in the diagnosis and monitoring system, which
is assumed to be more reliable than (S), corresponds to $\Delta A(t)$,
$\Delta B(t)$, ΔC, and $\Delta D(t)$.

   (c) When designing the on-line failure diagnosis system, one
must select D(t) to meet the following objectives:

i. Freedom in controlling the stability margin of (S) with respect to $A_S(t)$ and C_S and preserving the observability and controllability of (S) (see Section 1.3)

ii. Freedom in assigning the eigenvalues of $[A(t) - D(t)C]$, which will characterize the stability of the monitoring system

iii. Any single catastrophic failure of the type mentioned (except failures of the monitoring system) should correspond to well-discriminated changes in different sets of coordinates of $\epsilon(t)$, or in linear combinations of these coordinates (the signatures)

In the deterministic case it can be shown that

$$\dot{\epsilon}(t) = C[A(t) - D(t)C]x(t) + [CD(t)C_S - C_S A_S(t)]x_S(t)$$
$$+ [CB(t) - C_S B_S(t)]u(t)$$

The failure diagnosis unit thus monitors and computes the signatures $\epsilon(t)$ and applies a decision procedure to these measurements, e.g., a threshold comparison or a discriminant function classification. The equation for $\dot{\epsilon}(t)$ shows that the diagnostic performances can be strongly affected by modeling errors, noise, and feedback structure.

If requirement iii cannot be achieved with a single D feedback, then several monitoring systems can be used in parallel with different D's.

(d) It is usually advantageous to select all eigenvalues close to the imaginary axis. This makes (S) and the failure diagnosis slower but also gives lower feedback gains, which is desirable with respect to actuator failures.

As soon as a failure is detected, the feedback gains should be changed in order to maintain, if possible, the prescribed eigenvalues of the closed-loop system. This requires that the system be completely controllable after the failure modifies $D(t)$. In the event of a sensor failure, $D(t)$ should be modified to ensure separation of the new eigenvalues.

(e) There have been a number of successful aerospace applications of this design (analog signals).

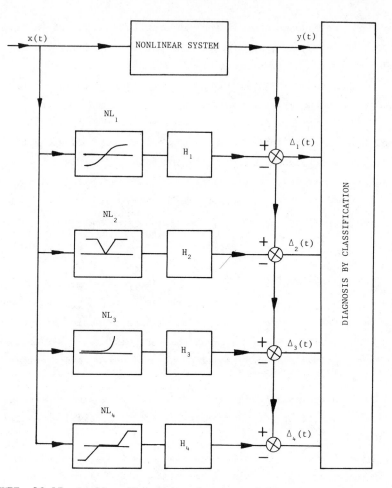

FIGURE   12-13   On-line diagnosis of some nonlinear systems.

6.4 Nonlinear Control Systems

We shall restrict ourselves to those systems having failure modes E_k which can be modeled by an adjustable nonlinear part NL_k (including a saturation) followed by a linear transfer function $H_k(p)$.

Denote by $\Delta_k(t)$ the difference between the output of the actual control system and a model of this system in the failed condition E_k. The final diagnosis is carried out using $\Delta_k(t)$, $k = 0, \ldots, n - 1$, as features.

The differences between failure modes E_k can be accounted for
to some extent by varying the type of nonlinear elements NL_k involved (see a list in Ref. B-28). See Figure 12-13.

7. DIAGNOSIS OF CONTROL SYSTEM CONDITION BY A BENCH OF PARALLEL MULTIVARIABLE OBSERVERS OR FILTERS

In Section 6.3, we considered a linear control system with a mis-
matched monitoring and diagnosis system operating on the measurement residuals $\epsilon(t)$. In Chapter 15, it will be indicated how a
recursive estimation of the system state $x_S(t)$ may lead to failure
diagnosis, although dual variables are more efficient features.

The use of multivariable observers or filters consists first
in convolving in parallel the system output $y_S(t) = s(t)$ with one
observer/filter for each possible condition E_k, $k = 0, \ldots, n - 1$,
of the system (S), and next in making a diagnostic decision from the
n corresponding estimated states $\hat{x}_k(t)$ as defined below. Let $H_k(p)$
be the transfer functions of the system and $F_k(p)$, $k = 0, \ldots, n - 1$,
the transfer functions of these observers/filters; then

$$\hat{X}(p) \triangleq F_k(p)Y_S(p) \qquad k = 0, \ldots, n - 1$$

These estimated states $\hat{x}_k(t)$ are in fact generalized features replacing $\epsilon(t)$.

Failure diagnosis is carried out by one of the following techniques:

i.   Decision thresholds on $\hat{x}_k(t)$ (see Chapter 15)

ii. Voting among some of all these $\hat{x}_k(t)$

iii. Merging all or some of the vectors $\hat{x}_k(t)$ into one feature
vector, to be classified as indicated in Chapter 10

The advantages of this method are well known from signal processing, where it is called a vocoder setup [A-8, A-31]. The flex-
ibility comes from degrees of freedom in selecting $F_k(p)$; the dis-
advantages come from the fact that not all conditions E_k, $k = 0,
\ldots, n - 1$, guarantee a stable and robust observer design; the
reader is referred to the literature on Luenberger observer design

[A-50, A-52]. One of the specific difficulties is to optimize the
observers for high sensitivity for some crucial condition-dependent
parameters while preserving their stability, minimizing the false
alarm rate, and maximizing the signal/noise ratio in case of failure
[F-64, F-70].

8. DIAGNOSIS IN A NOISY CONTROL SYSTEM
    WITH SENSOR FAILURES

   (a) So far, we have dealt only with deterministic control
systems; noise and stochastic perturbations are, however, very important. One procedure, applying to sensor failures or changes in
the observation equation, will be described in this section; other
aspects are presented in Chapter 15.

   Assume the observation equation to be (see Section 6.3)

$$y_s(t) = C_s x_s(t) + w_s(t) + a_k b \qquad (8.1)$$

where:

$\dim y_s = \dim a \triangleq m$

w_s: gaussian noise of mean 0 and covariance R

b: unknown scalar quantity

$a_k \triangleq [0 \ \ldots \ 0 \ 1 \ 0 \ \ldots \ 0]$, $k = 0, \ldots, n - 1$, the 1 being
              in position k

v_j: vector such that ${}^t v_j \cdot C_s = 0$, $j = 0, \ldots, n - 1$;
              $v_j \triangleq (v_{j\ell}, \ \ell = 1, \ldots, m)$; v_j is given; $v_{\cdot\ell} \triangleq (v_{j\ell}, j = 0, \ldots, n - 1)$

This observation equation model assumes that failures, including
sensor failures, occur by a jump of magnitude b in one of the coordinates of y_s, selected by a_k in terms of the actual failure mode
E_k, $k = 0, \ldots, n - 1$.

   These bias shifts in $y_s(t)$ are best measured in certain directions in the measurement space; we therefore introduce, for each
possible failure mode E_j, a detection statistic $p_j(y_s)$, obtained by
weighting by v_j the residual in (8.1):

$$p_j(y_s) \triangleq {}^t v_j(y_s - C_s x_s) = {}^t v_j w_s + v_{jk} b \qquad (8.2)$$

The distribution of $p_j(y_s)$ is consequently gaussian, with mean $v_{jk}b$ and covariance ${}^tv_j Rv_j$.

(b) A failure in the observation system may thus be detected by shifts of the mean of $p_j(y_s)$; thus, if b and E_k were known, the detection rule would be

$$E_0: \qquad E(p(y_s)) = 0 \qquad\qquad E(p^tp) = v^tv$$

$$E_1: \qquad E(p(y_s)) = bv_{\bullet k} \qquad\qquad Var(p(y_s)) = v^tv$$

where

$$V \triangleq ({}^tv_j,\ j = 0,\ \ldots,\ n-1) \qquad p \triangleq (p_j,\ j = 0,\ \ldots,\ n-1)$$

(c) The jump b must however be estimated, conditionally on the actual failure mode E_k:

$$\hat{b} = \frac{{}^tp(v^tv)^{-1}v_k}{{}^tv_k(v^tv)^{-1}v_k}$$

Consequently, the simple detection procedure (b), which assumed b to be known, must be replaced by the following:

$$DF_k \triangleq \frac{[{}^tp(v^tv)^{-1}v_k]^2}{{}^tv_k(v^tv)^{-1}v_k}$$

$$E_0: \ DF_0 > c_0$$
$$E_k: \ DF_k > c_k \qquad\qquad c_k \text{ threshold } k = 0,\ \ldots,\ n-1$$

The distribution of DF_k is approximately χ^2.

(d) Further analysis shows that good performances of the procedure (c) depend critically on:

i. The rank of V, for invertibility of v^tv, and also for discrimination among failure modes; (n - 3) rows of V must be linearly independent

ii. The conditional mean of DF_k versus E_k, which must be large. A good choice for V, and thus the v_k's, which fulfills these two requirements, is such that

$${}^tVV = I - c_s({}^tc_sc_s)^{-1\,t}c_s$$

9. APPLICATIONS

9.1 Impact Analysis

Signature analysis is carried out for diagnostic purposes in systems with mechanical impacts, where system movements are recorded both geometrically, optically, and acoustically. See for example Ref. F-14 : a computer card puncher unit [F-19].

9.2 Land Vehicle Engine Failures

Signature analysis implementation is beginning on trucks and tanks, where the signatures are vibratory, acoustical (including ultrasonic), or magnetic (by magnetometers based on the Hall effect). This is also a method for evaluating the overall condition of a motor before operational service. Research in this field has mainly dealt with the choice of measurements and sensor improvements, especially for moving parts. The failure modes studied are bearing breakdowns, piston breakdowns, faulty combustion, and fuel flow troubles. Correct diagnosis rates reach a level of 80%. See Figure 12-14.

9.3 Airborne Equipment and Actuators

Signature analysis also applies to the simpler parts of airborne equipment and actuators, especially those which are predominantly mechanical. It should be stressed that the important thing is to possess learning signatures $(e_k(\cdot), s_k(\cdot))$ $(k = 0, \ldots, n - 1)$ for each main flight configuration and to suppress noise.

9.4 Electronic Systems

Contrary to popular opinion, it is possible to perform external diagnosis on electronic systems if measurements are appropriately selected. However, if we restrict ourselves to measuring only the input and output voltages and dynamics of an amplifier with counter-reaction, diagnosis and especially failure detection in this amplifier proves to be practically impossible. The rate of counterreaction must also be measured to predict the failure that occurs when feedback can no longer compensate for circuit drift.

9.5 Ball Bearings and Pinions

Acoustical (generally ultrasonic, as well as vibrations pro-

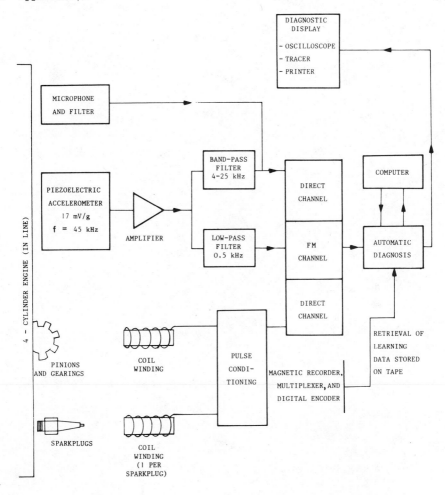

FIGURE 12-14 Instrumentation and sensors for the testing and diagnosis of a tank engine.

duced by a bearing in operation) signatures are analyzed by means of directional sensors. Deterioration/fatigue modes are wear of bearings, wear of a ball race, insufficient lubrication, etc. Major applications concern cyclical machines, gear bearings, radar scanners, compressor valves, and hydraulic pumps [F-18].

9.6 Tracking Systems

Signature analysis as evolved in Section 6 for feedback systems has been found to be useful.

Chapter 13

ACOUSTIC AND VIBRATION MONITORING

Our purpose in this chapter is to give a short introduction to those methods of sound and vibration analysis which are well suited for performance monitoring and hardware realization. The focus is on connections to failure diagnosis, rather than on a detailed presentation of the properties of the signal processing techniques involved. Many of the quantities that are defined can be considered as features in an automated diagnostic system for which signature analysis applies (as defined in Chapter 12). All the monitoring procedures described use external or remote transducers, although their locations are not always essential.

1. TIME DOMAIN AVERAGING FOR QUASI-PERIODIC SIGNALS

1.1 Signal Detection

(a) In many applications involving rotating machinery, a major problem that must be solved prior to further vibration analysis is the extraction of the signal from noise. The time domain signal averaging technique consists of synchronously adding up a number of signal records.

Assume that the period T of the signal to be extracted is known and that this signal $s(t)$ consists of the sum of a periodic signal $f(t)$ and additive noise (assumed to be uncorrelated):

$$s(t) = f(t) + n(t) \qquad (1.1)$$

When summing the subsequent s measurements, each one period T apart, the repetitive signal f will add up coherently and the noise uncoherently. After N summations we get the rms value:

$$s(t_i) = Nf(t_i) + \sqrt{N}\, n(t_i) \qquad t_i \in [0,T] \qquad\qquad (1.2)$$

and the signal/noise ratio is enhanced by a factor $\sqrt{N}$.

(b) This can be generalized to quasi-periodic signals by decomposing $f(t)$ into a mixture of k periodic (not necessarily harmonic) components:

$$s(t) = \sum_{\ell=1}^{k} f_\ell(t) + n(t)$$

where each f_ℓ is periodic of period T_ℓ. Averaging over periods of each type yields the rms value of each component, with a formula similar to (1.2).

The signal to be averaged $s(t)$ is digitized at the rate $\tau < \inf(T_\ell)$, resulting in samples $s(n\tau)$. If $m_\ell \tau = N_\ell T_\ell$ is the averaging period for the component ℓ, $\ell = 1, \ldots, k$, the average signal becomes

$$y_\ell(n\tau) = \frac{1}{N_\ell} \sum_{j=0}^{N_\ell - 1} s\left(n\tau - \frac{jm_\ell \tau}{N_\ell} \right) \qquad \ell = 1, \ldots, k \qquad (1.3)$$

This decomposition procedure is extremely useful when one is interested in separately monitoring different periodic signals of which the measurement $s(t)$ is only a mixture. Each component may then be designed in order to characterize one type of malfunction or one source at the time.

Example

i. In a gear train, one may define (a) malfunction of period T_1 = imbalance of the first shaft, (b) malfunction of period T_2 = imbalance of the second shaft, and (c) malfunction of period T_3 = roller bearing period.

ii. See Figure 13-1 for an aircraft engine example. ∎

(c) $y(n\tau)$ can be computed recursively:

$$y(n\tau) = y((n-1)\tau) + \frac{s(n\tau) - y((n-1)\tau)}{n}$$

An approximate $\tilde{y}$, leading to an exponentially time-weighted average, is obtained by replacing n (variable) by M (fixed):

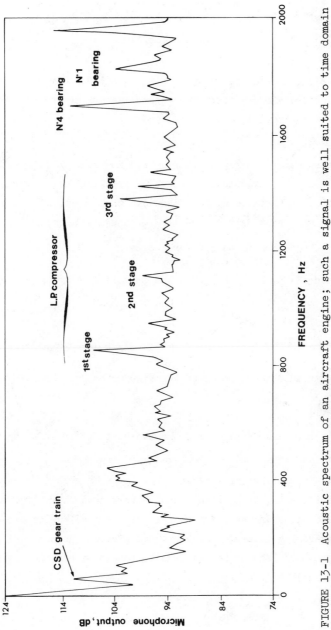
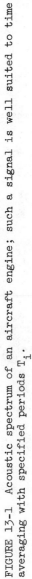

FIGURE 13-1 Acoustic spectrum of an aircraft engine; such a signal is well suited to time domain averaging with specified periods T_i.

$$\tilde{y}(n\tau) = \tilde{y}((n-1)\tau) + \frac{s(n\tau) - \tilde{y}((n-1)\tau)}{M}$$

$$\tilde{y}(n\tau) \# \frac{1}{M} \sum_{k=1}^{n} s(k\tau) \exp\left[\frac{-(n-k)}{M}\right]$$

Thus $\tilde{y}$ can be computed by an N-path analog or hybrid filter with track and store units. The generalization to the case of k components is trivial.

1.2 Rejection of Broadband Noise n

The number of averagings N required in order to reduce the noise $n(t)$ can be drastically reduced by prefiltering, since there is no sense in having a higher bandwidth than that dictated by the highest significant harmonic of $1/T$ for diagnostic purposes.

1.3 Rejection of Narrow Band Noise n
       and of Harmonic Signals

Braun [H-23, H-24] suggests the following:

$$N > \frac{\alpha}{\pi^2 F}$$

where

$\alpha \overset{\Delta}{=}$ attenuation imposed on the side lobes due to an interfering
signal at frequency φ

$F \overset{\Delta}{=} T\varphi$

This rule also applies for the rejection of interfering periodic signals.

1.4 Triggering Error Effect

Occasionally, triggering signal errors may occur. The main consequence is a decrease in the recovered signal due to mistuning of the averaging filter. The extracted signal (including all M first harmonics) should be required to remain within the bandwidth of the main lobe; thus,

$$T\varphi < \frac{0.45}{NM}$$

The triggering error is $\varphi - 1/T$. Jitter can be considered as a time-varying triggering error, depending on the correlation between the signal and the random jitter.

1.5 Use of the Phase After Time Domain Averaging

It is important to point out that, besides the rms levels computed by (1.3), the time-domain-averaged phase values are equally important for diagnostic purposes.

2. CEPSTRUM TECHNIQUES AND HOMOMORPHIC FILTERING

Cepstrum techniques are appropriate for a variety of diagnostic purposes, because of source separation properties. The critical issue is the noise level, which ought to be moderate.

2.1 Cepstrum Definition

(a) The cepstrum $Q(\tau)$ is defined to be the power spectrum of the logarithm of the power spectrum of the periodic signal $s(t)$ (of period T):

$$Q(\tau) = \left| \mathcal{F}\{\ln|S(f)|2)\right|^2 \qquad \text{in } (dB)^2 \text{ if } |S(f)| \text{ is in dB}$$

$$|S(f)|2 = 2\left| \int_0^T w(t)s(t) \exp(-2\pi jft) \, dt \right|^2 \tag{2.1}$$

where $w(t)$ is a symmetrical weighting function tapering to zero at each end in order to minimize the effects due to triggering errors (i.e., the Hamming window of Section 6.1 of Chapter 1).

(b) The quefrequency τ is the independent variable of the cepstrum and has the dimension of time, as in the case of autocorrelation. The quefrequency (in seconds) is the reciprocal of the frequency spacing (in hertz) of the original frequency spectrum $S(f)$ of a particular periodic component. Just as the frequency in a normal spectrum says nothing about absolute time but only about repeated time intervals, the quefrequency only gives information about frequency spacings and not about absolute frequency.

(c) The importance of $Q(\tau)$ in vibration monitoring is the ability of the logarithm to separate transfer functions that are multiplied in the frequency domain; this property is also called homomorphic filtering. If

$$|S(f)| = |H(f)||N(f)|$$

where

        $N(f)$ = source spectrum of the input to the system (transmitting path)

        $H(f)$ = spectrum of the impulse response of the system itself

then

$$\ln|S(f)|^2 = \ln|H(f)|^2 + \ln|N(f)|^2$$

and the effects of the source and of the system are separated.

As a consequence,

1. The cepstrum is only valuable when the interesting spectral rays of the source and of the system are well separated.

2. The amplitudes of the harmonic components in the cepstrum are in theory independent of the system transfer function $H(f)$ and thus independent of the location where the measurements are made.

3. The cepstrum is very sensitive to the relative rms value of the noise [included in $N(f)$]; noise should be filtered via the weighting function $w(t)$.

4. A linear cepstrum scale should be used to separate cepstral harmonics, rather than a scale in dB.

(d) The difficulties related to cepstrum computation are the following:

i. The width of the time window necessary for the spectrum computation: if it is too small, then the amplitudes of the cepstral rays become too small.

ii. The filtering function $w(t)$.

iii. It is impostant to initiate the signal records at the beginning of a period corresponding to the fundamental frequency in the quasi-periodic signal $s(t)$.

See Figures 13-2 and 13-3.

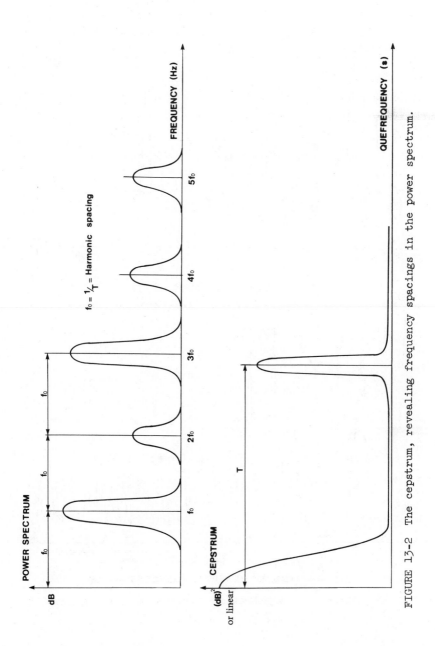

FIGURE 13-2 The cepstrum, revealing frequency spacings in the power spectrum.

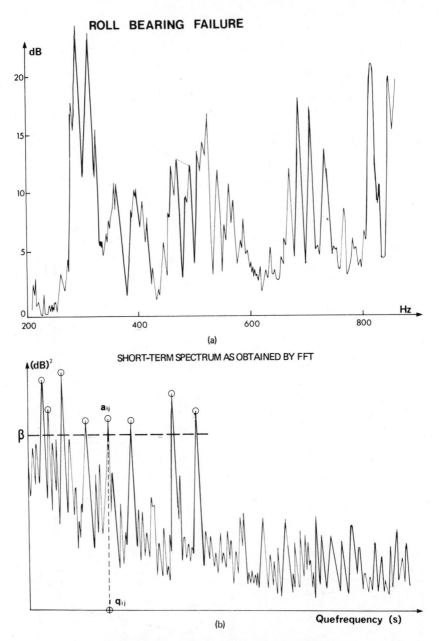

FIGURE 13-3 Example of a vibration spectrum and its cepstrum.

2.2 Application to Engine Monitoring

By using a microphone as sensor, the main cepstral ray generally gives a reliable indication of the engine firing rate, provided the low frequencies are filtered out. This holds even if the engine sound is deeply embedded in noise. Finding the peak of the ray involves thresholding problems, especially if it is low; the threshold can be set at a specified fraction of the highest cepstral ray over the whole working range.

Monitoring the engine firing rate is useful for vehicle classification [H-30]. It is also useful for diagnostic purposes because (in multicylinder engines) uneven pressure increases in the various cylinders can cause the overall waveform to be periodic at a subharmonic of the firing rate. These applications are feasible due to the following experimental findings which are based on the acoustic monitoring of a number of trucks, buses, and cars while driving at speeds from 0 to 80 km/hr [H-31]:

(a) The shape of spectral distributions is approximately independent of the driving speed over the 60- to 4000-Hz range; it depends only on the driving conditions and the angles between the microphone lobe axis and the wheels.

(b) The variance of the fluctuations in the acoustic level perceived is highly dependent on driving speed: small variance in idle position and at high speeds, large variance between.

2.3 Application to Gearbox Monitoring or Testing

In gearbox vibration analysis, a number of geometric faults tend to amplitude-modulate the tooth meshing frequency (i.e., tooth spacing errors), giving rise to sidebands in the frequency spectrum, spaced at multiples of the modulating frequencies (see Section 6.3 of Chapter 1 and Figure 1-4). It is possible for the cepstrum to detect sideband growth; by virtue of the logarithmic conversion, more weight can be given to low-level components. This is advantageous when the existence of periodicity and the modulating frequency must be determined (see Ref. H-27). However, for the separation of cepstral harmonics in assemblies and when frequency modulation is analyzed, a linear scale should be used.

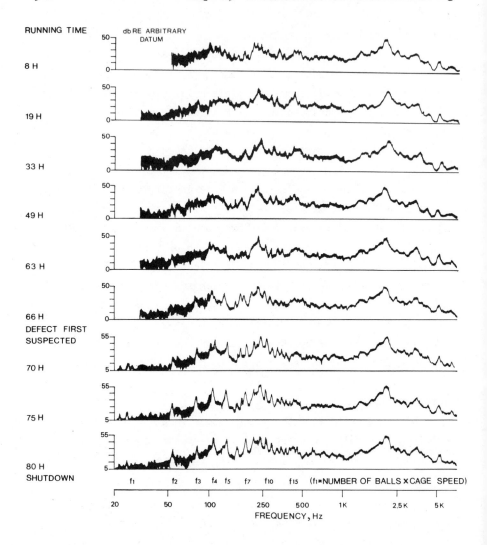

FIGURE 13-4   Variation of noise spectrum with time for Hoffman ball bearings running under heavy thrust and journal loads.

Frequency modulation appears in the case of noninvolutive action, because the mesh forces produce nonsinusoidal vibrations which appear as a proliferation of harmonics and sidebands.   These noninvolutive teeth are due to variations in the mesh teeth elasticity.

2.4 Application to Turbine Monitoring

Cepstrum techniques are very powerful for anomaly detection in turbine blades (rays and deformations of the profile). Figure 13-5 shows the spectrum of a failed turbine; it is obvious that the failure could be detected more easily by using the cepstrum.

2.5 Tracking Cepstral Rays for On-line Diagnosis [H-28]

(a) Assume that the cepstrum $Q_i(\tau)$ is obtained from the short-term power spectrum $S_i(f)$, estimated from the record of the signal $s(t)$ over the period $[t_i, t_{i+1})$.

The cepstral rays (q_{ij}, a_{ij}) of Q_i are defined as those que-frequencies q_{ij} corresponding to the jth highest peak in Q_i such that

$$a_{ij} = Q_i(q_{ij}) \geq \beta \tag{2.2}$$

where β is a fixed threshold (see Figure 13-3).

(b) If the system condition is modified or if the working conditions change, then the vectors $X_i \triangleq (q_{i1}, \ldots, q_{im})$ and $A_i \triangleq (a_{i1}, \ldots, a_{ip})$ will change. To distinguish between these two main reasons for X_i and A_i changes, we assume that a model F is given which relates X_i to the actual controls U_i applied (with proper consideration for delays) under normal system conditions. F can be determined by a suitable identification method (see Chapter 14) but is usually a consequence of the equations governing relations among the various parts of the equipment. In this way, we restrict the diagnostic process to the examination of the deviations:

$$DX_i \triangleq X_i - F(U_i) \tag{2.3}$$

Rather than X_i, DX_i only represents the changes of the internal condition; changing working conditions are determined by U_i.

(c) Suppose that the equipment condition can be classified into n mutually exclusive classes E_k, k = 0, ..., n - 1. Each of

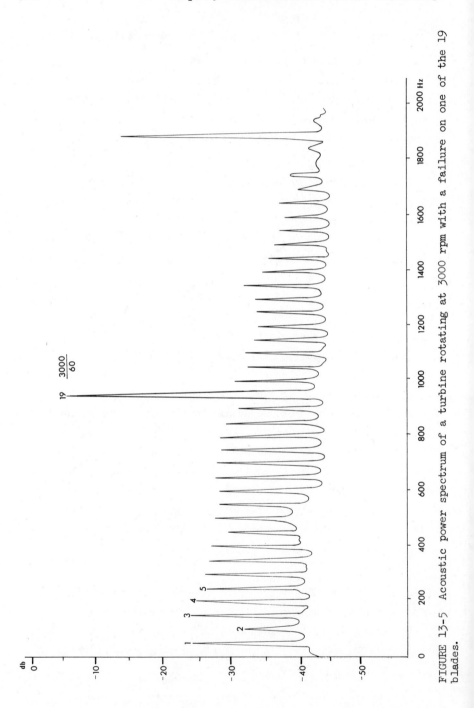

FIGURE 13-5 Acoustic power spectrum of a turbine rotating at 3000 rpm with a failure on one of the 19 blades.

these is defined on the basis of operational specifications of the equipment by standards and a priori measured condition parameters.

Assume that a number of learning or reference signatures (DX^k, A^k) are used for each such condition E_k (see Figure 13-4).

By using classification procedures such as those described in Chapters 10 and 12, it becomes possible to classify any observed vector (DX_i, A_i) in one of these n condition classes at the end of each signal record i. To obtain reasonable probabilities for correct diagnosis, n should be limited to n < 10 in most practical applications.

(d) The false alarm rates observed in practice using the preceding procedure tend to be lower than those where alarms are solely based on threshold detection, because it uses multidimensional features (DX_i, A_i). The classification procedure may compensate for the excessive deviations of one cepstral ray w.r.t. other rays.

2.6 Examples of On-line Diagnosis
via Cepstral Ray Tracking

Cepstral tracking and diagnosis are best suited for equipment having several interrelated moving parts, each with specific eigen-frequencies that are well separated.

For monitoring applications, it is not always possible to attain sufficient reproducibility of the learning signatures (DX^k, A^k); this may inhibit classification accuracy. Others may then contribute to better diagnostic performance. The same remark holds if there is a need for better failure localization; for example, an increase in the sound level and cepstral amplitudes a_{ij} at the load side of a bearing indicates a worn bearing, whereas an increase away from the load indicates wear or damage of the bearing race [F-18].

In the case of gearboxes, the control-dependent correction (2.3) mainly represents changes in the rotation speeds and tooth mesh frequencies vs. the actual driving speed.

The main applications of the procedure of Section 2.5 are the following:

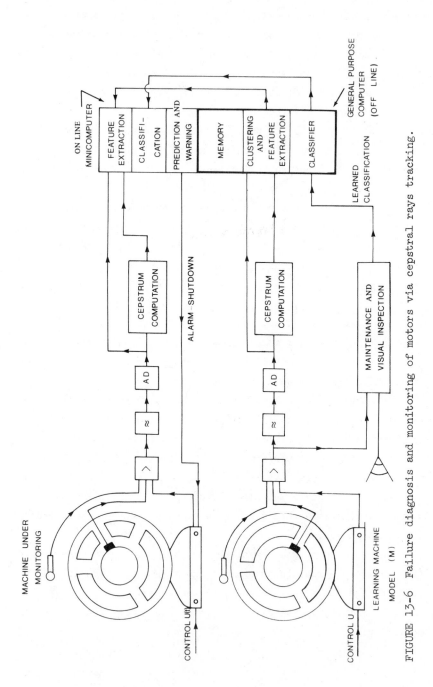

FIGURE 13-6 Failure diagnosis and monitoring of motors via cepstral rays tracking.

     i. Remotely controlled gearboxes [H-28]

    ii. Thermal turbomachines [H-28], with variations of the turbine blade eigenfrequencies and of the leading edge pressure

    iii. Engine monitoring (vehicles, submarines) (see Figures 13-4 and 13-6)

    iv. Fatigue in machinery and general deterioration (scuffing)

    v. Misalignment in power transmission systems

    vi. Speed converters

    vii. Generators

3. NARROW BAND ANALYSIS

Narrow band analysis is used mostly for fault localization in complex machinery via time-dependent variations or transients of natural frequency rms levels. The basic sensor is an accelerometer clamped to the assembly housing, tuned into a frequency window $[f_0 - \Delta f/2, f_0 + \Delta f/2]$, where f_0 is the natural mode. The accelerometer output $s(t,f)$ is filtered and eventually time-averaged:

$$\mu(t) = \int_{f_0 - \Delta f/2}^{f_0 + \Delta f/2} s^2(f,t)\, df$$

$$\bar{\mu} = \frac{1}{T} \int_0^T \int_{f_0 - \Delta f/2}^{f_0 + \Delta f/2} s^2(f,t)\, df\, dt$$

The filter-accelerometer can be replaced by a resonant transducer.

    3.1 Narrow Band Monitoring

    (a) The idea is to apply signal classification to the time-dependent feature $\mu(t)$ either by classifying each sampled value (see Chapter 10) or by adaptive classification (see Chapter 15).

    (b) Another approach, which is a variant of the preceding, is to encode $\mu(t)$ and then correlate the resulting binary signal $\mu c(t)$ with prestored attributes over sliding time horizons τ. This generalizes the concept of zero-crossing encoding to a band-crossing encoding scheme (see Figure 13-7).

3.2 Shock Pulse Monitoring

Damage or wear in a moving mechanical assembly initially takes
the form of surface irregularities; as a result, the relative movements of the pieces become irregular, and impacts may occur. Each
irregularity or impact causes a small conversion of kinetic energy
in a very short period of time, also called shock pulse. Spectral
analysis of shock pulses shows that, in general, they contain energy
over all frequencies from zero to infinity and that their spectrums
are continuous with no discrete frequency components. By measuring
the shock amplitude via narrow band analysis at a frequency f_0 well
above the normal range of machine component resonances, it is sometimes possible to gauge the condition of the dynamic assembly in a
manner that is independent of the structure on which it is mounted.
By the definition of $\mu(t)$, the amplitude of the pulse corresponds
to the rms energy content of that transient.

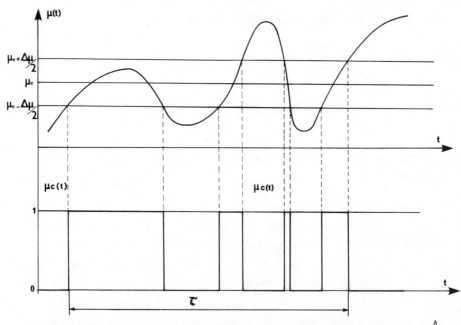

FIGURE 13-7 Narrow band monitoring by band-crossing encoding; $\mu_0 \overset{\Delta}{=}$
$E(\mu(t))$.

These pulses can then be converted to logarithms in order to
achieve a large dynamic range and be passed to a peak value detector
(Figure 13-8). The peak amplitude µp(t) is then displayed and trans-
ferred to a classification procedure. For most applications, a
knowledge of this peak value (sometimes called shock pulse reading
or SPR) is sufficient to detect a defect in the assembly. With a
little experience in classification, it is possible to indicate the
degradation condition.

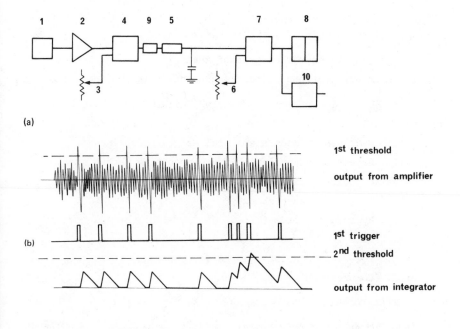

(a)

(b)

FIGURE 13-8 (a) Block diagram of a narrow band shock pulse monitoring device; (b) shock pulse peak detection; example of operation.

1. Transducer (accelerometer)   7. Second trigger (multivibra-
2. Amplifier   tor)
3. Reference voltage   8. Store
4. First trigger (multivibrator)   9. Shock amplitude calibration
5. Integrator   10. Classification setup.
6. Reference voltage

The peak amplitude µp(t) is obtained by sampling µ(t) when a peak
is detected.

3.3 Application to Vibration Monitoring
     of Aircraft Engines

Vibration monitoring of engines is helpful in detecting bearing
failures, gearbox failures, and mass imbalance. The vibrations
spectrum is closely tied to shaft speed (see Figure 13-4). For dual
spool engines, both N_1 and N_2 are significant. If measurements are
obtained only at 100% physical speed, narrow band filters with fixed
pass frequencies can be employed. Broken parts change the spectrum
because the harmonics of N_1 and N_2 are determined by the number of
blades in the compressor and turbine, the number of rollers in a
bearing, and the number of teeth in the gearbox.

3.4 Applications of Narrow Band Analysis

The main applications of narrow band analysis are the following:

   i.   Detection of rolling bearing failures (i.e., in heli-
copters)

   ii. Backlash in mechanisms such as gear couplings

   iii. Detection of failures in reciprocating mechanisms
(poppet valve motions, piston slope)

   iv. Radar antenna bearings

   v.   Hydraulic valves

   vi. Fans

   vii. Low-speed bearings (magnetic couplings)

   viii. Compressors

4. SPECTRAL MOMENT FEATURES

   (a) For acoustic or vibration monitoring problems for which
the measurements are stationary but not periodic, it may be worthwhile to characterize the state of the system by the first moments
of the short-term power spectrum of a record from the signal.

   The nth moment of the short-term power spectrum $|S(f)|$ is de-
fined by

$$M(n) \triangleq \int_0^{+\infty} |S(f)| f^n \, df \qquad \overline{f} \triangleq \frac{M(1)}{M(0)}$$

The central moments are obtained from

$$U(n) \triangleq \int_0^{+\infty} |S(f)| (f - \bar{f})^n \, df$$

and the normalized central moments are given by

$$N(n) \triangleq \frac{U(n)}{M(0)}$$

The moments give information about the shape or dispersion of the short-term power spectrum about its mean frequency $\bar{f}$:

  i. $U(2)$ is a measure of compactness.

  ii. $U(3)$ is related to the symmetry.

  iii. $U(4)$, or kurtosis, is a measure of the peakedness of the distribution.

Multivariate analysis (Chapters 7 and 8) can be applied to feature vectors made of these moments in order to find the best ones for diagnostic purposes.

   (b) Moment features have been used for performing automatic engine condition diagnosis via acoustic monitoring and also for vehicle classification (tracked, wheeled, diesel) [H-30].

   Other applications include the following:

  i.   Fluid dynamics effects such as cavitation in pumps

  ii. Rotating machinery

  iii. High-frequency bearing noise

  iv. Faults in combustion systems

  v.   Pipe leaks, in combination with ultrasound measurements

  vi. Bailing, in combination with ultrasound measurements

  vii. Valve leaks, in combination with ultrasound measurements

5. INTERPRETATION OF THE RESULTS OF ACOUSTIC OR VIBRATION MONITORING

It is worthwhile to point out some possible sources of uncertainties and thus misdiagnosis when acoustic or vibration measurements are used:

(a) Misuse of the techniques, e.g., unsuitable bandwidth.

(b) Faulty calibration of the instrumentation; the checking out of vibration monitoring equipment can be helped by carrying out a probability density estimate of the instrument output while disconnected from the assembly under test.

(c) Field-operator errors.

(d) Insufficient understanding of the basic physics of the test and masking of the signal by other phenomena (e.g., scatter in the interpretation rules, nonstationarity of the measurements, lack of sensitivity, inadequacy of the failure model, variability of the systems under test, inability to determine satisfactory signatures).

(e) Finite record lengths, introducing sampling errors.

(f) Background noise, i.e., for in-flight vibration monitoring on board aircraft, which is extremely difficult to carry out for that reason; one approach is then to monitor only the high-frequency range.

Recall (see Chapter 11) that internal diagnosis is closely related
to the identification of the transfer operator H of the actual system (S) under study. H transforms the exogenous input signal $e(\cdot)$
into the output signal $s(\cdot) = H(e(\cdot))$. To do so, a model (M) is
used which is characterized by the transfer operator $\hat{H}$ and by simulated outputs $\hat{s}(\cdot) = \hat{H}(e(\cdot))$ such that the identification error·
$\varepsilon(\cdot) = s(\cdot) - \hat{s}(\cdot)$ is minimized with respect to the condition $x(\cdot,e)$
of (S). See Figure 14-1.

The transfer operator $H = f(x(\cdot,e))$ depends on the internal
condition $x(\cdot,e)$ of (S) as estimated by $\hat{x}(\cdot,e)$. Diagnosis is carried
out by classifying the estimated internal condition $\hat{x}(\cdot,e)$ such that
$\hat{H} = \hat{f}(\hat{x}(\cdot,e))$ by means of a structural distance d_x.

In this chapter, we shall limit ourselves to the description
of a single identification method in order to stress the diagnosis
phase.

1. MODEL IDENTIFICATION USING A
SECOND-ORDER GRADIENT ALGORITHM

(a) To be identified is a system (S), not necessarily linear,
sampled at the rate τ during the time $T = N\tau$ using a linear model
(M) depending on p parameters: $\hat{H} = g(X)$, $X = [x_1, \ldots, x_p]$; X represents, for example, the coefficient vector in the transfer function $\hat{H}$. We assume that the output $s(\cdot)$ is one-dimensional.

The identification criterion I is minimized with respect to X;
it represents the mean quadratic error on the horizon $[0,T]$ when
$e(\cdot)$ is given:

FIGURE 14-1   Input $e(\cdot)$ and output $s(\cdot)$ of (S).

$$I(X) \overset{\Delta}{=} \sum_{\ell=0}^{N} \varepsilon^2(\ell\tau) \qquad \varepsilon(\ell\tau) \overset{\Delta}{=} s(\ell\tau) - \hat{H}(e(\ell\tau) - \hat{s}(\ell\tau)$$

(b) Depending on the ends sought, this criterion can be replaced by any of the following alternative criteria:

$$\sum_{\ell=0}^{N} \ell\tau\varepsilon^2(\ell\tau) \qquad \sum_{\ell=0}^{N} |\varepsilon(\ell\tau)| \qquad \sum_{\ell=0}^{N} \left\{ \varepsilon^2(\ell\tau) + a^2\left[\frac{d\varepsilon(\ell\tau)}{dt} \right]^2 \right\}$$

Identification corresponds to solving the nonlinear optimization problem

$$I(\tilde{X}) = \min_{X} I(X)$$

for instance, by a gradient algorithm where the gradient $\nabla I(X)$ is

$$\nabla I(X) \overset{\Delta}{=} \left[\frac{\partial I(X)}{\partial x_i};\ i = 1,\ \dots,\ p \right] \qquad \frac{\partial I}{\partial x_i} = -2 \sum_{\ell=0}^{N} \varepsilon(\ell\tau)\frac{\partial \hat{s}(\ell\tau)}{\partial x_i}$$

The quantities $\partial\hat{s}/\partial x_i$ represent the sensitivity of the model $\hat{H}$
to variations of the parameters X. The gradient method consists of
realizing successive displacements in the direction of $\nabla I(X^m)$,
starting from a point X^m, for the purpose of minimizing $I(X^m + \delta X)$
in this direction by a step adjustment $\delta X = X^{m+1} - X^m$. The process
then begins anew with X^{m+1}.

If $I(X^m + \delta X)$ is developed to the second order and if X^{m+1} is
a stationary point,

$$I(X^m + \delta X) = I(X^m) + {}^t\nabla I(X^m)\, \delta X + \frac{1}{2}\, {}^t\delta X\, \nabla^2 I(X^m)\, \delta X$$

$$\frac{dI(X^m + \delta X)}{dX} = 0 \Rightarrow \delta X = [\nabla^2 I(X^m)]^{-1}\, \nabla I(X^m)$$

$$X^{m+1} = X^m - k[\nabla^2 I(X^m)]^{-1}\, \nabla I(X^m) \qquad k \geq 0$$

The Hessian

$$\nabla^2 I(X) \triangleq \left[\frac{\delta^2 I(X)}{\delta x_i\, \delta x_j} : i = 1, \ldots, p;\ j = 1, \ldots, p\right] =$$

$$\sum_{\ell=0}^{N} [\nabla\hat{s}(\ell\tau)\, {}^t\nabla\hat{s}(\ell,\tau) + \epsilon(\ell\tau)\, \nabla^2\hat{s}(\ell\tau)]$$

is the sum of two terms, the first related to the sensitivity of the model $\hat{H}$ and the second negligible in the neighborhood of optimum $\tilde{X}$ because of the factor $\epsilon(\ell\tau)$. The terms $\epsilon(\ell\tau)$ and $\nabla^2\hat{s}(\ell\tau)$ are therefore to be left aside when calculating the Hessian at successive iterations m.

Like all identification procedures, this one requires that the initial condition X^0 of (S) be given. In most diagnostic problems, adequate knowledge of the system condition E_0 satisfying the specifications is used to specify the X^0 value. Identification can also be achieved using a low-order model $\hat{H}$, improving it gradually by consecutive identifications with increasing values of p.

(c) We shall briefly indicate the modifications required to take measurement noise into account. Let b_ℓ be the noise on the measurement $s(\ell\tau)$ of the output $s(\cdot)$ at time $\ell\tau$. The random variable measured is then

$$s^*(\ell\tau) = s(\ell\tau) + b_\ell \qquad E(b_\ell) = 0$$

Let $\delta\tilde{X}$ be the random error due to noise on the identified optimum $\tilde{X}$ for the model $\hat{H}$. It can be shown that

i. The mean value of $\delta\tilde{X}$ is $\overline{\delta\tilde{X}} = B^{-1}$ in which

$$B \triangleq \sum_{\ell=0}^{N} \nabla_{\widetilde{X}}\hat{s}(\ell\tau)^{t}\nabla_{\widetilde{X}}\hat{s}(\ell\tau) \qquad \beta \triangleq \sum_{\ell=0}^{N} b_{\ell}\nabla_{\widetilde{X}}\hat{s}(\ell\tau)$$

ii. The covariance matrix of X is equal to V^2B^{-1}, in which

$$V \triangleq \beta^{t}\beta \sum_{\ell=0}^{N} \nabla_{\widetilde{X}}\hat{s}(\ell\tau)^{t}\nabla_{\widetilde{X}}\hat{s}(\ell\tau)$$

2.   INTERNAL DIAGNOSIS USING THE IDENTIFIED MODEL

Internal diagnosis is made after learning; that is, a prototype
system for each failure/deterioration condition E_k must first be
identified. Note X_k, the corresponding vector of p parameters
characterizing the identified model $\hat{H}_k$ of E_k, k = 0, ..., n - 1.

To each of these vectors X_k, confidence limits proportional to
the variance of X_k are assigned.

During the operational phase, the N last output samples are
recorded, and the vector X of parameters of the system (S) is then
identified. X is classified into one of the classes E_k (k = 0,
..., n - 1) by comparison with the learning vectors X_k. See Figure
14-2.

To improve the quality of the identification, it is advisable
to make use of the same test signal e(·) and duration $N\tau$ = T for all
systems with the various conditions already mentioned.

Example

Take a system (S) to be identified by a second-order system

$$\hat{H}(p) = \frac{x_0 + x_1 p}{1 + x_2 p + x_3 p^2} \qquad X = [x_0, x_1, x_2, x_3]$$

for which two conditions E_0, E_1 are defined, where E_0 is the "good"
condition:

$$E_0: \quad |x_0 - 1.666| < \delta x_0 \qquad |x_1 - 0.333| < \delta x_1$$
$$\quad\;\; |x_2 - 1| < \delta x_2 \qquad\quad |x_3 - 0.666| < \delta x_3$$
$$E_1: \quad |x_0| < \delta x_0 + 1 \qquad\quad |x_1| < \delta x_1$$
$$\quad\;\; |x_2 - 1| < \delta x_2 \qquad\quad |x_3 - 0.666| < \delta x_3$$

$$\delta x_0 = 0.2 \qquad \delta x_1 = 0.05 \qquad \delta x_2 = 0.01 \qquad \delta x_3 = 0.2$$

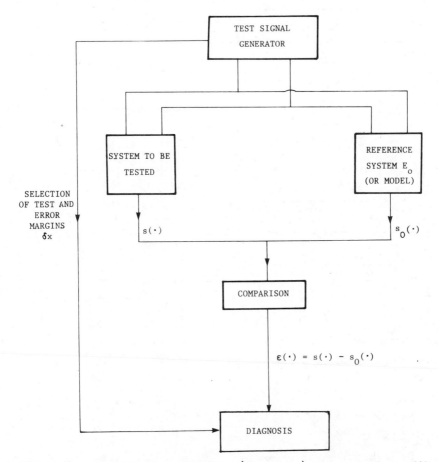

FIGURE 14-2 Case of two conditions (E_0 and E_1) and comparison with a physical reference system in good operating condition E_0.

The test signal is $e(t) = 5t$ for $0 \le t \le 2s$ and is equal to 10 for $2 \le t \le 6s$; the sampling period is $\tau = 0.2s$ with $N\tau = 6s$; that is, $N = 30$ samples. As the initial solution, the identification will use X^0, which are the parameters of the system in condition E_0. We classify the system (S) at each iteration of the identification algorithm using definitions of E_0 and E_1; there is rejection if (S) is neither in condition E_0 nor in condition E_1.

Iteration m	Estimated transfer function $\hat{H}$	Identification criterion I (X^m)	Diagnosis
0	$\dfrac{1.666 + 0.333\ p}{1 + p + 0.666\ p^2}$	1000	–
1	$\dfrac{1.11 + 0.02\ p}{1 + 0.988 + 0.566\ p^2}$	24.0	Rejection
2	$\dfrac{1.009 + 0.005\ p}{1 + 1.0015\ p + 0.516\ p^2}$	0.233	E_1
3	$\dfrac{1.0003 + 0.0003\ p}{1 + 1.0002\ p + 0.5015\ p^2}$	0.000315 Adequate precision	E_1

The conclusion is that the system (S), observed for a period $T = N\tau$, incurred the failure E_1, given the test signal $e(\cdot)$. See Figure 14-2.

3.   TESTING BY DETECTION OF HARMONIC DISTORTION IN THE SIGNATURE

The following is a simple method of system testing by measuring the harmonic distortion D in the signature $(e(t), s(t))$ when compared to the time-sampled E_0 condition signature $(e(t), s_0(t))$:

$$\varepsilon(t) \overset{\Delta}{=} s(t) - s_0(t) \qquad \varepsilon(t) \text{ of period } N$$

The usual method of measuring distortion D involves tuning a notch filter to remove the fundamental frequency from $s_0(t)$, so that the power in the harmonics can be compared to the power in the fundamental. The difficulty in adapting this method to automated failure diagnosis is the tuning requirement.

An alternate numerical method consists of fitting a sine wave to the sampled error signal $\varepsilon(t)$:

$$J(A,\gamma) \triangleq \sum_{t=1}^{N} [\epsilon(t) - A\sin(\omega t + \gamma)]^2$$

Because good initial guesses of amplitude A and phase γ can usually be made, the best fit is performed by solving the simultaneous equations

$$\frac{\partial J(A,\gamma)}{\partial A} = \frac{\partial J(A,\gamma)}{\partial \gamma} = 0$$

for $\tilde{A}$, $\tilde{\gamma}$ by a gradient algorithm (see Section 1).

The harmonic distortion D is defined as the ratio of quadratic power of $\epsilon(t)$, assumed of period N. If the best fit values are $\tilde{A}$, $\tilde{\gamma}$, it can be shown that
it can be shown that

$$D = \frac{2J(\tilde{A},\tilde{\gamma})}{N\tilde{A}^2}$$

A threshold value must then be specified on D such that a failure is detected if D becomes too large.

The method may also be applied to $s(t)$ instead of $\epsilon(t)$ if the signature itself is quasi-periodic.

4. FAULT DETECTION IN HYBRID CONTROL SYSTEMS

Hybrid control systems are characterized by the fact that analog subsystems interface with digital subsystems, such as digital controllers or filters.

The effect of interfaces such as A/D converters, D/A converters, sample-and-hold circuits, digital circuits, and memories is to modify profoundly the dynamic signatures of the analog subsystems in the time domain. Also, miscalibration in the clock controlling the digital subsystems and interfaces may lead to malfunctioning of other units. Altogether, fault diagnosis in hybrid control systems is very difficult.

Preliminary experiments suggest the following approach:

1. Carry out frequent recalibration of the clock and of all interfaces, especially the data converters (see Ref. G-36).

2.   Off-line testing without dismantling requires additional access to the clock frequency, the A/D converter output, the D/A converter input, and the hold circuits.

3.   Global off-line testing can be carried out using sinusoidal input stimuli e(t), the frequency of which must not be an integer multiple of the sampling frequency; because of the sampler, these stimuli generate high-frequency sidebands in the periodic signature s(t); failure detection is then carried out by the method of Section 3, by measuring the harmonic distortion in this signature. This distortion may then be due to either the digital subsystems or the analog ones. If the frequency of e(t) is a multiple of the sampling frequency, only the analog subsystem faults will be detected, as-suming the digital parts to be trouble-free.

5.   EXAMPLES OF APPLICATION

5.1 Gyroscopic Platform Errors

Internal diagnosis will be carried out periodically, especially for platforms operating permanently, in order to facilitate the maintenance and warn the users about changes in the drift rates.

5.2 Rotating Machines, Mills, and Pumps

Internal diagnosis, in addition to the histogram method (Chapter 12), is of great help in manufacturing line automation and for the remote monitoring of hydraulic pumps.

5.3 Aircraft Engines

(a) For application to aircraft engines, a number of different identification algorithms have been tested, all of them suffering from the nonlinearities of all equations involved [A-19].

(b) Another identification-based procedure is to use a non-linear regression of the state equations, with state X and control U:

$$\frac{dx_i}{dt} = f_i(X(t),U) \qquad i = 0, \ldots, n - 1 \qquad \dim(X) = \binom{n}{1}$$

$$f_i(X,U) \# K_{0i}(U) + K_{1i}(U)X + {}^tXK_{2i}(U)X$$

$$\dim(K_0) = \begin{pmatrix} 1 \\ 1 \end{pmatrix} \qquad \dim(K_1) = \begin{pmatrix} 1 \\ n \end{pmatrix} \qquad \dim(K_2) = \begin{pmatrix} n \\ n \end{pmatrix}$$

Assume also that the coefficients K_0, K_1, K_2 characterize the condition of the engine, in that sensitivity tests lead to the estimation of the following linearized relation between the variations of these coefficients and the variations ΔU of the control parameters (i.e., thermodynamic parameters):

$$\Delta K_j = A_j \Delta U \qquad \Delta U = A_j^+ \Delta K_j$$

If the failure or degradation modes are defined in terms of ΔU features, then on-line recursive regression leads to on-line failure diagnosis following the procedure of Figure 14-3.

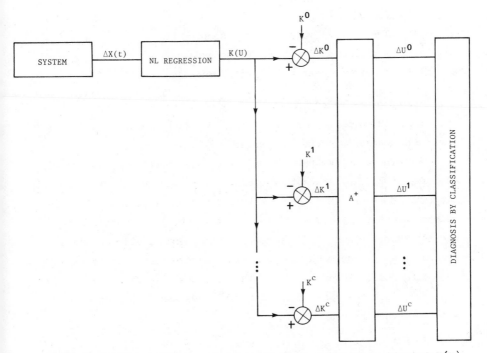

FIGURE 14-3 Regression-based internal diagnosis; the estimated $K(U)$ values are compared to stored K parameters associated to various system conditions: K^i, $i = 0, \ldots, n - 1$.

(c) An interesting application is engine diagnosis without
dismantling by identifying the engine parameters while a test run
is carried out on the ground. By carrying out predictive filtering
on these parameters and comparing them with earlier records, a
lower bound for the residual potential life of the engine can hopefully be obtained.

(d) A variant procedure is to carry out identification only
on measurements already compressed into a lower-dimensional space
by one of the procedures of Chapters 12 or 13.

5.4 Analog or Hybrid Filters and Microwave Components

(a) Internal diagnosis must be considered for those analog
devices of bad internal accessibility; the goal is then to estimate
the true component values by identification using:

i.   The diagram

ii. The nominal values of the components

iii. A series of input-output measurements, i.e., the gains
and phase measurements at different frequencies

Failed or degraded components may be localized by comparing
the estimated parameter values to the nominal values, allowing for
component and measurement tolerances.

(b) The actual parameter values can, in theory, be estimated
globally by solving the set of equations associated with the circuit
diagram. However, this approach rarely works out well in practice
because of nonlinearities and because the number of equations may
be less than the number of unknowns. The identification-based approach is an improvement, because of recursive parameter estimation,
including quasi-linearization of the previously mentioned equations.

(c) Take the case of a polynomial low-pass filter of order n,
with frequency response

$$F_i = f(g_1, \ldots, g_N; \omega_i)$$

where:

g_j: Actual component parameter, $j = 1, \ldots, N$

g_j^O: Nominal component parameter, $j = 1, \ldots, N$

ω_i: Time frequency of the sinusoidal test signal $e(t)$, $i = 1$, $\ldots, M$

F_i: rms frequency response of the filter to the test signal ω_i, and by definition,

$$F_{ij}^O(g_j) \triangleq f(g_1^O, \ldots, g_{j-1}^O, g_j, g_{j+1}^O, \ldots, g_N^O; \omega_i)$$

$$j = 1, \ldots, N$$

is the perturbated frequency response due to a change in g_j only.

(d) If we assume that there is only a single failed component, then a nonnominal value $g_j \neq g_j^O$ may be detected by testing the solution of the following nonlinear program for nominality:

$$\min_{g_1, \ldots, g_N} \sum_{i=1}^{M} \sum_{j=1}^{N} [F_i - F_{ij}^O(g_j)]^2 \tag{5.1}$$

When initiating the gradient search, one should select $(g_1^O, \ldots, g_N^O)$ as the initial solution; let $(\tilde{g}_1, \ldots, \tilde{g}_N)$ be the optimal solution of (5.1).

(e) If we want to refine the resulting failure localization, we can select a more complex criterion accounting for trimming errors. This time, $(\tilde{g}_1, \ldots, \tilde{g}_N)$ should be taken as the initial solution of

$$\min_{g_1, \ldots, g_N} \sum_{i=1}^{M} \sum_{j=1}^{N} [F_i - f(g_1, \ldots, g_N; \omega_i)]^2 \tag{5.2}$$

By testing the solution of this nonlinear program for nominality one may detect badly trimmed components or components that are out of tolerance without an actual failure occurring. See Figure 14-4.

5.5 Other Applications

The identification techniques help to carry out failure diagnosis from an identified transfer function. A change in the transfer

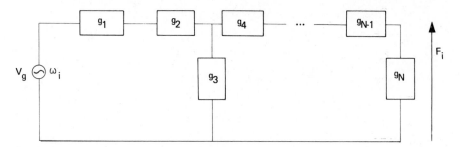

FIGURE 14-4   Failure localization in a quadruple filter by internal
diagnosis.

function is an indication of nonlinearity in the device under test;
higher-frequency components are also apparently enhanced because of
harmonic distortion of the output.   This holds in applications such
as:

1.   R-C coupled oscillators
2.   Regulated power supplies
3.   Transmission lines
4.   Linear analog control systems, e.g., autoland systems
5.   Aircraft actuators, e.g., autostabilizers

Chapter 15

ADAPTIVE FAILURE DIAGNOSIS
AND PERFORMANCE MONITORING

Adaptive failure diagnosis is used essentially for performance monitoring of devices undergoing slow degradation or periodic restoration through maintenance, and for some classes of control systems.

The underlying concept is the use of a model or charts in which
some condition-dependent parameters are estimated recursively using
a short sequence of past measurements. The failure or degradation
classes are then determined on line by classifying a vector of such
condition-dependent parameters, and the whole process is repeated
each time new measurements become available. This diagnosis leads
in turn to the activation of likely alarms by predicting the future
condition of the system.

Such a scheme is tremendously important in many high-performance
and high-safety systems such as in aerospace, nuclear, and manufacturing processes. Because the deteriorations are expected to be
revealed via the short-term fluctuations of the measurements made
on the system, one major difficulty is dealing with the conflicting
requirements of minimizing the false alarm rate and minimizing the
detection time for actual degradations.

A method (C) of adaptive signal classification is described
for a case example, and related to actual diagnostic problems in
monitored aircraft engines for which an input-output model is available. This new method is based on the prediction in parallel of the
output residual and of discriminant functions, thus yielding a predictive state classification into overall degradation classes.

Updating is achieved by monitoring the actual output and requesting an a posteriori classification from a "teacher."

1. TREND ANALYSIS

Trend analysis operates on one time series at a time either by smoothing out or estimating the parameters characterizing the shape of the time-dependent curve. Alarms result from extrapolations of this curve and from comparisons with fixed or variable thresholds.

1.1 Trend Models

(a) Let $s(t)$ be the measured process. If it is a slowly varying one, the time dependence can be described by a trend model, of which the following are the most common types:

    i.   Linear trend: $s(t) = a + bt$

    ii. Polynomial trend: $s(t) = a + bt + ct^2$

    iii. Exponential trend: $s(t) = a^{bt}$

    iv. Linear trend with exponential saturation: $s(t) = a + bt + ce^{dt}$

Curve-fitting algorithms are described in the literature for estimating the parameters of these trend models from a sequence of measurements; these estimation algorithms are global, as opposed to the recursive ones of Section 2.

(b) Forecasting can be carried out by computing the value of the trend outside the estimation interval. A by-product of this procedure is to compute the time at which the forecasted process will cross some thresholds corresponding, for example, to design or maintenance limits. This is a standard way of estimating the so-called residual life of a device.

1.2 Exponential Smoothing

(a) If $s(t)$ is the normalized measurement process, let $\bar{s}(t)$ be the smoothed process defined as follows:

$$\bar{s}(0) = s(0) \qquad 0 \le \alpha \le 1$$

$$\bar{s}(t) = \alpha s(t) + (1 - \alpha)\bar{s}(t - 1) \tag{1.1}$$

The goal is to produce a process $\bar{s}$ with bandwidth less than that of s by making a linear combination of all past measurements of s to which exponentially decreasing weights are assigned as a result of (1.1).

(b) Threshold comparisons for the activation of alarms are carried out on the smoothed process $\bar{s}(t)$, and forecasts are derived from the same trend analysis.

1.3 Cumulative Sum Charts to Monitor Successful Cycles of Operation

Consider a device with cyclic operations whose success rate we want to monitor, where the success rate is the probability of completing a task cycle successfully. A very simple procedure is the cumulative sum chart, obtained by programming a plotter as follows:

1. Go 1 to the right for any unit cycle.

2. Go 1 upward if the cycle was a success.

3. Go 9 downward if the cycle was a failure.

Then:

(a) A slope of +1 represents a success rate of 100%

0 represents a success rate of 90%

-1 represents a success rate of 80%

-2 represents a success rate of 70%

(b) The overall success rate is given by the slope of the line joining the end points of the trace.

(c) The average success rate between any two cycles is given by the slope of the line joining the corresponding points of the trace.

A visual inspection of the cumulative sum chart may easily reveal trends such as wear-out. See Figure 15-1.

1.4 Applications of Trend Analysis to Performance Monitoring

Trend analysis is an easy-to-implement performance monitoring technique which is applicable only to slowly varying degradation processes, generally at low sampling rates (see more details in Section 5.2):

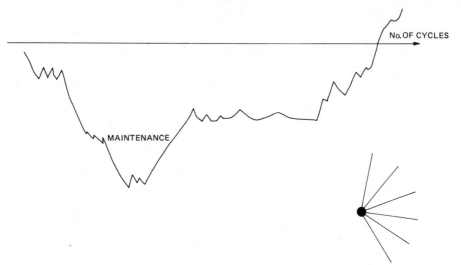

FIGURE 15-1 Cumulative sum chart.

    i.   Component monitoring on diesel or turbine ships

    ii. Component monitoring for condition maintenance, e.g., of aircraft engine components or of nuclear systems

    iii. Engine monitoring sensors [H-70]

2. DIAGNOSIS FROM RECURSIVE KALMAN FILTER STATE
    OR PARAMETER ESTIMATES

The concept of diagnosis from recursive Kalman filter state or parameter estimates is a generalization of straightforward trend analysis; a recursive algorithm is used to estimate a condition-dependent state or parameter vector. The basic Kalman filtering model and algorithm is presented in Section 5 of Chapter 1, from which the notation is used.

    2.1 Kalman Filter State Estimates for Diagnosis

    (a) The use of Kalman filter state estimates for diagnosis assumes the existence of a condition-dependent plant equation and measurement equation:

$$x_k = \varphi_c(k, \ k - 1)x_{k-1} + w_{k-1}$$

$$z_k = H_k x_k + v_k$$

where E_c, $c = 0, \ldots, N - 1$, represents the degradation class. In the following, $\hat{x}_k$ represents the state estimate obtained by Kalman filtering.

(b) If the goal is failure detection, a typical approach is to linearize the plant equation φ_0 around the state trajectory corresponding to the nonfailure class E_0. Another approach, called extended Kalman filtering, is to linearize φ_0 around the previous state estimate. Actual failure detection can then be implemented by one of the following decision rules operating on the $\hat{x}_k$ estimate:

    i. Threshold comparison (see Section 5.2)

    ii. Linear classification, by considering a linear mapping W_0 such that (see Section 3.2)

$$W_0 \hat{x}_k \text{ is} \begin{cases} \geq 0 & \text{the system is estimated to be in condition } E_0 \text{ at time } t = k \\ < 0 & \text{the system is estimated to fail (condition } E_1) \text{ at time } t = k \end{cases}$$

    iii. Sequential hypothesis testing via the likelihood ratio technique (Section 8.3 of Chapter 1), which assumes knowledge of the joint distribution of a sequence of state estimates.

(c) If the goal is failure diagnosis (with more than two alternate degradation or warning classes), the problem becomes much more difficult in general. One major reason is that it becomes necessary to properly model state evolutions in the degraded modes (φ_c functions), which may be very hard. Another reason is that the short-term fluctuations of both the measurements z_k and the state x_k tend, in physically degraded modes, <u>not</u> to satisfy additive Gaussian noise models. Deviations from normal operating conditions will very often be characterized by a shift and/or a skewness in the distribution of x_k.

Whenever applicable, a conservative design technique is to refer to the detection case (b) by testing at any time and for each of the N models whether a particular degradation mode is present or absent. If the system is found to be in several degradation classes simultaneously (due to the model dependency of the n estimates of $\hat{x}_k$), then decision logic must be used to choose.

(d) In all cases, the classical difficulty of selecting proper noise covariance remains. A pessimistic (large) covariance leads to slow filter convergence and long failure detection delays. An optimistic (small) covariance may destabilize the filter and multiply the number of false alarms.

In many practical implementations, especially in the multimodel technique (C), only steady-state Kalman filter gains are used (in order to reduce the computational load). However, the estimates may be improved by adding a stochastic approximation algorithm in series to the Kalman filter.

2.2 State Jumps Due to Abrupt Failures

(a) Reconsidering the failure detection problem (Section 2.1b), there are a few cases where one may want to estimate the size of the jump in the state vector. The corresponding technique is based on the assumption that such jumps occur only infrequently. Then one may implement a Kalman filter based on the assumption of no abrupt change and design a secondary system which monitors the measurement residual ϵ_k of this filter,

$$\epsilon_k \overset{\Delta}{=} z_k - H_k \hat{x}_k \tag{2.1}$$

to determine if a jump has occurred and to reinitialize the filter accordingly.

(b) The modified assumed plant equation becomes

$$x_k = \varphi_c(k, k-1)x_{k-1} + \delta_k\theta + w_{k-1} \qquad c = 0, \ldots, N-1 \tag{2.2}$$

where δ is the vector Dirac function and θ is a scalar jump parameter. (See also Section 8 in Chapter 12.)

Filtering in the absence of a failure is done with $\theta = 0$ and $c = 0$. The SPRT test (Section 2.1b of this chapter and Section 8.3 of Chapter 1), as applied to a finite sequence of measurement residuals ϵ_k, decides whether a state jump has occurred or not. If a jump is detected, then the jump size estimate $\hat{\theta}_k$ is specified by the following equation, and the filter state is reinitialized:

$$\hat{\theta}_k: \quad \hat{x}_k = \varphi_0(k, k - 1)\hat{x}_{k-1} + \delta_k\hat{\theta}_k$$

(c) A related approach is to consider a jump in a plant parameter. This is a special case of Section 3, where this parameter is assumed to be a steady-state coordinate.

(d) In some cases, the state jumps cannot, for physical reasons, take any set of values. This can be modeled via state jumps $\delta_k\theta$ constrained to lie among fixed subsets of states or of linear combinations of states. The feasible jumps $\delta_k\theta$ then lie in specified cones in state space (see Ref. H-69).

2.3 Applications

Applications are essentially limited to failure detection or diagnosis problems for which good models φ_c are available ($c = 0$, ..., $N - 1$). These applications are limited to those circumstances where physical reasons tell the designer that the purely measurement-based diagnosis is inadequate, obliging him or her to estimate unobservable condition-dependent parameters or state vectors.

1. Nuclear fast breeder core monitoring: The goal is to activate warnings based on recursive estimates of the reactivity parameter, as derived from power measurements.

2. Monitoring the sodium coolant temperature in fast breeder nuclear reactors: The thermocouple setup in the sodium coolant, especially the absence of physical contact for corrosion reasons, leads to a bias between the actual and measured temperature estimates, in addition to time delay effects. Kalman filter estimates provide a means of reducing the failure detection delays.

3. Recursive estimates for component monitoring and time between overhaul (TBO) updates: Assuming a trend model such as $\dot{x}(t) = a_t x(t) + b_t$, the Kalman filter provides recursive estimates of a_t

and b_t which are used to predict the crossing time of a specific
threshold for x. This time-to-go is then the residual life of the
equipment before the next overhaul. This technique has been investigated for ship engine maintenance.

4. Recursive updates of the failure rate of a component:
This usually corresponds to a nonlinear relation between the state
(failure rate) and the measurements, as expressed through a degradation model (see Chapter 3). Applications are mostly for structures
or electronic components.

5. Heat exchangers: The estimated parameter is the transmit-
tivity for which a second-order dynamic model is generally sufficient.

6. Inertial platforms: The estimated parameters are the characteristics of the accelerometers and the friction (or torque).

7. Spaceborne subsystems

3. DIAGNOSIS FROM THE RECURSIVE ESTIMATION OF AN AUTOREGRESSIVE MODEL OF THE MEASUREMENT RESIDUALS: THE ADAPTIVE SIGNAL CLASSIFICATION PROCEDURE (C)

In those cases where the confidence attributed to the model φ_c of
the degraded modes is rather small and where the spectral characteristics of the measurements are strongly condition dependent, a
very powerful approach is to recursively estimate an autoregressive
model of the measurement residuals (after normalization). The coefficients in such a model are shown to be directly related to the
measurement power spectrum, implying that the latter is being recursively estimated too. The diagnosis results from the classification of a vector of such coefficients.

This approach can be generalized to control systems with control-dependent residuals and to fault-tolerant hardware implementation.

This will be illustrated in the following sections through the
application of (C) to aircraft engine condition monitoring.

This section is devoted to the explanation of the assumptions and basic steps of (C). Specific portions of the algorithm and its implementation are discussed in Sections 4 and 5.

3.1 Constitution of the System (S)

The system (S) to be monitored (i.e., engine) is a time-sampled multidimensional control system for which a parameterized model ρ is available. If the sampling period is $\Delta t = 1$,

$e_n =$ p-dimensional control vector at time $t = n\,\Delta t$

$x_n =$ m-dimensional noisy observation vector of (S) at time t, given e_{n-q}, $\ldots$, e_{n-1}, e_n

$c_n =$ discrete-valued overall degradation class E_c of (S) at time t, $c_n = 0$, $\ldots$, $N - 1$

$\rho(e_n, e_{n-1}, \ldots, e_{n-q}; c_n) =$ m-dimensional nominal observation of (S) at time t, according to the model ρ, given the degradation class E_c of (S)

$s_n = x_n - \rho(e_n, e_{n-1}, \ldots, e_{n-q}; c_n) =$ m-dimensional noisy output residual at time t or deviation from the model

$s_n^* = (1, s_n) =$ extended $(m + 1)$-dimensional output residual at time t

$$(3.1)$$

In addition to (S), there is (Figure 15-2):

i. A teacher (T), who provides a posteriori the true condition c_n of (S) at time t, given e_n, e_{n-1}, $\ldots$ and x_n, x_{n-1}, $\ldots$

ii. A (learning) memory (M), which is a standard read-and-write memory, keeping the rolling records $\{x_{n-1}, \ldots, x_{n-k}\}$, $\{s_{n-1}, \ldots, s_{n-k}\}$, and $\{c_{n-1}, \ldots, c_{n-k}\}$ and updating them

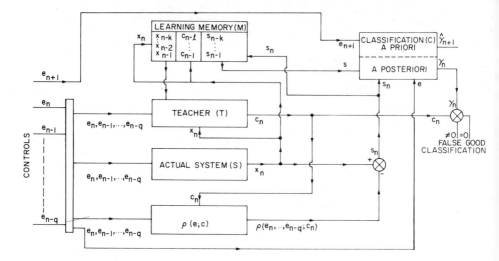

FIGURE 15-2 Adaptive signal classification system.

   iii. A classification device (C), which provides two estimated
conditions:

   i. An a priori condition $\hat{\gamma}_n$ of (S) at time t, given e_n, e_{n-1},
... and s_{n-1}, s_{n-2}, $\cdots$, s_{n-k-1}; $\hat{\gamma}$ is given at time t - 1.
   ii. An a posteriori condition γ_n of (S) at time t, given e_n,
e_{n-1}, ... and s_n, s_{n-1}, $\cdots$, s_{n-k}; γ_n is given at time t.

   The model ρ is assumed to apply to a fairly wide range of controls and operating conditions, and it may be obtained by identification (Chapter 14).

   The goal of the design procedure is to minimize the expectation
of the following error probabilities for the classification procedure (C):

   i. A priori error probability: $Pr(\hat{\gamma}_n \neq c_n)$
   ii. A posteriori error probability: $Pr(\gamma_n \neq c_n)$

   In the case of engine condition monitoring, the first of these
criteria is equivalent to minimizing the probability of having (C)
forecast for (S) a degradation class $\hat{\gamma}_n$ different from the actual

one, which may be a case of false alarm. The second criterion is
equivalent to testing the diagnostic performances of (C) against
those of the maintenance department.

3.2 The (C) Procedure for Adaptive Signal
      Classification

(a) The (C) procedure for adaptive signal classification uses
the following assumptions:

1. The sequence $\{s_n\}$ is modeled as a linear autoregressive
stochastic process of order k, assumed to be weakly stationary given
the sequence $\{e_n\}$:

$$s_n = u_n - a_{n-1}^1 s_{n-1} - \cdots - a_{n-1}^k s_{n-k}$$

$$= u_n - {}^t(S_{n-1})A_{n-1} \qquad k > m + 1 \qquad\qquad (3.2)$$

where:

$$A_{n-1} \triangleq [a_{n-1}^i \; ; i = 1, \ldots, k] \qquad \dim(A_{n-1}) = \binom{k}{1}$$

is a k-dimensional vector, updated at each step n

$$u_n \triangleq [u_{ni}; i = 1, \ldots, m]$$

is an m-dimensional zero-mean Gaussian white noise process with
independently distributed components and covariance matrix $(\Sigma_s {}^t\Sigma_s)$

$$S_{n-1} \triangleq [s_{n-1}, \ldots, s_{n-k}] \qquad \dim(S_{n-1}) = \binom{m}{k}$$

It should be recalled that s_n can only be defined once the teacher
(T) has produced c_n.

2. In the augmented $(m + 1)$-dimensional space of the output
residuals s_n^*, there exists at each time $t = n$ a subspace for each
degradation class $c = 0, \ldots, N - 1$, and these N subspaces are linearly separated for all n. Let the $m + 1$ vector $w_n = [w_{in} \; ; i = 0,
\ldots, m]$ represent the optimum discriminant mapping separating at
time $t = n$ the classes E_0, E_1, and minimizing the a posteriori
misclassification probability among them; w_n is recomputed at each
step n, given s_n, c_n.

3. The sequence $\{w_n\}$ is also modeled as a linear autoregressive stochastic process of order k, assumed to be weakly stationary given the sequence $\{e_n\}$:

$$w_n = z_n - b_{n-1}^1 w_{n-1} - \cdots - b_{n-1}^k w_{n-k}$$

$$= z_n - W_{n-1} B_{n-1} \tag{3.3}$$

where

$$B_{n-1} \triangleq [b_{n-1}^i \; ; \; i = 1, \ldots, k] \qquad \dim(B_{n-1}) = \binom{k}{1}$$

is a k-dimensional vector updated at each step n

$$z_n \triangleq [z_{ni} \; ; \; i = 1, \ldots, m + 1]$$

is an $(m + 1)$-dimensional zero-mean Gaussian white noise process with independently distributed components and covariance matrix $(\Sigma_z^t \Sigma_z)$

$$W_{n-1} \triangleq [w_{n-1}, \ldots, w_{n-k}] \qquad \dim(W_{n-1}) = \binom{m+1}{k}$$

w_n can only be defined once the teacher (T) has produced c_n, because it is an a posteriori discriminant mapping (see Section 4).

(b) By the definition of linear discriminant mappings the a posteriori estimated state γ_n depends on the sign of the scalar product:

$$^t w_n \cdot s_n^* = w_{0n} + w_{1n} s_{1n} + \cdots + w_{mn} s_{mn} \tag{3.4}$$

$$^t w_n \cdot s_n^* \begin{cases} \geq 0 & \begin{array}{l}\text{(C) classifies (S) at time } t = n^+ \\ \text{in the class } \gamma_n = E_0 \text{ at time } t = n\end{array} \\[2ex] < 0 & \begin{array}{l}\text{(C) classifies (S) at time } t = n^+ \\ \text{in the class } \gamma_n = E_1 \text{ at time } t = n\end{array} \end{cases} \tag{3.5}$$

(c) The a priori estimated condition $\hat{\gamma}_{n+1}$ is determined at time $t = n^+$ using e_{n+1} and extrapolating the linear models (3.2) and (3.3), which assumes that the degradation class does not change:

$$\hat{c}_{n+1} = c_n$$

1. $\hat{A}_n = A_{n-1}$ and $\hat{c}_{n+1} = c_n \Rightarrow \hat{s}_{n+1} = -{}^t\!\underbrace{s_n A_{n-1}}$

$+ \underbrace{\rho(e_{n+1}, e_n, \ldots, e_{n+1-q}; c_n) - \rho(e_n, e_{n-1}, \ldots, e_{n-q}; c_n)}_{\Delta\rho}$ (3.6)

2. $\hat{B}_n = B_{n-1}$ and $\hat{c}_{n+1} = c_n \Rightarrow \hat{w}_{n+1} = -W_n B_{n-1}$ (3.7)

$${}^t\hat{w}_{n+1} \cdot \hat{s}^*_{n+1} \begin{cases} \geq 0 & \begin{array}{l}\text{(C) classifies (S) at time}\\ t = n^+ \text{ in the class } \hat{\gamma}_{n+1} = \\ E_0 \text{ at time } n+1\end{array} \\[2em] < 0 & \begin{array}{l}\text{(C) classifies (S) at time}\\ t = n^+ \text{ in the class } \hat{\gamma}_{n+1} = \\ E_1 \text{ at time } n+1\end{array} \end{cases} \quad (3.8)$$

(d) Now observe that the fundamental idea of the procedure (C) is to perform adaptive and predictive filtering on the nonlinear scalar sequence $\{{}^t w_n \cdot s^*_n\}$, since the sign of each such scalar product determines the state classification. In (C), this filtering problem is decomposed into two linear adaptive identification problems (3.2) and (3.3), where:

i. The coefficient vector A_{n-1} of the $\{s_n\}$ process is updated on the basis of the bias $(s_{n+1} - \hat{s}_{n+1})$.

ii. The coefficient vector B_{n-1} of the $\{w_n\}$ process is updated on the basis of the bias $(w_{n+1} - \hat{w}_{n+1})$; however, this is done only if $c_{n+1} \neq \hat{\gamma}_{n+1}$; if $c_{n+1} = \hat{\gamma}_{n+1}$, B_n remains unchanged, and w_{n+1} is not even computed.

The adaptation schemes of (3.2) and (3.3) are described in Section 4. See Table 15-1, Figures 15-3 and 15-4.

3.3 Comparison with Other Methods

Many practical signal classification or pattern recognition problems involve nonstrictly stationary random processes such as $\{s_n\}$. However, very little theoretical work deals with such processes in a classification framework. Sequential pattern recognition schemes for slowly varying processes have been introduced with time as a supplementary exogenous control [B-30]. The identification of $\{s_n\}$ is performed either by stochastic approximation schemes repeated at each discrete instant [B-31] or by studying an innovations process. If statistical tests indicate nonwhite noise $\{u_n\}$ [F-41] or a sudden change in a plant parameter [F-40], then this is taken as theoretical evidence that a fault has occurred.

TABLE 15-1 Computation formulas for the classification procedure (C)

Discriminant mappings w_n $n \geq k$	Output signal residual s_n

Linear model

$$\tilde{w}_n = z_n - W_{n-1}B_{n-1} \qquad\qquad \tilde{s}_n = u_n - {}^tS_{n-1}A_{n-1}$$

Adaptation

$$B_n = B_{n-1} + R_n(w_n + W_{n-1}B_{n-1}) \qquad A_n = A_{n-1} + K_n(s_n + {}^tS_{n-1}A_{n-1})$$

Prediction

$$\hat{w}_n = -W_{n-1}B_{n-1} \qquad\qquad \hat{s}_n = -{}^tS_{n-1}A_{n-1}$$

Optimal dual Kalman filter gain

$$Q_n = Q_{n-1} + R_nW_{n-1}Q_{n-1} \qquad\qquad P_n = P_{n-1} + K_n{}^tS_{n-1}P_{n-1}$$

$$= \text{mean}[(B - B_n)^t(B - B_n)] \qquad\qquad = \text{mean}[(A - A_n)^t(A - A_n)]$$

$$R_n = -Q_{n-1}{}^tW_{n-1} \qquad\qquad K_n = -P_{n-1}S_{n-1}$$

$$\cdot (W_{n-1}Q_{n-1}{}^tW_{n-1} + \Sigma_z{}^t\Sigma_z)^{-1} \qquad \cdot ({}^tS_{n-1}P_{n-1}S_{n-1} + \Sigma_s{}^t\Sigma_s)^{-1}$$

$$R_n = -Q_n{}^tW_{n-1}(\Sigma_z{}^t\Sigma_z)^{-1} \qquad\qquad K_n = -P_nS_{n-1}(\Sigma_s{}^t\Sigma_s)^{-1}$$

$$\dim(R_n) = \begin{pmatrix} k \\ n+1 \end{pmatrix} \qquad\qquad \dim(K_n) = \begin{pmatrix} k \\ m \end{pmatrix}$$

$$\dim(Q_n) = \begin{pmatrix} k \\ k \end{pmatrix} \qquad\qquad \dim(P_n) = \begin{pmatrix} k \\ k \end{pmatrix}$$

However, the (C) procedure introduces adaptive learning via a controlling teacher as well as recursive identification schemes on the discriminant functions and the output residuals. It is thus related only to the theoretical paper of Ref. B-2 in which the observed state s_n is matched with a number of possible filtered outcomes of completely independent reference processes describing the condition classes c_n. The paper of Ref. B-2 introduces linear predictive filtering on the two first statistical moments of x_n, which is an interesting idea.

It should be noted that (C) can be combined with the techniques described in Chapter 12 for the diagnosis of closed-loop control systems.

Also, for purely numerical reasons, the recursive estimation of the A_{n-1} and B_{n-1} coefficients may be replaced by the recursive estimation of so-called reflection coefficients k_i, which are in one-to-one correspondence to the previous parameters. The advantage of the k_i's is that they allow for continuous stability tests and give a natural ladder form realization to the estimation procedure [A-41].

4. ADAPTIVE IDENTIFICATION OF AN AUTOREGRESSIVE PROCESS

In this section we shall detail the adaptive identification technique used in order to update A_{n-1}, B_{n-1} in (3.2) and (3.3) to provide for adaptive a posteriori and a priori state classifications (Sections 3.2b and 3.2c). We treat the case of the linear autoregressive relation (3.2):

$$s_n = u_n - {}^t S_{n-1} A_{n-1} \qquad n \geq k, \; k > m + 1 \qquad (4.1)$$

4.1 Recursive Linear Estimation of A_{n-1}

By using standard state space notations, (4.1) can be reformulated by considering a state variable χ_n belonging to the dual vector space to the original m-dimensional observation space:

$$(4.1) \Leftrightarrow \begin{cases} x_{n+1} = I x_n = x \\ y_n = -{}^t S_n x_n + u_{n+1} \end{cases} \qquad (4.2)$$

with:

$$x_n = A_n$$

$$A_{n+1} = A_n$$

$$y_n = s_{n+1}$$

where I is the $k \times k$ unit matrix.

Finding a recursive estimator of A_{n-1} is then clearly equivalent to finding a recursive estimator for the state vector x_n in (4.2). If we restrict ourselves to linear estimators, they will be of the following form:

$$x_n = x_{n-1} + K_n(y_{n-1} - \hat{y}_{n-1})$$

$$A_n = A_{n-1} + K_n(s_n - \hat{s}_n) \qquad \dim(K_n) = \binom{k}{p} \qquad (4.3)$$

$$\hat{s}_n \overset{\Delta}{=} -{}^t S_{n-1} A_{n-1} = \hat{y}_{n-1}$$

The gain matrix K_n weighs the influences of the bias between the actual deviation s_n and the predicted deviation $\hat{s}_n$. K_n is selected to minimize the variance of the estimation of x_n (the variance of A_n) over a given time window:

$$\min_{K_n} J \qquad J \overset{\Delta}{=} \text{trace } P_n \qquad P_n = \text{mean}[(A_n - A)^t(A_n - A)] \qquad (4.4)$$

Because of the transformation (4.2) into the dual state space of (4.1), any such gain K_n is called a dual filter gain. We consider the preceding derivation of (4.3) to be interesting by itself: It may also lead to generalizations of (4.1), i.e., by adding a noise term to the relation $A_{n+1} = A_n$, which is still within the framework of Kalman filtering.

4.2 Dual Kalman Filtering for Identification Purposes

It is well known that the discrete Kalman filter gain, applied to the recursive linear estimation of the state vector x_n of (4.2),

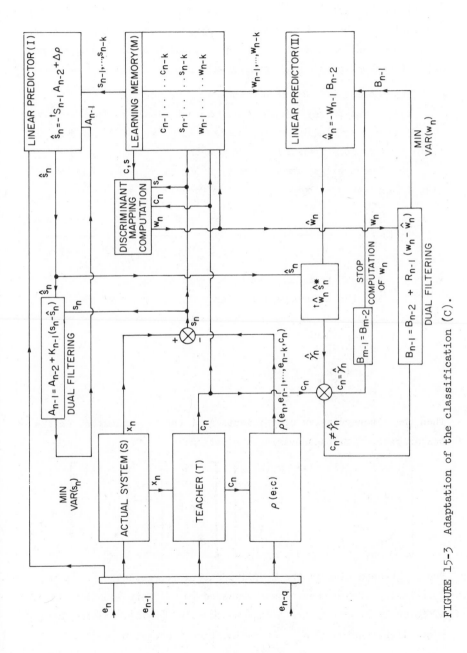

FIGURE 15-3 Adaptation of the classification (C).

is an optimal solution of the minimum variance problem (4.4). Due
to (4.2), this discrete multidimensional Kalman gain provides a recursive linear estimator of A_{n-1} in (4.1) and thus an adaptive identification of the sequence $\{s_n\}$. This result applies to the recursive linear estimation of B_{n-1} in (3.3), which leads to the optimal
identification formulas of Table 15-1.

4.3 Spectral Properties of the A_{n-1} Vector

Linear autoregressive all-pole processes such as $\{s_n\}$ [equation
(4.1)] have been studied in the scalar case m = 1 [A-38, A-39]; the
basic results follow when s_n is zero mean:

(a) The power spectral density $G_n(f)$ of s_n can be approximated
(for k large enough) by the following function of the frequency:

$$\hat{G}_n(f) = \frac{2|\Sigma_s{}^t\Sigma_s|}{|1 - a^1_{(n-1)} \exp(-2\pi if) - \cdots - a^k_{(n-1)} \exp(-2\pi kif)|^2}$$

where $0 \le f \le 0.5$ (sampling frequency $1/\Delta t = 1$).

(b) Let the autocorrelation function be estimated by

$$r_n(k) = \frac{E(s_{n+k}s_n)}{E(s_n^2)}$$

$$= \frac{1}{\ell} \sum_{i=1}^{\ell-|k|} \frac{s_i s_{i+k}}{E(s_n^2)}$$

Then the autoregressive coefficients A_{n-1} can be estimated, in the
scalar case, from the covariance equation:

$$\begin{bmatrix} 1 & r_n(1) & \cdots & r_n(k) \\ r_n(1) & 1 & \cdots & r_n(k-1) \\ \vdots & \vdots & \ddots & \vdots \\ r_n(k) & r_n(k-1) & \cdots & 1 \end{bmatrix} \begin{bmatrix} 1 \\ a^1_{(n-1)} \\ \vdots \\ a^k_{(n-1)} \end{bmatrix} = - \begin{bmatrix} r_n(1) \\ \vdots \\ \vdots \\ r_n(k) \end{bmatrix}$$

The right-hand side is the Toeplitz matrix representing the autocorrelation of the measurement sequence $\{s_n\}$. This equation can be
efficiently solved by the Levinson algorithm [A-40], and the asymptotic distribution of A_{n-1} is k-dimensional Gaussian [A-38].

4. Identification of an Autoregressive Process 345

It therefore appears that the dual Kalman filter presented here and in Ref. F-31 has a number of distinctive features, at least with respect to the derivation and the dimensionality.

(c) A recursive estimation algorithm has been proposed [A-41] which operates on better parameters than the A_n's. These coefficients are called PARCOR coefficients; they require less computation and are well suited for hardwired fixed-point realization.

4.4 Initialization

Still considering the specific case of the $\{s_n\}$ process (4.1), it is recommended that the dual Kalman filter be initialized as follows to allow for linear trend correction:

$$A_{k-1} \triangleq \left[\frac{1}{k} + \frac{k+1}{2(k-1)}, \ \frac{1}{k}, \ \ldots, \ \frac{1}{k}, \ - \frac{k+1}{2(k-1)} \right] \qquad (4.5)$$

$$P_{k-1} \triangleq \left\{ \zeta_p \exp\left[- \frac{1}{2}\left(\frac{i-j}{\theta_p} \right)^2 \right] : i = 1, \ \ldots, \ k; \ j = 1, \ \ldots, \ k \right\} \qquad (4.6)$$

where ζ_p, $\theta_p > 0$, and ζ_p is large.

With this initialization, the mean prediction error is zero, and the A_n's remain constant if the process is a linear ramp $s_n = an + b$.

Note that the choice of Σ_s will influence the rapidness of the dual filter, because the gain K_n is inversely proportional to $\Sigma_s{}^t\Sigma_s$. If this quantity is small in norm, the gain K_n will be large in norm, and A_n will be modified significantly; if this quantity is small in norm, then A_{n-1} will remain almost unchanged.

More generally, the matrices Σ_z, Σ_s (related to measurement and ρ modeling errors) will need a careful experimental adjustment to achieve a satisfactory compromise between the convergence rate of the two dual Kalman filters and their stability. The same remark applies to the initial conditions P_{k-1}, Q_{k-1}. However, these requirements are fairly easy to meet if all parameters A_{n-1}, B_{n-1}, w_n vary slowly. Computation time is not a limitation in this case.

The process noises u_n [equation (3.2)] and z_n [equation (3.3)] are assumed to be zero-mean white Gaussian. If the modeling errors due to the ρ model are significant, the innovations process of (3.2)

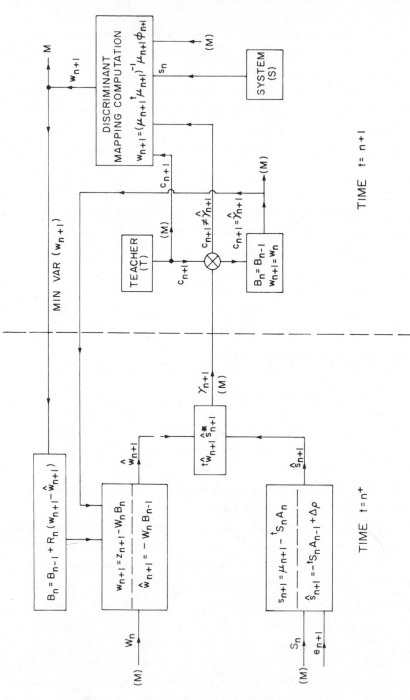

FIGURE 15-4 A priori predictive classification of (C). (M) is the learning memory.

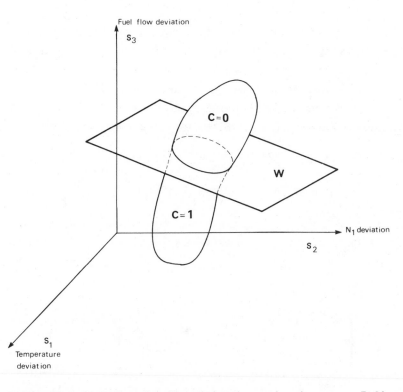

FIGURE 15-5 Example of a discriminant mapping in an m = 3-dimensional space, showing that the degradation classes may sometimes be defined on the basis of regions in the parameter space (or, equivalently, of linear combinations of the individual deviations s_i, i = 1, ..., m).

and (3.3) may be more complex; it may be necessary to introduce time-correlated Gaussian processes (Section 5.4 of Chapter 1).

4.5 Computation of the Discriminant Mappings w_n

The discriminant mappings w_n introduced in Section 3.2 are defined in the (m + 1)-dimensional space of the output residuals s_n^* (see Figure 15-6). We assume that all such residuals are drawn from one of N-multidimensional normal distributions each characterizing a degradation class E_i, i = 0, ..., N - 1. Both the first and second statistical moments of these distributions may vary with the time t = n.

In the adaptive signal classification procedure (C), the discriminant mapping w_n separating any two such classes E_0, E_1 is defined as a finite sample maximum-likelihood estimation of the optimal mapping minimizing the misclassification probability between E_0 and E_1. w_n is thus computed over a rolling horizon via the classical pseudoinverse equation (Ref. B-8, p. 101) using the following:

   i.   The N_1 most recent samples s_n classified into E_0 by the teacher (T)

   ii. The N_2 most recent samples s_n classified into E_1 by the teacher (T)

$$w_n \triangleq (\mu_n^t \mu_n)^{-1} \mu_n \Phi_n \qquad n \geq (N_1 + N_2) \qquad \dim(w_n) = \binom{m+1}{1}$$

$$(4.7)$$

where

$$\mu_n \triangleq \begin{cases} +1 & \text{iff } c_n = E_0 \\ \\ -1 & \text{iff } c_n = E_1 \end{cases} \qquad \dim(\mu_n) = \binom{m+1}{N_1+N_2}$$

$$\Phi_n \triangleq [\mu_{n-(N_1+N_2)}, \ \ldots, \ \mu_{n-1}] \qquad \dim(\Phi_n) = \binom{N_1+N_2}{1}$$

and $\mu_n \triangleq [s^*_{n-(N_1+N_2)}, \ \ldots, \ s^*_{(n-1)}]$ is the sample matrix.

Alternatively, one may use a construction which takes care of all class pairs (E_0, E_1) simultaneously (Ref. B-8, pp. 174 to 176). Quadratic discriminant functions might also be considered, as well as the nearest neighbor classification rule of Section 5 of Chapter 10 applied to the A_{n-1} vector for each n.

4.6 Applications of (C) to Failure Diagnosis and Performance Monitoring

Unlike in Section 2, the main application here is to control systems for which the knowledge or estimation of a state vector is not crucial as in Chapter 14. (C) is very well adapted to those cases where the short-term fluctuations of the measurements, as revealed eventually by their spectral characteristics, are essential

for fast failure or degradation diagnosis. As a result, the detection delays are shorter than those attained by other methods, and
the sampling rates can be fairly high, although limited by the computational load. Apart from engine condition monitoring, (C) has
been tested with success on the following:

1. Inertial/gyroscopic platforms

2. Turbomachines and ship engines

3. Unstationary flows in nuclear reactors

4. Pumps

5. Industrial processes

5. APPLICATION OF (C) TO ENGINE MONITORING

5.1 Formulation of the Engine Condition Monitoring (ECM) Problem

Engines in service on aircraft deteriorate. Their use must be
interrupted from time to time either in order to return them to
their original status (major scheduled overhaul) or for repair following a failure (premature partial overhaul). The major goal which
the engine maintenance department wants to achieve is to obtain the
best operational availability with full safety at minimum cost [C-14].
The following subgoals receive special attention because of the
possible benefits from engine condition monitoring programs [C-28,
C-29, H-13]:

i. Reduce the mean time to repair (MTTR).

ii. Reduce the number of spares.

iii. Define the least sets of repairable units (LRU), which
are the modules to be changed in order to bring the system back to
its operational status with the shortest delay and the smallest
number of spares.

iv. Reduce the time required by ground tests before and
after the repair.

v. Increase the mean time between repairs (MTBR) and between
scheduled overhauls (MTBO).

vi. Better control the causes of unscheduled partial overhauls and inefficient maintenance (which are very costly and upset
planning).

vii. Reduce unjustified premature landings and other false
alarms by initiating proper warnings only in the case of observed
increased overall degradation. The frequency of premature removals
has been estimated by some airlines to be 10 to 15% of all removals.

Despite cost and reliability problems, the implementation of
in-flight engine performance monitoring systems is generally considered a necessary step toward the achievement of these subgoals
[H-9, H-12]:

Mode A: Either by having the flight engineer log (register)
parameters once during each actual flight and at least every hour
in well-specified configurations such as cruise

Mode B: Or by operating a data-logging system, such as AIDS
(aircraft integrated data systems), FDAU (flight data acquisition
unit), or a maintenance recorder, with buffer, storage, and signal
preprocessing capabilities

Some airlines estimate that 25% of all justified premature
removals have been detected by automatic engine condition monitoring
programs, as compared to 10% by purely traditional means.

The computations of all monitored parameters pertaining to engine and flight conditions may be achieved in different ways:

i. By the central computer on board the aircraft in a time-
shared mode

ii. By a general-purpose computer on the ground, after assem-
bling the logs at this central location

iii. By a central real-time computer on the ground, based on
a postflight data link to the data-logging system contents, with
remote processing

The engine condition monitoring (ECM) programs should then,
together with the usual nondestructive testing procedures (boroscope,

vibration, SOAP, engine health monitoring, X rays, eddy currents), be able to identify the level of repair needed and those repairs not required. These levels, which we call overall degradation classes, range from complete overhaul to on-the-wing minor repair via the replacement of a major component (turbine disk blades or a fan rotor assembly). Taking the special case where only two over-all degradation classes are considered, the ECM should be able to make go/no go decisions at the end of each flight/mission, especially for engines which have had severe abnormal usage.

5.2 Trend Analysis Programs

The usual approach to these problems has been to perform trend analysis and exponential smoothing on each individual monitored parameter, after normalization with respect to the flight conditions [H-9, H-2, H-13] (see Section 1).

Alarms are then activated by means of a system of thresholds which are generally difficult to set properly but which are crucial to the actual usefulness of the ECM program (see Figures 15-6 and 15-7):

(a) Fixed recording threshold, below which no further pro-cessing is made of that given parameter

(b) Fixed tolerance limits, based on the accuracy and repeat-ability of the airborne sensors and of the following electronics

(c) Intermediate limits, below which no prediction is made

(d) Maximum thresholds for safety, maintenance, and design specifications

(e) Thresholds on the slope of the smoothed curves below the maximum limits

The thresholds, instead of being on the normalized signal, may be on the measurement prediction error ϵ_k (Section 2.2) when a Kalman filter is used in connection with trend analysis.

Consider, for example, excess speed. For the rotor speed, there may be three limits:

i. Maximum continuous angular speed

ii. Higher speed, which warrants postflight inspection of shaft and disk

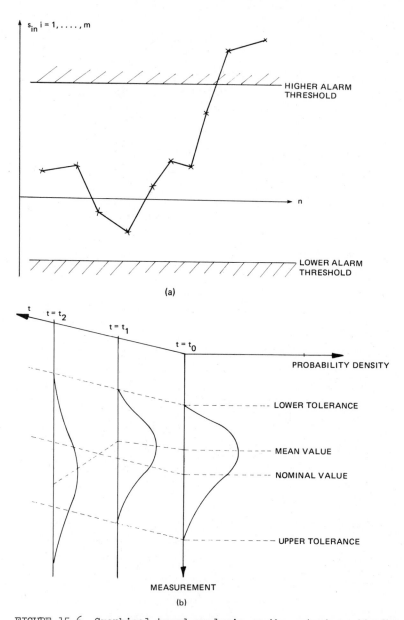

FIGURE 15-6 Graphical trend analysis on the output residual s_{in}, $i = 1, \ldots, m$; alarm thresholds can be defined either in absolute value or on the local slope of the curve. (a) Thresholds on the output residuals. (b) Time dependency of the probability density of the output residual and thresholds on this residual.

iii. Upper limit due to shaft critical speeds or centrifugal disintegration

In those cases where a prediction of the overall degradation is required before the next flight, these systems basically proceed as follows [H-9]:

i. The smoothed record of each parameter is extrapolated into the nearest future, eventually with some weighting of the most recent logs (see Section 1.2).

ii. The go/no go decision depends on whether all forecasts individually fulfill the major thresholds (a) through (e).

It is clear that such a procedure applies only to the two-class problem and does not therefore serve one earlier-stated requirement.

In addition, there are some other drawbacks:

i. Such systems operate on one measurement at a time, without taking into account correlations or fixed relations among the monitored parameters; thus, it may happen that one measurement gets close to a slope threshold (e) and to a maximum limit (d), leading to a warning, while this transient excursion is compensated for by the variations of a set of other parameters.

ii. A degradation may be the result of the joint observation of parameter values, all of these being below the alarm thresholds.

iii. Engine-to-engine variations may significantly influence the alarm probabilities when the ECM program is assigned to monitor a family of engines all of the same model number and installation. This is due to the difficulty in setting the thresholds properly because of engine-to-engine variation, which includes changing settings or tolerances on instrumentation.

iv. Following a partial overhaul, trend analysis on a particular engine is impossible for a while, because of missing performance information and evaluations. Improved methods should allow for the use of the flight engineer's judgment during the first flights and incorporate this into the system.

v. In the event an ECM mode B is available with a capability for continuous display of the engine parameters to the flight/maintenance crew, trend analysis may require a fair storage capacity. This will probably have to be decreased in improved systems in order to make this concept viable [H-12] even if cheap bulk storage is available in the future.

In the following, we shall describe a simple version of an ECM system which tries to compensate for drawbacks (i) through (iv) while keeping some thoroughly tested aspects of trend analysis. It also leads to a decreased sensitivity of the false alarms to threshold settings.

This system is largely based on the adaptive multidimensional signal classification procedure (C), which incorporates a continuously updated diagnosis of the engine condition as provided when necessary by the flight engineer or by the maintenance department (altogether called "teacher") [F-31]. The implementation by an airline engine maintenance department has been satisfactory, both in terms of a reduction in the probability of false alarms (which lead to unscheduled shop inspection or dismantling) and from the point of view of a more informative and flexible exploitation of the basic in-flight measurements.

5.3 Application of (C) to Engine Condition
      Monitoring in Mode A

Getting back to the ECM problem discussed in Section 5.1, we now give in detail its direct relations to the adaptive signal classification procedure (C) of Section 3. To make these connections clear, the same notation is used wherever possible and meaningful. Moreover, this section has a structure similar to that of Section 3.1.

The following exposition relies on experience gained during the actual implementation of procedure (C) with an airline.

Emphasis is placed on those aspects of general importance for an ECM system. The initializing phase, spanning k flights (typically three to five flights) is not detailed here.

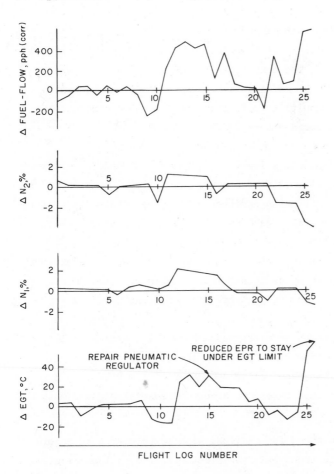

FIGURE 15-7 Evolutions of some output residuals for an engine monitored in mode A, where the sampling period is equal to one flight.
This record ends with damage to the second stage of the engine.
This example shows how important it is, for alarm and diagnosis purposes, to simultaneously analyze the evolutions of all individual
output residuals. ΔFF: output residual s for the fuel flow; ΔN_1:
output residual s for rotation speed of the first stage; ΔN_2: output residual s for rotation speed of the second stage; ΔEGT: output
residual s for nozzle temperature.

The system (S) individually monitors turbofan engines at the
same (or similar) standard, from which a set x_n of m parameters is

recorded once during each flight and at least once during each flying hour. The sampling period Δt follows from this monitoring mode
A (see Figure 15-7). The measurements x_n, as well as the logs of
the controls and flight conditions e_n, are made during so-called
stabilized flight conditions. This means that the engine has temporarily reached a permanent regime, conditional on e_n and independent of the previous controls e_{n-1}, ..., e_{n-q}; thus $q = 0$.

   e_n: The controls e_{in}, $i = 1$, ..., p, are the usual parameters
characterizing flight conditions: EPR, flight level, indicated air-
speed, Mach number, throttle position, etc. (see ARINC specifications
No. 563 and 573 for flight recorders); depending on the ρ model,
$p = 4$ to 8.

   x_n: Measurements x_{in}, $i = 1$, ..., m, of the usual major engine
performance values, such as those listed in Figure 15-7 or in Refs.
H-9 and H-12, depending on the type of engine considered, $m = 6$ to
14.

   c_n: Each degradation class must represent the overall level
of repair needed. Because of the existence of nonsymmetric maximum
and minimum limits on each scalar deviation s_{in}, $i = 1$, ..., m
(Figure 15-6), at least three different degradation classes must be
defined:

   E_0: Engine cleared for service, with performances in accord-
        ance with technical specifications; (no) action required:
        (1)

   E_1: Large positive excursions of the major measurements away
        from the class E_0; action required: (2)

   E_2: Large negative excursions of the same major measurements
        away from the class E_0; action required: (3)

   Depending on the engine type and the nature of the measurements
x_n, additional classes may be defined and interpreted in terms of
those parts of the engine which are likely to require maintenance
action with or without dismantling, i.e., rotor damage or gas path
flow irregularities. It is essential that all persons involved in
the operations or maintenance of the engine have a clear view of the
actual degradations associated with each class and that airborne

test equipment/sensors provide the necessary information to perform such an assessment.

It is important that the corresponding symptom-fault table be available to personnel in the main working documents (instruction sheet, maintenance handbook). Because the $N = 3$ degradation classes are each associated with a closed convex subspace in the s* space, the number of such subspaces determines in turn only the number of discriminant mappings w_n updated at each period n; a realistic choice is between the following two alternative designs (Figure 15-8):

    i. Two discriminant mappings $w_n \to N = 4$ degradation classes

    ii. Three discriminant mappings $w_n \to N = 7$ degradation classes (not all of which have to be used)

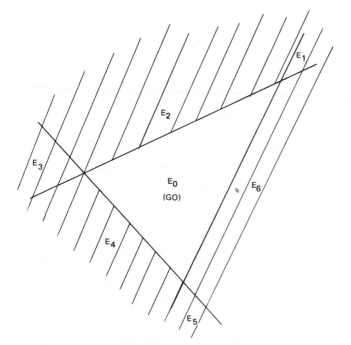

FIGURE 15-8 Classifier design in an $m = 2$-dimensional measurement space, with $N = 7$ degradation classes defined by three discriminant mappings at time $t = n$; only class E_0 corresponds to an unconditional go order.

$\rho(e_n;c_n)$: For all engines of the type considered and for each degradation class E_c, $c = 0, \ldots, N - 1$, a parameterized model $\rho(e;c)$ of the engine is available and provides the nominal values of the m parameters x_{in}, $i = 1, \ldots, m$, given the flight conditions e_n and the state of the engine [H-2, H-9]. Such a crude model is generally provided by the engine manufacturer, at least for the standard engine in class E_0. In a few cases, identification models [H-9] may be useful. However, such models may be imprecise for the case $c \neq 0$, especially when N gets large. Instead, so-called degraded performance tables must be used, originating either from prototype testing with simulated defects of each type or in previous actual logs leading to these failures. It is evident that the performances of (C) depend to a large extent on the validity of the ρ models.

Besides (S), there are (Figure 15-2) the following:

i. A teacher (T): In mode A, the position of teacher is held jointly by:

i. The last crew reporting about occasional deficiencies (pilot report), including those problems observed during the ground spin-up

ii. The maintenance team: functional check and sampling inspection between flights

It is important to describe how this position is exercised. Before the flight n (or during the previous flight hour if on-board computation is available, (C) automatically provides an estimated a priori engine condition $\hat{\gamma}_n$.

This decision is automatically kept as true (i.e., $c_n = \gamma_n$) if the derived a posteriori classification γ_n verifies $\gamma_n = \hat{\gamma}_n$ and if it has not been denied by either the crew or maintenance team for flight n. It can be seen that such a reinitialization rule without updating the discriminant mappings $\{w_n\}$ is compatible with the (C) algorithm (Figure 15-2). It also minimizes any additional burden caused by (C). If the operations engineer, crew, and maintenance personnel agree that the degradation class has changed (for better or worse), then their new classification c_n is transmitted (along with

x_n) to the processing facility before the following flight n + 1.
They receive the predicted estimated degradation condition $\hat{\gamma}_{n+1}$,
based on c_n; the discriminant function is then recomputed (Section
4 and Table 15-1). The final go/no go decision depends on the
available information, including the warning $\hat{\gamma}_{n+1}$.

ii. A memory (M): In mode A, it is ground based and communicated to maintenance and planning engineers in order to define the
scheduled partial and major overhauls.

iii. A classification program (C): This is a ground-based
program that operates for n ≥ k, as indicated in Section 3.2, with
the following detail: Classification rules (3.5) and (3.8) apply
only if all single deviations s_{in} and $\hat{s}_{i(m+1)}$ (i = 1, ..., m) lie
within the permanent extremum alarm thresholds defined in Section
5.2. If not, then appropriate threshold-based alarms are initiated.
It should be noted, however, that all other thresholds are eliminated
from (C), making the implementation of (C) easier in terms of trend
analysis programs.

k: The last parameter which must be selected in this ECM case
is the order k of the linear autoregressive models (3.2) and (3.3).
Depending on the sensor noise levels and the quality of the ρ model,
efficient time constants may be achieved in mode A for tracking
discontinuities and alarms in the $\{s_n\}$ or $\{w_n\}$ processes for k
ranging from three to six flights or flight hours (see Figure 15-7).

5.4 Additional Remarks

This section contains a brief review of some difficulties and
additional procedures related to the ECM case.

(a) Despite the correction $\Delta\rho$ in equation (3.6), when in mode
B or in case of violent changes in the controls e_n, procedure (C)
must be reinitialized as soon as new stabilized flight conditions
are reached (or the ρ model must include description of transient
engine performances). In any case, this reinitialization should be
performed for large n (> 300) because of accumulated round-off
errors in (4.3).

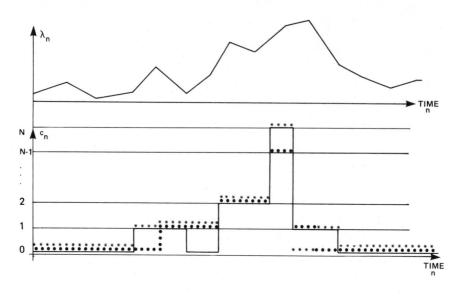

FIGURE 15-9 Plots of the alarm criterion λ_n and of the classification performance of (C). _____ c_n; .... $\hat{\gamma}_n$; * * * * * * γ_n.

(b) An automatic reinitialization or failure alarm may be
based on the following test quantity (Figure 15-9):

$$\lambda_n \triangleq ||A_n - A_{n-1}||^2 = {}^t(A_n - A_{n-1})(A_n - A_{n-1})$$

If λ_n (and/or the similar test quantity for B_{n-1}) becomes larger
than a given threshold, there is a noticeable shift between two
successive estimates of A_{n-1}. This may characterize either an important and sudden state change in the system (S) (i.e, a failure)
or a sudden change in the controls (such as the throttle position).
If λ_n exceeds this threshold, a new initialization should be performed. Experience shows that this test quantity is not very sensitive to noise.

(c) The trend analysis and plotting programs (Section 5.2)
may be used to follow the evolution of s_n, $\hat{s}_n$, A_{n-1}, w_n (one scalar
coordinate at the time; see Figure 15-7). In addition, the performances of (C) in terms of misclassification probabilities can be observed using diagrams such as Figure 15-9.

(d) The classification rules (3.5) and (3.8) may be made
Bayesian if appropriate a priori information is available [B-32].
It may be necessary to assign a priori probabilities for correct
classification to compensate for important aspects such as sensor
accuracy, tolerances in instrumentation, or noise characteristics.
However, this requires the estimation of these probabilities for
each engine. Experience has shown that the teacher is usually a
better estimator, since corrections made by him or her force an
update of (C) to take into account the sensor particularities of
the specific engine. The same remark applies to compensation for
transducer or BITE failures and reliability.

5.5 Clustering the Degradation Conditions of the System (S)

Let us consider the recursive linear identification (4.3) for
the m-dimensional residual s_n using the k-dimensional vectors A_{n-1}.
Except for the state-dependent correction (3.1),

$$s_n = x_n - \rho(e_n, e_{n-1}, \ldots, e_{n-q}; c_n)$$

A_{n-1} is estimated recursively without knowing the actual state of
the system (S) for $t = n - k, \ldots, n - 1$. Since the ρ model may be
weak, there are good reasons to perform nonparametric clustering of

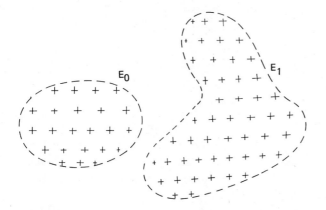

FIGURE 15-10 Clustering the conditions E_c of (S) by applying data
analysis to the vectors A_{n-1} of (4.1).

the vectors A_{n-1} to determine how many degradation classes can be
defined as time passes and how well discriminated they are (Figure
15-10). If this discrimination is unsatisfactory [large overlappings
between c-dependent subspaces (Figure 15-5)], this is an indication
that the degradation classes are not defined or understood correctly
(see Section 5.3: c_n). This task can be carried out using the feature extraction and clustering techniques described in Chapter 8.
This a posteriori evaluation of the ECM procedure (C) was found
useful during the initial implementation stage and in each extension
to another type of engine.

6.   TOLERANCE TO SENSOR FAILURES AND RECONFIGURATION OF MONITORING SYSTEMS

When adding performance monitoring to systems with high MTBF, a
critical issue is tolerance to monitoring sensor failures. Efficient
design techniques are discussed briefly below.

6.1 Sensor Failure Tolerance of a Diagnostic System Using Recursive State Estimates (Analytic Redundancy)

Assuming sensor multiplicity, it is essential to remember that
the outputs from these sensors are not independent but are related
by the process dynamics (as represented by the plant equation).
Consequently, fictitious redundant sensors can be obtained via recursive state estimators using as measurements any combination of
the outputs of all actual sensors.

It is at this stage necessary to elaborate further upon the
notion of sensor multiplicity. This means that several instruments,
eventually different in design or setup, are dedicated to the monitoring of specialized parts of the same process dynamics. As a
result, while the measurements z_k^1, z_k^2, ... are different in nature,
recursive filtering should provide for the estimation of the same
state vector x_k from these multiple sensors, unless x_k is only partially observable with respect to some of these.

Example

In the case of two different sensors, a third fictitious sensor results from computing a recursive state estimate $\hat{x}_k^3$ using z_k^3, a linear combination of the two sensor outputs z_k^1, z_k^2:

   i. Plant equation: $\quad x_{k+1} = A_k x_k + B_k u_k + w_k$

   ii. Measurement equation for sensor 1: $\quad z_k^1 = H_k^1 x_k + v_k^1$

          Measurement equation for sensor 2: $\quad z_k^2 = H_k^2 x_k + v_k^2$

          Measurement equation for sensor 3: $\quad z_k^3 = \alpha z_k^1 + \beta z_k^2$

   iii. Recursive estimators (see the notation of Section 5 of Chapter 1:

        Filter 1--from sensor 1: $\quad \hat{x}_k^1 = \hat{x}'^1_k + K_k^1(z_k^1 - \hat{z}_k^1)$

        Filter 2--from sensor 2: $\quad \hat{x}_k^2 = \hat{x}'^2_k + K_k^2(z_k^2 - \hat{z}_k^2)$

        Filter 3--from sensor 3: $\quad \hat{x}_k^3 = x'^3_k + K_k^3(z_k^3 - \alpha \hat{z}_k^1 - \beta \hat{z}_k^2)$

   iv. Fictive sensor 3: $\quad z_k^3 \overset{\Delta}{=} \alpha z_k^1 + \beta z_k^2$ (matrices α, β depending on reconfiguration controls)

If any single actual sensor fails, the reconfiguration procedure should replace the failed sensor by the fictitious sensor which uses a linear combination of the outputs of all actual sensors (that have not yet failed), so that the state vector x_k may still be estimated:

(a) To detect which sensor has failed, any of the previously described failure detection schemes will work. The simplest, but not necessarily the most reliable, is to perform pairwise comparisons of the state estimates $\hat{x}_k^i$, i = 1, 2, 3, from sensors (actual and fictive) to pinpoint any major deviation. Other schemes are discussed in Section 6.2 and Chapter 12.

(b) The reconfiguration should be done immediately either by feeding the redundant fictitious sensor output $\hat{z}_k^3$ into the recursive estimator of the failed sensor or simply by using the fictitious sensor state estimate $\hat{x}_k^3$. The latter scheme requires more state estimators (assuming no simultaneous multiple failures).

If it has been detected that sensor 1 has failed alone, then set $\alpha = 0$, $\beta = 1$; deliver $z_k^3 \triangleq z_k^2$ to filter 1; and set $\hat{x}_k = \hat{x}_k^1$, $\hat{x}_k^2$, or $\hat{x}_k^3$ (assuming all three filters will operate).

If it has been detected that sensor 1 has failed and that filter 1 has also failed, then set $\alpha = 0$, $\beta = 1$, and $\hat{x}_k = \hat{x}_k^2$ or $\hat{x}_k^3$ (assuming both filters 2 and 3 will operate).

Similar reasoning applies if sensor 2 fails and/or if other filters fail.

The crucial point with this implementation is that the software-based fictive sensor 3 should at any time be more reliable than any hardware filter 1 or 2 taken individually.   ∎

6.2 Sensor Failure Tolerance of a Diagnostic System Using an Autoregressive Model of the Measurement Residuals

Assuming sensor redundancy, the idea is to use the assertion that the spectral characteristics of the measurement residuals from different sensors should normally be similar even in case of measurement biases and such. Discrepancies between sensor outputs make it impossible to build redundant fictitious sensors. See Figure 15-11.

In case a single sensor fails, the reconfiguration procedure should simply eliminate it or replace it by a linear combination of the normalized A_n parameter vectors from the remaining sensors:

$$A_n^3 = \frac{A_n^1}{||A_n^1||} + \frac{A_n^2}{||A_n^2||}$$

To detect which sensor has failed, the simplest procedure is to perform pairwise comparisons of the normalized A_n parameter vectors; that is, $A_n/||A_n||$.

This scheme requires as many parallel A_n estimators as available actual sensors, plus one for the updates of B_n.

6.3 Applications

Cases where sensor fault tolerance in a diagnostic system is necessary are:

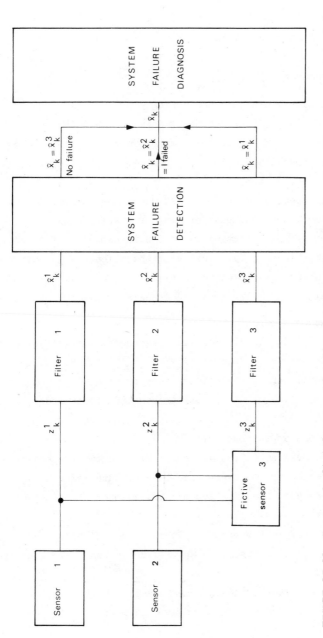

FIGURE 15-11   Sensor fault tolerance of a diagnostic system using two sensors and recursive state estimates.

    i.   Spaceborne control systems, especially for attitude control

    ii. Autopilots for automatic landing

    iii. Missiles and fighter planes

7.   OTHER METHODS AND APPLICATIONS

7.1 Adaptive Vibrations Monitoring

Because of the interpretation of an autoregressive model such as equation (4.1) in terms of the short-term spectrum of the measured signal s_n, adaptive diagnosis can be carried out in the spectral domain. (See Section 4.3.)

The power spectral density is estimated on-line by the autoregressive model; the features for diagnosis are, instead of A_{n-1}, the amplitudes of this spectrum for a finite number of frequencies. Diagnosis is carried out by classifying these feature vectors related to the short-term spectrum.

<u>Example</u>: Monitoring of the noise in a nuclear power plant.   ■

7.2 Control Networks

A network is obtained by linking together a number M of control systems, with individual conditions x_k^j, j = 1, ..., M, at time k. The overall condition of the network must be diagnosed from L measurements z_k^ℓ, ℓ = 1, ..., L. Faults propagate between nodes, and links may fail, adding to the complexity of the problem.

The possible approaches are:

    i. To consider $\{x_k^j$, j = 1, ..., M\} as a time-dependent statistical correspondence between nodes; after data compression of this correspondence, the time-dependent trajectories of the nodes may be tracked

    ii. To analyze the propagation rules among nodes, and to infer from them a syntactic parser, which will detect an overall change in the network behavior

This leads to a number of new problem areas:

    i. Distributed measurements and actuators

    ii.   Routing diagnostic measurements on the same lines

   iii.   Survivability

   iv.   Distributed memory for local diagnosis, and corresponding data queuing problems

    v.   Instrument and calibration diversity

   vi.   Discrimination between node failures, link failures, and overloads

   vii.   Replaceable units, and regeneration of some measurements

Examples: Network diagnostic problems arise in power systems, flight control systems, communications systems, and manufacturing systems.   ∎

Appendix 1

DEFINITIONS USED IN FAILURE DIAGNOSIS

The following standards, specifications, or documents may be examined: ARINC-203, British Council of Maintenance Associations Glossary, GOST 20417-75 (USSR), BS 3811-1964 (UK), ISO Publ. 271 (1975), GOST 20911-75 (USSR), CCT 1010 (France), MIL-STD-121-B (1961), MIL-STD-721-B (1970); most of the following definitions were compiled by IMEKO TC-10 (technical diagnostics).

Accelerated test: A test in which the applied stress level is chosen to exceed what is stated in the reference conditions in order to shorten the time required to observe the stress response of the item or magnify the response in a given time. To be valid, an accelerated test shall not alter the basic modes and mechanism of failure or their relative prevalence.

Acceleration factor: The ratio between the times necessary to obtain the same stated proportion of failures in two equal samples under two different sets of stress conditions involving the same failure modes and mechanisms.

Accessibility: A measure of the relative ease of admission to the various areas of an item.

Adjustment: The act of bringing any out-of-tolerance condition into tolerance by manipulating the equipment controls.

Availability: The availability of an item to perform its specified function at any instant of time. This characteristic is given as a ratio in one of the following forms:

(a) The ratio of the time that an item is available for
specified use in a stated period of time to the total length
of the stated period of time, or

(b) The ratio of the proportion of a single population of
items which is capable of performing their specified aim at a
specified instant of time to the total number of that population.

Built-in test equipment: Any device mounted in the prime equipment
and used for the express purpose of testing the prime equipment.

Catastrophic failure: Failure which is both sudden and complete.

Classification: Implies a decision rule where data or information
may be identified and grouped into classes.

Condition-based maintenance: Preventive maintenance as a result of
knowledge of the condition of an item from routine or continuous testing.

Condition monitoring: Action carried out continuously or at regular
or irregular intervals with measuring or indicating instruments
or similar methods in order to quantify qualitative properties
of an item, indicating its condition or fitness for service intended.

Corrective maintenance: Maintenance carried out to restore (including adjustment and repair) an item which has ceased to meet an
acceptable condition.

Degradation: The act of impairing or deteriorating a functional
condition or physical property, including the performance of a
specified task or mission.

Degradation failure: Failure that is both gradual and partial.

Destructive testing: Testing of any nature which may materially
affect the life expectancy of the item tested whether or not
a failure occurs during the test.

Detect: To affirm, discern, or sense the occurrence of a specific
statistic or discriminant.

Deterioration: Result of a degradation.

Diagnosis: The act or process of identifying a condition based on
an evaluation of its signs or symptoms.

Diagnostic: Pertaining to the detection and isolation of a mal-
    function.
Diagnostic routine: A logical sequence of tests designed to locate
    a malfunction.
Diagnostic test: A test performed for the purpose of isolating a
    malfunction in the system or confirming that there actually is
    a malfunction.
Discriminant: A statistic for which a detector can be specified.
Downtime: The period of time during which an item is not in a con-
    dition to perform its intended function.
Dynamic test: A test of one or more of the characteristics of the
    equipment or of any constituent components performed while the
    equipment is energized.
Engine condition monitoring (ECM): An observation for indication
    of a change in the condition of an engine or engine components.
Failure: A condition characterized by the inability of a material,
    structure, or system to fulfill its intended purpose (task or
    mission) and resulting in its retirement from usable service.
Failure detection: Act of identifying the presence or absence of a
    nonspecified failure mode in a specified system carrying out a
    given task or mission; this implies that a detection criterion
    has been specified.
Failure diagnosis: The act or process of identifying a failure mode
    (or condition) upon an evaluation of its signs and symptoms
    (including performance monitoring measurements).
Failure localization: If the outcome of failure detection is posi-
    tive, then failure localization designates the material, struc-
    tures, components, or systems which have failed.
Failure mechanism: The physical, chemical, or other process which
    results in failure.
Failure mode: The particular manner in which an omission of occur-
    rence or performance of a task or mission happens; it is a
    combination of catastrophic failures and degradation failures.
Failure path: The chain of events connecting a change of physical
    condition of one equipment component with changes in other
    components which can terminate in equipment failure.

Fault tree: An expression for a logic routine used to trace the
    sources of failures using a sequence of binary condition tests.
Functional test: A test performed to demonstrate that the item
    operates as specified.
Gradual failure: Failure that could be anticipated by prior exami-
    nation or monitoring.
Hard time limit: A maximum time interval for performing a mainten-
    ance or overhaul task.
Incipient failure: A condition prior to actual failure where the
    first signs of failure become observable by some acceptable
    means of detection.
Inspection: A careful and critical scrutiny of an item carried out
    with or without dismantling by using senses.
Intermittent failure: Failure of an item for a limited period of
    time, following which the item recovers its ability to perform
    its required function without being subject to any external
    corrective action.
Maintainability: A characteristic of design and installation which
    is expressed as a probability that an item will be retained in
    or restored to a specified condition within a given period of
    time when the maintenance is performed in accordance with pre-
    scribed procedures and resources.
Maintenance: A combination of any actions carried out to retain an
    item in, or restore it to, an acceptable condition.
Maintenance manual: Collated information and advice on the main-
    tenance requirements of an item.
Malfunction: Failure to operate in the normal, usual, or expected
    manner or level of performance; this may be intermittent and
    is due to either failures or degradations.
Monitoring: The act of observing indicative change or condition or
    function signals as warnings that possible corrections are re-
    quired.
Monitoring (performance or condition monitoring): Measurement and
    observation acquisition process accomplished by appropriate means
    for finding and resolving problems. To be monitored, a unit must

adversely affect operating safety or readiness, and its functioning must be viewable via measurement points and the like.

Nondestructive testing: Testing of a nature which does not impair
the usability of the item.

Observed failure rate: For a stated period in the life of an item,
the ratio of the total number of failures in a sample to the
cumulative observed operating time on that sample. The observed
failure rate is to be associated with particular and stated time
intervals (or summation of intervals) in the life of the items
and with stated conditions.

Observed mean life: The mean value of the lengths of observed times
to failure of all items in a sample under stated conditions.

Observed MTBF: For a stated period in the life of an item, the mean
value of the length of time between consecutive failures, computed as the ratio of the cumulative observed time to the number of failures, under stated conditions.

Observed MTTF: For a stated period in the life of an item, the ratio
of the cumulative operating time for a sample to the total number of failures in the sample during the period under stated
conditions.

Observed reliability: (a) of nonrepairable items: For a stated
period of time, the ratio of the number of items which performed
their functions satisfactorily at the end of the period to the
total number of items in the sample at the beginning of the
period; (b) of repairable items: The ratio of the number of
occasions on which items performed their functions satisfactorily for a stated period of time to the total number of occasions the items were required to perform for the same period.

Off-line testing: Any method of testing in which the unit under
test has been removed from its operational environment.

On condition: Repetitive inspections, tests, or measurement acqui-
sitions in order to determine the condition of units, systems,
or portions of structures.

On-line testing: Any method of testing which allows the unit under
test to be tested in its operational environment.

Overhaul: A comprehensive examination and restoration of an item,
or a major part thereof, to an acceptable condition.

Preventive maintenance: Maintenance carried out at predetermined
intervals or to other prescribed criteria and intended to reduce the likelihood of an item not meeting an acceptable condition.

Probability of false alarm: The likelihood of a decision being made
that a failure is imminent or has occurred when in fact this is
not true (the equipment is not failing).

Probability of reject or miss: The probability of not detecting an
imminent failure before or when it occurs.

Prognosis: The art or act of forecasting the future condition based
on present signs and symptoms observed.

Readiness: The ability of the system to carry out a specified task
or mission at a specified performance level, without interruption and catastrophic failure, when activated at any given
time; readiness is estimated either a priori or a posteriori.

Redundancy: In an item, the existence of more than one means for
performing a given function.

Reliability: The ability of an item to perform a required function
under stated conditions for a stated period of time.

Removal: Act of pulling down a component, module, structure, or
piece of equipment regardless of its condition.

Repair: To restore an item to an acceptable condition by renewal,
replacement, or mending of decayed or damaged parts.

Repairability: The probability that a failed item or piece of equipment will be restored to operability in no more than a specified
interval of active repair time when maintenance is performed
under specified conditions.

Restoration: Maintenance actions intended to bring an item back to
its original appearance or condition.

Screening test: A test, or combination of tests, intended to remove
unsatisfactory items or those likely to exhibit early failures.

Secondary effect: The effect of a condition change of one equipment
component on condition changes of other components tending to
extend component failure possibilities.

Secondary failure: Failure of an item caused either directly or
     indirectly by the failure of another item.

Self-test: A test or series of tests performed by the device upon
     itself which shows whether or not it is operating within desig-
     nated limits.

Sensor: A device used to provide an observation related to the con-
     dition of interest; i.e., such a device usually transforms
     physical quantities into an electrical output form or an image.

Sensor output format: The form of the signal or waveform supplied
     by the sensor, i.e., analog, pulse, frequency, digital, etc.

Signature: Refers to some characteristics of a signal or a combina-
     tion of signal characteristics which are specifically indicative
     of a component, assembly, or equipment status or condition.

Sonic vibration: Usually refers to dynamics of mechanical vibration
     waveforms in the frequency band of 1 Hz to 20 kHz.

Standby redundancy: That redundancy wherein the alternative means
     for performing a given function are inoperative until needed.

Statistic: A characteristic of a set of observables thought to
     provide a general description of the set as a whole; or a scalar
     function of a fixed number of measurements.

Stimuli: Any physical or electrical energy applied to a device in-
     tended to produce a measurable response.

System life cycle cost: The total cost of an item throughout its
     life, including initial, maintenance, and support costs.

Test: A test is a measurement procedure that provides sufficient
     information to determine whether or not all members of a par-
     ticular subset of elements are functioning properly. Each
     test is named by specifying a subset of elements operating or
     not operating all together.

Test point: A convenient safe access to a circuit or a system so
     that a significant quantity can be measured or introduced to
     facilitate maintenance, repair, calibration, alignment, and
     diagnosis.

Testing: To compare the response of an item to a suitable or de-
     fined application of stress, energy, or measurement against a
     standard.

Threshold element: The element following the detector which imple-
   ments a prescribed decision rule.

Transducer: A device used to change or condition the sensor output
   format for ease of computation, comparison, recording, etc.
   Note: A transducer is neither an A/D or D/A converter.

Trend analysis: The determination that if a signal is changing in
   some predictable manner, such as increasing in magnitude with
   respect to time, a forecast of failure probability can be made.

Troubleshooting: Locating and diagnosing malfunctions or breakdowns
   in equipment by means of systematic checking and analysis.

Ultrasonic vibration: Usually refers to the dynamics of mechanical
   vibration waveforms in the frequency range of more than 20 kHz.

Waveform: Usually a voltage-time record of a sensor output. Since
   a signal is related to a failure or impending failure, a waveform may or may not contain a signal.

Wear-out failure: Failure whose probability of occurrence increases
   with the passage of time and which occurs as a result of processes which are characteristic of the population.

PREVENTIVE MAINTENANCE OF MECHANICAL EQUIPMENT

1. Main Preventive Maintenance Steps:

(a) Burn-in of new or reconditioned machines

(b) Paint

(c) Cleansing of oil filters and sumps

(d) Lubrication

(e) Systematic operations

2. Organization of Preventive Maintenance: List of diagnostic tests aimed at eliminating the main failure causes.

Possible failure causes	No.	Diagnostic test to detect causes
1: Failure caused by jamming of a moving part, such jamming possibly occurring because of:	1	Check various points to be lubricated
	2	Check reservoirs, sumps, etc., in need of filling
Lack of lubrication	3	Check bearings for heating
Unsuitable oil/grease	4	Check nature of oil used
Dirty oil/grease	5	Drain sump if necessary
Leaks	6	Cleanse oil filters
Overloading	7	Cleanse oil sump
Inefficient cooling	8	Take samples to analyze
	9	Check for surplus oil
	10	Look for possible leaks
	11	Check oil pressures

Possible failure causes	No.	Diagnostic test to detect causes
	12	Check bearings for accidental loads
	13	Check pumps
	14	Check conduits for clogging
2: Failures caused by loosening of joining parts of mechanical and electrical gear (nuts, pins, corners, belt clips)	20	Tighten up bolts and screws
	21	Put corners and pins back into place
	22	Examine machine noise and vibrations
	23	Check belt clips
	30	Check coupling cones
	31	Check ferodos
	32	Check signs of wear and tear
	33	Check rollers for wear
	34	Check rail or race for wear and tear

3: Failures due to:
  Wear and tear
  Erosion
  Oxidation
  Overheating
  Chemical corrosion
  Electrical arcing
	35	Check ring and bearing wear

	36	Check shaft wear
	37	Check slide block wear
	38	Check pinions, sprocket wheels, and racks
	39	Check fork and ratchet wear
	40	Check drive chain wear
	41	Check universal joint
	42	Check coupling sleeves
	43	Check sliding pin wear
	44	Check conveyor belt wear
	45	Carry out necessary geometrical checkups
	46	Set regulating mechanism clearances
	47	Check state of paint and corrosion

Possible failure causes	No.	Diagnostic test to detect causes
4: Failures due to aging of materials such as electric insulators	50	Check insulating parts of contacts
	51	Check cable covering
	52	Check insulation
5: Jumping metals, overturning and other accidents due to race defects	60	Check rail gauge
	61	Check race level
	62	Check buffers at track end
	63	Check fixing to rails
	64	Check spragging
	65	Check rule observance

6. Failures due to collapse, elongation, or breaking of a part because of:
 	
    Misuse of equipment
    Material fatigue
    Defective design
    Unforeseeable accident
	70	Examine easily breakable parts

	71	Check flexible parts
	72	Check correct use of machines
	73	Check lifting cables and chains
	74	Check hooks and safety devices
	75	Check shackles
	76	Carry out static and dynamic checkups
	77	Restretch belts and chains
7. Failures due to power supply troubles such as excess or insufficient voltage	80	Carry out power checkups
	81	Check speeds

8. Wear and tear of controls:
 	
    Electric
    Pneumatic
    Hydraulic
	90	Examine state of power connections

	91	Check contact springs
	92	Check earth connections
	93	Check transformer protection
	94	Check motor bearing backlash
	95	Check dust gathering on motor

Possible failure cause	No.	Diagnostic test to detect cause
	96	Operate electric brakes
	97	Operate various safety devices
	98	Check power feed lines
	99	Check terminal clamping
	100	Check state of collector ring brushes
	101	Check dielectric state of collector rings
	103	Examine spark plugs
	104	Check platinated screws
	110	Check drive oil fill-up
	111	Check for possible fluid leaks
	112	Check valve operation
	113	Cleanse control oil sumps
9: Failures due to water inflow, humidity, or introduction of foreign body, causing:	120	Cleanse thrust blocks
	121	Cleanse slide bars
	122	Cleanse shafts
Short circuits	123	Report dirty machines
Clogging of thrust block	124	Check safety valves
	125	Check automatic stops
Filters not working	126	Check driving torque limiting devices
Greasy coupling		
Greasy or wet brakes	127	Check parachutes
Safety devices blocked	128	Examine brakes
	129	Examine thermal protection

VARIANCE OF ESTIMATED HISTOGRAMS

The use of fluctuations of the signature in external diagnosis (Chapters 11 and 12) is justified by the fact that it is natural to pay attention to the probability of observing a deviation in one interval at a time rather than investigating the probability density of this deviation throughout the whole measurement range. It is essential to find confidence intervals for this probability, because of the reduced sample size when carrying out interval-by-interval estimation. The computation of such confidence intervals is difficult; in this appendix, a technique is given which relies upon assumptions about the signal autocorrelation function and about the distribution of the fluctuations.

1. ASSUMPTIONS

The variance σ_h^2 of the estimator $\hat{h}(x)$ of the histogram of the signal deviation $\epsilon(t)$ is computed in accordance with the following assumptions:

(a) The random process $\epsilon(t)$ is stationary, ergodic, and normal $N(0,\sigma)$.

(b) The histogram is estimated from N discrete samples, $\epsilon(t)$ being sampled at the rate τ; these samples are assumed to be independent.

(c) The autocorrelation function $\underline{p}$ of $\epsilon(t)$ is estimated over a time interval $\tau_m \gg (N\tau)$; $\underline{p}(0) = 1$; $\underline{p}$ is assumed given.

(d) The histogram intervals are each of length Δx.

(e) Each interval δx is characterized by its middle x and by its length Δx: $\delta x \stackrel{\Delta}{=} [x - \Delta x/2; \; x + \Delta x/2]$; let $p = Pr[\epsilon(\ell\tau) \in \delta x]$, $\ell \leq N$; p depends on x, Δx, and $\underline{p}$.

(f) $p_k \stackrel{\Delta}{=} Pr\{\epsilon(\ell\tau) \in \delta x$ and $\epsilon(\ell + k)\tau \in \delta x\}$.

Following the previous assumptions (Cramer [A-28]),

$$p_k = \iint_{\delta x \cdot \delta x} w_{2k}(x_1, y_1, \underline{p}) \; dx_1 \; dy_1 \qquad x_1 \in \delta x, \; y_1 \in \delta x$$

$$x_1 \stackrel{\Delta}{=} \epsilon(\ell\tau) \qquad y_1 \stackrel{\Delta}{=} \epsilon((\ell + k)\tau)$$

$$w_{2k}(x_1, y_1, \underline{p}) \stackrel{\Delta}{=} \frac{1}{2\pi\sigma^2} \frac{1}{\sqrt{1 - \underline{p}^2(k\tau)}}$$

$$\cdot \exp\left\{ -\frac{1}{2\sigma^2} [1 - \underline{p}^2(k\tau)][x_1^2 + y_1^2 - 2\underline{p}(k\tau)x_1 y_1] \right\}$$

w_{2k} admits a Hermite polynomial series expansion (see Sections 2.10 and 4.7 of Chapter 1):

$$w_{2k}(x_1, y_1, \underline{p}) = \frac{1}{2\pi\sigma^2} \exp\left(-\frac{x_1^2 + y_1^2}{2\sigma^2} \right)$$

$$\cdot \sum_{j=0}^{\infty} H_j\left(\frac{x_1}{\sigma}\right) H_j\left(\frac{y_1}{\sigma}\right) \frac{\underline{p}^j(k\tau)}{j!}$$

where H_j is the Hermite polynomial of order j defined by

$$\left(\frac{d}{dx}\right)^j e^{-x^2/2} \stackrel{\Delta}{=} (-1)^j H_j(x) e^{-x^2/2}$$

2. VARIANCE OF THE HISTOGRAM ESTIMATE $\hat{h}(x)$

For $\hat{h}(x)$ we take the maximum-likelihood estimator:

$$\hat{h}(x) = \frac{N_{\delta x}}{N \, \Delta x} \qquad h(x) \stackrel{\Delta}{=} Pr(\epsilon(t) \in \delta x))$$

where $N_{\delta x}$ is the number of samples of $\epsilon(t)$ falling in the δx interval. The variance of that estimator is

$$\sigma_h^2(x) = \overline{\left[\hat{h}(x)^2\right]} - \overline{\left[\hat{h}(x)\right]}^2$$

$$= \frac{p}{N(\Delta x)^2} + \frac{2}{N(\Delta x)^2} \cdot \sum_{k=1}^{N} \left(1 - \frac{k}{N}\right) p_k - \frac{p}{(\Delta x)^2}$$

Let us replace p_k by its series expansion:

$$\sigma_h^2(x) = \frac{p}{N(\Delta x)^2} - \frac{p}{(\Delta x)^2}$$

$$+ \frac{1}{\pi N(\sigma \, \Delta x)^2} \sum_{k=1}^{N} \left(1 - \frac{k}{N}\right) \iint_{\delta x \cdot \delta x} \exp\left(-\frac{x_1^2 + y_1^2}{2\sigma^2}\right)$$

$$\cdot \sum_{j=0}^{\infty} \frac{p^j(k\tau)}{j!} H_j\left(\frac{x_1}{\sigma}\right) H_j\left(\frac{y_1}{\sigma}\right) dx_1 \, dy_1$$

Following term-by-term integration,

$$\sigma_h^2(x) = \frac{p}{(\Delta x)^2} \left[\frac{1 - p}{Np} + \sum_{j=1}^{r} \frac{b_j}{j}\left(\frac{d_j}{p}\right)^2 + R_r \right] \qquad (2.1)$$

where:

i. $\quad b_j \triangleq \frac{2}{N} \sum_{k=1}^{N} \left(1 - \frac{k}{N}\right) \underline{p}^j(k\tau)$ $\qquad\qquad\qquad$ (2.2)

remains bounded for $\tau \to 0$.

ii. $\quad d_j \triangleq \frac{1}{\sigma\sqrt{2\pi(j-1)!}} \int_{\delta x} \exp\left(-\frac{x_1^2}{2\sigma^2}\right) \cdot H_j\left(\frac{x_1}{\sigma}\right) dx_1$ (2.3)

is found to be almost independent of j.

iii. $\quad R_r \triangleq \sum_{j=r+1}^{\infty} \frac{b_j}{r}\left(\frac{d_j}{p}\right)^2$ $\qquad$ r: given integer

is a residual term which will be bounded in Section 6.

The advantage of formula (2.1) is therefore that all computations required to determine σ_h^2 with a specified numerical accuracy can be carried out fairly easily.

In practical cases, b_j, d_j, and p are tabulated vs. $N_{\delta x}$, N, and $\underline{p}$; these precomputations allow us to carry out external diagnosis by the histogram method still in quasi-real time.

3. COMPUTATION OF THE PROBABILITY p
   OF BELONGING TO THE δx INTERVAL

In the remainder of this appendix, x will be replaced by the normalized variable x/σ; thus the new variance of the signal becomes equal to 1.

   If the normal probability density function $w_1(x)$ is expanded in Taylor series vs. x and integrated over δx, we find

$$p = \frac{1}{\sqrt{2\pi}} \Delta x \cdot e^{-x^2/2} \left[\sum_{j=0}^{m-1} H_{2j}(x) \left(\frac{\Delta x}{2} \right)^{2j} \frac{1}{(2j+1)!} + R_{2m} \right]$$

$$|R_{2m}| \le \max_{x_1 \in \delta x} \left[|H_{2m}(x_1)| e^{(x^2 - x_1^2)/2} \right] \frac{(\Delta x/2)^{2m}}{(2m+1)!}$$

A simple way to obtain an upper bound on R_{2m} is to use the inequality

$$|H_j(x)| < 1.086435 \times \sqrt{j!} \exp\left(\frac{x^2}{4} \right)$$

Thus

$$|R_{2m}| \le \max_{x_1 \in \delta x} \left[\exp\left(-\frac{x_1^2}{4} \right) \right] \times 1.086435 \times e^{x^2/2} \frac{(\Delta x/2)^{2m}}{\sqrt{2m!}\,(2m+1)}$$

   This upper bound is less than 10^{-3} for $m \ge 6$ whenever $|x/\sigma| \le 4$ and $|\Delta x/\sigma| \le 2$, or for $m \ge 2$ whenever $|x/\sigma| \le 4$ and $|\Delta x/\sigma| < 0.1$.

4. COMPUTATION OF d_j

d_j can be computed exactly by integration:

$$d_j = \frac{1}{\sqrt{2\pi(j-1)!}} \left[H_{j-1}\left(x - \frac{\Delta x}{2} \right) \exp\left\{ -\frac{[x - (\Delta x/2)]^2}{2} \right\} \right.$$
$$\left. - H_{j-1}\left(x + \frac{\Delta x}{2} \right) \exp\left\{ -\frac{[x + (\Delta x/2)]^2}{2} \right\} \right] \qquad j \ge 1$$

where the Hermite polynomials are obtained recursively:

$$H_j = xH_{j-1} - (j - 1)H_{j-2}$$

If Δx is small, the following approximation can be established:

$$d_j \# \frac{1}{\sqrt{2\pi}} \frac{H_j(x)}{\sqrt{j!}} e^{-x^2/2} \cdot \Delta x$$

5.   COMPUTATION OF b_j

b_j is defined by an expression which can be computed numerically or analytically if $\underline{p}$ is given:

$$b_j \overset{\Delta}{=} \frac{2}{N} \sum_{k=1}^{N} \left(1 - \frac{k}{N}\right) \underline{p}^j(k\tau)$$

For example, if the autocorrelation function is $\underline{p}(k\tau) = e^{-k}$, then

$$b_j = \frac{2}{N} \frac{e^{-j}}{1 - e^{-j}} \left(1 - \frac{1}{N} \frac{1 - e^{-jN}}{1 - e^{-j}}\right)$$

6.   UPPER BOUND ON THE RESIDUAL R_r

To determine the number r of terms which ought to be considered in the limited expansion (2.1), it is useful to have available an upper bound for $|R_r|$,

$$|R_r| \leq \frac{1}{p^2} \sum_{j=r+1}^{\infty} \frac{|b_j| d_j^2}{j} \leq \frac{1}{p^2} \max\{|b_{r+1}|, |b_{r+2}|\} \cdot \sum_{j=r+1}^{\infty} \frac{d_j^2}{j}$$

because $b_{2j} \geq |b_{2j+1}|$ and $b_{2j} \geq b_{2j+2}$.

However,

$$\sum_{j=1}^{\infty} \frac{d_j^2}{j} = p(p - 1)$$

Thus

$$|R_r| \leq \max\{|b_{r+1}|,|b_{r+2}|\}\left[\frac{1-p}{p} - \sum_{j=1}^{r} \frac{1}{j}\left(\frac{d_j}{p}\right)^2\right]$$

One may establish a closer bound if Δx is small.

7.   IMPLEMENTATION CONSIDERATIONS

The convergence of the limited expansion (2.1) is improved by the fact that the decrease of the autocorrelation $\underline{p}(k\tau)$ may eventually be rapid when k increases. Smaller Δx values reduce the convergence speed.

It is essential to record $\varepsilon(t)$ for a time τ_m long enough to guarantee a stable estimate of the autocorrelation function.

Because of the crucial role played by $\underline{p}(t)$, this technique is well adapted to those cases where the system signature fluctuations vary slowly or periodically with time. This applies, for example, to rotating machinery such as pumps, mills, paper mills, and electric motors driving radar antennas.

RELIABILITY OF MAJOR SYSTEMS
WITH REDUNDANCIES OR STANDBY SPARES

SYSTEM		R_s = SYSTEMS RELIABILITY R_s	
Series	A_1 — A_j --- A_n	$R_s = \prod_{i=1}^{n} R_i = \exp\left(-\sum_{i=1}^{n} \lambda_i\, t\right)$	$R_i \triangleq$ Reliability of A_i = Survival probability
Parallel (duplex) active units	A_1 A_2	$R_s = 1 - (1 - R_1)(1 - R_2)$ $R_s = 1 - F_1\, F_2$	$F_i \triangleq (1 - R_i)$ = failure probability
Parallel (duplex) standby unit	A_1 A_2	$R_s = \dfrac{\lambda_1 R_2 - \lambda_2 R_1}{\lambda_1 - \lambda_2}$	A_1 = active unit A_2 = standby unit
Parallel (triplex) active	A_1 A_2 A_3	$R_s = 1 - \prod_{i=1}^{3} (1 - R_i)$ $R_s = 1 - F_1 \cdot F_2 \cdot F_3$	$F_i \triangleq 1 - R_i$

SYSTEM		R_s = SYSTEMS RELIABILITY	
Majority voting (m out of n for success)	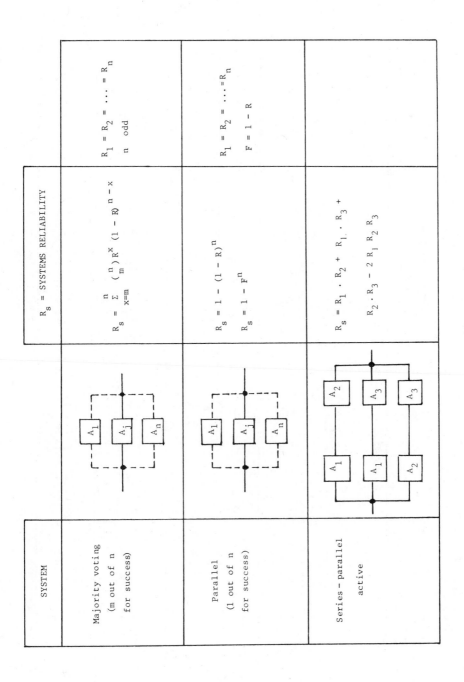	$R_s = \sum_{x=m}^{n} \binom{n}{m} R^x (1-R)^{n-x}$	$R_1 = R_2 = \cdots = R_n$ n odd
Parallel (1 out of n for success)		$R_s = 1 - (1-R)^n$ $R_s = 1 - F^n$	$R_1 = R_2 = \cdots = R_n$ $F = 1 - R$
Series-parallel active		$R_s = R_1 \cdot R_2 + R_1 \cdot R_3 + R_2 \cdot R_3 - 2 R_1 R_2 R_3$	

SYSTEM		R_s = SYSTEMS RELIABILITY	
Simple redundancy		$1 - P_o - P_c$	P_o = failure probability for an open circuit P_c = failure probability for a closed circuit
Series redundancy		$1 - (2 P_o - P_o^2) - P_c^2$	P_o, P_c as above
Parallel redundancy		$1 - P_o^2 - (2 P_o - P_c)^2$	P_o, P_c as above
Quadruple serial redundancy		$1 - (2 P_o - P_o^2)^2 - (2 P_c - P_c^4)$	P_o, P_c as above
Quadruple parallel redundancy		$1 - (2 P_c^2 - P_c^4) - (2 P_c - P_c^2)^2$	P_o, P_c as above

The following includes:

i. Sections A, B, and C: general references, in which some basic theoretical notions are further developed; these lists are obviously incomplete because of the large number of publications on these subjects.

ii. Sections D, E, F, G, and H: references specific to failure diagnosis and performance monitoring of nondigital systems; the most recent publications have been gathered, considering the fact that they are extremely scattered throughout the technical literature.

In addition to the last five sections, we have provided lists of journals or conferences likely to include papers on these specific subjects; some standards are also mentioned when considered useful. Not all references are cited in the text.

It has been considered essential to list references pertaining to a wide range of equipment types, so that readers may by themselves correlate the general techniques of this book, with special considerations related to specific applications.

Moreover, additional bibliographies on fault detection and location in analog or digital systems can be found in R. Saeks and S. R. Liberty, Rational Fault Analysis, Vol. 1, Electrical Engineering and Electronics Series, Dekker, New York, 1977.

A. GENERAL REFERENCES IN STATISTICS, PROBABILITY THEORY,
   DIGITAL SIGNAL PROCESSING, AND AUTOMATIC CONTROL

A-1 T. W. Anderson, An Introduction to Multivariate Statistical
     Analysis, Wiley, New York, 1958.

A-2 J. S. Bendat and A. G. Piersol, Measurement and Analysis of
     Random Data, Wiley, New York, 1966.

A-3 J. P. Benzecri (ed.), L'analyse des données, Vols. I and II,
     Dunod, Paris, 1973.

A-4 K. Gerdin, On histogram uncertainty for normal, stationary
     signals with an application to paper machine disturbances,
     Acta Polytech. Scand. MA-23, Stockholm (1971).

A-5 R. Baeyens and B. Jacquet, Applications of identification
     methods in power generation and distribution, Jour. A 15(4)
     (1974).

A-6 D. Graupe, Identification of Systems, Van Nostrand-Reinhold,
     New York, 1972.

A-7 W. Feller, An Introduction to Probability Theory and Its
     Applications, Vols. 1 and 2, Wiley, New York, 1968.

A-8 B. Gold and C. M. Rader, Digital Processing of Signals,
     McGraw-Hill, New York, 1969.

A-9 H. O. Lancaster, The Chi-Square Distribution, Wiley, New York,
     1969.

A-10 A. H. Jazwinski, Stochastic Processes and Filtering Theory,
     Academic Press, New York, 1970.

A-11 R. Kalman and R. Bucy, A new approach to linear filtering and
     prediction, ASME Trans.: J. Basic Eng. 35 (1960).

A-12 H. Kaufman and J. L. Groboillot, La prévision économique à
     court terme: méthodes générales de lissage exponentiel,
     Dunod, Paris, 1968.

A-13 M. G. Kendall, A Course in Multivariate Analysis, Hafner,
     New York, 1967.

A-14 E. O. Landeide, Statistical uncertainty of estimating corre-
     lation between signals in noise, SACLANTCEN Memorandum No. 185,
     La Spezia, Italy, 1972.

A-15 L. Lebart and J. P. Fenelon, Statistique et informatique ap-
     pliquées, Dunod, Paris, 1971.

A-16 Yu. I. Medvedev, Some theorems on the asymptotic distribution
     of a chi-2 statistic, Dokl. Akad. Nauk SSSR 192(5) (1970).

A-17 D. F. Morrison, Multivariate Statistical Methods, McGraw-Hill,
     New York, 1967.

A-18 L. F. Pau, Distributions et filtres linéaires, ENS de l'Aéro-
     matiques, ENS de l'Aeromautique, Paris, 1969, 35 pp.

A-19 J. Richalet, A. Rault, and R. Pouliquen, Identification des
      processus par la méthode du modèle, Gordon & Breach, New York,
      1973.

A-20 G. P. H. Styan, Notes on the distribution of quadratic forms
      in singular normal variables, Biometrika 57(3), 567 (1970).

A-21 A. P. Sage and J. L. Melsa, System Identification, Academic
      Press, New York, 1971.

A-22 G. E. P. Box and G. M. Jenkins, Time Series Analysis for Fore-
      casting and Control, Holden-Day, San Francisco, 1970.

A-23 P. I. Dhrymes, Distributed Lags, Oliver & Boyd, Edinburgh, 1971.

A-24 G. B. Mann and A. Wald, On the statistical treatment of linear
      difference equations, Econometrica 11, 173-220 (1943).

A-25 D. Graupe, D. J. Krause, and J. B. Moore, Identification of
      ARMA parameters of time series, IEEE Trans. Autom. Control
      AC-20 (Feb. 1975).

A-26 U. Grenander, On Toeplitz forms and stationary processes, Ark.
      Mat. Astron. Fys. 1, 555-571 (1951).

A-27 U. Grenander and M. Rosenblatt, Statistical Analysis of Sta-
      tionary Time Series, Wiley, New York, 1957.

A-28 H. Cramer, Mathematical Methods of Statistics, Almquist &
      Wiksell, Uppsala, 1945, or Princeton Mathematical Series No. 9,
      Princeton University Press, Princeton, N.J., 1946.

A-29 C. V. L. Charlier, Application de la théorie des probabilités
      à l'astronomie, in Traité de calcul des probabilités, Vol. 2,
      Part IV (E. Borel, ed.), Paris, 1931.

A-30 E. Dynkin and A. Yushkevich, Markov Processes: Theory and
      Problems, Plenum, New York, 1969.

A-31 L. R. Rabiner and B. Gold, Theory and Application of Digital
      Signal Processing, Prentice-Hall, Englewood Cliffs, N.J., 1975.

A-32 A. J. Duncan, Quality Control and Industrial Statistics,
      Irwin, Homewood, Ill., 1965.

A-33 R. C. K. Lee, Optimal Estimation, Identification and Control,
      M.I.T. Press, Cambridge, Mass., 1964.

A-34 E. L. Lehmann, Testing Statistical Hypotheses, Wiley, New York,
      1959.

A-35 D. R. Cox and P. A. W. Lewis, The Statistical Analysis of
      Series of Events, Methuen, London, 1966.

A-36 P. A. W. Lewis, Asymptotic properties and equilibrium condi-
      tions for branching Poisson processes, J. Appl. Probl. 6, 355-
      371 (1976).

A-37 E. J. Gumbel, Statistical Theory of Extremes, Columbia Univer-
      sity Press, New York, 1958.

A-38   H. Akaike, Power Spectrum identification through autoregressive
       model fitting, Ann. Inst. Stat. Math. 21, 407-419 (1969).

A-39   H. Akaike, Statistical predictor identification, Ann. Inst.
       Stat. Math. 22, 203-217 (1970).

A-40   F. Itakura and S. Saito, A statistical method for estimation
       of speech spectral density and formant frequencies, Electr.
       Commun. Japan 53-A(1), 36-43 (1970).

A-41   J. Markel and A. Gray, On autocorrelation equations as applied
       to speech analysis, IEEE Trans. Audio. AU-21(2), 69-79 (1973).

A-42   C. Derman, Finite State Markovian Decision Processes, Academic
       Press, New York, 1970.

A-43   R. C. Singleton, A comparison of FFT algorithms, AD-735920,
       Jan. 1972.

A-44   N. L. Mathiesen, Adjustment of inconsistent sets of measure-
       ments using linear programming, Automatica 10, 431-435 (1974).

A-45   L. F. Pau, Statistical Quality Control by Variables; Applica-
       tion to Instrumentation, Editions Chiron, Paris, 1978.

A-46   M. O. Hill, Correspondence analysis: a neglected multivariate
       method, Appl. Stat. Ser. C 23(3), 340-354 (1974).

A-47   H. O. Hirschfeld, A connection between correlation and con-
       tingency, Proc. Cambridge Philos. Soc. 31, 520-524 (1935).

A-48   R. A. Fischer, The precision of discriminant functions, Ann.
       Eugen. London 10, 422-429 (1940).

A-49   M. G. Kendall and A. Stuart, The Advanced Theory of Statistics,
       Vol. 2, Inference and Relationship, Griffin, London, 1961.

A-50   H. H. Rosenbrock, Computer-Aided Control System Design,
       Academic Press, New York, 1974.

A-51   A. G. J. MacFarlane and I. Postlethwaite, The generalized
       Nyquist stability criterion and multivariable root loci, Int.
       J. Control 23(1), 81-128 (Jan. 1977).

A-52   C. A. Desoer and M. Vidyasagar, Feedback Systems: Input-Output
       Properties, Academic Press, New York, 1975.

B.   PATTERN RECOGNITION

B-0   Journals: Pattern Recognition; Cybernetic Abstracts (from
       Russian); Communications of the ACM; Artificial Intelligence;
       Journal of Man-Machine Studies; Engineering Cybernetics (USSR)
       (from Russian); Kybernetik; Computer Graphics and Image Pro-
       cessing; Machine Intelligence; Automation and Remote Control
       (USSR) (from Russian); IEEE Transactions on Pattern Analysis
       and Machine Intelligence (PAMI), Automatic Control (AC), Computers
       (C), Information Theory (IT), Systems, Man and Cybernetics

(SMC); Bell System Technical Journal; IBM Journal of Research and Development

B-1   M. E. Hellman, The nearest neighbor classification rule with a reject option, IEEE Trans. Syst. Man Cybern. SMC-6(3), 179-185 (July 1970).

B-2   W. C. Martin and W. D. Hokins, A state space basis for sequential pattern classification, 1st International J. Conference on Pattern Recognition, Oct. 30-Nov. 1, 1973, Washington D.C., IEEE catalog 73-CHO-821-9C, pp. 159-165.

B-3   P. W. Becker, Recognition of Patterns Using the Frequencies of Occurrence of Binary Words, 3rd ed., Springer-Verlag, New York, 1978.

B-4   C. H. Chen, Statistical Pattern Recognition, Spartan Books, Hayden, New York, 1973.

B-5   J. Donio, Problèmes de diagnostic par construction d'espaces mesurables, Metra 11(2), 315-331 (1972).

B-6   E. Diday, Optimisation en classification automatique et reconnaissance des formes, RAIRO 3, 61-96 (Nov. 1972).

B-7   O. Duda and P. E. Hart, Pattern Classification and Scene Analysis, Wiley-Interscience, New York, 1973.

B-8   K. Fukunaga, Introduction to Statistical Pattern Recognition, Academic Press, New York, 1972.

B-9   U. Grenander, Foundations of pattern analysis, Q. Appl. Math. 27(1) (April 1969).

B-10 C. A. Kulikowski, Pattern recognition approach to medical diagnosis, IEEE Trans. Syst. Man Cybern. SMC-6(3) (July 1970).

B-11 D. O. Loftsgaarden and C. P. Quesenbury, A nonparametric estimate of a multivariate density function, Ann. Math. Stat. 36, 1049-1051 (1965).

B-12 W. S. Meisel, Computer Oriented Approaches to Pattern Recognition, Academic Press, New York, 1972.

B-13 J. Mendel and K. S. Fu (eds.), Adaptive Learning and Pattern Recognition Systems, Academic Press, New York, 1970.

B-14 M. Minsky and S. Papert, Perceptrons, M.I.T. Press, Cambridge, Mass., 1969.

B-15 E. A. Patrick and F. P. Fischer, A generalized k-nearest neighbor rule, Inf. Control 16(2), 128-152 (April 1970).

B-16 E. A. Patrick, Fundamentals of Pattern Recognition, Prentice-Hall, Englewood Cliffs, N.J., 1972.

B-17 L. F. Pau, Common theoretical formulation of the pattern recognition, identification and detection problems, IMSOR, Tech. Univ. Denmark, Lyngby, March 1972, 24 p.

B-18 L. F. Pau, Méthodes statistiques de réduction et de reconnais-
      sance des formes, Dr. ing. thesis, University of Paris-Sud,
      Orsay, CNRS Report No. A-0-8-165, May 29, 1972.

B-19 L. F. Pau, Statistical reduction and recognition of speech
      patterns, in Machine Perception of Patterns and Pictures,
      Conf. Publ. No. 13, Institute of Physics, London, 1972, pp.
      126-133.

B-20 L. F. Pau, Optimisation d'une métrique et déformations en
      reconnaissance des formes, Journées d'étude GALF 1973, Presses
      Université libre de Bruxelles, May 1973.

B-21 L. F. Pau, Applications de la reconnaissance des formes dans
      le domaine aérospatial, L'Aéronautique et l'astronautique 42,
      67-78 (1973-1974).

B-22 L. F. Pau (ed.), Topics in pattern recognition, IMSOR, Tech.
      Univ. Denmark, Lyngby, 1973, p. 159.

B-23 C. Roche, Information utile en reconnaissance des formes et
      en compression des données; application à la génération auto-
      matique de systèmes de reconnaissance optique et acoustique,
      Thèse d'état, University Paris VI (1972).

B-24 M. J. Sorum, Estimating the conditional probability of mis-
      classification, Technometrics 13(2), 333-353 (May 1971).

B-25 Ya. Z. Tsypkin, Adaptation and Learning in Automatic Systems,
      Academic Press, New York, 1971.

B-26 L. Uhr, Pattern Recognition, Learning and Thought, Prentice-
      Hall, Englewood Cliffs, N.J., 1973.

B-27 O. Spire, Détermination de l'importance relative de différents
      paramètres descriptifs pour l'obtention d'un diagnostic, RAIRO
      4(1), 85-99 (1970).

B-28 G. N. Saridis and R. F. Hofstadter, A pattern recognition ap-
      proach to the classification of non-linear systems, IEEE Trans.
      Syst. Man Cybern. SMC-4(4), 362-371 (July 1974).

B-29 H. Niemann, Methoden der Mustererkennung, Akademische Verlags-
      gesellschaft, Frankfurt am Main, 1974.

B-30 K. S. Fu, Sequential Methods in Pattern Recognition and Machine
      Learning, Academic Press, New York, 1968.

B-31 K. S. Fu (ed.), Pattern Recognition and Machine Learning,
      Plenum, New York, 1971.

B-32 S. Noguchi and T. Watanabe, On self-learning systems, J. Cy-
      bern. 3(1), 60-71 (1973).

B-33 L. F. Pau, Shape dependent similarity measures for oriented
      line patterns, Comput. Graph. & Im. Proc. 4, 388-395 (Dec.
      1975).

B-34 K. S. Fu (ed.), Digital Pattern Recognition, Vol. 10, Communications and Cybernetics, Springer, Berlin, 1976.

B-35 T. Pavlidis and G. S. Fang, A segmentation technique for waveform classification, IEEE Trans. Comput. C-21, 901-903 (Aug. 1972).

C. RELIABILITY AND MAINTENANCE THEORIES

C-0 Standards: MIL-STD-756-B, Reliability Prediction Procedures; MIL-STD-781-C, Reliability for Exponential Failure Distribution; CCT-1010, Maintenabilité des équipements électroniques

C-1 R. E. Barlow and F. Proschan, Mathematical Theory of Reliability, Wiley, New York, 1965.

C-2 S. H. Tsiang, G. Haugk, and H. N. Sekler, Maintenance of a large electronic switching system, IEEE Trans. Commun. COM-17, 1-9 (Feb. 1969).

C-3 N. R. Mann, R. E. Schafer, and N. D. Singpurwalla, Methods for Statistical Analysis of Reliability and Life Data, Wiley, New York, 1974.

C-4 J. de Corlieu, Fiabilité des systèmes, ENS de l'Aéronautique, Toulouse, 1971.

C-5 J. de Corlieu, Maintenabilité et vie des systèmes, ENS de l'Aéronautique, Toulouse, 1972.

C-6 G. L. Grellin (ed.), Special issue on Bayesian reliability techniques, IEEE Trans. Reliab. R-21(3) (Aug. 1972).

C-7 J. M. Dethoor and J. L. Groboillot, La vie des équipements: investissement, renouvellement et maintenance, Dunod, Paris, 1968.

C-8 A. M. Freudenthal (ed.), Structural Safety and Reliability, Pergamon Press, Elmsford, N.Y., 1972.

C-9 A. S. Goldman and T. B. Slattery, Maintainability, Wiley, New York, 1964.

C-10 A. M. Gorlin, Problems of selecting an optimal servicing mode for an automatic system, Izv. Akad. Nauk. SSSR Tekh. Kibern., 21(3), 79-85 (1967).

C-11 A. J. Gross, An approach to the minimization of misclassification in the repair of equipments, IEEE Trans. Reliab. R-19(1) 10-13 (Feb. 1970).

C-12 C. Lievens, Securité des systèmes aéronautiques, Cepadues Editions, Toulouse, 1977.

C-13 J. C. Wanner, Etude de la sécurité des aéronefs en utilisation, Service Technique Aéronautique, Paris, Oct. 1969.

C-14   H. L. Gilster, A statistical analysis of aircraft maintenance
       costs, Oper. Res. 18(5), 904-917 (Sept.-Oct. 1970).

C-15   J. M. Myhre and S. C. Saunders, Approximate confidence limits
       for complex systems with exponential component lives, Ann.
       Math. Stat. 42(1), 342-348 (1971).

C-16   NATO, Conference on Reliability Testing and Reliability Evalu-
       ation, The Hague, Sept. 4-8, 1972, Bureau of Business Services
       and Research, California State University, Northridge, Calif.,
       1972.

C-17   C. Neuman and N. M. Bonhomme, Optimal inspection and repair
       schedules for multicomponent systems, IEEE Trans. Syst. Man
       Cybern. 4(1), 68-75 (Jan. 1974).

C-18   B. G. Peyret, La fiabilité industrielle et ses bases mathé-
       matiques, Eyrolles, Paris, 1969.

C-19   B. L. S. Prakasa Rao, Estimation for distributions with mono-
       tone failure rate, Ann. Math. Stat. 41(2), 507-519 (1970).

C-20   B. L. Retterer, A design sensitive maintainability prediction
       technique, in Proceedings of the 1972 Annual Reliability and
       Maintainability Symposium, San Francisco, Jan. 25-27, 1972,
       Annals of Assurance Sciences, IEEE Catalog 72-CH 0577-7R, 1972,
       pp. 111-115.

C-21   V. L. Grose, Status of failure mode and effect analysis,
       fault-tree analysis and prediction, ASME Ann. Reliab. & Maint.
       10, 415-422 (1971).

C-22   V. V. Bolotin, Statistical Methods in Structural Mechanics,
       Holden-Day, San Francisco, 1969.

C-23   J. D. Esary, A. W. Marshall, and F. Proschan, Shock models
       and wear processes, Ann. Probability 1(4), 627-649, 1973.

C-24   Reliability Stress and Failure Rate Data for Electronic Equip-
       ments, MIL-HDBK-217-A/B, Dec. 12, 1971, and revisions.

C-25   C. Marcovicci and J. C. Ligeron, Utilisation des techniques
       de fiabilité en mécanique, PSI-Technique et documentation,
       Paris, 1974.

C-26   M. L. Shooman, Probabilistic Reliability: An Engineering Ap-
       proach, McGraw-Hill, New York, 1968.

C-27   RADC, Hybrid Micro-circuit Reliability Data, compiled by the
       Reliability Analysis Center, RADC, Rome, N.Y., Pergamon, Elms-
       ford, N.Y., 1975.

C-28   A. E. Davies, Principles and practice of aircraft power-plant
       maintenance, Trans. Inst. Mar. Eng. 84, Part 14, 441-457 (1972).

C-29   FAA, Handbook for Maintenance Control by Reliability Methods,
       Advisory Circular 120-17, FAA, Washington, 1965 (condition
       monitoring).

C-30 B. Gnedenko, Mathematical Methods of Reliability Theory, Academic Press, New York, 1969.

C-31 P. Kolesar, Minimum cost replacement under Markovian deterioration, Manage. Sci. 12(9), 694-706 (1966).

C-32 P. Kolesar, Randomized replacement rules which maximize the expected cycle length of equipments subject to Markovian deterioration, Manage. Sci. 13(11), 867-878 (1967).

C-33 M. Corazza, Techniques mathématiques de la fiabilité prévisionnelle, Cepadues Editions, Toulouse, 1975.

C-34 Reactor Safety Study, PB-248-201 to -208, Nuclear Regulatory Commission, Germantown, Md., Oct. 1975.

C-35 A. S. Goldman and T. B. Slattery, Maintainability: A Major Element of System Effectiveness, Krieger, New York, 1977.

C-36 Maintenance Engineering Techniques, AD-A-021390, 1975.

C-37 Development Guide for Reliability: Design for Reliability (Part 2), Reliability Prediction (Part 3), Reliability Measurement (Part 4), Mathematical Appendix (Part 6), AD-A-027370, AD-A-032105, AD-A-027371, AD-A-027372, Jan. 1976.

C-38 NTIS-Search: Replacement Theory, NTIS/PS-77/0540/3 PNB, NTIS, Springfield, VA., June 1977.

C-39 U.S. Naval Ordnance Systems Command, Maintainability Engineering Handbook, GPO, Washington, D.C., 1970.

C-40 G. V. Druzhinin, Reliability of Automated Systems, Energiya, Moscow, 1977.

C-41 Instruction générale sur la maintenance et l'entretien des équipements de télécommunications, Direction Générale des Télécommunications, Paris, 1971.

C-42 C. P. Tsokos and I. N. Shimi (eds.), The Theory and Applications of Reliability with Emphasis on Bayesian and Nonparametric Methods, Vols. I and II, Academic Press, New York, 1977.

C-43 G. V. Druzhinin, Reliability of Automated Systems, Energiya, Moscow, 1977.

C-44 Maintenance Engineering Techniques, AD-A-021390/PDM, June 1975.

C-45 Development Guide for Reliability, Part 2 (AD-A-027370), Part 3 (AD-A-032105), Part 4 (AD-A-027371), Part 6 (AD-A-027372), Jan. 1976.

C-46 L. F. Pau and G. G. Weber, A fault-tree approach to quality control by variables, IEEE Trans. Reliability R-28(3), 344-352 (Dec. 1979).

D. TEST SEQUENCING AND SEQUENTIAL DIAGNOSIS

D-0 Journals: Operations Research; Methods of Information in Medicine; Naval Research Logistics Quarterly; Technometrics; IEEE Transactions on Reliability (R); Management Science

D-1   G. Anthony and C. Octo Barnett, Sequential diagnosis by com-
       puter, JAMA 205(12), 141-146 (Sept. 16, 1968).

D-2   Yu K. Belyaeu and I. A. Ushakov, Mathematical models for prob-
       lems of detection and localization of failures, in: Cyber-
       netics in the Service of Communism, Vol. 2, Energiya, Moscow,
       1964 (in Russian).

D-3   R. G. Bennetts and D. W. Levin, Fault diagnosis of digital
       systems — a review, Comput. J. 4(2), 199-206 (1971).

D-4   R. W. Butterworth, A branch and bound method for optimal fault
       finding, Report ORC 69-21, College of Engineering, University
       of California, Berkeley, Aug. 1969, and grants DA-31-124-ARO-
       D-331, GN-1684.

D-5   G. Cardillo and K. S. Fu, On suboptimal sequential pattern
       recognition, IEEE Trans. Electronic Computers EC-17(8), 565-
       588 (Aug. 1968).

D-6   F. C. Reed, A sequential multidecision procedure, in Proceed-
       ings of a Symposium on Decision Theory and Applications to
       Electronic Equipment, U.S.A.F. Development Center, Rome, N.Y.,
       April 1960.

D-7   J. Donio, E. Hayat, and M. Tenenhaus, Le problème Bayésien:
       application des modèles bayésiens séquentiels au problème de
       l'aide à l'action médicale, Metra 9(2), 237-259 (1970).

D-8   K. S. Fu, Sequential Methods in Pattern Recognition, Academic
       Press, New York, 1968.

D-9   A. S. Ginsberg and F. L. Offensend, An application of decision
       theory to a medical diagnosis, IEEE Trans. Syst. Man Cybern.
       SSC-4(3), 355-362 (Sept. 1968).

D-10   B. Gluss, An optimum policy for detecting a fault in a complex
       system, Oper. Res. 7(4), 468-477 (July-Aug. 1959).

D-11   I. J. Good and W. I. Card, The diagnostic process with special
       reference to errors, Methods Inf. Med. 10(3), 176-188 (1971).

D-12   G. S. Pashkovskiy, Optimization of sequential fault detection
       procedures, Eng. Cybern. 9(2), 259-270 (March-April 1971).

D-13   L. F. Pau, Sequential pattern recognition methods applied to
       technical diagnosis and maintenance, IMSOR, Tech. Univ. Den-
       mark, Lyngby, April 1973, 54 pp.

D-14   L. F. Pau, Sequencing laboratory tests for improved sequential
       diagnosis, in Proc. MEDINFO 74, North-Holland, Amsterdam,
       1975, pp. 569-574.

D-15   V. I. Perov, Majority gradient method for the optimization of
       a sequential procedure for checking operability, Autom. and
       Remote Control USSR, 31(2), 282-288 (Feb. 1970).

D-16   E. Persoon, Dynamic Sequential Pattern Recognition Applied to
       Medical Diagnosis, AD-734292, Purdue University, Lafayette,
       Ind., July 1971.

D-17   E. E. Scheufens, Optimal lokalisering af en enkelt fejl i et
       system, in Ref. B-22, p. 19.

D-18   J. R. Slagle and R. C. T. Lee, Application of game tree search-
       ing techniques to sequential pattern recognition, Commun. ACM
       14(2), 103-110 (1971).

D-19   F. S. Sogomonyan, Testing operability and failure localization
       in functionally connected systems, Avtomatika i Telemekhanika
       25(6) (1964).

D-20   L. S. Timonen, Construction of optimal programs for diagnostics,
       Eng. Cybern., No. 4, 94-100 (1966).

D-21   A. Wald and J. Wolfowitz, Optimum character of sequential
       probability ratio tests, Ann. Math. Stat. 19, 326-329 (1948).

D-22   M. Cohn and G. Ott, Design of adaptive procedures for fault
       detection and isolation, IEEE Trans. Reliab. R-20(1), 7-10
       (Feb. 1971).

D-23   S. Firstmann and B. Gluss, Optimum search routines for auto-
       matic fault location, Oper. Res. 8, 512-523 (July-Aug. 1960).

D-24   W. W. Chu, Adaptive diagnosis of faulty systems, Oper. Res.
       16, 915-927 (1968).

D-25   D. Cameron, Advanced Electronic Troubleshooting, Reston Publ.
       Co., Reston, Va., 1977.

D-26   A. S. Serdakov, Automatic Control and Technical Diagnostics,
       Tekhnika, Kiev, 1971.

E.   STATISTICAL FAILURE AND DEGRADATION ANALYSIS; RELIABILITY AND
     MAINTENANCE DATA BANKS

E-0   Standards: NORME AIR 0116, Sept. 28, 1977 (France); MIL-STD-
       831, Test Report Summaries; MIL-STD-1556 (AF), Reliability
       Data Banks; NAS-NHB-4-1A-B, Reliability Data Banks

E-1   B. Schneider,Fejlmekanismer: monolitiske IC, Elektronikcen-
       tralen, ECR-43, Hørsholm, Sept. 1974 (in Danish).

E-2   L. F. Pau, Diagnosis of equipment failures by pattern recog-
       nition, IEEE Trans. Reliab. R-23(3), 202-208 (Aug. 1974).

E-3   E. Bolis and C. Chiara, Reliability of aircraft systems by
       field trials, NATO Congress on Statistical Design of Experi-
       mental Field Trials, Rapallo, Italy, Sept. 10-14, 1973,
       Noordhoff, Leyden, 1974.

E-4   K. Enslein and C. L. Rose, Computer based data analysis in
       longevity research, Comput. Biomed. Res. 4, 289-329 (1970).

E-5   R. Goarin, Application de l'analyse des correspondances à
       l'étude de la fiabilité des composants électroniques, Congrès
       national de fiabilité, Perros-Guirec, Sept. 1972.

E-6   R. Goarin and Y. Benoit, Etude de la dérive des condensateurs par l'analyse factorielle des correspondances sur des tableaux juxtaposées, CNET/CPM/FMI/14/74, CNET, Lannion, July 1974.

E-7   A. K. Head, P. Humble, L. M. Clarebrough et al., Computed Electron Micrographs and Defect Identification, North-Holland, Amsterdam, 1973.

E-8   O. Holst Jensen, Korrespondance analyse anvendt på reparation og vedligeholdelsespolitik for fly, in Ref. B-22, 83-94.

E-9   Operation of Reliability Analysis Center, RADC-TR 71-304, AD 738649, Jan. 1972.

E-10 L. F. Pau, Diagnostic statistique, 2nd ed., ENS de l'Aéronautique, Toulouse, 1973, 83 pp.

E-11 L. F. Pau, Diagnostic statistique: synthèse des informations relatives à la fiabilité et à la maintenance d'un matériel aéronautique, L'Aéronautique et l'astronautique, No. 34, 69-76 (1972).

E-12 L. F. Pau, Analysis and diagnosis of in-service failures, in Einführung in Methoden und Probleme der Zuverlässigkeit, KFK Report 1811 (G. Weber, ed.), Kernforschungszentrum Karlsruhe, Karlsruhe, 1973, No. 124.

E-13 L. F. Pau, Diagnostic statistique, Onde Electr. 54(10), 529-537 (Dec. 1974).

E-14 H. Solomon, A first application of clustering techniques to fleet material condition measurements, Tech. Report T-238, George Washington University, June 1970; project ONR-347 020, Office of Naval Research.

E-15 N. P. Taylor and Lt. R. Linck, An Air Force engineering look at reliability prediction, laboratory testing, and service usage experience, AIAA Paper No. 70-392, AIAA, New York, 1970.

E-16 H. W. Young, Specifying the interface between design and test organisations, in Proceedings Conference on Automatic Test Systems, Institute of Electronic and Radio Engineers, London, 1970, 204-220.

E-17 J. C. Trichet, L'AIDS: un moyen de diagnostic permanent, Télonde, 10(3), 11-13 (Dec. 1973).

E-18 C. Rosiaux, Fiabilité des allumeurs déterminée à partir des ventes-échanges, Proc. 2nd Congrès National de fiabilité, Perros-Guirec, Sept. 17-20, 1974, pp. 563-583. Published by CNET, Lannion (France).

E-19 J. C. Ligeron and R. Goarin, Economie de déverminage par la reconnaissance des composants porteurs de gênes de défaillance, Proc. 2nd Congrès National de fiabilité, Perros-Guirec, Sept. 17-20, 1974, pp. 639-653. Published by CNET, Lannion (France).

E-20 P. W. Borg, Field reporting system for reliability analysis on telecommunication equipment, paper III-A, in Ref. C-16, pp. 156-174.

E-21   E. Ullman (ed.), Seminar on reliability data banks, FTL Report
       A-16-41, Försvarets tekleniska laboratorium (FOA-3), Stockholm,
       Oct. 15-17, 1973.

E-22   H. Broberg, Failure rate functions from test data, FTL Report
       A-16-28, FOA-3, Stockholm, April 1973 (failure rates vs. time).

E-23   S. Adnot, R. Goarin, and C. Guyot, The reliability at CEN-
       Saclay and CNET, paper 11, in Ref. E-21, pp. 124-126.

E-24   L. F. Pau, Emploi des techniques de diagnostic statistique
       pour la synthèse des rapports sur l'exploitation et la main-
       tenance des matériels, ENS Télécommunications, Paris, Sept.
       1975.

E-25   V. Joksimovic, Statistical fault analysis method applied to
       advanced gas-cooled reactors, J. Br. Nucl. Energy Soc. 8(4),
       275-302 (Oct. 1969).

E-26   K. Yakuwa, T. Nakazawa, and H. Sugiki, Failure analysis of
       transformers and coils for communication equipment, Fujitsu
       Sci. Tech. J. 6(3), 45-67 (Sept. 1970).

E-27   H. Huppmann, Haüfigkeit und Ursachen von Schäden an Bauteilen
       grosser Dampfturbinen, Der Maschinenschaden 43(1), 1-6 (1970).

E-28   P. A. Engel, Impact Wear of Materials, Elsevier, Amsterdam,
       1976.

E-29   Conditions générales d'établissement et de fourniture du
       mémoire d'organisation de la maintenance des matériels de
       télécommunications, DGA/DTCA, Norme Air 0116, Sept. 28, 1977.

E-30   M. Woerner, La fiabilité appliquée aux atterrisseurs et à
       l'hydraulique, L'Aéronautique et l'Astronautique, No. 60,
       63-71 (1975-1976).

E-31   B. Friedland, Maximum-likelihood estimation of a process with
       random transitions (failures), in Proceedings of the 1978
       IEEE Conference on Decision and Control, San Diego, Jan. 10-
       12, 1979, IEEE Catalog 78 CH 1392-0CS, 427-432.

F.   AUTOMATED FAILURE DIAGNOSIS AND RECONFIGURATION

F-0   Journals and Conferences: IEEE Transactions on Reliability (R),
       Automatic Control (AC), Aerospace and Electronic Systems (AES),
       Nondestructive Evaluation, Circuits and Systems (CAS); Pattern
       Recognition; Nondestructive Testing (Chicago); Engineering
       Cybernetics (USSR) (from Russian); Automation and Remote Con-
       trol (USSR) (from Russian); Control Engineering; Production
       Engineer (London); Mathematical Biosciences; Avtomatika (in
       Russian); All union conferences on technical diagnostics in
       the USSR; IMEKO Biannual International Conference on Technical
       Diagnostics; Sicherheit und Zuverlässigkeit in Wirtschaft,
       Betrieb und Verkehr; Neue Technik; IEEE decision and control
       conferences

F-1   P. Andersen, Automatisk diagnosticering af tekniske systemer, IMSOR, Tech. Univ. Denmark, Lyngby, 1973, 158 p. (in Danish).

F-2   M. V. Zhukov et al., First all union conference on technical diagnostics, Avtomatika i Telemakhanika, 31(7), 186-192 (July 1970).

F-3   G. Bracchi and M. Somalvico, The correlation method for computer-aided statistical analysis, IEEE Trans. Reliab. R-20(3), 96-101 (Aug. 1971).

F-4   J. Chinal, La logique des pannes, ENS de l'Aéronautique, Toulouse, 1973.

F-5   E. Cortina, H. L. Engel, and W. K. Scott, Pattern recognition techniques applied to diagnostics, Society of Automotive Engineers Report 700497, Midyear meeting, Detroit, May 18-22, 1970.

F-6   E. Cortina, Automatic diagnostic equipment studies, USATACOM TR-11289, Jan. 29, 1971.

F-7   D. B. Drane and W. B. Martin, Pattern recognition applied to sleep state classification, Electroencephalogr. Clin. Neurophysiol., 15(26), 238 (1969).

F-8   J. L. Frarey, Mechanical basis for pattern analysis, Society of Automotive Engineers Report 700496, Midyear meeting, Detroit, May 18-22, 1970.

F-9   A. A. Burrows and W. L. Miles, Aircraft fault isolation based on patterns of cockpit indications, Aeronaut. J. (Sept. 1972).

F-10 G. Dube and J. C. Rault, La détection et la localisation des défauts dans les circuits analogiques, Rev. Tech. Thomson-CSF 6(1), 71-80 (March 1974).

F-11 A. I. Yermochenko, Improving control system performance in the presence of parameter variations by introducing redundancy, Sov. Autom. Control (Avtomatika) 8(4), 1-6 (July-Aug. 1975).

F-12 W. J. Hankley and H. M. Merrill, A pattern recognition technique for system error analysis, IEEE Trans. Reliab. R-30(3), 148-153 (Aug. 1971).

F-13 A. Hannavy, New detection devices help predict potential failures, Prod. Eng. (London), 37-44 (March 27, 1967).

F-14 R. L. Hoffman and K. Fukunaga, Pattern recognition signal processing for mechanical diagnostics signature analysis, IEEE Trans. Comput. C-20(9), 1095-1100 (Sept. 1969).

F-15 A. Van Court Hare, Systems Analysis: A Diagnostic Approach, Harcourt Brace, New York, 1967.

F-16 J. A. Jones, The analysis of metallurgical data using pattern recognition techniques, in Proceedings of the National Aerospace Electronics Conference, May 17-19, 1971, IEEE Publ. 71-C-24-AES, IEEE, New York, 1971.

F-17 P. I. Kuznetzov and L. A. Pchelintzev, The application of some
      mathematical methods in medical diagnostics, Math. Biosci. 5,
      365-377 (1969).

F-18 F. J. Lavoie, Signature analysis, product early-warning system,
      Mach. Des. 23, 151-160 (Jan. 1969).

F-19 V. S. Levadi, Automated learning applied to fault diagnosis,
      IEEE Trans. Aerosp. Electron. Syst. AES-3(6), 941-946 (Nov.
      1967).

F-20 C. Y. Hsiung and C. W. Cox, Pattern classification in scan-
      type nondestructive tests, Int. J. Nondestr. Test. 4, 231-247
      (1972).

F-21 G. S. Britov and L. A. Mironovskiy, Checking of linear control
      systems, Eng. Cybern. USSR 10, 63-70 (Jan.-Feb. 1972).

F-22 G. O. Martens and J. D. Dyck, Fault identification in elec-
      tronic circuits with the aid of bilinear transformations,
      IEEE Trans. Reliab. R-21(2), 99-104 (May, 1972).

F-23 Statens Byggeforskingsinstitut, Fejlfinding ved ventilations
      anlaeg, SBI-Anvisning 97, Copenhagen, 1973.

F-24 J. Page, Recognition of patterns in jet engine vibrations
      signals, IEEE Publ. 1651, pp. 102-105, IEEE, New York, 1968.

F-25 P. P. Parkhomenko, O. Tekhnickeskey diagnostike, Znaniye
      Press, Moscow, 1969.

F-26 L. F. Pau, Applications of pattern recognition to the diag-
      nosis of equipment failures, Pattern Recognition 6(3), 3-11
      (Aug. 1974).

F-27 L. F. Pau, Applications of pattern recognition to the diag-
      nosis of equipment failures, in Cognitive Verfahren und Sys-
      teme, Lecture notes in economic and mathematical systems No.
      83 (T. Einsele, W. Gilai, and H. H. Nagel, eds.), Springer,
      Berlin, 1973, pp. 291-306.

F-28 L. F. Pau, Procédé et dispositifs de reconnaissance des formes,
      French patents No. F 72-22958 (June 26, 1972), F 75-15202
      (May 15, 1975).

F-29 L. F. Pau, Conditions d'utilisation de la reconnaissance des
      formes en vue du diagnostic des pannes et du contrôle de
      qualité automatisés, ENS Télécommunications, Paris, Oct. 1975.

F-30 L. F. Pau, Diagnosis of Equipment Failures from Dynamic Meas-
      urements, Siemens Foundation, Copenhagen, Dec. 1973, 106 p.

F-31 L. F. Pau, Adaptive on-line failure diagnosis and predictive
      pattern recognition, 2nd International J. Conference on Pattern
      Recognition, Copenhagen, Aug. 13-15, 1974, IEEE Catalog 74-CH-
      0885-4C, pp. 6-9, IEEE, New York, 1974.

F-32 G. Pfurtscheller and W. Koch, Eine maschinelle Methode zur
      EEG-Klassifikation, Methods Inf. Med. 11(4), 233-237 (1972).

F-33 F. N. Pokrowsky, On reliability prediction by pattern classi-
      fication, in Proceedings of the 1972 Annual Reliability and
      Maintainability Symposium, San Francisco, Annals of Assurance
      Sciences, IEEE Catalog 72-CH-0577-7R, pp. 367-375, IEEE, New
      York, 1972.

F-34 J. C. Rault, D. Bastin, and E. Girard, La détection et la lo-
      calisation des pannes dans les circuits logiques: principes
      généraux, Rev. Tech. Thomson-CSF 4(1), 49-88 (March 1972).

F-35 S. Seshu and R. Waxman, Fault isolation in conventional linear
      systems, IEEE Trans. Reliab. R-15, 11-16 (May, 1966).

F-36 W. A. Glaesser, The application of oil analysis techniques to
      the diagnosis of condition and prediction of failures in U.S.
      Army construction vehicles, AD 770461, Nov. 1973.

F-37 S. Toida and F. J. Allan, A diagnosing algorithm for networks,
      Inf. Control 29, 141-148 (Oct. 1975).

F-38 R. N. Clark, D. C. Fobth, and W. M. Walton, Detecting instru-
      ment malfunctions in control systems, IEEE Trans. Aerosp. Elec-
      tron. Syst. AES-11(4) (July 1975).

F-39 R. B. Broen, A fault tolerant estimator for redundant systems,
      IEEE Trans. Aerosp. Electron. Syst. AES-11(6) (Nov. 1975).

F-40 M. H. A. Davis, The application of non-linear filtering to
      fault detection in linear systems, IEEE Trans. Autom. Control
      AC-20(2), 257-259 (April 1975).

F-41 R. K. Mehra and J. Peschon, An innovations approach to fault
      detection and diagnosis in dynamic systems, Automatika 7,
      637-640 (1971).

F-42 A. S. Willsky and H. L. Jones, A generalized likelihood ratio
      for the detection and estimation of jumps in linear systems,
      IEEE Trans. Autom. Control 21(1), 108-112 (Feb. 1976).

F-43 P. Sanyal and C. N. Shen, Bayes decision rule for rapid de-
      tection and adaptive estimation scheme with space applications,
      IEEE Trans. Autom. Control 19, 228-231 (June 1974).

F-44 A. I. Yermachenko and V. V. Zdor, Automatic classification
      and pattern recognition diagnostics and reliability, Sov.
      Autom. Control 8(4), 1-5 (July-Aug. 1975).

F-45 O. A. Solheim, Some integrity problems in optimal control sys-
      tems, in Advances in Control Systems, AGARD Conf. Proc. No.
      137, AGARD, Paris, 1975.

F-46 D. E. Small, Classification of overlapping waveforms with
      pattern recognition techniques, AD-741734, March 1972.

F-47 R. Bellman, Dynamic programming, pattern recognition and loca-
      tion of faults in complex systems, J. Appl. Prob. 3, 268-271
      (1966).

F-48 W. W. Chu, A mathematical model for diagnosing system failures,
      IEEE Trans. Electron. Comput. EC-16(3), 327-331 (June 1967).

F-49 R. Weiss and I. Nathan, An ultra-reliable sensing system for vehicles with limiting sparing capacity, J. Spacecr. Rockets 4(9), 1151-1158 (Sept. 1967).

F-50 J. T. Ephgrave, Optimum redundant configurations of inertial sensors, TR-1001 (9990)-5, Aerospace Corp., El Segundo, Sept. 1966.

F-51 J. C. Wilcox, Competitive evaluation of failure detection algorithms for strapdown redundant inertial instrument, J. Spacecr. Rockets 11(7) (July 1974).

F-52 G. S. Fang and T. Pavlidis, Signal classification through quasi-singular detection with application in mechanical fault diagnosis, IEEE Trans. Information Theory IT-18(5), 631-636 (Sept. 1972); also Proceedings of the 1972 International Conference on Cybernetics and Society, Washington, Oct. 9-12, 1972, pp. 199-205, IEEE, New York, 1972.

F-53 T. Sankar and G. Xistris, Failure prediction through the theory of stochastic excursions of extreme vibration amplitudes, ASME Publ. 71-Vibr. 60, ASME, New York, 1971.

F-54 K. P. Seshagiriprabhu, On the detection of a sudden change in system parameters, IEEE Trans. Information Theory IT-16(4), 497-500 (July 1970).

F-55 J. D. Brule, R. A. Johnson, and E. J. Kletsky, Diagnosis of equipment failures, IRE Trans. Reliab. Qual. Control RQC-9, 23-34 (April 1960).

F-56 A. J. Gross, Minimization of misclassification of component failures in a two-component system, IEEE Trans. Reliab. R-19(3), 120-122 (Aug. 1970).

F-57 J. H. Maenpaa, C. J. Stehman, and W. J. Stahl, Fault isolation in conventional linear systems, IEEE Trans. Reliab. R-18(1), 12-14 (Feb. 1969).

F-58 D. R. Stevens, G. E. Ott, and J. R. Tudor, Frequency modulated fault locator for power lines, IEEE Trans. Power Systems PAS-91(4), 1760-1768 (1972).

F-59 H. Schaffhausen and L. Heger, Leckerkennung und Ortung von Verlusten beim Betrieb von Mineral-ölfernleitungen, Teil 1-3, Tech. Uberwach. 11(5), 135-137 (May 1970); 11(6), 213-215 (June 1970); 11(7), 236-237 (July 1970).

F-60 J. V. Harrison and E. G. Gai, Evaluating sensor orientations for navigation performance and failure detection, IEEE Trans. Aerosp. Electron. Syst. AES-13(6), 631-643 (Nov. 1977).

F-61 J. V. Harrison and T. T. Chien, Failure isolation for a minimally redundant inertial sensor system, IEEE Trans. Aerosp. Electron. Syst. AES-11(3) (May 1975).

F-62 P. P. Parkhomenko (ed.), Principles of Technical Diagnostics, Vol. 1, Energiya, Moscow, 1976 (diagnosis of digital or logical circuits).

F-63   Verzakov, Kinšt, Rabinovič, and Timonen, Vvedenie v technicěskuju diagnostiku, Energiya, Moscow, 1968.

F-64   R. N. Clark, Instrument fault detection, IEEE Trans. Aerosp. Electron. Syst. AES-14(3), 456-465 (May 1978).

F-65   R. A. Hughes, M. A. Fischler, and H. E. Rauch, Using pattern recognition in product assurance, in Proceedings of the 1977 Annual Reliability and Maintainability Symposium, Philadelphia, Jan. 18-20, 1977, IEEE, New York, 1977.

F-66   T. T. Chien and M. B. Adams, A sequential failure detection technique and its applications, IEEE Trans. Autom. Control AC-21(5), 750-757 (Oct. 1976).

F-67   T. J. Rollins and T. D. Martin, Assured Performance Calibration Program, North American-Autonetics, Anaheim, CA., April 20, 1965.

F-68   R. C. Gonzalez, D. N. Fry, and R. C. Krytter, Results in the application of pattern recognition methods to nuclear reactor core component surveillance, IEEE Trans. Nucl. Sci. NS-22(21), 750-756 (1974).

F-69   R. C. Gonzalez and L. C. Howington, Machine recognition of abnormal behavior in nuclear reactors, IEEE Trans. Syst. Man Cybern. SMC-7(10), 717-728 (1977).

F-70   R. N. Clark, A simplified instrument failure detection scheme, IEEE Trans. Aerosp. Electron. Syst. AES-14(4), 558-563 (July 1978).

F-71   Cable-fault locator, PB-80-973180, and U.S. Patent No. 4,110,683.

F-72   E. Y. Ho, An efficient analog circuit pack fault diagnosis algorithm, IEEE Paper CH 1584-2/80/0295, IEEE, New York, 1980.

F-73   J. A. Jacquez, Computer Diagnosis and Diagnostic Methods, Charles C Thomas Publishing, Springfield, Ill., 1977.

F-74   Human Failure Diagnosis, Proc. NATO ASI (J. Rasmussen, ed.), Roskilde, Denmark, Aug. 1980, Plenum, New York, 1981.

F-75   Special issue on automatic analog fault diagnosis, IEEE Trans. Circuits and Systems CAS-26(7) (July 1979).

F-76   L. F. Pau, Design of a suboptimal Kalman filter of very high reliability and speed, with internal reconfiguration and failure localization, in Ref F-75, pp. 565-574.

G.   FAULT TESTING AND AUTOMATIC TEST SYSTEMS

G-0   Journals and Conferences: International Journal of Nondestructive Testing; Microelectronics and Reliability; IEEE Transactions on Reliability (R), Computers (C); Maintenance (France); Circuits Manufacturing; annual IEEE automatic testing conferences (U.K.); annual IEEE/AIAA AUTOTESTCON confer-

ence; annual IEEE WESCON conference; Elecktrotechnische Zeit-
schrift, Ausgabe B (ETZ-B); IBM Nachrichten; Bell System
Technical J.; IBM J. of Research and Development; AFIPS con-
ferences; IEEE COMPCON conferences; IEEE FTC (fault-tolerant
computing) conferences
Standards: MIL-STD-883, Test Methods and Procedures for
Microelectronics, May 1, 1968; MIL-STD-761, Accelerated Life
Testing; MIL-STD-1309-A, Definition of Terms for Automatic
Electronic Test and Checkout, April 12, 1972; MIL-STD-1519,
Preparation of Test Requirement Documents, Sept. 17, 1971;
State Standard GOS 20417/75 (USSR), Principles for the Process
of Elaboration of Diagnostic Systems; MIL-STD-2084, Modularity,
Test Point Locations, Accessibility, BIT, FD/FL and Testability
Verification; MIL-STD-2076 (AS), Unit Under Test Compatibility
with ATE, General Requirements for, March 1, 1978; NAVMAT INST
4120.105A, ATLAS Test Language Specification; NAVMAT INST 3960.9,
BIT Design Guide for Navy-Procured Systems; XWS-19621A, Weapon
Design for Testability (Spec. Guidelines, Oct. 1978); IEEE-STD-
416, ATLAS Language Specification (a DoD standard); TR-3826,
Testability into Electronics Systems, May 1978; MIL-STD-1519,
Test Requirements Documentation (TRD) as Input for ATE Test
Program Sets (TPS); IEEE-STD-488, Standard Test Equipment Bus
Requirements

G-1   R. Knowles, Automatic Testing and Applications, McGraw-Hill,
      New York, 1976 (survey and use of ATS).

G-2   L. Yu Abramova, Testing instruments used for monitoring the
      dimension of parts during mechanical processing, Measurement
      Techniques 19(1), 75-78 (Jan. 1976).

G-3   S. H. Shinners, Considerations for automatic testing of com-
      plex shipboard systems, Comput. Electr. Eng. 1(1), 73-81
      (June 1973).

G-4   G. Jumarie, Test automatique et auto-organisation, Onde Electr.
      50(2), 95-102 (Feb. 1970).

G-5   J. R. Humphrey and C. H. Dale, Innovations are key to fully
      automated testing, Microwaves, 54-56 (June 1973).

G-6   H. Y. Chang, E. G. Manning, and G. Metze, Fault Diagnosis of
      Digital Systems, Wiley, New York, 1970.

G-7   M. Depeyrot, Computer component and system testing as a part
      of computer-aided production and manufacturing, Report No. 83,
      IRIA-Laboria, Rocquencourt, France, 1974.

G-8   R. J. Preiss, Fault-test generation, in Design Automation of
      Digital Systems, Vol. 1, Theory and Techniques (M. A. Breuer,
      ed.), Prentice-Hall, Englewood Cliffs, N.J., 1972, Chap. 7.

G-9   W. A. Plice, in Techniques for the automatic generation of
      fault isolation tests for analog circuits, Proceedings of
      NAECON-76, Dayton, Ohio, May 18-20, 1976 (parameter identifi-
      cation from a factored transfer function, IEEE, New York, 1976.

G-10 R. Bussett, Microwave measurements on 3rd generation ATE,
      IEEE-AES Newsletter, 23-30 (May 1976).

G-11 R. J. Brachman, The Army multi-purpose inspection and diag-
      nostic technology program, IEEE-AES Newsletter, 27-31 (April
      1976).

G-12 W. Weibull, Fatigue Testing and Analysis of Results, Pergamon,
      Elmsford, N.Y., 1961.

G-13 Computer Systems Reliability, Infotech State of the Art Report
      No. 20, Infotech Information, Maidenhead, Berkshire, 1974.

G-14 W. Görke, Fehlerdiagnose digitaler Schaltungen, Teubner Verlag,
      Stuttgart, 1973.

G-15 FAA workshop on the grounding of electronic systems, AD 785 858,
      1974.

G-16 C. I. Hubert, Preventive Maintenance of Electrical Equipment,
      2nd ed., McGraw-Hill, New York, 1969 (electric motors trouble-
      shooting).

G-17 R. L. Goodman, Trouble-shooting with the Dual-Trace Scope,
      Tab Books, Blue Ridge Summit, Pa., 1976 (color TV chassis).

G-18 J. G. Langset, Teroteknologi: oversikt over metoder for til-
      standskontroll, SINTEF Report STF 18-A 76007, Trondheim, Jan.
      29, 1976 (nondestructive testing for condition monitoring)
      (in Norwegian).

G-19 E. C. Harmon, A Bayesian analysis of avionic sub-systems
      built-in test, IEEE Trans. Aerosp. Electron. Syst. AES-$7(5)$,
      982-987 (Sept. 1971).

G-20 R. Gustafson, Modular automatic test equipment for commercial
      airlines, Aircr. Eng. $44(1)$, 24-27 (Jan. 1972).

G-21 D. G. Mullens, Automated testing of the SAS—an experiment,
      IEEE Trans. Instrum. Meas. IM-$20(4)$, 235-238 (Nov. 1971).

G-22 Testing Philosophy and Methods for Guidance and Control Sys-
      tems and Sub-systems, AGARD Lecture Series No. 60, AGARD,
      Paris, 1974.

G-23 Modern Methods of Testing Rotating Components of Turbo-machines
      (Instrumentation), AGARD Monographs No. 167 (1972) and No. 207
      (1975), AGARD, Paris.

G-24 O. Horenburg, Schäden an Kesselspeisepumpen, Der Maschinen-
      schaden $43(4)$, 135-147 (1970).

G-25 V. V. Karibskii, Analysis of systems for efficient inspection
      and troubleshooting, Autom. Remote Control USSR $16(2)$, 305-310
      (Feb. 1965).

G-26 R. Saeks, S. Pal Singh, and R. W. Liu, Fault isolation via
      components simulation, IEEE Trans. Circuits and Systems CS-
      $19(6)$, 634-640 (Nov. 1972).

G-27 H. Weigel, Funktions prüfung bei elektronischen Grenzwertmel-
      dern, Regelungstech. Prax. Prozess-Rechentech. $15(1)$, 17-19
      (Jan. 1973).

G-28   NTIS-Search, Electric Fault Location, NTIS/PS-77/0691/4 PNB,
       NTIS, NTIS, Springfield, Va., Aug. 1977.

G-29   J. D. Lenk, Handbook of Basic Electronic Troubleshooting,
       Prentice-Hall, Englewood Cliffs, N.J., 1977.

G-30   V. Robinson, Handbook of Electronic Instrumentation, Testing
       and Troubleshooting, Reston, Reston, Va., 1974.

G-31   M. Mandl, Handbook of Electronic Testing, Measurement and
       Troubleshooting, Reston, Reston, Va., 1976.

G-32   G. Schlesinger, Testing Machine Tools, 8th ed., Pergamon,
       Elmsford, N.Y., 1978.

G-33   F. Liguori (ed.), Automatic Test Equipment: Hardware, Soft-
       ware, and Management, IEEE Press, New York, 1974.

G-34   J. Kozak, Diagnostische Einrichtung zur Feststellung des tech-
       nischen Zustandes von Maschinen und Anlagen, Technik 31(1),
       23-27 (Jan. 1976).

G-35   J. Waidelich, Methoden der Mustererkennung zur Fehlerdiagnose
       von Digitalrechnern, T.R. KFK-PDV-127, Kernforschungszentrum
       Karlsruhe, Karlsruhe, Nov. 1977.

G-36   L. F. Pau, Tast testing and trimming of high accuracy data
       converters, Proceedings of AUTOTESTCON '78, IEEE Catalog 78
       CH1416-7-AES, Nov. 1978, pp. 268-274, IEEE, New York, 1978.

G-37   W. C. Carter, Hardware Reliability, IBM Research, Yorktown
       Heights, N.Y., July 1978.

G-38   F. Liguori (ed.), Special issue on automatic test equipments,
       IEEE Trans. Instrum. Meas. IM-27(2) (June 1978).

H.   PERFORMANCE MONITORING, ACOUSTIC MONITORING, AND
     FAILURE DIAGNOSIS IN CONTROL SYSTEMS

H-0   Journals: Automatic Monitoring and Measurement; Soviet Auto-
       matic Control (Avtomatika); Nuclear Science Abstracts; Journal
       of Sound and Vibration; IEEE Transactions on Automatic Control
       (AC), Acoustics and Signal Processing (ASSP), Instrumentation
       (IM); Measurement Techniques (USSR) (from Russian); Der Ma-
       schinenschaden; Technische Überwachung (Berlin); IEEE decision
       and control conferences

       Standards: MIL-STD-1553 A/B, Avionics Multiplex System

H-1   R. L. Aronson, Production monitoring survey: diagnostic sys-
       tems, Control Eng. 19(3), 62-65 (March 1972).

H-2   M. F. Fry, Importance des moyens de surveillance d'état des
       moteurs, l'Aéronautique et l'Astronautique, No. 42, 25-32
       (1973); No. 44, 63-74 (1974).

H-3   R. B. Tatge, Acoustical techniques for machinery diagnostics,
       in Acoustical Society of America Conference, Ottawa, May 21-
       24, 1968, ASA, New York, 1968.

H-4   H. N. Taylor, Monitoring data from jet engines, in <u>Aircraft Flight Instrumentation Integrated Data Systems</u>, AGARD Conference Publication No. 6, AGARD, Paris, Nov. 1967, pp. 141-159.

H-5   R. B. Lumsden, The identification of aircraft powerplant dynamic response from flight tests using power spectral techniques, Report TR 73049, Royal Aircraft Establishment, Farnborough, 1972.

H-6   E. Handschin (ed.), <u>Real Time Control of Electrical Power Systems</u>, Elsevier, Amsterdam, 1972.

H-7   R. Savage, Surveillance problems, <u>Naval Res. Logistics Q</u>. <u>9</u>, 187-209 (1962).

H-8   M. Mazumdar, Use of statistical theory of extremes in hot channel analysis of a liquid metal fast-breeder reactor, <u>Nucl. Sci. Eng</u>. <u>47</u>, 187-194 (1972).

H-9   Diagnostics and engine condition monitoring, <u>AGARD-CP-165</u>, AGARD, Paris, 1975.

H-10   A. Poujol, G. Zwingelstein and J. C. Marc, Etude pratique de l'estimation en ligne de paramètres de Kalman, <u>SES/PUB/SAI/73-206</u>, CEA/CEN Saclay, Oct. 1973, and report CEA-N-1695, Saclay, Dec. 1973.

H-11   Y. Shinohara and R. Oguma, Estimation of time-varying reactivity using a method of non-linear filtering, <u>Nucl. Sci. Eng</u>. <u>52</u>, 76-83 (1973).

H-12   Aircraft flight instrumentation integrated data systems, <u>AGARD CP-6</u>, AGARD, Paris, 1967.

H-13   A. Mihail, Fiabilité et maintenabilité sur les réacteurs aéronautiques, <u>L'Aéronautique et l'astronautique</u>, No. 44, 60-75 (1974).

H-14   E. S. Eccles, Monitoring and control of aerospace vehicle propulsion, in <u>Principles of Avionics Computer Systems</u> (J. N. Bloom, ed.), AGARDograph No. 183, AGARD, Paris, 1974.

H-15   D. G. Lainotis and F. L. Sims, Sensitivity analysis of discrete Kalman filters, <u>Int. J. Control</u> 12(4) (1970).

H-16   N. Suda and S. Shirai, Estimation of reactor parameters by optimal filtering method, <u>J. Nucl. Sci. Technol</u>. <u>8</u>, 438-443 (Aug. 1971).

H-17   AIDS, <u>AD-752882</u>.

H-18   D. W. Botstiber, Wear-monitoring systems, <u>Mach. Des</u>. <u>26</u>, 170-176 (Oct. 1967).

H-19   W. M. Hawkins, Stopping vibration with dynamic analysis, <u>Mach. Des</u>. <u>31</u>, 86-91 (May 1973).

H-20   Acoustic signatures of engines, <u>AD-876216</u>.

H-21   Experiments in line quality monitoring, <u>IBM Syst. J</u>. <u>15(2)</u>, 124-142 (1976) (telecommunications).

H-22 K. B. Kochanski, Condition monitoring, ASME Paper 69-GT-66,
      March 1969.

H-23 S. Braun, The extraction of periodic waveforms by time domain
      averaging, Acustica 32(2), 69-77 (1975).

H-24 S. Braun, Signal analysis for rotating machinery vibrations,
      Pattern Recognition 7, 81-86 (1975).

H-25 G. M. Jenkins and D. G. Watts, Spectral Analysis and Its Ap-
      plications, Holden-Day, San Francisco, 1968.

H-26 A. M. Noll, Cepstrum pitch determination, JASA 41, 293 (1967).

H-27 R. B. Randall, Cepstrum analysis and gearbox fault diagnosis,
      Brüel & Kjaer Application Notes 13-150, Brüel & Kjaer, Noerum,
      Denmark, 1973.

H-28 L. F. Pau, Adaptive failure mode diagnosis based on pattern
      recognition of acoustical spectral measurements, in Inter-
      national Conference on Monitoring Diagnostics in Industry,
      Prague, Aug. 18-22, 1975; čislo publikace 60/797/75(1010),
      Vol. II, pp. 139-147, ČVTS DT, Prague, Aug. 1975.

H-29 G. Sapy, Diagnostic vibratoire des ruptures d'aubes mobiles
      de turbines à vapeur, in Ref. H-28, pp. 137-146.

H-30 D. W. Thomas and B. R. Wilkins, The analysis of vehicle sounds
      for recognition, Pattern Recognition 4, 379-389 (1972).

H-31 S. A. Storeheier, K. Skaalvik, and M. Ringheim, Noise from
      motor vehicles, SINTEF Report STF-44-A 73103, Laboratory for
      Acoustics, ELAB, Trondheim, 1973.

H-32 P. A. Boto, Detection of bearing damage, SKF Ball Bearing J.,
      No. 167 (1971).

H-33 ISVR, Workshop in on-condition maintenance, Southampton Uni-
      versity, Jan. 5-6, 1972, Institute for Sound and Vibration
      Research (includes long bibliography), Southampton, 1972.

H-34 C. W. Cox and C. J. Renken, The application of signal process-
      ing techniques to signals from non-destructive test systems,
      Mater. Eval. 28, 173-181 (Aug. 1970).

H-35 R. Friedrich, D. Barschdorf, W. Hensle, and D. Wentland,
      Untersuchung über den Zusammenhang zwischen der Veränderung
      des Geräuschspektrums und dem Betriebszustand thermischer
      Strömungsmaschinen, Motortech. Z. 35(3), 67-72 (March 1974).

H-36 H. K. Kohler, A. Pratt, and A. M. Thomson, Dynamics and noise
      in parallel-axis gearings, in Gearing in 1970, Institute of
      Mechanical Engineering, London, 1970, 54-62.

H-37 D. R. Houser, M. J. Drosjack, and C. W. Hogg, Vibration diag-
      nostics in helicopter power trains, Paper 12 in Ref. H-9.

H-38 A. R. Kramer, J. Mathieson, and S. Pergament, The deviation
      concept: a tool for preventive maintenance of marine power
      plants, Mar. Technol. (Oct. 1972).

H-39   K. H. Drager and H. Liland, A Computer System for Process
       Control and Predictive Maintenance of a Diesel Engine on a
       Seagoing Vessel, Det Norske Veritas, Oslo, 1972.

H-40   J. Wotipka and R. Zelensky, Identification of failing mechan-
       isms through vibration analysis, ASME Publ. 71-Vibr.-90,
       ASME, New York, 1971.

H-41   E. Downham and R. Woods, The rationale of monitoring vibration
       on rotating machinery in continuously operating process plant,
       ASME Publ. 71-Vibr.-96, ASME, New York, 1971.

H-42   R. Baumster and V. Donanto, Signature analysis of turbomachine-
       ry, J. Sound Vibr. 15, 14-21 (Sept. 1971).

H-43   H. Sandtorv, M. Rasmussen, and G. Fiskaa, Datatrend: A Com-
       puterized System for Engine Condition Monitoring and Predictive
       Maintenance of Large Bore Diesel Engines, Ship Research Insti-
       tute of Norway, Trondheim, 1974.

H-44   I. B. Tartakovskii, Forecasting the wear of machine components,
       Russ. Eng. J. 53(6) (1973).

H-45   L. F. Pau, Analyse continue des fluctuations d'un paramètre
       de fonctionnement: application au diagnostic automatique des
       changements de régime d'une machine, RAIRO 11(1), 5-15 (March
       1977).

H-46   W. Marsh and H. R. M. S. Ferguson, The development of a system
       for collecting and analysing service failures, Nucl. Eng. Des.
       13, 322-336 (1970).

H-47   H. P. Balfanz, Bestimmung von Ausfallraten und Ausfallarten
       mechanischer und elektrischer Bauteile mit der Fehlerbaum
       methode und der Ausfalleffektanalyse, Kerntechnik 13(9), 392-
       399 (1971).

H-48   B. Döring, Anlagen sichern mit Melde- und Auslösseinrichtungen,
       Teil 1-3, Elektrotechnik 53(9), 18-20; 53(10), 16-19; 53(11),
       20-23 (1971).

H-49   D. N. Ewart and L. Kirchmayer, Automation and utility system
       security, IEEE Spectrum 8, 37-42 (July 1971).

H-50   H. S. Witsenhausen, Sets of possible states of linear systems
       given perturbed observations, IEEE Trans. Autom. Control AC-
       13, 556-558 (Oct. 1968).

H-51   A. W. Astrop, The Rayleigh computerized inspection system,
       Mach. Prod. Eng. 114(2943), 562-566 (April 1969).

H-52   H. J. Bohnstedt, Die Grenzen der Körperschallmessung bei der
       Überwachung von Dampfturbinen, Der Maschinenschaden 43(3),
       111-115 (1970).

H-53   T. S. Sankar, Failure prediction through the theory of sto-
       chastic excursions of extreme vibration amplitudes, J. Eng.
       Ind. 94, 133-138 (Feb. 1972).

H-54   F. Schöllahammer, Beitrag zur Deutung von Relativ-Wellen-
       schwingungsmessungen an gropzen Turboaggregaten, Der Maschin-
       enschaden 44(1), 1-11 (1971).

H-55   H. Dreiheller and K. H. Waechter, Ortung eines Lecks in einer
       Kesselanlage, Tech. Überwach. 8(2), 61-63 (Feb. 1967).

H-56   A. Sturm, R. Meyer, and D. Brauer, Früerkennung von Fehlern
       als Möglichkeit zur Rationalisierung der Anlagenerhaltung in
       Kernkraftwerken, Energie-technik 22(4), 162-168 (April 1972).

H-57   W. Nürnberg, Untersuchung und Betriebsüberwachung grosser
       elektrischer Antriebe, Der Maschinenschaden 41(5), 165-173
       (1968).

H-58   E. Hayd, Störungen des stationären Betriebs von Rohrfernleit-
       ungen, Tech. Überwach. 10(6), 181-184 (June 1969).

H-59   B. Szabados, C. D. Dicenzo, and N. K. Sinha, Dynamic measure-
       ments of the main electrical parameters of a DC-machine,
       IEEE Trans. Ind. Gen. Appl. IGA-7(1), 109-115 (Feb. 1971).

H-60   M. B. Adams and T. T. Chien, A sequential failure detection
       technique and its applications, IEEE Trans. Autom. Control
       20, 824-827 (Oct. 1976).

H-61   Power plant reliability, AGARD Conference Proceedings, AGARD-
       CP-215, AGARD, Paris, 1977.

H-62   R. W. Smeaton, Motor Application and Maintenance Handbook,
       McGraw-Hill, New York, 1969.

H-63   R. H. Waring, Handbook of Noise and Vibration Control, Trade
       and Technical Press, Morden, Surrey, 1973.

H-64   A. S. Serdakov, Automatic Control and Technical Diagnostics,
       Tekhnika, Kiev, 1971.

H-65   G. P. Shibanov, A. E. Artemenko, A. A. Meteshkin, and N. I.
       Tsiklinskiy, Monitoring the Functioning of Large Systems,
       Mashinostroyeniye, Moscow, 1972.

H-66   Integrity in electronic flight control systems, AGARDOGRAPH
       No. 224, AGARD, Paris, April 1977.

H-67   J. R. Sturgeon, Flight data acquisition for fatigue load mon-
       itoring and conservation, Colloque sur la maintenance des
       structures d'avion, CEAT, Toulouse, June 19-21, 1973.

H-68   H. Sriyananda, D. R. Towill, and J. H. Williams, Voting tech-
       niques for fault diagnosis from frequency-domain test data,
       IEEE Trans. Reliab. R-24(4), 260-267 (1975).

H-69   J. S. Liu and H. L. Jones, Linear manifold constrained GLR,
       IEEE Trans. Autom. Control AC-22(6), 988-989 (Dec. 1977).

H-70   R. C. Corley and H. A. Spang, Failure detection and correla-
       tion for turbofan engines, in Proceedings of the 1977 J. Auto-
       matic Control Conference, June 22-24, 1977, IEEE, New York,
       1977.

H-71   R. S. Kryter, Application of the FFT algorithm to on-line
       reactor diagnosis, IEEE Trans. Nucl. Sci. NS-16, 120 (1976).

H-72   K. R. Piety and J. C. Robinson, An on-line reactor surveillance
       algorithm based on multivariate analysis of noise, Nucl. Sci.
       Eng. 59(4), 369-380 (1976).

H-73   J. D. Birdwell, D. A. Castanon, and M. Athans, On reliable
       control systems designs with and without feedback reconfigura-
       tions, in Proceedings of the 1978 IEEE Conference on Decision
       and Control, San Diego, Jan. 10-12, 1979, IEEE Catalog 78 CH
       1392-0CS, pp. 419-426, IEEE, New York, 1980.

H-74   J. C. Doyle, Robustness of multiloop linear feedback systems,
       in Ref. H-73, pp. 12-18.

H-75   L. F. Pau, An adaptive signal classification procedure: appli-
       cation to aircraft engine monitoring, Pattern Recognition 9(3),
       121-130 (Oct. 1977).

H-76   J. F. Dopazo, S. T. Ehrmann, O. A. Klitin, A. M. Sasson, and
       L. S. Van Slyck, Implementation of the AEP real-time monitor-
       ing system, IEEE Trans. Power Systems PAS-95(5), 1618-1624
       (Sept. 1976).

H-77   E. Handschin, F. C. Schweppe, J. Kohlas, and A. Fiechter, Bad
       data analysis for power system state estimation, IEEE Trans.
       Power Systems PAS-94(2), 329-337 (March 1975).

H-78   E. Lechner, Untersuchung des Betriebs- und Geräuschverhaltens
       einer verstellbaren Axialkolbenpumpe, Springer, Berlin, 1980.

H-79   Synchronous transfer circuits for redundant systems, PB-80-
       975940.

H-80   K. C. Daly, E. Gai, and J. V. Harrison, Generalized likelihood
       test for FDI in redundant sensor reconfigurations, J. of
       Guidance and Control 2(1), 9-17 (Jan. 1979).

H-81   G. P. Shibanov, A. E. Artemenko, A. A. Meteshkin, and N. I.
       Tsiklinskiy, Monitoring the Functioning of Large Systems,
       Mashinostroyeniye, Moscow, 1972.

H-82   Michael Naele Assoc. (Farnham, Surrey), A Guide to the Condi-
       tion Monitoring of Machinery, Committee on Terotechnology,
       Dept. of Industry, HMSO, London, 1979.